RE-ORDERIN

RE-ORDERING NATURE

THEOLOGY, SOCIETY AND THE NEW GENETICS

edited by
Celia Deane-Drummond and
Bronislaw Szerszynski
(with Robin Grove-White)

T & T CLARK
A Continuum imprint
LONDON • NEW YORK

T&T CLARK LTD

A Continuum imprint

The Tower Building	370 Lexington Avenue
11 York Road	New York 10017–6503
London SE1 7NX	USA

www.continuumbooks.com

First published 2003

ISBN 0 567 08878 2 (paperback)
ISBN 0 567 08896 0 (hardback)

British Library Cataloguing-in-Publication Data
A catalogue record for this book is available from the British Library

Typeset by Fakenham Photosetting Ltd, Fakenham, Norfolk NR21 8NN
Printed and bound in Great Britain by Bookcraft, Midsomer Norton

Contents

Contributors

MICHAEL BANNER is F. D. Maurice Professor of Moral and Social Theology at King's College London. Revd Professor Banner is a member of the Royal Commission on Environmental Pollution, chair of the Home Office's Animal Procedures Committee, and chair of the Department of Health's CJD Incidents Panel. He was formerly a member of the Church of England's Doctrine Commission and its Board for Social Responsibility. Recent publications include *Christian Ethics and Contemporary Moral Problems* (Cambridge University Press, 1999).

JOHN HEDLEY BROOKE is Andreas Idreos Professor of Science and Religion and Director of the Ian Ramsey Centre, University of Oxford, where he is also a Fellow of Harris Manchester College. He is the author of *Science and Religion: Some Historical Perspectives* (Cambridge University Press, 1991), and, with Geoffrey Cantor, of *Reconstructing Nature: The Engagement of Science and Religion* (T&T Clark, 1998).

DONALD M. BRUCE is Director of the Society, Religion and Technology Project, Edinburgh, Scotland. He has been a member of the bioethics working group of the Conference of European Churches since 1993. He is a member of the Scottish Science Advisory Committee and the Public Issues Advisory Group of the Biotechnology and Biological Sciences Research Council. He is also an official observer to the International Bioethics Committee of UNESCO and the Global Summit of National Bioethics Committees. He is a director of the John Ray Initiative for promoting environmental education and awareness in churches. Publications include *Engineering Genesis:*

The Ethics of Genetic Engineering in Non-human Species (Earthscan 1998, co-edited with Ann Bruce) and *Modifying Creation* (Paternoster 2001, co-edited with Don Horrocks for the Evangelical Alliance). He is also a member of the International Association of Bioethics, the European Society for Agriculture and Food Ethics, Christians in Science and the Science Religion Forum. He is a director of the John Ray Initiative for promoting environmental education and awareness in churches, and is on the steering committee of the Eco-Congregation Project of the UK Government's 'Going for Green' initiative. With Ann Bruce he is co-editor of *Engineering Genesis: The Ethics of Genetic Engineering in Non-Human Species* (Earthscan, 1998).

STEPHEN R. L. CLARK is Professor of Philosophy at the University of Liverpool. His research interests include Greek philosophical thought, animals and the environment, and the philosophy of biology. His publications include *How to Think about the Earth: Models of Environmental Theology* (Mowbrays, 1993), *Animals and Their Moral Standing* (Routledge, 1997), *God, Religion and Reality* (SPCK, 1998) and *Biology and Christian Ethics* (Cambridge University Press, 2000).

CELIA DEANE-DRUMMOND is Professor of Theology and the Biological Sciences and Director of the Centre for Religion and Biosciences, both at Chester College. Recent publications include *A Handbook in Theology and Ecology* (SCM Press, 1996), *Ecology in Jürgen Moltmann's Theology* (Mellen, 1997), *Theology and Biotechnology: Implications for a New Science* (Geoffrey Chapman, 1997) and *Creation Through Wisdom: Theology and the New Biology* (T&T Clark, 2000).

ROBIN GROVE-WHITE is Professor of Environment and Society and Chair of the Centre for the Study of Environmental Change, at the Institute for Environment, Philosophy and Public Policy, Lancaster University. He is Chair of the Board of Greenpeace UK and a Trustee of Greenpeace International, and from 1991 to 1998 was a Board Member of the Forestry Commission. He is co-author of *Uncertain World: Genetically Modified Organisms, Food and Public Attitudes in Britain* (CSEC, Lancaster University, 1997) and *Wising Up: The Public and New Technologies* (CSEC, Lancaster University, 2000).

MAIRI LEVITT is Senior Lecturer in the Centre for Professional Ethics, University of Central Lancashire. Her research is in the area of social and bioethics, including the EU-funded projects Biocult, Euroscreen and Empire. She is the author of *Nice When They Are Young: Contemporary Christianity in Families and Schools* (Avebury, 1996) and of recent articles in the *BMJ, New Genetics and Society, Human Reproduction* and *Genetic Ethics.* She is also co-editor of *The Right to Know and the Right Not to Know* (Ashgate, 1997) and of *Ethical Issues in Community Health Care* (1998). She was a member of the Food Ethics Council's working party on novel foods.

MICHAEL S. NORTHCOTT is Reader in Christian Ethics at the University of Edinburgh and Academic Chair of the Centre for Human Ecology in Edinburgh. He is a priest in the Scottish Episcopal Church. His publications include *The Environment and Christian Ethics* (Cambridge University Press, 1996), *Urban Theology: A Reader* (Cassell, 1998) and *Life After Debt: Christianity and Global Justice* (SPCK, 1999). He was a co-author of *Engineering Genesis* (Earthscan, 1998).

ARTHUR PEACOCKE was until 1999 the Director of the Ian Ramsey Centre for interdisciplinary study of the relation between the sciences and religion in the Faculty of Theology, Oxford University. For twenty-five years he had a career as a physical biochemist and later, after becoming a priest in the Church of England, he was Dean of Clare College, Cambridge. He is now an Honorary Canon of Christ Church Cathedral, Oxford, and has been a Bampton and a Gifford Lecturer. He was awarded the 2001 Templeton Prize for Progress in Religion. His most recent books are *From DNA to Dean* (Canterbury Press, 1996), *God and Science: The Quest for Christian Credibility* (SCM Press, 1996) and *Paths from Science towards God: The End of All Our Exploring* (Oneworld, 2001).

MICHAEL J. REISS is Professor of Science Education and Head of Science and Technology at the University of London Institute of Education, a priest in the Church of England and a former Vice-President of the Institute of Biology. He is an adviser to a range of organisations on biotechnology issues and is a member of the UK Government's Advisory Committee on Novel Foods and Processes (ACNFP) and Chair of EuropaBio's Advisory Group on Ethics. He is the author of a number of books, including (with Roger Straughan) *Improving Nature? The Science and Ethics of Genetic Engineering* (Cambridge University Press, 1996).

PETER SCOTT is Lecturer in Theology at Cheltenham and Gloucester College of Higher Education. Author of *Theology, Ideology and Liberation* (Cambridge, 1994) and articles on political and ecological theology, he is currently writing a book on the political theology of nature.

CHRISTOPHER SOUTHGATE is a poet, editor, and Honorary University Fellow in Theology at the University of Exeter. He also serves as a mental health chaplain. His publications include *A Love and Its Sounding: Explorations of T. S. Eliot* (University of Salzburg, 1997), *God, Humanity and the Cosmos: A Textbook in Science and Religion* (T&T Clark, 1999), of which he was the co-ordinating editor, and *Beyond the Bitter Wind* (Shoestring Press, 2000).

JACQUI STEWART is Senior Lecturer in Theology and Religious Studies and Co-Director of the Centre for Science and Religion at the University of Leeds. She has a Ph.D. and research experience in Population Genetics as well as a background and Ph.D. in Theology. Her research interests include theology, hermeneutics and the sciences, and her most recent publication is *Reconstructing Science and Theology in Postmodernity: Pannenberg, Ethics and the Human Sciences* (Ashgate, 2000).

BRONISLAW SZERSZYNSKI is Lecturer in Environment and Culture at the Centre for the Study of Environmental Change, Institute for Environment, Philosophy and Public Policy, Lancaster University. His research interests include religion and environment, citizenship and social movements, on which subjects he has published articles in *Worldviews, Environmental Values* and *Studies in Christian Ethics*. He was co-editor with Scott Lash and Brian Wynne of *Risk, Environment and Modernity: Towards a New Ecology* (Sage/TCS, 1996).

BRIAN WYNNE is Professor of Science Studies at the Centre for the Study of Environmental Change, Institute for Environment, Philosophy and Public Policy, Lancaster University. He was co-editor with Alan Irwin of *Misunderstanding Science? The Public Reconstruction of Science and Technology* (Cambridge University Press, 1996) and, with Scott Lash and Bronislaw Szerszynski, *Risk, Environment and Modernity: Towards a New Ecology* (Sage/TCS, 1996).

Acknowledgements

The editors would like to thank the following persons, who contributed to lively debate and discussion at the colloquium Reordering Nature: Theology and the New Genetics, held on 30 March 2000, where the first four papers and the replies to them were presented and discussed: Margaret Atkins, Sam Berry, John Brooke, Anne Bruce, Nigel Cooper, Tim Cooper, Sarah Franklin, Robin Grove-White, Harriet Harris, Alan Holland, Karim Labib, Lucy Larkin, Mairi Levitt, Andy Lowe, Neil Messer, Michael Northcott, Michael O'Dowd, Clare Palmer, Arthur Peacocke, Michael Reiss, John Rodwell, Peter Scott, Chris Southgate, Linda Woodhead and Brian Wynne. Regrettably, Michael Banner was unable to attend the colloquium, which resulted in his contribution to this volume taking the form of preliminary remarks, rather than a full-length paper. The Centre for the Study of Environmental Change at Lancaster University provided the venue for the colloquium, and Kate Lamb and Michelle Needham of CSEC supplied able administrative support.

We would also very much like to thank the Christendom Trust for providing the grant which made the colloquium and this collection possible, and for supporting the joint research by Celia Deane-Drummond, Bronislaw Szerszynski and Robin Grove-White which was published as an article in *Studies in Christian Ethics* (2001) and appears here as chapter 1. We would like to thank the University of Notre Dame Press for permission to include chapter 5, an earlier version of which was published in Philip R. Sloan (ed.), *Controlling Our Destinies: Historical, Philosophical, Ethical and Theological Perspectives on the Human Genome Project* (Notre Dame: University of Notre Dame Press, 2000). Celia Deane-Drummond would like to thank those who participated in the Association of Teachers in Moral Theology's meeting in Leeds in November 2001 for constructive criticism on her chapter. The editors would also like to thank Robin Grove-White, who played a key role in nurturing the book into its final state, and the commissioning editor, Stratford Caldecott, for his helpful comments and his patience and forbearance in waiting for the final manuscript to be delivered.

Introduction
Celia Deane-Drummond and
Bronislaw Szerszynski[1]

Many societies are now in the middle of debates about the new genetics, particularly in relation to genetically modified crops and food. The sheer intensity of the controversies about genetically modified organisms (GMOs), especially in European countries such as the UK, suggests their deep cultural significance in a period of great social change. But what *is* their cultural significance? Is genetic modification simply a continuation of the long history of human transformation of nature, or are we moving into a qualitatively different stage in our relationship with the natural world? Is the unease about GMOs expressed in many quarters simply a familiar and irrational failure of nerve when faced by a new technology – rooted, perhaps, in a pre-modern religious or even pagan notion of an immutable natural order? Or can critical or dissenting voices that draw on religious language and Christian theological insights offer us helpful clues for how to navigate some difficult dilemmas? Are we, as the title of this book suggests, witnessing a profound re-ordering of things – of nature itself, of the human role in nature, and even of the very boundaries between humans and nature? If so, how might the idea of 'the natural' – itself one of the central concepts in Western thought, especially when contrasted with 'the monstrous', 'the human', 'the

[1] The authors would like to thank Robin Grove-White for helpful comments on earlier drafts of this introduction, as well as for his important role in facilitating and shaping this collection.

1

artificial', or 'the divine' – itself be being reordered? What decisions do we face, whether at the level of specific interventions or at the more general one of societal trajectories? And do we already have the necessary cultural resources, especially those rooted in Christian theological traditions, to respond to these challenges and decisions, or do we need quite new ones?

Official secular orthodoxy – and much associated analysis – has tended to answer these questions in the manageable but reductionistic terms of relative risks and benefits. But it is our contention that genetic technologies also involve profound challenges to our ways of thinking about human identity and relationship with the natural world – challenges that have to be seen as at least implicitly theological in nature. Moreover, we suggest that theologians need to take into account such shifts in our understanding both of anthropology and the natural world in a way that is sensitive to these developments. This book, the result of a collaboration between the editors supported by a grant from the Christendom Trust, endeavours to explore the meaning of biotechnology at this deeper level. It takes the form of a dialogue between disciplines (theology, sociology, philosophy and history in particular) and between worlds (academia, the churches and public policy).

While it might have been possible to include a number of different religious traditions in response to the new genetic technologies, this book has focused on the resources available in Christian theology, rather than attempting to move wider into consideration of other religious responses, such as those rooted in Buddhism or Hinduism. Nevertheless, within many of the contributions of the book, Christian theological responses are subjected to the more general approach to the understanding of religion offered by a religious studies perspective. Thus, while we cannot claim that the book is comprehensive in its consideration of all possible religions, it does seek to locate Christian responses to biotechnology within a wider understanding of religion.

The resulting multidisciplinary conversation that the reader will find in this book raises a number of issues for debate, especially concerning how the need for such a conversation is accentuated by the new developments in biotechnology. Each part of the book offers a broad framework within which the debates can take place, and opens with an introduction that summarises the arguments made by each contributor. A final chapter discusses and critically evaluates the key themes explored in the book.

At root, all the contributions to the present volume are animated by two core questions: What contribution does, can and should Christian theology and religious insights make to debates about genetic technologies? And, in turn, what (if any) major challenge might the new genetics pose to our existing Christian theological resources for thinking about the human place in the world? Part I of the book opens up these questions with four wide-ranging core chapters from a number of disciplinary perspectives (by Celia Deane-Drummond, Robin Grove-White and Bronislaw Szerszynski; John Hedley Brooke; Michael Banner; and Michael Northcott), each chapter being followed by a critical response from another contributor. The opening chapter by the editors argues that the contemporary public response to GM foods should be understood as religious in nature, and in doing so lays down a serious challenge to regulators, sociologists and religious authorities alike. In contrast, Brooke takes us back to the seventeenth century and asks us to consider how far some of the religious ambiguity towards the natural world that we are aware of today has important historical precedents. Banner explores how far the concepts of the sublime and of holy dread can be of use in articulating human reactions to genetic modification, concluding that it is rather in the concept of the Sabbath rest that our attitudes to nature should be grounded. Northcott raises another important question in relation to the genetic modification of food, namely, whether it should simply be regarded as an extension of the destructive culture of modern farming, and goes on to ask whether we might recover more traditional Christian attitudes associated with affinity with the land and stewardship.

Given the centrality to biotechnology of scientific forms of knowledge, and the long and complex relationship between science and religion, the fact that many of the book's contributors have one foot firmly planted in the natural sciences has helped greatly to enrich the debate. In the past, however, debates about science and religion have tended to focus on the way theology and religious studies might simply respond to new developments in science, or alternatively how scientists are themselves also in some sense religious in their approach to their scientific pursuits. Such an analysis, while helpful in challenging the hostility commonly supposed to exist between science and religion, tends to assume that the philosophy of science is a fixed given that is set by scientists alone. In addition, while such an analysis may be helpful in challenging unwarranted dogmatism in theological analysis, this only places *theology* under pressure to change its way of thinking, rather than science as well. Brooke reminds us of the way that the ambiguity in human attitudes to science manifests itself in religious traditions and discourse, and this is certainly true in the current mixed responses to the new genetic technologies. Nonetheless, in the dominant framing of debates about science and religion the task of theologians is understood as merely responding to the powerful precedents set by the scientific community enshrined in logical positivism, and in modernity more generally.

Technology has, in the past, received rather less attention from those involved in the science and religion debates. The four chapters of Part II (by Arthur Peacocke, Michael Reiss, Donald Bruce and Stephen Clark) focus on specific issues, questions and dilemmas raised by genetic technology. Peacocke asks whether many of the most ambitious claims made for the technology rest on an erroneous, reductionistic understanding of the relationship between different kinds of knowledge. Bruce asks us to consider another question: how might alternative theological interpretations of the natural world bear on the way that we should regard risk in relation to genetic technologies? Or with Reiss and Clark, can received understandings of the boundaries between species, and those between permissible and impermissible acts, be used to select between possible genetic interventions – or are such boundaries challenged and made to seem less plausible by scientific, technological and cultural change?

It is the concern of this book to address another area that has flourished more recently in sociological debates about the place of science in contemporary culture, namely, the nature and extent of the public response to the new developments in biotechnology, particularly in the context of agriculture. A more 'respectful' consideration of the public response represents a novel approach, both in respect of current debates in science and religion and theological analysis of scientific and technological developments. This consideration has been assisted by recent advances in the sociological analysis of the practice of science and technology. For some years such analyses have been uncovering and exploring the values implicit in scientific and technological developments, to such an extent that many scientists will also admit that their work is not 'value free' in the way understood by many of the philosophers of science of the last century. This shift has problematised the conventional meaning imposed on the public's apparent reluctance to accept official reassurances of the safeness of new technologies. In expert circles, such hostile public reactions are generally treated as the mirror-image of science's neutrality and epistemic authority – as epistemologically vacuous, as driven by irrational overestimations of the actual physical risks that are posed by genetic engineering. The contributors to Part III (Levitt, Szerszynski and Wynne) counter this trend by seeking to attend closely and empathetically to what the public are trying to express when they talk about their concerns in this area.

The current debates about biotechnology have to be seen against the background of debates about the relationships between science, society and human flourishing. This is an era when science appears to be becoming increasingly central to public policy and social welfare and, in the eyes of governments and industry at least, to national 'wealth creation' and 'competitiveness'.[2] By contrast, in many parts of society there is growing ambivalence about society's relationship with 'science', fed by a number of successive controversies, from CFCs and the ozone layer, through BST and BSE, to the current GM upheavals.[3] The chapters of Part IV (by Jacqui Stewart, Peter Scott and Celia Deane-Drummond) and the final chapter by the editors, draw on theology in a number of different ways to explore these

---

[2] Successive official pronouncements, for example the White Paper *Excellence and Opportunity: A Science and Innovation Policy for the 21st Century*, CM4814 (London: HMSO, 2000), underline this reliance.

[3] Signals of concern are also coming from 'official' quarters – for example: the Royal Commission on Environmental Pollution's 21st Report, *Setting Environmental Standards*, Cm 4053, (London: HMSO, 1998); the House of Lords Science and Technology Committee's 3rd Report, *Science and Society*, HL 38, (London: HMSO 2000); Mike Gibbons, 'Science's New Social Contract with Society' *Nature*, 402, 6761 (Suppl), 1999, C81–C84.

wider issues. In particular, the way theology may serve to contribute to shifting debates in technology towards more political questions is raised by Stewart and Scott, while Deane-Drummond offers a way of exploring the usefulness of a virtue ethic rooted in a Thomistic understanding of wisdom and prudence. Finally, the closing chapter by the editors revisits many of the themes and arguments advanced in earlier chapters, against the background of a consideration of the implications of the contemporary rise of uncertainty as a key principle in risk debates.

A key argument of the book is that the richness of religious insight on these matters has been underexplored – hence the theological perspectives explored in the chapters that follow. But if this book is a challenge to biotechnologists and regulators to take seriously the contribution that can be made by religion, specifically Christian theology, it should also be seen as a challenge to theologians and religious institutions. Most of their interventions in this area have been characterised by a deference towards the problem-definitions given by science, and by a condescension towards the public that mirrors that, noted above, to which scientists are often prey. If religious institutions are usefully to add a distinctive theological voice to the wide-ranging debate that is sorely needed, they may need to develop new roles for themselves. This book is a start in this direction and is intended to stimulate debate amongst not just theologians but all those currently concerned with what it means to reorder nature through the new genetic technologies. Hence one of the purposes of this book is to help break down the compartmentalisation commonly existing between different academic approaches to the natural world and scientific interventions in it in particular. While issues in science and religion begin to foster debate between apparently disparate areas, it is our contention that the new genetics poses a much wider and more complex conversation between different parties with different interests in the issues involved. Indeed, it is our belief that the way forward in the public debate and policy formation is through taking such conversations seriously as a wider framework in which to reflect on these issues.

PART I

Current Debates in Theology

Introduction to Part I

The first section of the book offers four chapters, each with a response from another author, which illustrate the range of approaches and disciplines that can shed light on current theological debates over biotechnology – sociology, history, philosophy, as well as theology. In chapter 1, Celia Deane-Drummond, Robin Grove-White and Bronislaw Szerszynski encourage us to consider the public response to current issues in agricultural genetics as encompassing ethical issues that have been previously missed by regulatory and ethical frameworks which focus narrowly on particular risks and benefits. However, they argue that the public response is not just *ethically* significant; deeper religious issues about the ordering of the natural world, the place of God in such ordering, and the nature of human identity can also be discerned through a sensitive reading of lay voices. Such a religious dimension to the public response has been missed by policy-makers and has been marginalised in sociological analysis of the debates.

The authors argue that this public response is theologically significant. In contrast to the official responses of the churches, where there has been a relatively slow engagement with the theological significance of issues in genetic engineering of organisms other than humans, the public response seems on some levels at least to carry a greater degree of sophistication. As a survey of recent church statements shows, the official response of the churches towards the new technologies has been varied, though tending towards an anthropocentric

orientation. While there are those who argue that human
beings may or indeed should improve the natural world
through human intervention, for others this seems to break the
God-given natural order of things. The public response seemed
to be less riven by such a dichotomy, with most people
reasoning for genetic change in some circumstances, but not in
others. Yet such lay discriminations seemed to be grounded not
so much in a narrow cost–benefit analysis, but in judgements
about the motives and intentions lying behind such development. For the public, biotechnology companies and
regulators are not approaching the issue in a similar spirit of
reverence and seriousness. Making a guarded parallel with the
choices faced by Jewish theology after the Holocaust, but
stopping short of arguing that the biotechnology revolution
demands a radically new theology, the authors nevertheless ask
'what truths this historically unprecedented event may be
revealing about the nature of human existence in the world'.
They conclude by suggesting that what is needed is not greater
scientific, ethical or theological certainty, but increased societal
wisdom and discernment in the face of complexity and uncertainty, and that one element of such a project has to be a more
inclusive public debate about the deeper, ontological significance of genetic science and technology.

Christopher Southgate's response to this chapter takes a
more sceptical stance towards the capacity of focus group
discussions with members of the public to produce wisdom on
this or any other issue. He also suggests that young adults may
be at once more fatalistic and more pragmatic about biotechnology than the older adults quoted in the chapter, with far less
fundamental misgivings about tampering with natural order
(although see chapter 9 for findings about the attitudes of even
younger people). At the same time, he argues that people seem
to be more accepting of medical applications of biotechnology,
perceiving them as having clearer benefits and being subject to
more stringent testing procedures, than agricultural applications, seen as being developed with far less precautions and
by an industry suspected of being overly concerned with the
benefits to themselves rather than those to society at large. He
concludes by doubting that the emergence of the new genetics
is sufficiently significant an event as to serve as a serious
challenge to theology to seek new resources; nevertheless, he

suggests that theology needs to look to its 'treasure-houses' for less hubristic models of the rightful human relationship to creation.

In chapter 2, the historian John Hedley Brooke reminds us that swings between optimism and pessimism towards science and new technologies have historical precedents, dating even from the start of experimental science in the seventeenth century. The human ambivalence towards nature as such may be expressed religiously, either through fostering a passive contemplation of the natural world, or through activism in bringing in the new kingdom, a reconstruction of nature. He thus suggests that the theological justification of human intervention in nature is not new, being expressed in the works of, for example, Hugh Miller and Francis Bacon. Miller, for example, saw 'Man' [*sic*] as 'fellow-worker' with the Creator and a 'mighty improver of nature', working according to exactly the same principles as God. But while there were those, such as alchemists, and those from dissenting traditions, such as Joseph Priestley, who believed that religion legitimised almost anything that was possible for science, others were more conscious of the weakness of human nature. Even those promoting a view of nature as mechanised or 'artificial' could feel that there were theological limits to human intervention. Such voices of disquiet are heard even in the midst of optimism about the possibilities for God and humanity, namely, whether the quality of life will be eroded by an over-reliance on new technologies. Above all, Brooke's chapter asks us to consider Newton's question: does human intervention enhance divine power or detract from it? In leaving us with a question in this way, Brooke encourages us to explore the issues in a way that refuses to accept any simple opposition between technological progress and religious faith.

In a meditative response to Brooke's chapter, Arthur Peacocke finds other historical examples of belief in the idea that human beings partake in divine creativity. He firstly draws our attention to the art and writing of fifteenth-century thinkers such as Giannozzi Manetti and Marsilio Ficino, who, surrounded in Renaissance Florence by so many examples of human creativity, formed a powerful sense of human beings as being 'second creators', actively continuing the work that God had started. Peacocke then cites William Blake as a further example, as evidenced in that writer's call for all Christians to play their part in 'building Jerusalem'. He concludes by expressing hope that this 'wisdom of former times' can help inform the way that we respond today to the dilemmas that face us in this domain.

In chapter 3, Michael Banner discusses two recent papers by the moral philosophers Bernard Williams and David Wiggins, which both try to make philosophically respectable the notion that there are limits to what we can legitimately do to nature, limits that cannot be captured within the cost–benefit framework that dominates biotechnology debates. Williams tries to do this through the notion of *Promethean fear*, a quite reasonable fear of nature as an 'unbounded and potentially dangerous enemy, which requires respect'. Wiggins, for his part, echoing a theme in chapter 1, suggests that the idea of *holy dread* is useful as a way of capturing that moral response that many people felt was sorely lacking among farmers and agricultural feed manufacturers in the events that led up to the BSE crisis. Such a dread, Wiggins suggests, would be the reasonable result of recognising 'the severe limitation on our knowledge of the sum of factors to which we owe our survival ... and the near limitlessness of our ignorance of how things will turn out if we change those factors'.

Banner argues that such attempts fail exactly because of their concern to avoid what both authors see as a discreditable association with religious ideas. Both concepts add little more than a prudential caution to consequentialist notions of weighing costs and benefits. Neither will the notion of the 'sublime', that tries to capture the experience of awe and terror before nature, do justice to the idea of limits to our treatment of nature – it could just as easily justify an attitude of domination as one of respect (see chapter 10 for a more positive assessment of the sublime). Drawing on the theological doctrine of God's Sabbath rest, Banner argues that humanity has to learn not to fear nature but to love and enjoy it, and that it is only in that religious, rather than philosophical, truth that there is hope for a future in which we live with, not against, nature.

In his response, Michael Reiss presents his own survey of theological responses to biotechnology, broadly comparable to that presented in chapter 1. Reiss identifies three main positions taken by theological writers: *rejection* (on the basis that it reduces non-human nature to slaves or mere resources), *hesitancy* (particularly over developments that might blur the line between humans and other species) and *acceptance with caveats.* In this last category Reiss includes those who use the idea of humans as being co-creators with God as justification for the genetic alteration of species (see also chapter 2). Reiss then identifies three specific ways in which his own position departs from that of Banner. First, he professes little confidence in the experience of moral revulsion at certain actions which, Banner suggests, Wiggins fails to capture with his secularised, merely prudential rereading of 'holy dread'. Such feelings, Reiss suggests, are a very unreliable guide to right and wrong, and so often merely reflect untutored prejudices. Secondly, Reiss criticises Banner for his emphasis on Christian ideas, suggesting that Christians should look outwards to secular society and seek a wider consensus in language to which all can assent. Thirdly, Reiss suggests that Banner, in insisting that 'this God creates, as another god may or may not, out of love for human kind' is being too anthropocentric in his understanding of the value of nature. Reiss uses evolutionary arguments to suggest that, far from other species existing for our good, they exist in large measure for their own. He concludes by lending implicit support for the third of the positions he identified in his survey of theological writings on biotechnology, asking 'whether genetic engineering, for all its frequent, current ethical shortcomings, can yet function as an agent of restoration'.

In chapter 4, Michael Northcott asks us to consider whether current issues in agricultural genetics are really new, or part of a complex plethora of changes which have been going on for some time in technologically enhanced agriculture. He suggests that genetic engineering of food is symptomatic of the wider problem of human alienation from the land. For him the place to start both theologically and ethically is from an examination of the relationships with the land as portrayed in the biblical account, rooted in the Christian belief in God as Creator-Redeemer of the material world. In pre-modern societies agriculture is not simply about food production, but engenders complex social relationships between people and the land, expressed in symbols and traditions that inform religious and cultural existence. By contrast, he suggests that modern society has largely lost this vision of the interdependence and diversity of life expressed in agriculture, though it is retained to some extend in the works of Fritz Schumacher and Aldo Leopold.

From a theological point of view Northcott invites us to consider the demise of the Christian idea of stewardship alongside the rise in industrial forms of agriculture. For Northcott the jubilee and Sabbath laws are significant here (see also chapter 3). The Sabbath is a reminder of the covenant relationship between people and land, issuing in social justice and respect for land. Northcott's chapter is a pithy reminder of the seriousness with which the God of the Old Testament treated those who failed to show respect for the mutual covenant between God, humanity and the land. He finds an echo of such a critique in those who write about the devastating social and ecological consequences of globalisation and the industrialisation of agriculture. In place of responsible stewardship, we find systematic ecological devastation on an unprecedented global scale. He suggests that pesticide overuse, poor diet and junk food are global problems, leading to mineral deficiencies along with other associated health risks. The enforced increase in productivity and availability of cheap food eclipses wider social and ecological concerns. Biotechnology viewed in this light is just one further development in the trend towards the mechanisation of agriculture and government-sponsored industrialised farming. His answer to such a severe crisis is theological, namely, a return to the land ethic of Aldo Leopold and the stewardship ideal of Wendel Berry. Above all, Northcott wishes to identify the modern industrialisation of agriculture with idolatry against God and set in its place a restatement of the notion of the divine command to love God and neighbour under the sovereignty of Jesus Christ. Northcott's chapter is provocative in the sharpness of its critique and his proposed alternative.

The response by Peter Scott invites us to explore a little further the question of whether the traditional ideal of Christian stewardship necessarily provides the answer to modern farming practices. In particular, he challenges the premise in Northcott's chapter that genetic engineering does not represent a radically new departure, and thus does not raise radically new issues for theology. He suggests, indeed, that our power to manipulate nature itself is producing a new 'structure of feeling', from which a new notion of nature – fully commodified and stripped of agency – is emerging, and with it a new self-understanding of the human being. In developing this thought, Scott's worry about stewardship becomes clear. He suggests, provocatively, that it is not, in the end, a sufficiently distinct model for our right relation with nature from the instrumental subjugation of nature implied by genetic manipulation, since both in different ways deny the agency of nature. The *stewardship* of nature thus deconstructs all too easily into the *mastery* of nature, and in another twist the mastery of *nature* turns into the mastery of *humanity*, as 'we who would be "masters" of nature find ourselves "mastered" '. Scott concludes by wondering if consequentialism may be more useful for moral guidance in biotechnological issues than is often acknowledged, if only 'the consequences for the marginalised – the poorest, non-human nature – were written into ethical reflection'.

1

Genetically Modified Theology: The Religious Dimensions of Public Concerns about Agricultural Biotechnology[1]

Celia Deane-Drummond, Robin Grove-White and Bronislaw Szerszynski

Introduction

The latest massive controversies about genetically modified (GM) crops and foods in the UK and mainland Europe have underlined the novelty and complexity of the *human* issues raised by advances in biotechnology. Not only have the controversies found governments such as the British Government unprepared for the unprecedented surges in public hostility towards this emerging technology, but they have also suggested the extent to which dominant 'expert' opinion, which has overwhelmingly favoured reliance on 'scientific' safety assessments of GM products on an individual case-by-case basis, may have been missing the point.

But what *is* the point? How *are* recent events to be understood? In this chapter, we want to argue that the current public anxiety about the genetic engineering of plants and animals has been radically misunderstood in a number of ways. First, when

[1] The authors would like to express their gratitude to the Christendom Trust for their financial support for the collaboration that produced this paper.

viewed in their own terms, public reactions can be seen as reasonable and sensitive, rather than irrational and 'emotional'. Secondly, they are better understood as responses at the level of ontology and theology rather than simply as concerns about physical risk and health. Thirdly, whilst people are concerned about the technologies themselves, their deepest unease seems to be in relation to the *spirit* in which these technologies are being developed and encouraged – the motives that animate this development, the level of seriousness and respect with which it is proceeding, and the assumptions about human beings and their place in the world that seem to underlie it.

The urgency of the need to develop a richer understanding of the dynamics of human responses to biotechnology cannot be doubted – the more so because, hitherto, such dimensions have been given only residual attention in countries like the UK. Genetic modification is a profoundly important techno-logical process, for which huge scientific, political and economic expectations have been generated.[2] As fruits of the immense advances in molecular biology over the past three decades, such developments are claimed to have deep potential implications for future human welfare and development around the globe. Yet this potential will be nugatory if it is rejected by the human beings who are its supposed future beneficiaries. And the possibility of such rejection has been made credible for the first time by the continuing events in Europe.

From the early 1970s, there has been recognition of the moral and ethical challenges posed by advances in biotech-nology.[3] Countries like Britain have developed a patchwork of advisory committees (Advisory Commission on Releases into the Environment (ACRE), Advisory Commission on Novel Foods and Processes (ACNFP) and so on), reflecting the agreed 'precautionary' approach prescribed in European Union

[2] Ernst & Young, *Biotechnology's Economic Impact in Europe: A Survey of Its Future Role in Competitiveness* (London: Ernst & Young, 1994); CEC, *White Paper on Growth, Competitiveness and Employment* (Brussels: Commission of the European Communities, 1993).
[3] For recent discussions, see C. Deane-Drummond, *Theology and Biotechnology: Implications for a New Science* (London: Geoffrey Chapman, 1997); A. Holland and A. Johnson (eds), *Animal Biotechnology and Ethics* (London: Chapman & Hall, 1998).

member states. More recently, there has been a succession of reports and reviews by bodies such as the Royal Society, the Nuffield Council on Bioethics and the Royal Commission on Environmental Pollution. Overwhelmingly, such studies have focused on particular products and processes, either narrowly on questions of risk and safety or more broadly on their moral acceptability. The core problem tends to be pictured as being how to arrive at adequate moral, ethical (or even theological) *evaluations* (which are seen, by implication, as soft, if socially very important, issues of judgement) of matters of scientific *fact* (which, by contrast, are purported to reflect hard and objectively specifiable ontological reality).

In the present context, one immediately awkward implication of this approach is that it tends to give implicit support to an understanding of 'the public' which is in itself demeaning – and indeed thoroughly question-begging. If the task of moral, ethical and theological reflection becomes seen as being the provision of a distinctive form of 'expert' appraisal of developments in the physical-biological domain, then 'ordinary people' who react against such developments in ways which appear to be at odds with approaches emanating from such expertise will tend to be pictured, by implication, as by contrast less than 'expert' – their reactions untutored, 'emotional' or even, in the worst case, 'irrational'. Indeed, much 'informed' comment on recent events, in news media and by politicians, has had this flavour. When the GM controversy erupted in Britain in early 1999, commentators from all sides of the argument – politicians, leader-writers, and scientific institutions alike – sought to distinguish between supposedly 'rational' (i.e. scientifically or politically justified) concerns about GM developments and those which are simply 'hysterical' or 'media induced'.

Our own approach has a different starting point. To understand the human dynamics now in play, there appears to us an urgent need to focus in a far more sensitive and discriminating fashion on the quality and texture of the actual reactions of 'ordinary people' themselves in relation to such matters. From a Christian perspective, this means focusing with empathic sensitivity – with what Simone Weil calls *attention* – on the integrity of what particular people are saying, singly and in groups, about their own reactions, both to the new GM issues and to the ways in which such technological artefacts are now

being handled by governments and regulatory bodies.[4]
Respectful examination and interpretation of such reactions,
we suggest, may offer insights into the deeper human
significance of biotechnology's current travails.

It happens that research by the authors and their associates
provides a body of raw material for such a task. In particular, the
1997 study at the Centre for the Study of Environmental
Change, *Uncertain World: Genetically Modified Organisms, Food and
Public Attitudes in Britain,* offers insight into the finer grain of a
range of relevant public responses.[5] The material in question
was generated through focus group discussions involving
people from a spectrum of social classes and life stages, as part
of an attempt in late 1996 and early 1997, *well in advance of the
recent upsets,* to gain insight into then-latent concerns and
anxieties about GM prospects and developments.

A key finding from *Uncertain World* was the glaring gap
between the often unspecific and inchoate character of 'lay'
public concerns about biotechnology ('Where is this leading?';
'Won't it lead to unanticipated problems, as has tended to
happen with novel technologies in the past?'; 'Who on earth
can we trust in this post-BSE world?'; 'What crucial, and by
definition unspecifiable, unknowns are yet to be identified?')
and the hard-edged, one-issue-at-a-time, reductionist scientific
assessments of the official political oversight bodies (Ministerial
Advisory Committees, Scientific Advisers, EU Expert Scientific
Panels and so on). The sense of such a gap – and the understandable if largely unarticulated unease it engenders, even in
individuals untutored in the nuances of constitutional political
accountability – was all the more striking for the fact that at that
stage (i.e. in early 1997) there was no acknowledgement
whatsoever by the powers-that-be that any such mismatch
existed. The authors of *Uncertain World* concluded that the
political legitimacy of the prevailing regulatory arrangements
was probably highly brittle – a conclusion which appears now to
have been vindicated by the turbulent GM events of 1999 and

---

[4] S. Weil, *Gravity and Grace* (London: Routledge, 1952).
[5] R. Grove-White, P. Macnaghten, S. Mayer and B. Wynne, *Uncertain World:
Genetically Modified Organisms, Food and Public Attitudes in Britain* (Lancaster: Centre
for the Study of Environmental Change (CSEC), Lancaster University, 1997).

the associated bewilderment of the responsible regulatory bodies.[6]

A corollary was that more useful analytical insights for interpreting the *Uncertain World* focus group discussions were found to be available more in the domains of the sociology of knowledge – particularly, recent insights concerning the social dynamics of contending conceptions of 'scientific uncertainty' and 'public risk perceptions' – than in more mainstream moral and ethical commentaries.[7] In other words, the concepts and vocabularies of 'risk society' and from recent social scientific understanding of human responses to contemporary cultural change, turned out to help constitute more accurate 'predictions' of public responses than did the officially dominant tools of analysis.[8] There are now signs, in the wake of the current brouhaha, that such insights are beginning to have an impact on public policy reflection.[9]

Nevertheless, the *Uncertain World* focus group materials pointed to a host of further questions of a normative kind, not addressed in the study itself. It is these that provide a useful starting point for the present article. For example, in articulating their concerns about biotechnology developments (the same concerns left unaddressed within the official regulatory frameworks), what implicit picture of the human-nature relationship were people tacitly assuming? What tacit 'cosmology', or even 'ontology', is being predicated? What accommodations with 'uncertainty' were being assumed as normal, from which GM developments were intuited to be a

---

[6] Environmental Data Services (ENDS), 'The Spiralling Agenda of Agricultural Biotechnology', *ENDS Report*, 283, August 1998, 18–30; ENDS, 'Applying a Biodiversity Brake to Genetically Modified Crops', *ENDS Report*, 289, February 1999, 21–7; ENDS, 'Government Still Struggling to Master the Biotechnology Agenda', *ENDS Report*, 292, May 1999, 28–32; *Nature*: Editorial, 'GM Foods Debate Needs a Recipe for Restoring Trust', *Nature*, 398, 6729, 1999, 639.

[7] S. Lash, B. Szerszynski and B. Wynne, (eds), *Risk, Environment and Modernity: Towards a New Ecology* (London: Sage, 1996).

[8] U. Beck, *Risk Society: Towards a New Modernity*, tr. Mark Ritter (London: Sage, 1992); U. Beck, A. Giddens and S. Lash, *Reflexive Modernization: Politics, Tradition and Aesthetics in the Modern Social Order* (Cambridge: Polity Press, 1994); R. Grove-White and B. Wynne, *Science, Culture and the Environment* (Lancaster: CSEC, Lancaster University, 1998).

[9] Royal Commission on Environmental Pollution, *Response to the Review of the Framework for Overseeing Developments in Biotechnology* (London: RCEP, 1999); ESRC Global Environmental Change Programme, *The Politics of GM Food: Risk, Science and Public Trust*, Special Briefing No. 5 (Brighton: University of Sussex, 1999).

departure? Were people *really* hostile to human-induced changes to the 'natural' world, or could the anxieties being expressed on this score be palliated if there was greater confidence in their overall political supervision? What normative model of the very notion of 'rationality' is appropriate when issues concerning human intervention in the very processes of life itself are at issue?

As we argue below, questions of these kinds touch on deep issues concerning the nature of human personhood – indeed of human nature itself. It seems conceivable that the intensity of current controversies around GM crops and foods arises in part from the fact that, in their regulation in the public domain, *conflicting ontologies of the person* are making themselves felt in the politics of everyday life. If this is the case, then Christian theological understandings of the person may be of central analytical significance for helping throw light on what has been going on.

It is this intriguing possibility – that theological perspectives may now be indispensable in helping explain to largely secular institutions the sources and dynamics of conflicts now threatening to paralyse the development of what is being posited as a key technology for the twenty-first century – that we seek now to outline. In the next section we discuss relevant features of the *Uncertain World* focus group transcripts. This leads, in the third section, to a consideration of the ways in which prevailing strains of theological reflection have been considering broadly these same phenomena. And in the last section, we try to set out some of the challenges posed by our analysis, both for political institutions and for the role of theology itself.

The Nature of Public Concerns

The year 1999 was one of immense controversy around Europe concerning GM food and agricultural products. Yet, in Britain at least, the outlines of tensions resulting in such upheavals had been evident in qualitative research undertaken three years previously, in 1996–7, as part of the research study *Uncertain World*. Focus groups involving people from a variety of social groups and life stages provided the framework for an exploration of *public* views, actual or emergent, about GM prospects, as well as a basis for subsequent comparisons with *official* responses.[10]

In the research, the single most recurrent unease to emerge concerned the issue of *tampering*. At one level, GM developments were felt to be yet another stage in intensifying patterns of industrial interference in the 'natural' character of foods:

M: It sounds dangerous and unnatural ... I get the impression that all the food's been meddled with in a laboratory before it reaches the supermarket ... It's like, you know, these fruits they inject with stuff to keep apples redder for longer and things. I want food to be fresh. I don't want it to have all this stuff in it ... But that's like scientifically taking natural food and making it unnatural.

T: [T]hey're going to do a lot more messing about and I don't know why they don't just miss that bit out and hurry up and make three pills, breakfast, dinner, and tea. We'd all have a lot less to worry about [laughter] ... You get shades of Adolph Hitler, you know, you get the supreme fruit and veg ...
                        (North London Working Mothers' group)

But beyond this, GM crops and foods seemed to point to a qualitatively new phase in interference with *nature itself*:

R: It's messing about with nature, isn't it? I'm not sure if that's a good or bad thing ... That's it. Tampering with nature. What damage is it going to do? They're messing around with nature like that, what damage is it going to do to the environment? In twenty or thirty years time? I mean, maybe you won't be able to grow your own vegetables then. Because of the damage to the ozone layer or something like that ...
                        (North London 'Green Consumers' group)

J: When I look at it I think oh, they're dabbling in nature aren't they? You read scientific developments, that jumps out at me, scientific developments ... You think, well they're trying to,

[10] Nine focus groups were held in November and December of 1996. Four of these were held in North London, and consisted of non-working mothers, working mothers, fathers and green consumers (mixed gender), respectively. The other five were held in Lancashire, and were made up of working women, non-working mothers, churchgoers (mixed gender), male risk takers, and schoolgirls. For more details of the groups, and of the topic guide used to guide the discussion, see Grove-White et al., *Uncertain World*. We are grateful to Phil Macnaghten for allowing us to perform this secondary analysis of the transcripts.

you know, genetically change things and all this, well what are they putting in it to genetically change it?

(Lancashire Working Women's group)

M: It doesn't seem natural ... for man to interfere with the nature of things. I know processes of evolution, everything goes through changes, sometimes for the better, sometimes for the worse, but I'm not sure whether man should play God and change things for the better, for the lucre at the end of the day ...

(Lancashire 'Risk Takers' group)

Strong as such concern was, however, it was less than absolute. Many people were prepared to discriminate between different potential uses of GMs, according to the particular purposes to which they might be put:

C: Annoyed I can't have any control over it. But then in the next breath I understand that change has to happen, but I don't always think it happens for the right reasons. I think medicine is the right reason. I think productivity levels, to increase consumer power, to increase profit, are not. Not when it means injecting sheep and getting different kinds of milk from them ...

(Lancashire Working Women's group)

B: [Looking at a picture] ... struggling up a path to the bright sunlight ahead and that's what I feel we're doing at the moment. We're struggling through a path of tangled weeds and don't knows and worries and decisions and we don't know what we're going to find when we get to the end.

Mod: A good path or a bad path?

B: I think it's a rocky path.

(Lancashire Churchgoers' group)

Such ambivalence recurred in a number of the groups. There was extensive and profound unease at the prospect of the imagined increased pervasiveness of GM foods. This was in 1996/7, when there had so far been little or no *public* discussion of the implications of GM crops in Britain. But at the same time there was little evidence of any *reflex* hostility to the technology, or of any wish to avoid engagement with the complexity of what was at stake. When seen in context, the unease that people expressed was seldom comprehensively dismissive. Interference with nature was acknowledged frequently to be a reality of human existence and development – but at the same time the *reasons* for and motives behind particular classes of such interference, and the terms on which it might be undertaken, demanded review and extreme caution:

M: ... [T]here's a saying that 'if it isn't broke, don't bother trying to fix it' – and there's nothing wrong with food as it is naturally except that it hasn't got a long shelf life. So really I can see pound signs all over that ... that's all it's really to do with.
(Lancashire Working Women's group)

P: ... [I]n a world where the population is expanding at a high rate you've got to, in all areas, be as efficient and use technology in the most efficient manner, and in this respect, although I'm not particularly happy perhaps with choosing that food myself, I think it's something which has to progress to help everybody, or at least to test whether or not the results would be beneficial to help everybody.
(Lancashire Churchgoers' group)

H: ... [W]ell the other one I suppose, in a sense it had a purpose behind it – it was going to help some one with a serious, hopefully serious, illness and there might possibly be an argument for it. But I don't think there's an argument for feeding an animal to make it grow more quickly ... just so that we can kill them more quickly and eat them more quickly. I don't like that. That's immoral to me ...
(Lancashire Churchgoers' group)

Such tentative and highly selective acknowledgement of possible benefits was tempered, repeatedly, by deep anxiety about the ill-defined prospect of potentially enormous adverse – and irreversible – consequences:

S: Once you've genetically engineered a pig, it's always going to stay genetically engineered. But how are you going to reverse it?

R: If you find out there's a problem in 10 years ...

S: You can't and it will go on for ever, not just for the near future. This is permanent, once you've genetically engineered something. I don't think it will alter naturally, although nature will probably take over at one time and cause a problem.

R: Right, so if you tinker with something then ...

S: It will be passed on to the future ...
Mod: It will be passed on?
S: It's irreversible though isn't it, with genetics I would imagine.
                                    (Lancashire 'Risk Takers' group)

L: ... I'm not in control of this. I have no control over this. It's
        gonna happen and I can't ... you know ...
                                    (Lancashire Working Mothers' group)

G: They're messing around with food. The next thing is going to
        be human beings ...
                                    (Lancashire Churchgoers' group)

What theological significance might this have? We suggest that a fruitful approach is to explore what might be inferred *ontologically* about people's various reactions, viewed from the perspective of Christian understandings of the human person and of human interdependence.

Seen in this light, several points stand out. First, people appeared to be responding from within a sense of a given *order* – a *natural* order, the boundaries of which were felt to be challenged radically by the prospect and potentialities of genetic modification: fundamental categories in 'nature' were being threatened through human intervention, with unforeseeable potential consequences.

Yet secondly, there was tacit acknowledgement that human beings might be *justified* in certain circumstances in creative interactions (interference) in such *order*. But this should only occur if the purposes were somehow the *right* ones – which appeared to mean, governed by genuine compassion and charity towards other beings.

However, thirdly, such a condition was felt unlikely to be met. There was a recurrent fatalism and cynicism about the prospect of modifying the momentum of GM developments in order to respect 'moral' boundaries and the true range of uncertainties. The supposed collusion of governments and interested corporations was seen as making the widespread introduction of GM products inevitable, with scientific reassurances operating, as in the recent BSE–CJD (mad cow disease – Creutzfeldt-Jakob disease) disaster, to reinforce such momentum, neglectful of possible as-yet unidentified dangers.

In our view, when combined, such findings suggest that at the core of the concerns emerging from the focus group discussions were issues about human *responsibility* and *control*, under conditions of fundamental – indeed, ontological – uncertainty and ignorance. Whilst prepared to countenance the transcendence of 'natural' boundaries for specified benign purposes through processes of genetic modification, people tended tacitly to dismiss the possibility that the appropriate surrounding conditions or safeguards could or would ever be achieved. One pointer to this in the focus groups was the recurrent and disturbing fatalism and sense of disablement pervading people's discussion of their own lack of agency in relation to the ways in which matters were now developing. Sometimes the resulting sense of impotence took a heightened, even poetic, form:

S: I started out not too bad when I had the discussion. I thought I'd have an open mind about it, but I've changed my mind. As soon as I saw that about the human gene, suddenly the enormity of it made me feel really awful. I got an awful feeling about it, because I thought it was something that ... I think we're touching things that we don't realise and I think we're taking things out of the earth, and we're now trying to correct it by using things like genetic engineering, because mistakes were made. And I feel time's just ticking by and we don't realise what's going to happen in the future. I think something terrible could happen. It's given me a bad feeling really.

Mod: So it's as if we're trying to fix something which is mixed up with something ...?

S: Yes, because the earth hasn't got what it used to have. We feel we have to put something back into the food to make it better, and maybe we're correcting things in the wrong way. I don't know ...

T: It's a frightening thought to think that time's ticking away though ...

S: Yes. It's something that I'd like to put at the back of my mind now. I wouldn't like to think about it again. I probably wouldn't – but when we talk about it, it does bring it to your mind. But then I'll probably put it to the back of my mind now ...

(Lancashire Working Women's group)

In the *Uncertain World* report, a key empirical finding concerned the stark contrast that emerged between the broad open-ended character of such concerns about GMs on the part of lay people, and the narrowly constrained positivistic scope of the official regulatory frameworks of GM regulation in Britain.[11] Where people in the focus groups consistently highlighted their unease about broad trajectories of GM developments (*Why* was this being done? In whose interest? With what cumulative implications and as-yet unknown consequences?), the panoply of official Advisory Committees and authorisation processes had a narrow one-product-at-a-time evaluation focus, and avoided such wider questions. This, *Uncertain World* argued, amounted to 'a de facto process of political denial, on a matter of substantial public importance'. And the subsequent 1999 GM brouhaha appears to have followed precisely the fault lines between these two contrasting representations of what was at stake.[12]

In the context of the present paper, that same contrast between the two outlooks might fruitfully be represented as a conflict between two different *implicit theologies of the person* – between an 'official' picture which, through its normative insistence on the relevance for social decisions of only a restricted number of scientifically measurable parameters, implied one version of what were to be recognised as justified human concerns and a 'lay' picture in which a far wider range of implications of GMs pointed to deeper issues of human relationships with the natural order under real-world conditions of contemporary political economy. Alongside this tension there are clearly differences in the value being given to science. In the 'official' picture there is a positivistic view of science; that is, it is deemed to be the only worthwhile source of knowledge. In contrast, the 'lay' picture is more likely to view science in its context as a human endeavour. Yet it seems to us that contrasting views of science presuppose the implicit theologies of the person and that it is these differences that are of particular significance in the interpretation of current events.

Hence, we suggest that picturing the tensions in *theological* terms may yield a richer and more convincing account of the intensity of recent controversies in Britain than some of the

---

[11] The dismissal of intrinsic ethical views by influential spheres of government, academia, industry and commerce has been noted by D. Bruce and A. Bruce, *Engineering Genesis: The Ethics of Genetic Engineering in Non-Human Species* (London: Earthscan, 1998), 82.

[12] ESRC Global Environmental Change Programme, *Politics of GM Food.*

accounts which have been offered so far – for example, that public 'emotionalism' and 'irrationality', fanned by a hysterical media, has overwhelmed the 'objective' scientific facts, or that environmental pressure groups have somehow directed public sensibilities in unprecedentedly effective fashion. Rather, it appears to us that the dominant UK approaches to GM food/crop promotion and regulation may have been *insulting* the self-understanding of 'ordinary people' about matters of considerable existential moment to them – and that such experience may have been intensified by the chronic lack of any adequate public discourse or context in which such matters can be acknowledged adequately and given respectful shared public *attention*.

In short, what has burst forth in recent GM events, we suggest, has been the long-burgeoning crisis in societies like our own concerning *conflicting representations of the human* – of tensions between different tacit understandings of human essence, in a way that is inclusive of the relation between human beings and 'nature', and to one another.

And it is only when considered through the conceptual resources of *theology*, deployed in new ways, that insights into such matters – of mounting social and political importance in increasingly technologically-driven democracies like our own – can begin to be generated.

The Religious Debate

So far, we have raised issues arising from the focus group research in *Uncertain World*, and suggested some fresh interpretative perspectives that explore implicit religious dimensions. But how far does our approach match the 'official' theological debate conducted by church groups, religious organisations and theologians? A comprehensive survey of the literature in this area is beyond the scope of this paper; even more so would be an attempt to discuss the unofficial responses of the churches to genetic engineering of non-humans, which, in the case of the Church of England, for example, take the issue with much greater seriousness.[13] Nonetheless, we can point to a number of trends.

---

[13] For further discussion, see C. Deane-Drummond, 'Come to the Banquet: Seeking Wisdom in a Genetically Engineered Earth', *Ecotheology*, 9, 2000, 27–37.

First, certainly prior to the early 1990s in the Protestant Churches and even later in the Roman Catholic Church, there has been a strong emphasis in the religious interventions on potential *impacts* on human beings. The implicit (and even sometimes explicit) premise of this emphasis seems to be that the genetic modification of non-human animals and plants raises no fundamental ethical issues per se. The most clearly *ethical* responses, for example in the official booklets produced by the Church of England and the Roman Catholic Church, have concerned *human* genetic technology.[14] The World Council of Churches, similarly, has been primarily concerned with the possibility of manipulation of human life by geneticists and what this might mean for theology and ethics.[15] While at the popular level there has initially been fear, mistrust and suspicion of genetic engineering in the churches, the official position is more often positive. Dyson suggests that this is related to the number of participants who are also scientists.[16]

Interventions that *have* addressed the issue of non-human genetic engineering prior to the 1990s have tended to suggest it is amenable to simple cost–benefit calculations concerning the impact on humans. Since the 1990s the Scottish and Methodist churches have been particularly active in promoting a more rounded view of the ethical implications of non-human genetic engineering.[17] However, a view that is dismissive of the

---

[14] *Personal Origins* (London: Church of England Board for Social Responsibility, 1985); *Genetic Intervention on Human Subjects* (London: The Catholic Bishops' Joint Committee on Bioethical Issues, 1996).

[15] The issue was first discussed at the 1979 conference in Cambridge, Massachusetts, entitled 'Faith, Science and the Future'. See Paul Abrecht (ed.), *Faith and Science in an Unjust World*, vol. 2 (Geneva: WCC, 1980). Later documents update the same theme, such as *Manipulating Life* (Geneva: WCC, 1982).

[16] A. Dyson, 'Genetic Engineering in Theology and Theological Ethics', in A. Dyson and J. Harris (eds), *Ethics and Biotechnology* (London: Routledge, 1994), 259–71, (263). His view is supported by the observation that where the debate is broadened to include issues such as environment and justice, it tends to exhibit a more hostile approach to both science and genetic technology. John Williams believes that the suspicion of genetics found in some WCC documents is related to the emphasis on justice. J. R. Williams, *Christian Perspectives on Bioethics: Religious Values and Public Policy in a Pluralistic Society* (Ottawa: Novalis, 1997), 57–61.

[17] The Church of Scotland General Assembly Reports on animal cloning in the context of Genetic Engineering (1997), patenting (1997) and Genetically Modified Food (1999), alongside Society, Religion and Technology submissions to the Banner Committee on animal technologies (1994), and to Nuffield (1995) and the Department of Health (1996) on xenotransplantation, are just some examples of reports that present a fuller picture of the ethical issues involved. See

significance of the genetic engineering of non-humans still persists in official documents. For example, even as late as 1998, in the Church of England response to the Nuffield Consultation document on modified crops, the team, chaired by the scientist John Polkinghorne, found no real reason for concern about genetic modification of plants on theological or ethical grounds.[18] So far there has been no official Roman Catholic response to genetic engineering outside that of humans. However, Pope John Paul II has indicated positive approval of 'beneficial applications in the field of animal and vegetable biology which can be useful in food production'.[19] Very recently the Pontifical Academy for Life produced a slim volume, published only in Italian, dealing with the religious implications of genetic engineering of non-humans. It appeared to be similarly positive in line with the earlier papal statement about the possible benefits of genetic engineering of animals and plants for humanity, with the caveat that environmental issues needed to be taken into account.[20]

Secondly, the interventions have exhibited a second kind of narrowing, with a repeated tendency to reduce theological considerations to 'ethics'. The recent impressive book *Engineering Genesis* by the Society, Religion and Technology project of the Church of Scotland that we have already mentioned does consider the non-human realm in some detail.[21] However, it focuses on ethical and social concerns, rather than on theological issues. Its approach seems to be an

---

Bruce and Bruce, *Engineering Genesis.* The Methodist Church has also addressed the specific question of making debates about genetic engineering accessible to a wider Church audience in the publication of study packs, such as the most recent *Making Our Genes Fit: Christian Perspectives on the New Genetics* (London: Methodist Church, 1999).

[18] Response of the Church of England Board for Social Responsibility to the Nuffield Council on Bioethics Consultation Document on Genetically Modified Crops, August 1998. The earlier report of the Ministry of Agriculture, Fisheries and Food's Committee, chaired by John Polkinghorne, similarly found no fundamental objections to genetic modification of food on religious grounds. MAFF, *The Ethics of Genetic Modification and Food Use* (London: HMSO, 1984).

[19] Pope John Paul II, 'The Ethics of Genetic Manipulation', speech to World Medical Association, *Origins*, 13, 23, 17 November 1983, 339.

[20] G. Ancora, E. Benvenuto, G. Bertoni, V. Buonomo, B. Hoinings, A. Lauria, F. Lucchini, P. A. Marson, V. Mele, A. Pessina and E. Sgeccia, *Biotechnologie, animali e vegetali; Nuove fontiere e nuove responabilita* (Vatican City: Libreria Editrice Vaticana, 1999).

[21] Bruce and Bruce, *Engineering Genesis.*

exploration of ethical dilemmas from a Christian perspective in
the light of scientific facts, rather than a direct theological
engagement with the significance of genetic modification or its
associated human and social dynamics.

Thirdly, 'ethics' itself has tended to be interpreted so that
consequential ethics is given priority over other ethical frameworks. For example, the submission of the Church of England
to the House of Commons Science and Technology
Committee's Inquiry into Human Genetics welcomed genetic
engineering where it led to improvement of health or
treatment of disease, but objected to it where it was used for
mere cosmetic purposes.[22] John Williams has argued that, in
those cases where a deontological ethics is the dominant stance
amongst religious groups dealing with public policy issues, such
an approach will not be heard in the public domain, as secular
language is primarily consequential.[23] Michael Banner,
similarly, has observed that ethical debates on regulatory
committees are all too often drawn to a narrow consequentialism.[24] *Engineering Genesis* can be welcomed for including a
spectrum of ethical positions – but here, too, the consequential
approach seems to dominate. In their research the authors
found relatively few cases of intrinsic objections to genetic
engineering of non-humans.

Fourthly, stances taken toward genetic engineering within
the debate in the churches have tended to be polarised between
hostility and resistance at one end, associated with a more
popular response, and the gradual acceptance or even growing

---

[22] General Synod of the Church of England Board for Social Responsibility's
submission to the House of Commons Science and Technology Committee's
Inquiry into Human Genetics, chaired by the Bishop of Liverpool, David
Sheppard, January 1995. For a range of Roman Catholic views on the ethics of
genetic engineering, with a focus on human genetics, see M. Junker-Kenny and
L. S. Cahill (eds), *The Ethics of Genetic Engineering* (London: Concilium/SCM Press,
1998).

[23] Williams believes that arguing from principles, by which he means arguing from a
deontological perspective, is a general characteristic of the churches' response to
policy issues surrounding the new reproductive technologies. He believes that it
accounts for the poor reception to their statements at a secular level. However, his
extrapolation of this finding to a general conclusion that churches prefer arguing
from principles is not really justified, especially in view of the consequential
approach discussed here. See, Williams, *Christian Perspectives on Bioethics*, 73, 135.

[24] M. Banner, 'Ethics, Society and Policy: A Way Forward', in A. Holland and A.
Johnson (eds), *Animal Biotechnology and Ethics* (London: Chapman and Hall
1998), 325–39.

enthusiasm at the other, associated with more official statements.[25] While the Society, Religion and Technology Project
quite deliberately takes a mediatory view in the case of genetic
engineering of non-humans and promotes this in the churches
at the official and popular level, we suggest that a *measure* of
tension still exists that reflects the tension we discussed earlier
between lay and official secular statements. The more hostile
responses may be associated with a general suspicion of science
and in some cases are undergirded by a reassertion of more
traditional theological positions, but this is not always the case.
For example, radical eco-feminist approaches to the
relationship between God, humanity and the natural world
lend themselves to a critique of science, and at least indirectly
to all aspects of genetic engineering. In Norway, for example,
new groups are developing that search for critical feminist
approaches to biotechnology that includes the genetic engineering of non-humans and its impact on the environment.[26]
More accommodating or accepting responses for the case of
human genetic engineering often draw on traditional Christian
notions of stewardship, or even claim that genetic engineering
can allow us to become created co-creators with God. While the
context of the discussions about humanity as creating with God
is primarily the genetic manipulation of humans, this is then
extrapolated to include ideas such as the redemption of nature
as such.[27]

Fifthly, up to the early 1990s there has been a shift in official
responses of the Church to a more positive stance towards
genetic engineering, where, as we noted earlier, the discussion
was primarily around the genetic engineering of humans
(including the proviso that human greed and irresponsibility

[25] For example, the chairman of Christian Ecology Link, Tim Cooper, has specifically called for the Church Commissioners to disinvest in companies that are
involved in GM trials, exploring opportunities for investment in organic foods
instead. He rejects the idea that the Church of England has arrived at an agreed
policy on this issue. Press Release, *Christian Ecology Link*, 25 November 1999.

[26] D. Kaul, 'Eco-News from across the World: Eco-Feminism in the Nordic
Countries', *Ecotheology*, 2, 1997, 100–8.

[27] T. Peters, *Playing God, Genetic Determinism and Human Freedom* (London:
Routledge, 1997); R. Cole-Turner, *The New Genesis: Theology and the Genetic
Revolution* (Louisville: Westminster/John Knox, 1993); Philip J. Hefner, *The
Human Factor: Evolution, Culture, and Religion*, (Minneapolis: Fortress Press,
1993). For a further discussion and critique of Peters's views, see P. Scott, this
volume.

needs to be checked).[28] A relatively positive stance seems to have been retained and persisted in many of the later official statements about genetic engineering of non-humans. There may be parallels here with the religious shifts that occurred at the time of the industrial and mercantile revolution at the end of the seventeenth century. The Church's original position was to condemn the market and human greed. However, there were increasing moves amongst certain Puritan divines towards a position that sanctioned and celebrated economic individualism itself as a divine calling.[29] Notions of humans becoming co-creators with God through genetic engineering appear to echo this response.

Thus what seems to be lacking overall is a specific theology which takes account of the profound challenges to human beings' self-image, and to their relationships with one another and with the natural world, that are posed by the new genetic technologies.[30] The focus on nature through notions of stewardship or trends to see humans as created co-creators with God appear to be ignoring the ambiguities of response of the kind which have surfaced in the focus groups and the implications of scientific uncertainty and ignorance for truly shared *responsibility*. Eco-feminism has pointed to the distortion in the human relationship with the natural world, but has not considered adequately the shifts in human identity through genetic engineering; the latter is rather castigated along with the rest of male-dominated science. Pointers to the ways in which the insights from focus groups might create a map for richer theological approaches are proposed in the section that follows.

[28] Such as those from the World Council of Churches.

[29] W. Coleman, 'Providence, Capitalism and Environmental Degradation: English Apologetics in an Era of Economic Revolution', *Journal of the History of Ideas*, 37, 1, 1976, 27–44.

[30] While there has been much fluent discussion amongst theologians and ethicists of the relationship between humanity and nature, this is in the context primarily of environmental concerns, rather than genetic engineering as such. See, for example, M. Northcott, *The Environment and Christian Ethics* (Cambridge: Cambridge University Press, 1996); R. Page, *God and the Web of Creation* (London: SCM Press, 1996). Of course in this volume, in contrast to our own position, Michael Northcott argues that there is essentially nothing new about genetic engineering in defining our relationship with nature and seems to elaborate a theology based on stewardship.

A Genetically Modified Theology?

We have argued above that the examination of lay speech about agricultural biotechnology reveals a deep sense that biotechnology is challenging people's sense of existential order, as well as society's capacity for shared responsibility. We want to suggest that theological perspectives can help us better understand the character and significance of these public anxieties – and also that listening sensitively to lay discourse can assist theology, by offering clues towards a different kind of theological response to the issues thrown up by biotechnology.

The members of the public who took part in the *Uncertain World* focus groups seemed to have a profound sense both of mystery about the character of the universe, and of the essential openness of nature. This sense appeared to be profoundly at odds with the sense of certainty with which government regulators seemed to be handling biotechnology at the time that the discussions were held in late 1996. Both the consequentialist language and reductionist evaluation framework embodied in the regulatory processes, and the deontological ethics that often comes more easily to the churches, look like inadequate responses in the context of these ambiguities. A consequentialist approach to ethics is less than satisfactory for reflection on the new biotechnologies, not least because of the unknown extent of the uncertainties involved in their diffusion. However, the deontological ethics that has been favoured by some church groups is unhelpful as it speaks a language that often appears to be disconnected from the secular ethical debate and is unlikely to be heard outside the churches.

Perhaps a more promising ethical vocabulary for the present situation may lie in the wisdom tradition in Jewish and Christian theology. In situations of rapid change and radical uncertainty ethics arguably needs to be carried out in a way that relies less on abstract rules or on knowledge of outcomes and more on insights arising from the cultivation of character, virtue and judgement. Wisdom signifies discernment, the ability to choose when confronted by a plurality of different factors. The wise person chooses not as an isolated individual but as a person in community with God, neighbour and the natural world. Those who develop the virtue of wisdom re-examine such a wider sense of self and discern how it might be expressed through particular actions in the human and non-human community of which they are a part. Furthermore, wisdom in the theological sense includes the idea of goodness; that any wise action is one of righteousness before God.[31] Wisdom is not so much truncated knowledge-as-information but the ability to embrace all perspectives and to integrate them. An ethic of wisdom flows from this inner transformation of the person. While the ability to show wisdom has been analysed from a psychological perspective, it is essentially a theological concept. For example, Birren and Fisher suggest that '[j]ust as the belief in an all-knowing deity is widespread, there is implicit in our culture a conviction that something like wisdom exists'.[32] They suggest, further, that a fuller appreciation of wisdom 'will help to develop useful tools to assist world and national leaders in the increasingly complex problems facing humanity'.[33]

Just as lay discourse about biotechnology poses a challenge to our understanding of 'ethics' so it does to existing notions of 'natural order'. In this regard, we would argue, the biotechno-logical *revolution* – and the challenges its handling poses both to human social relations and to human relations with the natural order – might also be seen as a *revelation*. The various reactions of Jewish theologians to the Holocaust may be instructive here. Many writers attempt to make sense of the Holocaust using existing theological understandings of God's relation to God's creatures, and to the Jewish people in particular. Eliezer Berkovitz, for example, argues that there was nothing in the sheer scale of the Holocaust that made it any more problematic than any other disaster in Jewish history for traditional under-standings of a God who alternately hides his face and intervenes in history.[34] Other writers, by contrast, interpret the Holocaust as a *novum*, as a revelation after which everything has to be different. For Emil Fackenheim, the Holocaust as an event uniquely resists being seen as part of a cosmic plan; it is nothing

---

[31] On the idea of the relationship between wisdom and goodness, see D. Hardy, 'The God Who is with the World', in F. Watts (ed.), *Science Meets Faith* (London: SPCK, 1998), 136–53.

[32] J. E. Birren and L. M. Fisher, 'The Elements of Wisdom; Overview and Integration', in R. J. Sternberg (ed.), *Wisdom: Its Nature, Origins and Development* (Cambridge: Cambridge University Press, 1990), 319.

[33] Birren and Fisher, 'Elements of Wisdom', 332.

[34] E. Berkovitz, *Faith after the Holocaust* (New York: Ktav, 1973).

more than a turning point in history, after which the maintenance of faith takes on a special significance as a militant resistance to evil.[35] Finally, a third set of responses invite us to see the Holocaust as a revelation not just in the sense of a break with the past but as an event which sharply reveals what must always have been the case. Richard Rubenstein takes this route to argue for the radical conclusion that after the Holocaust the Jewish people should abandon any traditional notion of a benevolent, omnipotent deity altogether.[36] For Martin Buber, by contrast, the Holocaust demands from Jews a return to the fundamentals of their faith, in order to work back from them to a more adequate understanding of God.[37]

We suggest that theology is faced by a comparable set of options in relation to biotechnology. In suggesting this we do not mean to liken genetic engineering to Nazism, nor genetically modified organisms (GMOs) to the victims of the Holocaust. We simply want to suggest that the options for theology in its response to the biotechnology revolution are formally similar to those of Jewish theologians after the Holocaust. First, theologians might take the position that theology can go on much as before, simply regarding genetic engineering as a new, additional domain about which they might be asked to make interpretative or ethical judgements. Secondly, they might understand it as ushering in a radically new situation – interpreted either as one of elevation of humans to being 'created co-creators with God', or as a situation of great potential evil – which demands of them a newly militant intervention in the public domain. Or, thirdly, they might see themselves as participants in a public debate about what truths this historically unprecedented event may be revealing about the nature of human existence in the world.

It is at this third level of response, we would suggest, that the novel human dynamics of the new genetics appear to lie. In a number of ways they seem to point towards a kind of theological response that is anything but simple-minded. People, quite prudently, want to resist the enthusiastic rush to embrace the

[35] E. Fackenheim, *God's Presence in History* (New York: New York University Press, 1970).

[36] R. Rubenstein, *After Auschwitz: Radical Theology and Contemporary Judaism* (New York: Bobbs-Merrill, 1966).

[37] M. Buber, *Good and Evil: Two Interpretations* (New York: Scribner's, 1953).

possibilities offered by these new technologies, but they are not closed to the use of the technologies themselves in principle. Indeed, their current hostility may be aimed less at the level of the specific technologies and their applications, and more at that of the model of the human person and its place in the world implicit in the actions of the industry and its regulators. At the same time, people appear to want to hold on to some notion of order and of a limit to human interference – and yet seem surprisingly open to the idea that our specific understandings of cosmic order and of human identity and responsibility may be on the verge of change. Above all, the public seem to sense the very notion, let alone the practice, of genetic engineering as bringing with it profound and challenging questions about humanity's place in the world. Yet they experience the institutions responsible for these technologies as apparently not recognising the existence of such questions at all. The conversation that we as a society need to have – and that the public seems to be demanding – is a theological one. The role of theologians must surely be to find a theology adequate to that task.

Response to Chapter 1

Christopher Southgate

If ever an academic paper found its time it was this one, delivered as it was the week after the electoral instincts of the Prime Minister told him he must track the nation's mood by publicly acknowledging the 'potential for harm'[1] in respect of GM crops. The questions the chapter raises as to the underlying causes of public suspicion of GM in this country, so much greater than in the US, are both academically topical and politically pressing.

The data for the chapter are extracted from work with focus groups. It is a sign of my crusty elitist recidivism that I find myself continuing to sound cautionary words as to the public's level of access to wisdom. Had the focus groups been on capital punishment, for example, the study might have discovered that it was the so-called 'Old Testament God' of vengeance and retribution who represented the theological model of the majority of our society. A recently published focus group study of the Christian Church in this country tended to suggest that the Church is now an irrelevance, a set of institutions without meaning. Since I would strongly resist both these theological conclusions I bite the bullet of political incorrectness and raise the question as to the extent to which this focus-group work, however empathetically performed and interpreted, necessarily

[1] T. Blair, 'The Key to GM is its potential, both for harm and good', *Independent on Sunday*, 27 Feb. 2000.

39

taps into any deep vein of truth, on GM any more than on the single currency or any other complex issue.

I do endorse the insight that it is BSE in particular which has had an enormous influence on the public mood. The taxi-driver who took me to Euston en route to the colloquium at which the paper was delivered made the connection immediately. That tragic and still-unresolved story grips the British people at two very vulnerable loci in our imaginative life – the fear of being poisoned and driven mad, on the one hand, and the sense of blasphemy against the purity and wholesomeness of the countryside, on the other. The vague picture most people have of millions of cattle being slaughtered and incinerated grates, I believe, deep in our craws – far more than it ever could in a vaster, more diffuse and more agriculturally specialised country such as the States. And GM, emerging while the science of BSE is still in the melting pot, has struck at those two same loci – fear of poisoning and blasphemy against the countryside.

As it happens I have been conducting my own entirely unscientific and anecdotal research with student groups on this issue. And my methodologically unsound gleanings do I think reflect something of interest about the attitudes of the generation that are now nineteen and will provide the Prime Minister of thirty years hence. The first sense I have from that generation is that technological change is basically unstoppable – this is the fatalism to which the chapter referred. There *will inevitably be*, my students tend to think, ever more sophisticated ways to use human tissue to overcome infertility and disease, there *will be* human cloning, there *will be* GM of all kinds. And the 'yuk factor' that I detect in my own friends on some of these issues is weak in this new generation. Rather there is a very strong sense of *cui bono* – who are the beneficiaries of these new techniques? This is a generation born under the star Thatcher, very aware that everything has costs, and that someone somewhere is profiting.

There is an interesting contrast to be drawn here with the public's rapidly softening attitude to various forms of fertility treatment. IVF and its successors raise huge ethical issues, but because the public can see that the procedures may benefit humans who could be helped in no other way, opposition to the new technologies seems to be fading. With GM crops the innate fear of the technology is less, but there is a much stronger sense that it has arrived for Monsanto's benefit rather than that of its users, or yet society at large.

The specimen student on the Exeter omnibus also notes the cavalier attitude to environmental risk taken by some of the companies concerned. Here there is a comparison to be made with the pharmaceutical industry. Many lament, but most accept, the vast profits made from drugs consumed by humans. Drugs, it is known, are subject to very stringent testing before general release, though still there are disasters like thalidomide. What has become evident over GM, as over BSE, is that new agricultural practice, though it has profound implications for the overall health of a human society and the ecosystems on which it depends, involves relatively few precautions. In retrospect Monsanto must be wishing they had cloned a few Millennium Domes so that they could show that they were testing cross-pollination rates in genuinely controlled conditions.

I pass now to the theological choices in this area. It seems to me that the alarmingly polarised nature of the GM debate leads to some strange theological bedfellows. Against GM one might find the most anthropocentric of creationists and the most biocentric of deep ecologists. For GM one might find endorsers of Hefner's created co-creator anthropology[2] alongside the scientistic atheist and the Chinese Government – the biggest single player in the ongoing global debate about food.[3] These strange marriages go to reinforce in my mind the importance of ethics being truly underpinned by theological positions, rather than theologies of humans and nature being devised to buttress a pre-formed ethical position. We need to move, as Michael Banner suggests in chapter 3, beyond a narrow consequentialism, and derive our ethics from a developed model of humans' relation to God and to the non-human world.

I must lay my own cards on the table and say with Hefner and Peters[4] that I think we humans will fail to be true to our nature unless we do deploy our ingenuity and technological innovation to help us through the mess we are in. We have a

[2] Philip J. Hefner, *The Human Factor: Evolution, Culture, and Religion* (Minneapolis: Fortress Press, 1993).
[3] N. Nuttall, 'China sows the seeds of GM crop expansion', *The Times*, 29 Feb. 2000.
[4] T. Peters, *Playing God? Genetic Determinism and Human Freedom* (London: Routledge, 1997).

calling to co-creativity. But again, I have to endorse another of
the key themes of the chapter, which is that the search for
wisdom is of the essence of that calling. And I would quote from
the same essay of Dan Hardy's cited by Deane-Drummond et al.
Hardy says:

> Wisdom is therefore the *configuration* of insight – both theoretical
> and practical – into the multi-dimensionality of the world and God,
> *not only how they are related but how they should be related* [this emphasis
> mine].[5]

We may be co-creators, possessed of vast ingenuity – that
ingenuity is the fruit of an evolutionary process in which we are
now, inescapably, ourselves a potent force. But there is also a
givenness to nature in its relation to God, before and apart from
our modification of it. That givenness is far harder to define, in
the context of Darwinian understandings, than most people
realise, but there is still a case for saying that we are stewards of
nature, even, some would say, priests of the relationship
between nature and God. Stewardship and priesthood are both,
properly understood, concepts based on humility. We are
moreover commanded to take our Sabbath rest within the
world, as God rested God's self.

I conclude by asking: *Do* we need a genetically modified
theology? Is the question of GM a radical new one calling for a
radical response? I do not myself think so. I cannot see it as
anything like the Holocaust as a disclosure of our capacity for
organised evil, or Hiroshima as a disclosure of our capacity
for self-extermination, or even Louise Brown, the first 'test-tube
baby', as a disclosure of the level of control implied by our
capacity to form, hold and manipulate healthy human life in a
Petri dish. But the GM debate does sharpen helpfully questions
already posed about our relationship to the non-human world.
So let us draw out from our treasure-houses both old insights
and a keenly informed awareness of the new genetics, so that
our ethical stances are appropriately underpinned by a
nuanced theology of the God–world relation.

---

[5] D. Hardy, 'The God Who is with the World', in F. Watts (ed.), *Science Meets Faith*
(London: SPCK, 1998), 136–53 (137).

2

Detracting from Divine Power? Religious Belief and the Appraisal of New Technologies

John Hedley Brooke

In a somewhat rueful letter to Joseph Priestley, Benjamin Franklin once expressed the bittersweet hopes of an Enlightenment vision. The power over matter promised by a science-based technology seemed unfettered:

> The rapid progress the sciences now make occasions my regrets sometimes that I was born too soon. It is impossible to imagine the heights to which may be carried in a thousand years the power of man over matter ... All diseases may by sure means be prevented or cured, not excepting even that of old age, and our lives lengthened at pleasure, even beyond the antediluvian standard.[1]

It remains just as impossible to imagine the heights, but within far less than a thousand years that optimistic vision of improving on nature had become clouded with pessimism. When Gordon Rattray Taylor published his *Biological Time Bomb* in 1968, the possibility of gene warfare and lethal doomsday bugs loomed large in a text that included the chapter: 'The Future – If Any'. His publishers made the most of it: 'You may marry a semi-artificial man or woman ... choose your children's sex ... tune out pain ... change your memories ... and live to be 150 if the scientific revolution doesn't destroy us first'.[2]

---

[1] I. Kramnick, 'Eighteenth-Century Science and Radical Social Theory: The Case of Joseph Priestley's Scientific Liberalism', in A. Truman Schwartz and J. McEvoy (eds), *Motion toward Perfection: The Achievement of Joseph Priestley* (Boston: Skinner House, 1990), 57–92 (68).

[2] R. Bud, *The Uses of Life: A History of Biotechnology* (Cambridge: Cambridge University Press, 1993), 172.

Had Franklin come into that foreign land of the future he might, perhaps, have concluded that he had been born too late. There was a price to be paid for improving on nature, and as the twentieth century taught us, the costs could be exorbitant. At the highest level of generalisation, confidence in the omnipotence of technology has given way to ambivalence. Reference to omnipotence reminds us that there are indeed theological questions not far below the surface. My purpose in this paper is to uncover some of them through historical example. What we find, I shall argue, is another kind of ambivalence and one that has recurred in religious appraisals of new technologies. The source of the ambivalence lies in the tension between contemplative modes of apprehending a created 'natural' order and activist programmes for the amelioration of man's estate, which have also received a transcendental blessing. To identify this and other sources of ambivalence through the recovery of theological voices from the past may help us to understand the inarticulacy when the echoes of such voices are heard today.

There is an extreme position that can be taken on the contemplative mode, though it is one usually ascribed to religious thinkers for polemical purposes rather than a fair representation of their position. It was stated by the atheist radical Richard Carlile in the late 1820s when the category of the 'natural' was already under pressure from the expansion of the artificial. It was a cheap point, but succinctly made. 'With the doctrine of intelligent deity', he wrote, 'it is presumption to attempt anything toward human improvement. Without the doctrine, it is not any presumption.'[3] The very fact of improving the world through technology rendered a natural theology obsolete. There was, however, a degree of presumption in Carlile's polemic. To expose it may be a good place to start because there is a way of showing that thoughtful Christian writers need not be in the bind that he implied. Historically there had been, and would be again, ways of construing the relationship between God and humankind which made techno-logical innovation a fufilment of Providence rather than an indictment. To make the point I shall introduce a

---

[3] R. Carlile, *Lion*, 2, 1828, 488–9.

contemporary of Carlile, a Scottish evangelical and prolific populariser of geology: Hugh Miller.

Miller is well known for his participation in the Disruption of the Scottish Church in 1843 when Thomas Chalmers led the breakaway movement. Miller was the irrepressible editor of *The Witness*, the organ of the Free Church, and equally energetic in demonstrating to his readers that Genesis and geology could be harmonised.[4] His posthumous book *The Testimony of the Rocks* (1857) contains elaborate essays on how an enlightened evangelical (unlike many south of the border!) should welcome the new science for its disclosure, in the fossil record, of a coherent pattern of progressive creation. But the key point for our purposes is the construction Miller places on the applied sciences rather than the pure. His position suggests that there were resources within a conservative Protestantism with which to legitimate a technological activism. He was not responding to Carlile but, in urging a *collaboration* between man and his maker, he presented human beings as 'fellow-workers' with the Creator.[5] One facet of the doctrine of *imago dei* was that the human and divine minds shared the same aesthetic sensibilities – a crucial plank in Miller's natural theology – and this allowed the 'deputed lord of creation' to further God's creative ends through whatever techniques were beneficial. For Miller, there was evidently nothing sacrilegious in attempting to improve the world the deity had made:

> Man was the first, and is still the only creature of whom we know anything, who has set himself to carry on and improve the work of the world's original framer, – who is a planter of woods, a tiller of fields, and a keeper of gardens, – and who carries on his work of mechanical contrivance on obviously the same principles as those on which the Divine designer wrought of old, and on which He works still.[6]

No threat after all to the argument for design! A longer passage is worth quoting in full because it completely deflates the objection we have seen in Carlile. Man as 'fellow-worker' with the Creator is a 'mighty *improver* of nature':

---

[4] M. Shortland (ed.), *Hugh Miller and the Controversies of Victorian Science* (Oxford: Oxford University Press, 1996).

[5] H. Miller, *The Testimony of the Rocks* (Edinburgh: Nimmo, 1869), 142.

[6] Miller, *Testimony*, 198.

> We recognise that as improvement which adapts nature more thoroughly to man's own necessities and wants, and renders it more pleasing both to his sense of the aesthetic and to his more material senses also. He adds to the beauty of the flowers which he takes under his charge – to the delicacy and fertility of the fruits; the seed of the wild grasses become corn under his care ... the wild produce of nature *sports* under his hand ... the productions of his kitchen-garden, strangely metamorphosed to serve the uses of his table ... Nor is his influence over many of the animals less marked. The habits which he imparts to the parents become *nature*, in his behalf, in their offspring ... The udders of the cow and goat distend beneath his care far beyond the size necessary in the wild state.[7]

In Miller we see a willingness to embrace the instability of the *natural*. It may belong to the world of becoming. Since the late arrival of man on earth, human history has been one of process – a process of collaboration with the deity. Miller was no evolutionist. He disparaged the development hypothesis of Robert Chambers as despicably atheistic. But there was an overarching progress in human history and, in passages that seem to presage the vision of Teilhard de Chardin, Miller would write of a convergence towards a focal union of Creator and created that had been prefigured in the person of Christ:

> In the doctrine of the two conjoined natures, human and Divine, and in the farther doctrine that the terminal dynasty is to be peculiarly the dynasty of Him in whom the natures are united, we find that required progression beyond which progress cannot go ... Creation and the Creator meet at one point, and in one person. The long ascending line from dead matter to man has been a progress Godwards, – not an asymptotical progress, but destined from the beginning to furnish a point of union.[8]

It is just such a single overarching vision that we have lost in the modern world. It was lost to the Catholic modernist George Tyrrell a hundred years ago.[9] But it is important to appreciate that ameliorative technologies could be comfortably accommodated within such schemes. If a personal reminiscence may be forgiven, it was when reading Teilhard de Chardin's *Le Milieu*

---

[7] Miller, *Testimony*, 200–1.

[8] Miller, *Testimony*, 143.

[9] J. Brooke and G. Cantor, *Reconstructing Nature: The Engagement of Science and Religion* (Edinburgh: T&T Clark, 1998), 163–4.

Divin in the 1960s that I first encountered this notion of *collaboration* with a Creator.[10] It was sufficiently different from other images that I had previously assimilated to register with some force – just as one usually remembers one's first encounter with the Darwinian demonstration of how nature may counterfeit design. Had I been better read in the history of Christian theology, I would almost certainly have been less surprised. There had, after all, been a long tradition in which our ability to imitate the creative activity of the deity had been part of what it meant to be made in the image of God.

I do not wish to privilege Hugh Miller's stance. It simply serves to illustrate that there were conceptual resources within a Christian theism that allowed for a positive appraisal of beneficent technologies. On one level this may sound so all-embracing as to be facile. But Miller's theology, and others like it, could also supply critical perspectives. Miller's discussion of our collaborating with the deity takes place within a framework of evangelical theology with its discourse of the 'fall'. It is possible to choose not to work with God, even to work against him. Railways might be progressive but not when railroad companies planned to run their trains on Sunday. As Roy Porter has observed, so wretched a prospect gave rise to a visionary ecstasy in which Miller foresaw the collapse of civilisation: Edinburgh in ruins, villages burned, railway lines broken, engines rusting and churches derelict.[11] Leaving such a scene, we might turn to other historically significant schemata to bring out comparable tensions between the appropriation and the suspicion of new technologies.

We might begin with a tale of two Bacons – Roger the Franciscan friar, who advocated new technologies to stave off the forces of evil and to resist the guile of the Antichrist,[12] and Francis, lawyer, politician and diplomat for the sciences, who saw in their application the promise of power for the English monarchy.[13] One contrast between them would be that for Roger there was no prospect of sustained technical progress. As

[10] P. Teilhard de Chardin, *Le Milieu Divin* (London: Collins, 1957), 62.
[11] Shortland, *Hugh Miller*, 280.
[12] D. Lindberg, 'On the Application of Mathematics to Nature: Roger Bacon and His Predecessors', *British Journal for the History of Science*, 15, 1982, 3–25.
[13] J. Martin, *Francis Bacon, the State, and the Reform of Natural Philosophy* (Cambridge: Cambridge University Press, 1992).

far as this world was concerned, time was short before the
pending apocalypse. The future held no prospect of progress.
There would be struggle against the enemies of Christendom
and then the end of the world. The Last Judgement was as real
a presence as it was depicted to be over cathedral doorways.
And the efforts of the cathedral builders to improve technical
skills 'were not conceived as a means of improving the
condition of man within the present order of things; but rather,
they were reaching forward to meet an eternal order, a New
Jerusalem, which the cathedral itself symbolised'.[14] The
important point is that technology and other-worldliness were
not necessarily mutually exclusive: the aim was to reach out to
the immaterial through the material, in the hope of gaining
fleeting visions of God.

By contrast the seventeenth-century world of Francis Bacon
strikes us as unashamedly of *this* world. As with Marlowe's Dr
Faustus, there is a world of power, of profit and delight awaiting
the studious artisan. If the seeds of modern attitudes are more
clearly visible in Francis than in Roger, they were nevertheless
deeply planted in theological soil. Sustained progress there
would be. The technologies associated with printing,
gunpowder and compass testified to that. But the framework
was still one in which one focused on Christ's second coming.
Improvement through the applied sciences was a legitimate
goal in what Bacon called 'this autumn of the world'. This was
because it promised the restoration of a dominion over nature
which had been intended for humanity, but which had been
sacrificed at the 'fall'.[15] One of Bacon's many objections to
scholastic philosophy was that it had been sterile in this respect.
By rendering 'improvement' as *restoration* Bacon could take the
presumption out of technological aspiration. In general terms
at least, a critical apparatus was also in place. Christian virtues of
humility and altruism were invoked as criteria by which to judge
the pretensions of those who might seek to control nature for
their selfish gain. Bacon's twin ideals of collaborative research
and shared knowledge (qualified, though, if the knowledge be
dangerous) allowed him to reproach the Renaissance

---

[14] A. Pacey, *The Maze of Ingenuity: Ideas and Idealism in the Development of Technology*
(Cambridge, MA: MIT Press, 1976), 58.
[15] C. Webster, *The Great Instauration: Science, Medicine and Reform 1626–1660*
(London: Duckworth, 1975), 21–5.

magicians.[16] It would be difficult, however, to deny a certain ambivalence in his position. On the one hand there is a utopian vision that strikes us as deeply secular: the vision of a future in which the application of the sciences will be driven by the will to 'effect all things possible'. On the other the vision is of a restored Eden, a millenarian hope grounded in Old Testament prophecy. According to prophecies in Daniel, to which Bacon explicitly referred, one of the signs of the last things was an increase in knowledge, the cultivation of which therefore had divine sanction and was ultimately a religious duty.

Among the Renaissance magicians, whose practical skills if not their moral probity Bacon could admire, there had been other ways of finding theological justification for improving upon nature. The alchemists, for example, who sought to speed up natural processes in their quest for gold, and slow them down in their quest for immortality, would often present their efforts as deeply pious. In the iconography of alchemical texts, the adept is often shown at prayer, the *oratorium* adjacent to the *laboratorium*.[17] The act of prayer might help to engender the appropriate spiritual state, one might pray for success in one's experiment, and alchemical processes themselves – such as purification – could be symbolic of spiritual refinement. It is possibly in the context of alchemy that one first sees the forging of a vocabulary of collaboration in the perfecting of nature's (and ultimately of divine) ends. To the fourteenth-century alchemist Bernard Trevisan it was clear 'from many irrefutable and uncontestable testimonies that nature by itself procreates and prepares seed-bearing creatures whereas the art [of alchemy] works together with them toward the end which nature creates'.[18] The justification could be extended further. In the *Summa Perfectionis* attributed to Geber it was argued that the ability to improve on nature was part of human nature itself.[19] The alchemist's task was no different in kind from the farmer's use of grafting to improve his stock.

Critical reaction to alchemical practices could also be couched in theological terms, revealing once again the tensions

[16] P. Rossi, *Francis Bacon: From Magic to Science* (London: Routledge, 1968).
[17] Brooke and Cantor, *Reconstructing Nature*, 318.
[18] W. Theisen, 'John Dastin: The Alchemist as Co-Creator', *Ambix*, 38, 1991, 73–8 (74).
[19] W. Brock, *The Fontana History of Chemistry* (London: Fontana, 1992), 21–2.

between and within communities of those who took a keen interest. The Jesuits Martin del Rio and Athanasius Kircher, for example, differed on the topical issue whether the practice of transmutation was likely to involve demonic forces. For del Rio this was not necessarily the case; Kircher was the more suspicious. Neither was averse in principle to the imitation of nature. Indeed Kircher wanted alchemical apparatus to imitate the shapes of the caverns, veins and rivers of the underground world.

But moral scruples certainly found expression. Del Rio worried about the spiritual temperament of the initiates. Some may have had the requisite attributes of piety and humility, but others manifestly did not. He also took exception to those who pretended the Bible was an alchemical text to be decoded and to those who hid their chemical secrets under the cloak of biblical imagery.[20]

Prophets as well as profits needed critical scrutiny. When Paracelsus (allegedly) claimed that, given the right recipe, it would be possible to create a human being, there was no shortage of revulsion. The past can be strangely topical and it is worth remembering that Paracelsus himself had been champion of a chemistry that, in the service of medicine, could be given a Christological gloss (healing as a divine art) and which, in extracting the pure and efficacious ingredients from natural resources, could be given additional meaning in terms of the *redemption* of nature.[21] Referring to the last stage of the alchemical process, the tincturing of a substance to change its colour, Paracelsus stated that it 'makes all imperfect things perfect, transmutes them into their noblest essence'.[22] To improve the world through chemistry had perfect sanction in Scripture given that the creation of the world could itself be read as a chemical process. It is well known that Paracelsus and his disciples were vilified, in large measure because of their censure of Galenic physicians; but the existence of a theological ambivalence should also be registered. The promise to make all things new through chemistry drew a retort from the Calvinist

[20] M. Baldwin, 'Alchemy and the Society of Jesus in the Seventeenth Century', *Ambix*, 40, 1993, 41–64.

[21] O. Hannaway, *The Chemists and the Word* (Baltimore: Johns Hopkins University Press, 1975).

[22] Brooke and Cantor, *Reconstructing Nature*, 322.

Oswald Croll that, in the last analysis, it was God alone who could instigate such a change.[23]

The dialectic between a theology of technology and theological critiques of overreach is visible in the writings of a seventeenth-century natural philosopher, Robert Boyle, who did more than anyone to turn chemistry from the dubious art of sooty empirics into a respectable science. Boyle is usually associated with the reduction of nature to machinery, a movement epitomised by Descartes and deeply qualified by Newton. This process of reduction, sometimes called the 'death of nature', was itself profoundly ambivalent from a theological point of view. For one thing it could obliterate the distinction altogether between nature and art. As Henry Power put it: all things are artificial because 'nature itself is nothing else but the art of God'.[24] A mechanised universe could be turned to theological advantage, as it was by Boyle, because it could be used to eliminate intermediate agencies between Creator and creation, thereby saving the sovereignty of God. It could also find favour for its reinforcement of arguments for design. Boyle was genuinely overawed by the machinery of mites, by the manner in which the source of all life had packed life itself into so minute a creature.[25]

However, a mechanical universe could also give solace to deists and freethinkers who sought to rid the world of an active providence. The great naturalist John Ray worried when he first read Boyle that he was reading the work of a deist, whose clockwork analogies for the universe placed the Creator at arms length. For which he later apologised to Boyle when he realised there was more to Boyle's universe than the Strasbourg clock.[26] In fact the latest scholarship has revealed a Boyle who, particularly towards the end of his life, rekindled his interest in alchemy as a way of unveiling spiritual dimensions of reality.[27]

---

[23] Hannaway, *The Chemists*, 52.

[24] Brooke and Cantor, *Reconstructing Nature*, 323.

[25] For an introduction to Boyle scholarship, including his natural theology, see M. Hunter (ed.), *Robert Boyle Reconsidered* (Cambridge: Cambridge University Press, 1994).

[26] For the theological ambiguities associated with the mechanical philosophies, see J. Brooke, *Science and Religion: Some Historical Perspectives* (Cambridge: Cambridge University Press, 1991), 117–51.

[27] L. Principe, *The Aspiring Adept: Robert Boyle and His Alchemical Quest* (Princeton: Princeton University Press, 1998), 188–213.

Boyle's religious commitment generated critical perspectives from which he would deem it a *mis*application of the 'new philosophy' if it were used to deny a world of the spirit.

The ambivalence I particularly wish to stress, however, can be categorised in other ways. Boyle, along with many of his contemporaries, illustrates a profound change in sensibility towards the natural world, recently documented by Peter Harrison.[28] The process of change was gradual and rarely complete but natural objects ceased to be read as emblems or symbols having an immediate religious meaning and were studied instead for their utility. An anthropocentric conception of Providence allowed nature to be trawled for anything and everything of human benefit. It was in this mode that Boyle would observe how even the most despicable of God's creatures might furnish something of value for the empire of knowledge. In this spirit Boyle would confess to having dissected *even* rats and mice. The usefulness of natural philosophy, on which he wrote at length, could mean utility in the sense of mental and spiritual edification. It emphatically did mean that for Boyle. But it could also mean utility in the technical sense of improving the human condition. No apology was required for experiments on fellow men, one of whom he hired to be bitten by a viper.[29] This seems to speak of callousness rather than ambivalence; and yet there was a counterpoise. Boyle, to a degree, was sensitive to animal suffering. In animal experiments the end could justify the means; but once a specific animal had done its bit for humanity, and survived, it was to be released rather than used again. As Malcolm Oster pointed out some years ago, one detects a degree of compassion and discomfiture here.[30]

Boyle's theory of matter forged a link between chemistry and a limited process theology. John Beale told him in 1666, 'you will conduct the two rivulets of mechanism and chemistry into the ocean of theology'.[31] There was much more to this than a

---

[28] P. Harrison, *The Bible, Protestantism and the Rise of Natural Science* (Cambridge: Cambridge University Press, 1998).

[29] Brooke and Cantor, *Reconstructing Nature*, 325.

[30] M. Oster, 'The "Beame of Divinity": Animal Suffering in the Early Thought of Robert Boyle', *British Journal for the History of Science*, 22, 1989, 151–79.

[31] S. Shapin and S. Schaffer, *Leviathan and the Air Pump: Hobbes, Boyle and the Experimental Life* (Princeton: Princeton University Press, 1985), 322.

contemplative natural theology. It required Boyle to seek the Creator's indulgence. To change God's creatures, to improve upon nature, was, in Boyle's own words, a 'great honour, that the indulgent Creator vouchsafes to the naturalist'.[32] Such language clearly raises the question whether there might not be limits to the Creator's indulgence. For Newton there were, certainly as far as the vulgar were concerned. But for a select few initiates, imitation of the Creator's work was a high and privileged calling.[33] In Newton an argument from natural theology underpins the symbol of created co-Creator, better known perhaps from the writings of the contemporary theologian Philip Hefner.[34] Newton's version is, however, engaging precisely because the fact of a mediating role in the execution of divine power is seen to enhance that power, not detract from it:

> If any think it possible that God may produce some intellectual creature so perfect that he could, by divine accord, in turn produce creatures of a lower order, this so far from detracting from the divine power enhances it; for that power which can bring forth creatures not only directly but through the mediation of other creatures is exceedingly, not to say infinitely greater.[35]

If Newton intended that we should count as co-creators, then here was a capacious accommodation of human ingenuity. It would be instructive to look more closely to see what controls, if any, Newton envisaged. Given his pessimistic reading of human history, in which every nation had succumbed to idolatry and corruption, it is difficult to believe he would not have required some.

Mapping all the theological moves that have been made to accommodate technological entrepreneurship would be a major undertaking; but the map must be extended to include the appeal to technological progress in movements for political

---

[32] Brooke and Cantor, *Reconstructing Nature*, 325.

[33] J. Golinski, 'The Secret Life of an Alchemist', in J. Fauvel, R. Flood, M. Shortland and R. Wilson (eds), *Let Newton Be!* (Oxford: Oxford University Press, 1988), 147–67.

[34] Philip J. Hefner, *The Human Factor: Evolution, Culture, and Religion* (Minneapolis: Fortress Press, 1993).

[35] I. Newton, Portsmouth Collection MS Add. 4003, Cambridge University Library; B. J. Dobbs, *The Janus Faces of Genius* (Cambridge: Cambridge University Press, 1991), 36.

reform. Historians have often seen a correlation between
dissenting religion and the advocacy of an education in science
and technology.[36] The dissenting academies of the eighteenth
century are often invoked, the name of Joseph Priestley
associated with the Warrington Academy.[37] Like Newton,
Priestley was staunchly anti-Trinitarian in his theology, deeply
critical of the 'arbitrary power' of the established Church, and
incensed that dissenters like himself were obliged to pay tithes.
Reacting fervently against a Calvinist upbringing, Priestley jetti-
soned many doctrines that had been seen as constitutive of
Christianity: original sin, atonement, election, the immortality
of the soul, the direct influence of the deity on human minds.[38]
His political sympathies with the French Revolution and
sometimes unguarded censure of government led to the oppro-
brium he suffered as 'Gunpowder Joe'. We are, he once wrote,
as it were 'laying gunpowder, grain by grain, under the old
building of error and superstition, which a single spark may
hereafter inflame'.[39] Science and technology had a strategic
role to play in the displacement of a corrupt polity.
Government had every reason to tremble before an electrical
machine. Science, technology and a purified, rational, religion
were allies in the fight against superstition.

Priestley had no difficulty in justifying technological
innovation in theological terms. It was part and parcel of a
process theology grounded in the fundamental moral
principle that a benevolent deity willed nothing other than
human happiness. As with some Puritan leaders of the seventeenth century, Priestley embraced the applied sciences as a
liberating force, linked as they were with commercial realities
and millenarian hope. Oxford and Cambridge, he assured
William Pitt in 1787, resembled 'pools of stagnant water
secured by dams and mounds, and offensive to the neigh-
bourhood'.[40] Canals, bridges, roads, libraries and laboratories

---

[36] The classic and controversial statement is that of R. Merton, 'Science, Technology
and Society in Seventeenth-Century England', *Osiris*, 4, part 2, 1938, 360–632;
republished New York: Harper 1970.

[37] R. Schofield, 'The Professional Work of an Amateur Chemist: Joseph Priestley', in
Truman Schwartz and McEvoy, *Motion toward Perfection*, 1–19.

[38] J. Brooke, ' "A Sower Went Forth": Joseph Priestley and the Ministry of Reform',
in Truman Schwartz and McEvoy, *Motion toward Perfection*, 21–56.

[39] Kramnick, 'Eighteenth-Century Science', 67–8.

[40] Kramnick, 'Eighteenth-Century Science', 68.

were destined to remove the 'idle pageantry of a Court'. The fate of Priestley's own laboratory and his own personal fate are reminders that he did not take the world with him, despite his conviction that all the world should, one day, conform to his supremely rational monotheism. There may have been very little ambivalence in Priestley's own mind. Every gas that he 'discovered' he was convinced would have a beneficial use. But so direct a linkage between technology and theological radicalism could not be to everyone's taste. Even among his dissenting friends it was a question whether in the wake of his purge there was any theology left. His chemical account of the resurrected body, based on a monistic philosophy of the human person, left the Unitarian preacher Richard Price dissatisfied.[41]

Priestley's notoriety serves as a useful reminder that the appraisal of new technologies can depend on the content of one's theology as well as one's political sympathies. The possibility of improving on nature was disclosed through his chemistry when he realised that his de-phlogisticated air (our oxygen) supported combustion and respiration better than ordinary air. It might even be exploited commercially as a fashionable luxury article. Indeed Priestley held the optimistic view that each of his newly expanding pool of gases would bring both utility and prosperity: fixed air (our carbon dioxide) shaken with water might even be a cure for scurvy. But here was another niche that critiques might occupy – in the gap between promise and delivery. The medical uses of gases enjoyed a certain vogue at the end of the eighteenth century, the radical chemist Thomas Beddoes setting up a Pneumatic Institute in Bristol which he hoped would be commercially viable. It soon proved not to be. His story is an early parable of the uncomfortable truth that the efficacy of medical technologies can often be judged only in retrospect.[42]

If Priestley tried to deliver a chemistry of improvement to the people, Humphry Davy tried the same for a London elite and

---

[41] J. Priestley, *A Free Discussion of the Doctrines of Materialism and Philosophical Necessity in a Correspondence between Dr. Price and Dr. Priestley* (London: Johnson and Cadell, 1778), 73.

[42] D. Stansfield, *Thomas Beddoes M.D. 1760–1808* (Dordrecht: Reidel, 1984); R. Porter, *Doctor of Society: Thomas Beddoes and the Sick Trade in Late-Enlightenment England* (London: Routledge, 1992).

the landed gentry.[43] His proposals for a chemicalised agriculture suffered from a similar gap between promise and delivery. A balanced assessment of his sustained research in this field is impossible in a few lines; but it was Morris Berman's view that Davy's 'profound impact on farming circles' was 'not so much in actual scientific contribution as in reinforcing the belief that science was something in which one could invest'.[44] It certainly did not always work. The effect of a 'grow-fast' mixture that Davy had devised was reported by Lord Egremont to Arthur Young:

> I was fool enough to send to Mr Accum the Chymist ... & get six gallons of Mr Davies mixture to accelerate vegetation, & I steeped all my turnip seed in it & the consequence is that not one seed has vegetated & I have the trouble of sowing a hundred acres over again.[45]

I have introduced Davy, however, to highlight two other sources of ambivalence that might have theological connotations. In campaigns for the use of chemical fertilisers, there could be a further blurring of the natural and artificial when it was argued, as it was by Liebig, that the artificial was necessary to restore the natural, which would otherwise be exhausted. The refusal to use chemical fertilisers was an 'interference in the divine world order'.[46] A similar rhetoric would be used in the defence of pesticides later in the century.[47] A concentration of crops in confined spaces was not 'natural' and consequently remedial steps were necessary to reduce an unnatural concentration of pests. The second, more conceptual, ambivalence arose through the use of chemistry in debates over reductionism – a philosophical issue in which theologians emphatically have a stake.

Much of the current debate over genetic engineering presupposes a genetic reductionism, even down to the journalistic 'a

---

[43] J. Golinski, *Science as Public Culture: Chemistry and Enlightenment in Britain, 1760–1820* (Cambridge: Cambridge University Press, 1992), 50–128, 188–235.

[44] M. Berman, *Social Change and Scientific Organization: The Royal Institution, 1799–1844* (Ithaca, NY: Cornell University Press, 1978), 61.

[45] Berman, *Social Change*, 59.

[46] O. Sonntag, 'Religion and Science in the Thought of Liebig', *Ambix*, 24, 1977, 159–69.

[47] J. Clark, 'Eleanor Ormerod (1828–1901) as an Economic Entomologist: "Pioneer of Purity even more than of Paris Green"', *British Journal for the History of Science*, 25, 1992, 431–52.

gene for this and a gene for that'. But it is interesting that Davy (Coleridge too) saw in chemical synthesis the symbols of an anti-reductionist holism. Against Lavoiser's contention that oxygen was the principle of acidity, Davy relished the opportunity to embarrass the French by showing that there were acids devoid of oxygen. Even more to the point, the properties of compounds appeared not to depend exclusively on their material components: different combinations of nitrogen and oxygen yielded gases of widely different properties – gases that would make you laugh or cry, anaesthetise or kill you.[48] Davy was no orthodox Christian but a defiant Romanticism permeated his understanding of the forces of nature. The need to recapture a sense of wholeness of the kind Davy would not renounce was a prescription favoured by Arnold Pacey in a prescient conclusion to his analysis of technology and culture some twenty-five years ago. 'The trouble with conventional technology as a discipline', he wrote, 'is just that: it does exclude "wholeness".' And he quoted, as Davy might well have, from *Poetry Review*:

> machines will destroy
> what's natural only if
> directed by men who oppose
> a part of themselves to the wholeness
> of their nature.[49]

In such appraisals there is clearly space for a theology to express itself even if it is not positively demanded. We have a convenient bridge here between past and present; but, before crossing it, we should perhaps note a theological concern of another kind, this time from the Victorian age when so many promises of improvement congealed in an ideology, some would say religion, of progress – a surrogate religion fed, in part, by naturalistic theories of evolution.[50]

The concern was not merely that the encroachment of naturalistic explanation might make for a redundant deity, but that technology's promise of a life of luxury and ease could serve as a distraction from the spiritual life. It is

---

[48] D. Knight, *The Transcendental Part of Chemistry* (Folkestone: Dawson, 1978), 61–90.
[49] Pacey, *Maze of Ingenuity*, 318.
[50] P. Bowler, *The Invention of Progress: The Victorians and the Past* (Oxford: Blackwell, 1989).

perhaps difficult to see how such a concern could plausibly
be transplanted into our consumer culture when even Hugh
Miller's precious Sabbath day has been lost; but such a voice
from the past may remind us that even those biotechnologies
that can be justified in terms of eradicating disease leave
unanswered questions about the quality as distinct from the
quantity of life.

There is yet another ambivalence, so fundamental that a
further historical reflection may not be out of place. It can best
be introduced with reference to a remark of Keith Thomas in
his book *Man and the Natural World*. His suggestion was that a
major revolution in European thought had occurred towards
the end of the seventeenth century, one to which historians had
paid too little attention, and through which anthropocentric
readings of nature were displaced. The transformation he had
in mind was epitomised by John Ray's remark that it used to be
said that all things were made for man but 'wise men nowadays
think otherwise'.[51] It is not difficult to identify the trends in
seventeenth-century natural philosophy that might have
encouraged such decentring. There was the cosmological
decentring associated with the Copernican innovation,
reinforced by telescopic discoveries that revealed myriads of
stars of no earthly use, and reinforced further by the prospect
of extraterrestrial life. There was the decentring associated with
the mechanical philosophy, which broke the bonds between
microcosm and macrocosm, and which in the philosophy of
Descartes had banished the search for final causes from the
practice of the sciences. No wonder wise men now thought
otherwise.

But did they? There were ways of countering these
centrifugal tendencies, as I have argued elsewhere.[52] Even
cosmologically, human centrality could be preserved, as when
Kepler insisted that we occupy the central orbit around a sun
which he conceived to be the brightest and best in the universe.
Centrality could be preserved epistemologically: through the
divine gift of reason, and a mind that could uncover
the geometry of the universe, progress was actually possible in

---

[51] K. Thomas, *Man and the Natural World* (Harmondsworth: Penguin, 1984), 167.
[52] J. Brooke, ' "Wise Men Nowadays Think Otherwise": John Ray, Natural Theology
and the Meanings of Anthropocentrism', *Notes and Records R. Soc. London*, 54,
2000, 199–213; Brooke and Cantor, *Reconstructing Nature*, 221–8.

the sciences, as the Copernican achievement showed.[53] The mechanisation of nature was accompanied by anthropomorphic images of the deity, which arguably enhanced human prowess in the imitation of the divine artisan. The prominence given to aesthetic sensibilities in the appraisal of scientific theories (not least the Copernican) tended to exalt precisely those qualities of the human mind: man alone, it was often said, had the capacity to appreciate the beauty of God's creation. Nor were final causes, after all, excluded from natural philosophy – certainly not by Boyle who rebuked Descartes for discarding the most potent argument for God's existence. Even more to the point, a careful reading of the natural theology literature of the late seventeenth and early eighteenth centuries suggests an ambivalence of major proportions. It is true that Ray rejected the scholastic premise that all things were made for man *alone*; but that is not the same as saying that some things are not for man's use. The latter Ray did not say and it is a saying very hard to find. In a recent critique of the well-known thesis of Lynn White, that the roots of our ecological crisis can be traced to the Christian doctrine of creation, Peter Harrison has observed that a new *emphasis* on the subjugation of nature for human use came into being through seventeenth-century natural philosophy, certainly legitimised by new readings of Genesis but (contrary to White) having no real equivalent in medieval theology.[54] Even if some natural objects appear not to be of use today, their utility, said Ray, will be revealed in the future. There is perhaps a question whether Keith Thomas's 'revolution' amounted to much in practical terms. In the formula that not everything had been made for man alone there was, at the very least, an ambivalence, allowing for as much mastery of nature as the new rhetoric required. It is hard to believe that a hefty anthropocentrism did not win the day. We saw in Miller that what he meant by 'improvement' was that which adapts nature more thoroughly to human necessities. And so the process has continued. As Celia Deane-Drummond, Robin Grove-White and Bronislaw Szerszynski point out in their contribution to this

---

[53] N. Jardine, *The Birth of History and Philosophy of Science: Kepler's* A Defence of Tycho against Ursus, *with Essays on Its Provenance and Significance* (Cambridge: Cambridge University Press, 1984).

[54] P. Harrison, 'Subduing the Earth: Genesis 1, Early Modern Science, and the Exploitation of Nature', *Journal of Religion*, 79, 1999, 86–109.

volume, a strong anthropocentrism survives even in the evaluation by religious bodies of the genetic modification of non-humans.

In her *Theology and Biotechnology*, Deane-Drummond identified several respects in which theology ought to supply a critique of current practices, at least of the grosser kind. It might expose the hubris in identifying human enterprises with absolute value; it might expose the dishonesty of using environmentalist language to conceal materialist goals; it might criticise the alignment of genetic engineering with consumerism; and it might help to transcend a not uncommon impasse between anthropocentric and holistic assumptions: 'A theocentric perspective, by keeping the dignity of humanity but relativising all human achievements from the perspective of a God who loves all creation, can give us a guide through some of the dilemmas.'[55] I have been suggesting in this paper that there have indeed been spaces where attitudes towards the greater control of nature have been shaped by theological assumptions. But I have also tried to expose different levels of ambivalence where that shaping has occurred. It is an ambivalence detectable in competing readings of the Genesis text where the gift of dominion over nature has been construed both as a licence to dominate and an invitation to stewardship. If there are inarticulate religious concerns informing public attitudes towards scientific manipulation, it is perhaps not surprising that they should lack coherence and precision.

This need not mean that they cease to be relevant. It is clear from a recent collection of essays on animal biotechnology and ethics that there are contexts in which religious sensibilities may still leave their mark.[56] Least attractively perhaps is the manner in which advocates of blanket resistance to genetic manipulation have played on the sensibilities of American fundamentalists.[57] Religious views of the unique value of all human life have undoubtedly shaped answers to such questions as whether human parts taken from a subject in a vegetative

---

[55] C. Deane-Drummond, *Theology and Biotechnology: Implications for a New Science* (London: Geoffrey Chapman, 1997), 97.

[56] A. Holland and A. Johnson (ed.), *Animal Biotechnology and Ethics* (London: Chapman and Hall, 1998).

[57] A. Johnson, 'Needs, Fears and Fantasies', in Holland and Johnson, *Animal Biotechnology*, 133–42, especially 136–7.

state should ever be preferred to animal parts in an organ trans-plantation.[58] A revulsion to the patenting of onco-species may be the expression of the inarticulate conviction that God alone deserves the patent; for we act only as a demiurge (not strictly a creator or inventor) in modifying the pre-existing substrate. The moral issue becomes all the more poignant when, in the weighing of animal suffering against human gain, scientists themselves begin to doubt the gains, as when they express reser-vations about the utility of onco-mice in the development of anti-cancer drugs.[59] Ethical codes can of course be formulated independently of theological discourse, but historically they have been reinforced by them. The morality of altering an animal's genetic structure with the express purpose that it should develop a painful, lethal disease constitutes an issue on which religious belief may surely impinge. And there is, finally, that issue of humility. Back in the seventeenth century Francis Bacon advocated an experimental philosophy in part on the ground that it would encourage the Christian virtue of humility. It struck out against the hubris of the scholastic philosophers who, like spiders, spun ideas from their brains without troubling to consult nature. They had presumed to know how the world must be without examining which of the many worlds God might have made had actually *been* made. Humility still has its advocates in the appraisal of biotechnological programmes. David Cooper asserts that 'a person abandons humility not *because* animal life has an integrity which he or she dishonours. Rather, integrity is said to be dishonoured when proper humility has been abandoned.' And where humility is absent, he reminds us, there is likely to be what Jung, remembering the vivisections he had unwillingly performed as a student, experienced as 'alienation ... from God's world'.[60]

Such language is not the most congenial to policy-makers, especially perhaps to those in America who operate on the principle that, where possible, decisions should not be based on

[58] R. Frey, 'Organs for Transplant: Animals, Moral Standing, and One View of the Ethics of Xenotransplantation', in Holland and Johnson, *Animal Biotechnology*, 190–208, especially 204–5.

[59] P. Stevenson, 'Animal Patenting: European Law and Ethical Implications', in Holland and Johnson, *Animal Biotechnology*, 288–302, especially 296–8.

[60] D. Cooper, 'Intervention, Humility and Animal Integrity', in Holland and Johnson, *Animal Biotechnology*, 145–55, especially 154–5.

the vision of any one group as to what constitutes quality in human life. Instead 'policies are designed to serve peaceful and ordered societies, where individuals and groups are free to pursue their own traditions, at least to the extent that they cause no harm to others'.[61] Whether such a neutralising stance is possible in the context of genetic engineering has become a critical question. Recently, attention has been given to what is called the 'ethics of description'. The language used by legislators when describing genes is not ultimately neutral. As Mark Hanson has observed, 'legal rulings have reinforced the biotechnology industry's interest in describing genes as "mere chemicals", and patents on them as "legal mechanisms" for "compositions of matter", "invented" for human scientific and commercial purposes'.[62] Isolating a discourse of genes in this way and adopting such reductionist language for their description may reasonably be judged not to be morally neutral and certainly not inconsequential. One may even detect two forms of reductionism here. Other, more holistic, accounts of what genes contribute to the organism are simply excluded, and this in turn gives at least tacit support for ontological as well as methodological forms of reductionism in the understanding of living systems. Reductionist language when thus embedded can be uncongenial to secular and religious critics alike. The irony, as Hanson also points out, is that if such wider public concerns (however inarticulately expressed) continue to be ignored, we may end up not with neutral policies but with the very situation policy-makers seek to avoid: the imposition of a vision that may be said to be that of only one particular group in society.

Conclusion

I have argued in this paper that ambivalent attitudes towards ambitious technologies are neither new nor surprising. We hardly expect them to be surprising given that many new technologies have proved a mixed blessing. But the cultural issues run deeper than one might suppose on the basis of a calculus of consequences. Indeed in the variety of contemporary

---

[61] M. Hanson, 'The Depths of Reason: Biotechnology's Challenge to Public Policy', *Science and Spirit*, 10, 5, 2000, 22–3.
[62] Hanson, 'Depths of Reason', 22.

public concerns one sees the legacy of a theological ambivalence in which 'improvements' on, or to, nature could seem either presumptuous or providentially sanctioned. Theological commentators have found it easy to be caught between contemplative and activist approaches to nature. Diplomats for the applied sciences, typified by Francis Bacon, have found themselves caught between two different readings of the Genesis 'fall' narrative: in one there is presumption in seeking forbidden knowledge; in the other humankind has an ethical duty to work for the restoration of a blighted world. If one thought in terms of collaborating with God, as Hugh Miller did in the nineteenth century, there was (and still is) the obvious question as to how one knew one was working with the deity or against. Distended bovine udders that, for Miller, were symbols of human progress are the very items seized by critics today to expose a sinful anthropocentrism.[63] There is a pointer here to deeper tensions: between those, such as the Renaissance architect Alberti, who have welcomed the aspiration of the engineer or architect to come closer to God through God-like creative activity, and those harbouring an Augustinian suspicion of such assimilation, given the flaws in human nature. Teilhard de Chardin, to whom I referred earlier, could write with equanimity that 'since I can never set a boundary to the perfection of my fidelity nor to the fervour of my intention, this commerce enables me to liken myself, ever more strictly and indefinitely, to God'.[64] For the critic of an uncontrolled technology it is precisely that assimilation that is dangerous.

The machines of modern technology have provided an ever increasing stock of metaphors for the redescription of nature – a process already well under way in seventeenth-century Europe. As I have indicated, however, there could be a deep ambivalence associated with the mechanisation of the world picture. To erode the Aristotelian distinction between 'nature' and 'art' could be a way of either elevating humanity or demeaning God through anthropomorphic reduction. Not only that but clockwork models of the universe were deeply ambiguous in terms of the theological construction to be placed

---

[63] J. D'Silva, 'Campaigning against Transgenic Technology', in Holland and Johnson, *Animal Biotechnology*, 92–102.
[64] Teilhard de Chardin, *Milieu Divin*, 63.

upon them. They could enhance arguments for design but at the same time relegate the Creator to the role of a redundant clockmaker. They could be deployed against intermediary spirits or intelligences to underscore absolute divine sovereignty, as they were by Robert Boyle, nevertheless sacrificing in that very process a sense of divine immanence. They could be used to sharpen the boundaries between nature and supernature, providing more rigorous criteria for discrimination between miracles and mere marvels; or they could be used to eliminate references to the supernatural altogether. Design arguments for a deity could be formulated, as they often were, with pious intentions; but how easily they were desacralised to provide grounds for the promotion of science and technology![65] Ambivalence over what counts as sacred and what counts as secular can be illustrated once again by reference to Francis Bacon, whose vision of a restored world could be presented in all humility within a framework of biblical prophecy, but whose inspiration included a more secular imperative: if it can be done it shall be done. In Boyle's partial discomfiture over vivisection we see the classic ambivalence over whether such an end always justifies the means.

The Newtonian argument, from which this paper took its title, has a decisive air. That we should be permitted to be created co-creators enhances rather than detracts from divine power. But this has proved a high-risk stratagem. One is reminded of those aphorisms that abounded in the wake of the Darwinian impact – that a God who makes things make themselves is wiser and more powerful than one who simply makes things.[66] The problem, conceded by Darwin's correspondent Asa Gray, is that without the eye of faith one simply sees things making themselves. As we progress to the 'cloning' of human organs is that problem not writ anew and writ large?

---

[65] J. Topham, 'Science and Popular Education in the 1830s: The Role of the *Bridgewater Treatises*', *British Journal for the History of Science*, 25, 1992, 397–430.

[66] Such aphorisms are to be found in Charles Kingsley and Frederick Temple among others. Brooke and Cantor, *Reconstructing Nature*, 161–7; G. Elder, *Chronic Vigour: Darwin, Anglicans, Catholics, and the Development of a Doctrine of Providential Evolution* (Lanham: University Press of America, 1996), 158.

Response to Chapter 2

Arthur Peacocke

We have had from Professor Brooke a typically convincing exposition of how religious belief is involved, even if only subliminally, in the appraisal of new technologies. Such appraisal is, it seems, sensitive particularly to the degree to which the religious believer conceives of him- or herself as capable of enhancing God's creation as a 'co-creator'. This stirred echoes in my mind of a perception I once received of an earlier stance of this kind to be found among those who participated in what we now call the Italian Renaissance.

The actual occasion was when, some years ago, on successive days I was able to see two magnificent thirteenth-century pulpits, one in Siena and the other in Pisa, the work of the Pisano family. Both of these splendid walled platforms, with their lecterns from which the Word of God was to be proclaimed, were supported on elaborate arrangements of pillars depicting the substructure, one might say, that underlies the proclamation of the gospel. In addition to the obvious representations of prophets and Evangelists, these supports included representations of the arts of the Trivium and Quadrivium, the seven Liberal Arts – grammar, rhetoric and dialectic and music, arithmetic, geometry and astronomy – both the prolegomena to the study of theology and its cultural support. Here we were seeing the visible representation of the spirit of that re-won *Christian* humanism of the Italian Renaissance. This came to be expressed verbally and more explicitly by such later fifteenth-century Florentine writers as

65

Giannozzi Manetti (1396–1459), whose concept of creation in the image of God and whose vision of humanity's heavenly destiny represented 'an important new conception of man [humanity] as actor, creator, shaper of nature and history, all of which qualities he possesses for the very reason that he is made "in the image and likeness" of the Trinity'.[1] For Manetti 'man's ingenuity or inventiveness was so great that man himself should be regarded as a second creator of the human historical world that was superimposed on the original divine creation of the natural world'.[2] The Florentine Marsilio Ficino (1433–99) too had 'an irrepressible admiration for the works of human industry with which he was surrounded in Renaissance Florence … he cannot help seeing in man's mastery of the world … further evidence of man's similarity to God if not of his divinity itself'.[3]

Here we seem to have the germ of the idea of human beings *sharing* in the creative work of God – being, as it were, *co*-creators with God, but not with a capital 'C', for human creativity is a created and derived one, endowed by God the Creator, spelt with capital 'C'. The thinkers and creative artists of the Renaissance were in fact recovering something already implicit in the biblical tradition and specifically expressed in its Wisdom literature, the significance of which is only now being again recovered in recent biblical scholarship, as Celia Deane-Drummond continues to remind us (see chapter 14). In that remarkable and famous passage of Wisdom 7, and indeed throughout that book, 'Wisdom' is (be it noted) the female personification of the outgoing activity of God in all creation, an activity that is mirrored in the creative activity of that part of creation capable of responding to God and able itself also to be creative – namely, human beings.

Coming into the period of Professor Brooke's paper, I cannot help thinking too of William Blake who at least saw human beings as co-creating creatures of and with God. For he exhorted us to exercise our God-given creative capabilities in 'building Jerusalem'. We recall that marvellous series of illustrations of his for *Book of Job*. It begins with Job and his family

---

[1] C. E. Trinkhaus, *In Our Image and Likeness: Humanity and Divinity in Italian Humanist Thought* (London: Constable, 1970), 248.
[2] Trinkhaus, *In Our Image*, 247.
[3] Trinkhaus, *In Our Image*, 482.

depicted as worshipping God – so-called 'worship' Blake would have us understand – all of them *sitting* under the Tree of Life from which hang musical instruments, as 'untouched as on a Calvinist Sabbath', as Kathleen Raine describes them.[4] After Job's redemption through suffering and restoration to full life, the family all now *stand* under the Tree playing the instruments and enthusiastically joining in making the music of both heaven and earth. As Blake himself said, the Christian life is 'the liberty both of body and of mind to exercise the Divine Arts of Imagination … Let every Christian, as much as in him lies, engage himself openly and publicly before all the World in some Mental pursuit for the Building up of Jerusalem.'[5]

Perhaps we can learn today in our dilemmas concerning genetics from this wisdom of former times? We certainly need to do so.

---

[4] Kathleen Raine, *William Blake* (London: Thames and Hudson, 1970).
[5] Quoted by Kathleen Raine, *William Blake*, 186–7.

3

Burke, Barth and Biotechnology: On Preferring the Sabbath to the Sublime – Some Preliminary Thoughts

Michael Banner

The advent of biotechnology, with its offer of seemingly newly subtle, thoroughgoing and radical possibilities for the reshaping of nature, gives a contemporary urgency to the posing of a question which is by no means itself new: what are the ethical limits, if any, to the human Re-Ordering of nature?

In two recent papers[1] two eminent moral philosophers, Bernard Williams and David Wiggins, share not only an interest in this problem, but also similar doubts about the adequacy of many approaches to it, similar ideas about what notions or concepts we might need if we are to think properly in this area and similar anxieties about the fact that these ideas and concepts may be damaged – fatally – by their being supposed to have something to do with religion. It is undoubtedly a sign of grace that both are concerned to try to make sense of an unease about the use of biotechnology which cannot be explained by reference to the standard, broadly utilitarian, risk/benefit framework typically favoured by contemporary policy-makers;

[1] B. Williams, 'Must a Concern for the Environment be Centred on Human Beings?', *Making Sense of Humanity and Other Philosophical Papers 1982–1993* (Cambridge: Cambridge University Press, 1995), 233–40; D. Wiggins, 'Nature, Respect for Nature, and the Human Scale of Values', *Proceedings of the Aristotelian Society*, 100, 1, 2000, 1–32.

an unease which is often dismissed as irrational.[2] But I shall go on to suggest that whilst both reach after concepts which would render this unease explicable, these concepts fall short of providing a constraint markedly different from the one they both reject. I shall note that the concept of the 'sublime', which both entertain, seems more promising, but that on closer inspection it is not without problems. Indeed and in addition (and this will allow me to approach more nearly what mostly concerns me, namely, the character of a properly theological answer to the question first mentioned), the concept is fundamentally ill-suited to a theological outlook, which rather than beginning with an attempt to re-pristinate this concept would do well to begin with and think out of the meaning of the Sabbath.

In his paper Bernard Williams asks what sense can be made of certain characteristic attitudes towards the environment. Having argued that economic analysis, reflection on animal experience or the interest of non-humans offer false directions, he contends that 'our ideas of nature must play an important part in explaining our attitudes towards these matters' and further that 'nature may be seen as offering a boundary to our activities, defining certain interventions and certain uncontrolled effects as transgressive'.[3]

He notes, however, that this outlook may be thought religious, which will, of course, be a source of embarrassment to the religious sceptic. Indeed others might try to talk those who have concerns for the environment out of them 'just by referring these attitudes back to religion'. Williams parries this attack by reference to what he terms 'Feuerbach's Axiom':

> [I]f religion is false, it cannot ultimately explain anything, but itself needs to be explained. If religion is false, it comes entirely from humanity (and even if it is true, it comes in good part from humanity). If it tends to embody a sense of nature that should limit our exploitation of it, we may hope to find the source of that sense in humanity itself.[4]

---

[2] For a discussion of the problems with this approach, see my 'Why and How Not to Value the Environment', *Christian Ethics and Contemporary Moral Problems* (Cambridge, Cambridge University Press, 1999).

[3] Williams, 'Must a Concern for the Environment be Centred on Human Beings?', 238.

[4] Williams, 'Must a Concern for the Environment be Centred on Human Beings?', 238.

But what might that source be? Williams offers what he describes as 'no more than a speculation to encourage reflection'. And the speculation is this: 'Human beings have two basic kinds of emotional relations to nature: gratitude and a sense of peace, on the one hand, terror and stimulation on the other ... The two kinds of feelings famously find their place in art, in the form of its concern with the beautiful and with the sublime.' He continues:

> If we think in these terms, our sense of restraint in the face of nature, a sense very basic to conservation concerns, will be grounded in a form of fear: a fear not just of the power of nature itself, but what might be called *Promethean fear*, a fear of taking too lightly or inconsiderately our relations to nature. On this showing, the grounds of our attitudes will be very different from that suggested by any appeal to the interests of natural things. It will not be an extension of benevolence or altruism; nor, directly, will it be a sense of community, though it may be a sense of intimate involvement. It will be based rather on a sense of an opposition between ourselves and nature, as an old, unbounded and potentially dangerous enemy, which requires respect. 'Respect' is the notion that perhaps more than any other needs examination here – and not first in the sense of respect for a sovereign, but that in which we have a healthy respect for mountainous terrain or treacherous seas.[5]

He concludes:

> We should not think that if the basis of our sentiments is of such a kind, then it is simply an archaic remnant which we can ignore. For, first, Promethean fear is a good general warning device, reminding us still appropriately of what we may properly fear. But apart from that, it is something that many people deeply feel, then it is something that is likely to be pervasively connected to things that we value, to what gives life the kinds of significance that it has ... it is not these feelings in themselves that matter. Rather, they embody a value which we have good reason, in terms of our sense of what is worthwhile in human life, to preserve, and to follow, to the extent that we can, in our dealings with nature.[6]

In a paper entitled 'Nature, Respect for Nature, and the Human Scale of Values', David Wiggins, acknowledging

[5] Williams, 'Must a Concern for the Environment be Centred on Human Beings?', 239.

[6] Williams, 'Must a Concern for the Environment be Centred on Human Beings?', 239.

Williams's paper, takes up and advances some of Williams's concerns. Like Williams he is concerned to understand the sort of unease about our treatment of nature which might, for example, have prevented us following the path which led to BSE, namely, the addition of sheep offal to feed destined for herbivores. And like Williams he thinks that religion is a danger here, the danger being that of 'making the case against certain attitudes to the environment seem to depend on religion, on speculation, on ancient vacuities about living in accordance with Nature, or on that which is suspect in folk wisdom. The danger is real.'[7] However, if we react with horror to the BSE episode, for example, we 'owe it to ourselves to try to say *what* feeling or outlook it is that should have restrained the manufacturers and farmers ... There is a temptation here, for the sake of having a name, to call the feeling or outlook they lacked *holy dread*.'[8]

Now, says Wiggins, such an idea will be treated with suspicion: John Passmore has no use for the category of the sacred; Leszek Kolakowski treats the whole idea of respect for nature with distrust. 'The temptation we are under in this department, having dispensed with many or most other forms of respect specifically for Nature as such, is to superannuate holy dread entirely and put into its place, to be afforced by ordinary workaday moral ideas, the secular notions of risk that are imparted to us by all the various specialists.'[9] But we should resist this temptation, since this calculation does not take up everything which is involved in the concept.

> Maybe the one *irreplaceable residue* of holy dread is the mental state of one who acknowledges the fragility and the complexity of the interacting systems which make up the habitable world and have served us so far, and who grasps also the crucial role within these systems of very small differences ... It is the state of conscious being in which one never forgets the severe limitation on our knowledge of the *sum* of factors to which we owe our survival and well-being up to this point and the near limitlessness of our ignorance of how things *will* turn out if we change those factors, nor ever forgets our predictive ignorance of social processes and poor grasp of the

[7] Wiggins, 'Nature, Respect for Nature, and the Human Scale of Values', 27.
[8] Wiggins, 'Nature, Respect for Nature, and the Human Scale of Values', 27.
[9] Wiggins, 'Nature, Respect for Nature, and the Human Scale of Values', 27–8.

conditions under which human beings will be able to live in
serenity and contentment. Does not holy dread *live on*, even now, in
the bitterness of the righteous indignation that makes itself felt
wherever we think things have gone wrong because alteration has
been made to the world we are used to in ignorance of the
mechanisms at work in Nature or else in ignorance of the human
and animal purposes that were threatened by the alteration? The
simple thought is: how *dare* they put at risk, for the sake of rather
trivial benefits, the lives or the livelihoods of countless people that
depended on some concatenation of factors that had never been
reckoned or enumerated?[10]

Now we shall hardly want to do without the concepts and
categories which Williams and Wiggins examine and the
general caution which they advocate; however, we cannot but
note that, on examination, what this all delivers is remarkably
modest, and remarkably more modest than the words used
suggest. It turns out, in fact, that the reclamation of the concept
of 'holy dread' by Wiggins, or the invitation to 'Promethean
fear' from Williams, gives us, in actual fact, very little (in theory
or in practice) in addition to the prudential risk/benefit
analysis that Wiggins and Williams both scorn. After all, what
does Wiggins's 'holy dread' really amount to when he has
explained it? The concept of 'holy dread' will, of course, have
different resonances and there is no way of fixing it precisely –
except perhaps by reference to the classical literature to which
Wiggins refers. But it makes us think, perhaps, of the feeling
one might have at the prospect of eating human flesh. What,
however, has Wiggins given us with the cleaned-up concept, or
Williams with Promethean fear? Little more than a caution.
What both seem to say is: be careful, things are more complicated than you think. And this may be sensible and right, and it
might add a further pause to the weighing and balancing
procedures of the current policy process; but this is very far
from that holy dread which comes across someone on realising
that they are about to taste human flesh. The holy dread the
philosophers vindicate seems to be the dread of realising that
the aetiologies of various diseases have yet to be fully explored
and explained, so that it is on the whole more prudent to avoid
unusual foods and to stick to a plain and regular diet.

[10] Wiggins, 'Nature, Respect for Nature, and the Human Scale of Values', 30.

Now it would be too much to claim that because Williams's and Wiggins's particular attempts to re-pristinate the notion of 'boundaries' and 'holy dread' without recourse to religion seemingly end so disappointingly, all such attempts must do so. And both mention a concept – that of the sublime – which might well be thought to take us further, without risking that dangerous contact with religion, revealed or otherwise, which they are concerned, studiously, to avoid. Perhaps this can do the trick they seek to perform; that of vindicating a certain sort of respect for nature without reliance on what they would regard as dubious metaphysics. I suggest, however, that this strategy has weaknesses, and indeed is wrong-headed from a specifically theological viewpoint. In the first place, the experience of the sublime, rather than being a ground for respect, might in fact be taken as a gauntlet thrown down to humankind by nature which technology takes up. In the second place, the sublime is traditionally associated with fear and dread, and yet this fear and dread cannot be foundational for Christianity, which properly takes up its reflection on the natural not from any such experience, but from the idea of the Sabbath.

Any treatment of the origins and range of the concept of the 'sublime' would properly take in Edmund Burke's influential treatment of it.[11] Here it must suffice to say that the sublime has often and characteristically been identified with that in nature which affects the human mind with a sense of overwhelming grandeur or irresistible power, inspiring awe, fear, terror or dread. Now if this is held to be in some sense an authentic perception and response to the natural world, then perhaps this will give us more than Williams and Wiggins – perhaps, that is to say, an experience of the natural world as sublime will serve to ground respect for nature and a sense of there being proper limits to our engagement with it. But the thought is no sooner in place than reservations seem bound to arise, from the side of pure reason, as it were, as well as from the side of revealed religion.

First of all an experience of the sublime, with its associated feelings, does not seem to deliver what Williams and Wiggins

---

[11] E. Burke, *A Philosophical Enquiry into the Origin of our Ideas of the Sublime and Beautiful* (Oxford: Blackwell, 1987).

were looking for, namely, a basis for boundaries and limits in our handling of nature. For if one response to the great and the overwhelming and the grand in nature may be respect or reverence, there is surely another, no less characteristic, which finds in the great and the overwhelming and the grand a challenge to human accomplishments and mastery – that reaction and response which is implied in that clichéd reason for climbing Everest, namely, its being there. The desert, or the forest, or the Antarctic, which lie before us in all their inhospitable immensity must be tamed; the ocean, with its boundless and unpredictable power, must be charted; those other species of animal than our own, in all their recalcitrant otherness, must be subdued. The sublime, that is to say, is as often a challenge as it is a check. It is a gauntlet thrown down to humankind, which technology takes up with all its ingenuity and application.

But there is another and deeper reservation regarding the sublime, this time from the standpoint of revealed religion, and in particular the religion revealed in the life, death and resurrection of Jesus Christ, and this reservation relates just as well to the holy dread and Promethean fear of Wiggins and Williams as to the sublime. And it is, to be blunt, that terror and fear, whatever place they may properly have in our experience of and attitude towards nature, cannot properly be the foundation and basis for it. Why not?

Amongst the many politically incorrect things that Christians say – or at least ought to say – is this: that creation is for the sake of Christ and the Church, to use Karl Barth's formulation of the point. From a purely philosophical point of view, the existence of something rather than nothing may be wholly inexplicable; from a general religious point of view, the existence of this universe could, presumably, be explained by countless possible reasons, by a love of variety or beauty on the part of God, or, in a Hardyesque mood of despair, by a divine taste for suffering and pain. From a Christian point of view, however, there is one answer – that the end for which God created is the existence of that fellowship between God and humankind which will be achieved in the unity of Jesus Christ with that community which is owned and known by, and owns and knows, him.

Now if this is so, there may be much to be said about nature and our engagement with it, but from this place we must begin – that when in the book of Genesis God voices that appraisal of creation as 'very good', this is not some abstract appreciation of which we cannot make sense, as if what it might be good *for* remains a mystery to us. Creation is for the sake of Christ and the Church; this God creates, as another god may or may not, out of love for humankind. We can hardly think then, that fear could be the original and proper basis of our attitude to nature, to that order in which we are placed. We can hardly think that this is an order which we need, first of all, to subdue, tame, discipline or dominate. We should think instead that this is an order which, existing for our good, is one which we should first of all love and cherish. We should think that our proper and authentic engagement with the created order is that which is learnt by our responding to God's invitation to share in his Sabbath rest, a rest in which, in contemplation of this creation, and in utter conviction as to God's loving purpose in its ordering, we may put away anxiety, fear, dread or awe and learn instead a simple enjoyment of this order in its complexity, vitality, beauty and magnificence. We should think and expect that our created good at least exists in living in and with this order, not in triumphing over it. (It will have occurred to the reader that these thoughts require some further reference to the problem of evil and the fall.)

Karl Barth, to mention him again, once wrote:

> The last war, with all that led up to it and all its possible consequences, has posed afresh the problem of humanity from the particular angle of the question of the rights, dignity and sanctity of the fellow-man. Humanity stands at the crossroads. In its future development as humanity, will it be for man or against him?[12]

Biotechnology, we might say in paraphrase, with all its possible consequences, has posed afresh the problem of nature from the particular angle of the question of the limits of our reshaping of it. Humanity stands at a crossroads. In its future development as humanity, will it be for nature or against it? What I have sought to suggest, and no more than suggest, is that various attempts to discover and chart these limits, and so make sense of certain deep-seated commitments towards the natural world, without recourse to religion, fail to provide that which

---

[12] K. Barth, *Church Dogmatics*, Vol. III/2, tr. H. Knight et al. (Edinburgh: T&T Clark, 1960), 228.

they seem to promise, and offer us little more than the sort of cautions which might be advanced from within the matter-of-fact, everyday and rather shallow world of comparisons of costs and benefits. Perhaps there are other ways of understanding these commitments and hence the limits to which they point, but insofar as fear is thought to be basic to our proper appreciation of the natural, it does not seem to promise limits, but rather provokes us to rise to the challenge posed by a recalcitrant other. If humankind is to be for nature and not against, it may be that it has to learn not to fear nature, but to love it; and it may be that it will learn this from the religion of Jesus Christ, and from nowhere else; for here we learn what cannot be learnt from just anywhere, namely, that what stands before us is made for our good, and that our good will surely consist in enjoyment of it in God.

Response to Chapter 3
Possums on the Pill: How to Save Nature

Michael J. Reiss

Under the heading 'Possums on the Pill: Contraceptive Carrots Will Stop the Spread of Marauding Marsupials', the *New Scientist* of 4 March 2000 carried a piece, the first paragraph of which read:

> The explosion in New Zealand's possum populations could be reined in by sterilising the female possums with genetically modified carrots. Scientists who developed the carrots say they are a humane and environmentally sound alternative to managing wildlife with poisons or viruses.[1]

This piece carries sufficient information for a future scholar to have little difficulty in working out most of the essential issues in the current secular debates about the use of modern biotechnology even if all other written sources had perished. There is the confident editorial sub-heading – 'Contraceptive Carrots Will Stop the Spread of Marauding Marsupials'; images of profligate nature – 'The explosion in New Zealand's possum populations'; an assumed right for humans to control nature – 'managing wildlife'; a modern technology to the rescue with science's blessing – 'genetically modified carrots' developed by scientists; and evidence of a recent ethic of care – the carrots are 'a humane and environmentally sound alternative'.

---

[1] D. Graham-Rowe, 'Possums on the pill: Contraceptive Carrots Will Stop the Spread of Marauding Marsupials', *New Scientist*, 4 March 2000, 18.

Theological Analyses

But the *New Scientist* piece has no theology, explicit or implicit.
The arguments as to whether or not these novel carrots should
be employed are both secular and entirely consequentialist.
Recent years have seen something of a flourishing of applied
moral philosophy in the field of biotechnology. The, to some
surprising, allocation of significant funds, first in the USA and
then in the European Union and elsewhere, towards research
into the ethical, legal and social implications of the human
genome project has meant that the number of writings in the
area of the new genetics has increased dramatically. Nor have
theologians been slow to write in this field, though Michael
Banner does not review their contributions. I shall concentrate
on genetic engineering as this is the technology most
concerned with a possible re-ordering of nature, though other
technologies such as cloning and embryo transfer need analysis
too.

Most of what has been written about genetic engineering
from a theological perspective is the product of Christian
writers.[2] Three main approaches can be identified: rejection,
hesitancy and acceptance with caveats.

Some theologians reject genetic engineering on the grounds
that it entails humans having too much power over animals.
Andrew Linzey, for example, considers genetic engineering to
be a form of slavery:

> [G]enetic engineering represents the concretisation of the *absolute*
> claim that animals belong to us and exist for us. We have always
> used animals, of course, either for food, fashion or sport. It is not
> new that we are now using animals for farming, even in especially
> cruel ways. *What is new is that we are now employing the technological*

---

[2] R. Cole-Turner, *The New Genesis: Theology and the Genetic Revolution* (Louisville,
Kentucky: Westminster/John Knox Press, 1993); J. R. Nelson, *On the New
Frontiers of Genetics and Religion* (Grand Rapids, Michigan: William B. Eerdmans
Publishing Company, 1994); A. Dyson, 'Genetic Engineering in Theology and
Theological Ethics', in A. Dyson and J. Harris (eds), *Ethics and Biotechnology*
(New York: Routledge, 1994), 259–71; M. J. Reiss and R. Straughan, *Improving
Nature? The Science and Ethics of Genetic Engineering* (Cambridge: Cambridge
University Press, 1996); C. Deane-Drummond, *Theology and Biotechnology:
Implications for a New Science* (London: Geoffrey Chapman, 1997); T. Peters,
Playing God? Genetic Determinism and Human Freedom (New York: Routledge,
1997).

means of absolutely subjugating the nature of animals so that they become
totally and completely human property.[3]

One obvious problem with this argument is that certain
animals, not to mention plants, have been considered human
property in practically every society since time immemorial.
Farm animals and pets, in particular, are always owned by
people.

Another possible reason for rejecting genetic engineering is
that it involves too exploitative a view not just of animals but of
all of nature. Martin Heidegger argued that in technology we
make objects according to some blueprint that we determine.
We design things to satisfy our purposes rather than allow our
purposes to be affected by, and find creative expression
through, the qualities of the objects themselves.[4] Heidegger's
point is particularly apposite when applied to genetically
engineered organisms.

The most frequent response by religious writers to the issue
of genetic engineering is one of caution or hesitancy. In
particular, some people may hesitate about the movement of
genes between humans and other species, fearing that this
somehow diminishes the distinctiveness of being human. For
example, the notion that humans are made *imago Dei* may cause
some with a Christian faith to feel uncomfortable about a
technology that apparently threatens to blur the dividing line
between humans and the rest of the created order. Note too 1
Corinthians 15.39: 'For not all flesh is alike, but there is one
kind for men, another for animals, another for birds, and
another for fish.' Of course, others may feel differently, perhaps
believing that all of creation is, in a way, *imago Dei*, in the sense
that how can that which is created do other than reflect its
Creator, Sustainer and Redeemer.

Then, though this category overlaps with the previous one,
there are religious writers who accept genetic engineering,
though typically with certain specific caveats. Phil Challis,

---

[3] A. Linzey, 'Human and Animal Slavery: A Theological Critique of Genetic
Engineering', in P. Wheale and R. McNally (eds), *The Bio-Revolution: Cornucopia or
Pandora's Box* (London: Pluto Press, 1990), 175–88. The same point is made in A.
Linzey, *Animal Theology* (London: SCM Press, 1994).
[4] M. Heidegger, *The Question concerning Technology and Other Essays. Translated and
with an Introduction by William Lovitt* (New York: Harper Colophon, 1997).

arguing against Andrew Linzey's rejection of genetic engineering considered above, writes:

> We are co-creators with God, 'fearfully and wonderfully made' (Ps.
> 139:14). With our finite freedom we are called by Him to act
> responsibly as we continue the process of genetic manipulation of
> domestic organisms. A theology that emphasises embodiment
> rather than body–spirit dichotomy, that emphasises becoming
> rather than immutability as an essential part of God's nature, that
> emphasises relationship within the web rather than domination
> from outside the system, such a Christian theology may provide a
> critical framework that can realistically embrace the potential of
> genetic engineering for good.[5]

Ronald Cole-Turner[6] has explored the implications of a
distinction between humans as co-creators with God – a concept
which, he feels, contains a number of difficulties – and humans
as participants, through genetic engineering, in redemption.
Here redemption is being used in the sense of 'restoration'.
The idea is that genetic engineering can help to overcome
genetic defects caused by harmful mutations. In this way genetic
engineering can help to restore creation to a fuller, richer
existence and can, Cole-Turner maintains, play an important
role without encroaching on the scope of divine activity.

It can perhaps be argued, in this vein, that humans may have
a theological responsibility, even a duty, to use genetic engineering to root out imperfections in the natural world, including
those found in humans. Viewed in this light, genetic engineering can be seen as a tool with the potential to eliminate
harmful genetic mutations, reduce suffering and restore
creation to its full glory.

---

[5] P. Challis, *Genetic Engineering and Its Applications: Some Theological and Ethical Reflections* (Cambridge: Wesley House, 1992), 39–40. C. Deane-Drummond, 'Reshaping Our Environment: Implications of the New Biotechnology', *Theology in Green*, 5, 1995, 19–33, argues that 'A theological approach encourages those involved to see the wider social and religious consequences of these decisions. It does not necessarily ban all genetic engineering, but seeks to transform it so that it more clearly represents a fully human enterprise' (26).

[6] Cole-Turner, *New Genesis*.

Christian Theology in a Pluralist Society

One of the things I like about Michael Banner's chapter is its refusal to accept the sufficiency of a consequentialist ethic. Indeed, one of Michael Banner's significant achievements, as Chair of the Banner Committee, was to get that committee to argue that it would be unacceptable, through genetic modification, for certain agricultural ends to be met whatever their positive utility. For example, it would, the committee maintained, be unacceptable for a scientist to increase the efficiency of food conversion in pigs by reducing their sentience and responsiveness, thereby decreasing their level of activity, on the grounds that 'the proposed modification is morally objectionable in treating the animals as raw materials upon which our ends and purposes can be imposed regardless of the ends and purposes which are natural to them'.[7]

In his chapter, Michael Banner goes on to examine the concepts of 'holy dread' and of 'the sublime' and looks at recent attempts by two philosophers to use these terms when considering why people hesitate to do particular things. For myself I rather like the idea of reclaiming certain words from a somewhat exclusive religious domain for the use of a wider constituency. See, for example, Dworkin's attempt[8] to use the word 'sacred' in a non-religious sense and so discern just what it is about human life that almost everyone finds special even when there are major differences in the views held by people in such areas as abortion and euthanasia.

But my own approach to these issues differs from Michael Banner's in at least three ways – I do realise that this says at least as much about me as it says about Michael Banner. First, Michael Banner is more confident than I am of the value of notions of holy dread as illuminating what is right and what is wrong. He talks 'of the feeling one might have at the prospect of eating human flesh'. Now, thankfully, I have never been in such a situation but I suspect my reaction would be one of extreme disgust rather than holy dread. I am all in favour of

---

[7] Ministry of Agriculture, Fisheries and Food, *Report of the Committee to Consider the Ethical Implications of Emerging Technologies in the Breeding of Farm Animals* (London: HMSO, 1995), 15.

[8] R. Dworkin, *Life's Dominion: An Argument about Abortion and Euthanasia* (London: HarperCollins, 1993).

taking disgust seriously. I do not, for instance, believe in rejecting out of hand the 'yuk factor' argument in the evaluation of biotechnology. But just as disgust cannot be disregarded in ethical debates on the grounds that it is irrational nor can it be accepted as binding. After all, just as some people once found the notion of women training to be doctors disgusting, so some people now find same-sex sexual relationships disgusting or the eating of horse meat or pork disgusting. But that does not necessarily make such actions wrong.

Secondly, I am more interested than Michael Banner seems to be in how we make political decisions in a society when Christian values no longer hold sway. Unlike Ezra and Nehemiah, I am more concerned at how we can worship in Babylon than return to Jerusalem. My reading of Michael Banner's article is that his particular focus is on establishing a Christian understanding of the issues at hand. For myself, I consider the careful explication and articulation of a range of Christian positions an essential first step to be followed by attempts to reach a broader consensus[9] outside of the Temple.

Thirdly, if I read Michael Banner aright, his is an anthropocentric vision of salvation. It is possible that I am wrong here. I am aware that his passage 'the end for which God created is the existence of that fellowship between God and humankind which will be achieved in the unity of Jesus Christ with that community which is owned and known by, and owns and knows, him' can be interpreted in a non-anthropocentric manner. However, his closing lines, 'If humankind is to be for nature and not against, it may be that it has to learn not to fear nature, but to love it; and it may be that it will learn this from the religion of Jesus Christ, and from nowhere else; for here we learn what cannot be learnt from just anywhere, namely, that what stands before us is made for our good, and that our good will surely consist in enjoyment of it in God' suggest a narrower focus that I would wish.

I am interested in how we can save the possum. And the various resonances in the word 'save' suit my purpose well. I'm

---

[9] J. Habermas, *Moralbewusstsein und Kommunikatives Handeln* (Frankfurt am Main: Suhrkamp Verlag, 1983); J. D. Moreno, *Deciding Together: Bioethics and Moral Consensus* (Oxford: Oxford University Press, 1995).

the sort of person who would try to save an individual possum, male or female, if it was hurt. If the possum were an endangered species I would also give money to save it. My view of nature is informed both by a Christian analysis and by an evolutionary perspective. Let me conclude by saying a little about how I could imagine an evolutionary perspective might inform our view of nature.

It needs to be emphasised how firmly rooted contemporary biology is in an evolutionary framework. It is, of course, possible, to be a practising biologist, even a research biologist, without accepting that the world is very old and that all today's living creatures share a common ancestor. However, such biologists are in a small minority. The assumption by the overwhelming majority of today's biologists is that all of the abundance of life we see around us today has evolved slowly over some three and a half thousand million years, ultimately from inorganic (i.e. non-living) precursors.

Indeed, we can go further. The great majority of biologists believe that natural selection, as first described in any detail by Charles Darwin and Alfred Wallace in 1858, is either the sole or the most important driving force behind evolution. The essence of natural selection is that organisms (or, more strictly, the genes they carry) act in their own interests.[10] From an evolutionary perspective, an entity successfully acts in its own interests when it leaves copies of itself behind once it has ceased to exist. Thus, an elephant (or, for that matter, a toad, an oak tree, a dandelion, a virus or a gene responsible for one of an organism's enzymes) tries unconsciously to act in its own interests by mothering or fathering lots of baby elephants (or toads, oak trees, dandelions, viruses or genes for enzymes). The meaning of life for a toad is to produce baby toads.[11]

Given this, the fascinating thing about evolution is how, after all this time, humans alone of the ten million or so species on

---

[10] For discussions of the extent to which natural selection acts on genes, individuals or other units, see R. Dawkins, *The Extended Phenotype: The Gene as the Unit of Selection* (Oxford: Oxford University Press, 1982); R. Dawkins, *The Selfish Gene*, 2nd edn (Oxford: Oxford University Press, 1989); and E. Sober and D. S. Wilson, *Unto Others: The Evolution and Psychology of Unselfish Behavior* (Cambridge: Harvard University Press, 1998).

[11] M. J. Reiss, 'On Suffering and Meaning: An Evolutionary Perspective', *Modern Believing*, 41, 2, 2000, 39–46.

this planet have evolved the ability consciously to discern meaning and to save ourselves. But for all our uniqueness and value, I for one cannot imagine that 'what stands before us is made for our good' in a straightforward reading of those words. I would affirm both that it was created by God and that it made itself for its own good. Indeed, there are sufficient scriptural passages that talk of creation existing not for our sakes for it to be difficult for someone inhabiting a Christian viewpoint to maintain a purely anthropocentric position with respect of the worth of nature.

The more interesting question for me is whether genetic engineering, for all its frequent, current ethical shortcomings, can yet function as an agent of restoration, variously understood, just as conventional medicine, for all its past and present failings, can function as an agent of healing and wholeness. Sometimes the way to save nature is to have the wisdom to know when to stand back and let it take its course. But sometimes it is to have the knowledge of when it is right to step in and get involved.[12]

---

[12] See M. M'Gonigle, 'A New Naturalism: Is There a (Radical) "Truth" beyond the (Postmodern) Abyss?', *Ecotheology*, 8, 2000, 8–39.

4

'Behold I have set the land before you' (Deut. 1.8): Christian Ethics, GM Foods and the Culture of Modern Farming

Michael S. Northcott

Under virtually all ethical systems, except possibly those of the Jains, human life is reckoned to be of greater moral value than non-human life. In the Hebrew and Christian traditions the supreme moral value of human life is underwritten by the doctrinal belief that humans are more god-like than other life forms; they are said to reflect the 'image of God'. For Christians this god-likeness finds definitive form in the Incarnation of God in Jesus Christ, the Incarnate Word, who comes to creation as both Creator and Redeemer.

If the supreme ethical good in creation is human life, then the biological, social and intellectual enhancement of human life becomes a central task of any civilisation which has ethical purposiveness. The collective pursuit of this central ethical good – life – involves a quest for all those things which are essential to a good life including adequate nutrition, physical security, knowledge, sociability and the procreation and nurture of children who experience life in their turn as gift from parents, and ultimately from God the Creator. The ethical prioritisation of life puts agriculture at the heart of Christian ethics for without food and nutrition there would be no life. It also makes agriculture ethically significant in a way that, say, plastics science is not, although the modern tradition of Christian ethics is strangely silent about agriculture as compared to say economic inequality or medical ethics.

Agriculture represents a particular set of practices which together constitute the means by which humans produce food and fibre for nutrition, clothing, shelter and warmth – for life. In premodern societies food growing and gathering are central activities to society in which every person plays a part. In the hunter-gatherer culture each member from child to adult has a particular set of tasks, while in settled agrarian societies everyone will participate in agricultural production at certain points in the year, such as the harvest. Viewed in this light agriculture has an ethical significance which goes beyond the production of food, for through participation in the practices of food production and animal husbandry people are socialised into a cooperative relationship with the land and with nature which is expressed in symbols and rituals and which in their turn give shape to human life itself. Agriculture is more than human survival or food production. In some senses agriculture *is* civilisation as most of humanity has traditionally understood the meaning of this word. In premodern society agricultural rituals are not only focused on the production of food but are also concerned with the integration of land and life, humanity and nature, with cosmic harmony and peace with the divine.

This understanding of agriculture is not absent from modern society but it is more frequently found in the imagined farms of the artist or the photographer, or in the dreamy quest for authentic wholeness in the urbanite's quest for rural self-sufficiency on a smallholding. E. F. Schumacher believed agriculture had three purposes, only one of which was the production of food: the others are to keep people in touch with living nature, and the humanisation and ennoblement of the whole habitat of humanity. Schumacher also saw the spiritual significance of agriculture which was ecologically as well as humanistically sound:

> Although ignorance and greed have again and again destroyed the fertility of the soil to such an extent that whole civilisations foundered, there have been no traditional teachings which failed to recognise the meta-economic value and significance of 'the generous earth'. And where these teachings were heeded not only agriculture but also all other factors of civilisation achieved health and wholeness. Conversely, where people imagined that they could not 'afford' to care for the soil and work with nature, instead of

against it, the resultant sickness of the soil has invariably imparted sickness to all the other factors of civilisation.[1]

The American ecologist Aldo Leopold was pointing to the same interconnection between agriculture and civilisation, agriculture and human relations, and agriculture and religion when he said there are spiritual dangers in not owning a farm: 'one is the danger of supposing that breakfast comes from the grocery, the other that heat comes from the furnace'.[2]

Agriculture in premodern society is essentially the cultivation and nurture of life in all its diversity. It represents a set of practices and of inherited wisdom by which human life and non-human life are brought into a community of interest for a range of goals including the nurture of the landscape, the preservation of natural resources for future generations, the celebration of the cyclical nature of life, the quest for harmony between human and divine purposes, and the nurture of the soul.

Industrial Agriculture and the Demise of Stewardship

In the Christian tradition this sense for the spiritual significance of food and farming takes a range of forms including the covenantal and Sabbath traditions in the Old Testament, the teachings of Jesus about jubilee, justice and stewardship, his many parables and actions around food and feasting, the focus of worship on the eucharistic feast, and the Benedictine and Cistercian traditions of agrarian religious life which did so much to shape the practice of farming in Europe in the premodern era. The ancient Israelites treated the land as part of their ethical, covenanted community.[3] Their Torah charged them to respect the land, and to recognise moral constraints on its use, because they understood that it was given to them as gift:

> When you enter the land which I am giving you, the land must keep Sabbaths to the Lord. For six years you may sow your fields and prune your vineyards and gather the harvest, but in the seventh

[1] E. F. Schumacher in his *Small Is Beautiful: Economics as if People Mattered* (London: Abacus, 1974), 90.
[2] Aldo Leopold, *A Sand County Almanac and Sketches Here and There,* first published 1949, (paperback edition New York: Oxford University Press, 1968), 6.
[3] See further Michael S. Northcott, *The Environment and Christian Ethics* (Cambridge: Cambridge University Press, 1996), 187.

year the land is to have a sacred (sabbatical) rest, a Sabbath to the lord ... in the seventh year the land shall keep a sacred rest.[4]

Agriculture was practised by the Egyptians, the Babylonians and the Persians as well as the ancient Israelites but Israelite agriculture was to be distinguished from these other nations precisely by the tradition that the land was not Israel's possession but rather the gift of God received after the Exodus. This tradition meant that great inequality in land ownership was proscribed by Jubilee and Sabbath laws in order to prevent members of the tribes of Israel from becoming again serfs or slaves on the lands of others: 'No land may be sold outright, because the land is mine, and you came to it as aliens and tenants of mine.'[5]

According to Walter Bruegemann land in ancient Israel was understood primarily in terms of covenant: the land was gifted to Israel and to be distributed fairly and justly according to the terms of the covenant.[6] This covenantal concept of God's ownership of the land has major implications not only for patterns of land tenure but also for land use: the Israelites were not to abuse the land, to plough it harshly as the Egyptians were said to do, nor to use up so much of the land in their farming that no space was left for wild animals.[7] Preservation of the fragile soil of this dry region of the Eastern Mediterranean was therefore enshrined in the laws which God gave to the children of Israel for guidance in their use of the land. The Israelites were also warned that however successful their farming they must never forget that the fertility of the land arises from God's care for nature rather than simply human manipulation.[8] They should not look for security in the products of the land alone but rather seek the goodness of the whole created order, for in their relationship with God, and in their just and righteous treatment of land, animals and neighbours, lay real security, sufficiency and welfare. The God who redeemed his people from slavery promised that they shall not again be landless and without food or livelihood, so long as they

[4] Lev. 25.2–4. All biblical citations are from the Revised New English Bible.
[5] Lev. 25.23.
[6] Walter Bruegemann, *The Land: Place as Gift, Promise and Challenge in Biblical Faith* (Philadelphia: Fortress Press, 1977), 45–70.
[7] See further Northcott, *Environment and Christian Ethics*, 164–74.
[8] Deut. 8.11–18.

followed Torah which conferred livelihood on all who stood in the covenant community and received the promise of land.

In the cultic traditions of Israel, and in particular in certain of the Kingly Psalms, the fertility of the land is rhetorically linked to divine justice as reflected in the society of God's people:

> O God, endow the king with thy own justice,
> and give thy righteousness to a king's son,
> that he may judge thy people rightly
> and deal out justice to the poor and suffering.
> May hills and mountains afford thy people
> peace and prosperity in righteousness.[9]

The fruits of the land, its original redemptive abundance, are said to be dependent upon Israel keeping the terms of the covenant. Where God is worshipped in truth, where every household in the covenant community has access to the means of livelihood, where neighbour does not oppress neighbour with usury or debt slavery, where the poor, the widows and the fatherless are offered hospitality, and where the animals are not cruelly abused, then the land will meet the needs of God's people, and meet them with abundance. And correlatively the neglect of the worship of God, and neglect of the respect for land and social justice which the covenant required, would bring about real threats to livelihood and security. According to Jeremiah the divinely originated created order of the cosmos was subverted when the rulers of the people failed to worship God and respect the covenant law:

> But this people has a rebellious and defiant heart,
> they have rebelled and gone their own way.
> They did not say to themselves,
> 'Let us fear the Lord our God,
> who gives us the rains of autumn
> and spring showers in their turn,
> who brings us unfailingly
> fixed seasons of harvest.'
> But your wrongdoing has upset nature's order,
> and your sins have kept from you her kindly gifts.[10]

---

[9] Ps. 72.1–3.
[10] Jer. 5.23–5.

The prophet linked ecological devastation with the abandonment of the worship and commands of the Lord. Because the people of Israel had turned from the Lord, their land, its mountains and streams, animals and crops, was being laid waste, polluted and destroyed:

> Does the snow of Lebanon vanish from the lofty crag?
> Do the proud waters run dry, so coolly flowing?
> And yet my people have forgotten me; they burn their incense to a Nothing.
> They have lost their footing in their ways, on the roads of former times, to walk in tortuous paths, a way unmarked.
> They will make their country desolate, everlastingly derided:
> every passer-by will be appalled at it and shake his head.[11]

The prophetic reading of ecological breakdown points to a conflict between the unequal society spawned by the late Hebrew monarchy and the fertility of the land, the welfare of the created order. The pride of kings had denuded valleys of tree cover for their massive building projects, wealthy landowners were abusing the earth from greed, generating soil erosion, while the new landless poor went hungry. Consequently the land suffered and shared in the alienation that human corruption produces:

> Woe to those who add house to house and join field to field until everywhere belongs to them and they are the sole inhabitants of the land.
> Yahweh Sabaoth has sworn this in my hearing,
> 'Many houses shall be brought to ruin, great and fine,
> but left untenanted;
> ten acres of vineyard will yield only one barrel,
> ten bushel of seed will yield only one bushel'.[12]

Jeremiah and Isaiah argued that such ecological effects as soil erosion, desertification and declining rainfall, as well as the Exile of the people of Israel from their once fertile land, were connected consequences of the abandonment of the terms of the covenant under which the people of God had become resident in the land. They were the consequence of

---

[11] Jer. 18.14–16.
[12] Isa. 5.8–10.

the practices of landlordism, economic inequality and idolatry; the consequence in other words of sin.

The contemporary devastation of rural communities in Europe, North America and in much of the Southern hemisphere, the enforced exile of rural communities to the cities, and the ecological impacts of modern farming methods on the health of the soil and on resident species, are described in similar terms by critics of the industrialisation and globalisation of agriculture and the technologisation of agricultural practices. Wendel Berry, farmer, conservationist and writer, describes the condition of his own rural farming community in Kentucky:

> Counting the post office, the town has five enterprises, one of which does not serve the local community. There is now no market for farm produce in the town or within forty miles. We no longer have a garage or repair shop of any kind. We have had no doctor for forty years and no school for thirty. Now, as a local economy and therefore as a community, Port Royal is dying.
>
> My part of rural America is, in short, a colony, like every other part of rural America. Almost the whole landscape of this country – from the exhausted cotton fields of the plantation South to the eroding wheatlands of the Palouse, from the strip mines of Appalachia to the clear cuts of the Pacific slope – is in the power of an absentee economy, once national and now increasingly international, that is without limit in its greed and without mercy in its exploitation of land and people.[13]

The long-running BBC Radio programme *The Archers* in the spring of 2000 described the misery and bankruptcy which the current agricultural economy is visiting on small mixed farmers and their rural communities through the storyline of the gradual slide into bankruptcy of the Grundy family. In his book *The Killing of the Countryside* the agricultural story editor of *The Archers*, Graham Harvey, charts the ecological as well as the human impacts of modern industrialised farming and the heavy public subsidies for output quotas which sustain it. Not only have post-war subsidies and tax breaks for large-scale, chemicalised and mechanised farming reduced employment on the land to the point that many rural communities are now little more than commuter belts for the urban economy, but

---

[13] Wendel Berry, *Sex, Economy, Freedom and Community* (New York: Pantheon Books, 1992), 6–8.

the communities of life of all kinds which once lived on
farmland are rapidly disappearing because of the rain of
pesticides and herbicides which government policies have
directed on to Britain's industrialised and increasingly silent
fields:

> Scores of arable land species are currently under threat. Among the
> flowering plants corn gromwell, pheasant's eye, shepherd's needle·
> and corn buttercup, while endangered bird species include the
> corncrake, stone curlew, Montagu's harrier, the cirl bunting and
> the grey partridge. Half a century of public funding has given
> farmers unprecedented power to re-design rural Britain. Their
> legacy to a new generation is a sterile, lifeless landscape.[14]

Over-reliance on chemical inputs, the use of heavy farm
machinery, and the abandonment of traditional crop rotation
methods are having devastating effects on the condition of the
soil. Whereas traditional farmers regarded as their first duty
the stewarding of the land, and in particular, as Harvey says, to
pass on their land in better condition than they found it to the
next generation, the modern industrial farmer, and the scientists and agronomists who advise and subsidise him, is
responsible for the systematic degradation of soil fertility and
levels of soil erosion which, if sustained for another fifty years,
will turn arable areas into deserts:

> Topsoils are disappearing from susceptible land throughout the
> length and breadth of Britain. The rush to intensive farming is
> robbing a future generation of its capacity to grow food. We are
> stripping away the nation's true wealth and dumping it in our rivers
> and streams. Not that soil erosion is new. The signs have been there
> for decades. But farm support policies that make intensive arable
> cropping profitable on marginal land have added enormously to
> the scale of loss. Everywhere old grassland has been ploughed up,
> particularly on the marginal land of hill and chalk down. The shift
> to arable crops leaves the land bare or thinly covered in the autumn
> and winter, when most of the damaging rains are likely to fall.[15]

Vandana Shiva charts a similar process in farming in India.
Again government subsidies for the chemicalisation and industrialisation of farming, and in particular the move to the

---

[14] Graham Harvey, *The Killing of the Countryside* (London: Random House, 1998), 21.
[15] Harvey, *The Killing of the Countryside*, 142.

monocrop planting of high-yield varieties of rice and other cereal crops associated with the Green Revolution have had major impacts on plant and animal biodiversity while damaging the sustainability of formerly self-sufficient rural farmers.[16] The new technologically enhanced high–yield seeds only offer a high yield with the expensive application of herbicides and pesticides, the high cost of which has created much indebtedness in rural communities. The widescale planting of single strains of foreign seeds have created major problems of pest control and disease which makes the new crops much more chemically dependent, and susceptible to climatic and other environmental threats, than traditional plantings of different seed varieties. Similarly the abandonment of traditional systems of rotation planting has led to a reliance on expensive chemical inputs which make the new agriculture too expensive for many small farmers, driving them into debt, even though small farmers remain the principal source of food in agrarian communities in the South:

> The Green Revolution created the perception that soil fertility is produced in chemical factories, and agricultural yields are measured only through marketed commodities. Nitrogen fixing crops like pulses were therefore displaced. Millets which have high yields from the perspective of returning organic matter to the soil, were rejected as 'marginal' crops.
>
> By treating essential organic inputs that maintain the integrity of nature as 'waste', the Green Revolution strategy ensured that fertile and productive soils are actually laid waste. The 'land-augmenting' technology has proved to be a land-degrading and land-destroying technology.[17]

In addition to deleterious effects on rural communities, on the economics of small and subsistence farms, on biodiversity, and on the quality of the soil, the global embrace of intensive agriculture by science-informed official agricultural agencies in partnership with corporate lenders and seed and chemical companies has been accompanied by changes in the quality of diet and the availability of fresh food for poor communities in both North and South.

[16] Vandana Shiva, *Monocultures of the Mind: Biodiversity, Biotechnology and the Third World* (Penang: Third World Network, 1993), 74.

[17] Shiva, *Monocultures of the Mind*, 58.

The UK is a prime example of this tendency. Not only does the UK have one of the most intensively farmed land areas in Europe but it also supports one of the most heavily processed and centralised food supply systems in the world. From the Enclosures of the eighteenth century to the subsidised silent fields of the twenty-first century, British agriculture is characterised by a growing alienation between the food consumer and the food producer. Supermarkets control two-thirds of British food supply and they, along with the largest farmers, are the principal beneficiaries of the subsidy system which has laid waste rural communities and the quality of the soil. Supermarkets are purveyors of a vast range of processed and junk foods of which the British eat far more than any other nation in Europe. The British also eat much less fresh and locally produced food than their continental counterparts, and suffer correlatively higher rates of dietary disease of the kind that consumption of fresh fruit and vegetables are known to protect against.[18] Pesticide residues in fresh foods are also high in British supermarkets: one third of foods showed residues above recommended levels in a 1995 government survey.[19] If the quality of diet is generally poorer in fresh foods in Britain than on the continent, the diet of the poor in Britain is particularly damaging to the health of themselves and their children. Residents of many inner-city estates often have no local access to purveyors of fresh foods, and the limitations of the minimum wage or government social security payments mean that they are forced to resort to the cheapest available calories which are to be found in frozen and processed foods such as cheap burgers and pasties.

What Harvey calls the 'famine at the heart of the feast' is also a consequence of the declining quality of chemically farmed foods. Industrially produced cereals, fruit and vegetables have fewer minerals and nutrients naturally occurring in them than traditionally grown produce and this means that dietary deficiencies in certain key minerals such as zinc and selenium are increasing in Western countries. Food manufacturers sometimes put back certain essential dietary elements into foods; for example, into factory-produced bread and breakfast cereals. Consumers in the West may also take food supplements

[18] Harvey, *Killing of the Countryside*, 126.
[19] Harvey, *Killing of the Countryside*, 131.

as awareness has grown that the vitamin and nutrient content of industrial foods is lower than traditional foods. However consumers in the South are unable to supplement their diets in this way and malnutrition is increasing in many rural communities where farmers have been encouraged by governments and seed and chemical companies to adopt the new seeds and growing methods.[20]

Even more serious are the many millions of people whose ability to grow their own food has completely collapsed as a consequence of changes in food production systems. These changes have often been visited on developing countries by agronomists deployed by such agencies as the World Bank and the International Monetary Fund. Somalia is a particularly tragic example of Western-directed agricultural 'improvement'. Until the 1970s Somalia was self-sufficient in food. However, IMF- and World-Bank-imposed policies forced a shift in land use from nomadic pastoralism and subsistence agriculture to food production for export, which resulted in growing dependence on imported grain. Cheap surplus wheat and rice had the effect of undermining local producers of traditional crops such as maize and sorghum. In addition World-Bank-enforced privatisation of veterinary services and water supplies decimated the livestock herds of pastoralists.[21] Similar policies imposed upon Ghana greatly increased the amount of land devoted to the cultivation of cocoa in the 1980s. At the same time enforced devaluation of Ghana's currency reduced the value of export earnings, and in particular of cocoa, while enforced trade liberalisation measures encouraged the importation of cheap surplus cereals and vegetable oils from Europe and North America. Once again local food producers were hit very hard, and malnutrition in poor communities has greatly increased in Ghana, as in many countries in sub-Saharan Africa in recent years.[22]

---

[20] Harvey, *Killing of the Countryside*, 139.
[21] Michel Chossudovsky, *The Globalisation of Poverty: Impacts of IMF and World Bank Reforms* (Penang: Third World Network, 1997), 102–4.
[22] Ross Hammnon and Lisa McGowan, 'Ghana: The World Bank's Sham Showcase', in Kevin Danaher (ed.), *Fifty Years Is Enough: The Case against the World Bank and the International Monetary Fund* (Boston, MA: South End Press, 1994), 78–84. See also Michael S. Northcott, *Life after Debt: Christianity and Global Justice* (London: SPCK, 1999).

Biotechnology, the Saviour of the Soil?

In *The Spirit of the Soil* Paul Thompson argues that the current global shift towards unsustainable industrial agriculture is closely related to cultural processes amongst both farmers and agricultural scientists which have generated a focus on the goals of enhancing agricultural technology and reducing the cost of food above other competing goals such as preserving rural communities, conserving the soil, or improving human health through dietary improvement.[23] The development of the productionist approach to agriculture was, he suggests, reinforced by the Protestant belief that hard work is rewarded by God, and in particular that the work of biological production is rewarded by increased fertility of plants and animals under the care of the industrious farmer. Utilitarian economics was the other key influence upon the development of industrial agriculture, and in particular the belief that human welfare is enhanced by the satisfaction of preferences: when consumers need to spend less of their income on food they are able to spend more on other consumption activities. Farmers are therefore encouraged to take up technologies which both enhance crop yields and reduce the cost of food.

Thompson finds similar processes at work in the shaping of agricultural research, including that of biotechnology:

> Despite the positivist ethic of value neutrality and the doctrine of academic freedom, the work ethic of farmers has been carried over into agricultural science with little revision. The scientist's products are a sign of worth as much as the farmer's bales and bushels. Agricultural scientists regard their work as successful when it is widely adopted, and the surest path toward adoption is to increase the productivity of a farming operation. Thus, scientists have laboured hard to increase productivity as a sign of their own virtue.[24]

The principal justification for biotechnological research, and in particular for the genetic modification of plants and animals, is the enhancement of farming productivity. Scientists and agronomists claim that genetic modification is the only way,

---

[23] Paul Thompson, *The Spirit of the Soil: Agriculture and Environmental Ethics* (London: Routledge, 1995), 47ff.
[24] Thompson, *Spirit of the Soil*, 47–71.

with current levels of soil erosion, that it will be possible to feed the growing population of the world into the next century.[25] Such assertions are made with no reference to the social scientific literature on hunger and malnutrition and its causes even though we know from this literature that the principal cause of global hunger is not low farm productivity but land hunger and poor distribution systems of available food and other resources of the kind described above.[26]

The argument that the world needs ever greater quantities of cheap cereal crops to feed a growing population allows scientists to continue to ignore the unsustainable features of the agricultural revolution they have already visited on rural communities and the soil. In particular it fails to provide an answer to the central question raised by opponents of the technology, which is that the apparent benefits of the new technology appear to be heavily outweighed by the risks. The most certain outcome of GM crops will be further enhancements to crop yields, which will in turn exacerbate already existing problems in rural societies and economies, and make available even larger surpluses of grains, with their damaging effects on subsistence farmers and indigenous agriculture in the South. GM crops will also not address the environmental problems already attendant on intensive monocropping. The planting of crops designed to be resistant to herbicides will enhance the already serious reductions in biodiversity on chemically treated farm land, will exacerbate existing costs of treating and filtering poisoned ground water, and will not address the problems of soil erosion associated with productionist agriculture, which in the long term is the biggest threat to the ability of the population of the world to feed itself.

The real beneficiaries of GM foods will not be consumers or the environment or small or subsistence farmers. On the contrary, faster-growing crops, pest-resistant crops, frost-resistant crops, all of these will enhance the economic power of the largest producers and companies in the agricultural industry.

[25] See, for example, Michael Appleby, David Atkinson et. al., 'Developing Country Issues', in Donald Bruce and Anne Bruce (eds), *Engineering Genesis: The Ethics of the Genetic Modification of Non-Human Species* (London: Earthscan, 1998), esp. 245–8.

[26] See the definitive study of the causes of famine by Jean Dreze and Amartya Sen, *Hunger and Public Action* (Oxford: Clarendon Press, 1989).

Each such enhancement throws more small farmers out of work, reduces the need for agricultural labour, and increases the need for government subsidy for output to maintain prices in the shops even as farmers produce food more 'cheaply'. When set in the context of the current economic and social condition of the farming industry in both North and South the likely costs would seem to far outweigh the benefits. In the current governmental and corporate framing of agriculture in the European Union, in North America and in much of the South, GMOs seem set merely to enhance existing deleterious tendencies in agriculture, making food ever more heavily subsidised and chemically laden, at the expense of the tax-payer and at the risk of the health of the food consumer.

It is now well known that public resistance to GM foods in Britain arises from growing public concern at the methods and quality of modern food production systems, at their environmental effects, and their effects on human health. The single biggest concern expressed by UK consumers about food, aside from the recent BSE crisis, relates to pesticide and herbicide use. This concern is dismissed as unreasonable or irrational by most agrarian scientists, by food corporations and by many politicians. However, the highly toxic carcinogen lindane is still found as a residue in non-organic British dairy produce (it is commonly linked with breast cancer) while in government surveys organophosphates, which are nerve toxins, have been found at unsafe levels in various fresh produce, a finding which led to government advice that certain vegetables and fruits should be thoroughly peeled before consumption.[27]

The largest unmet demand for food in the UK is for food free of agricultural chemicals, and in particular for organic food. There is also a growing interest in forms of food marketing which enable people in cities and rural areas to buy direct from farmers. If the more than 1.5 billion pounds spent on output subsidies in the UK were redirected from the large farmers who benefit most from such subsidies to small mixed farms and organic farms the pain which many rural communities are currently experiencing would be alleviated as

---

[27] It is in any case unclear that there is a safe level of exposure to neurotoxins. There is a growing belief for example that the increasing incidence of immune system diseases such as ME, MS and Chronic Fatigue Syndrome may be due to the levels of neurotoxins in modern foods.

employment opportunities on the land would be enhanced. At the same time the quality of food available to consumers in the long term would increase, while the environmental costs of its production would decrease. Government and corporate funders of agricultural research teams are not, however, planning to invest heavily in these unmet consumer demands. Their already heavy investments in biotechnology mean that large amounts of public and private monies will continue to be made available for forms of agricultural research and technology which pursue the productionist metaphor, and increase output efficiency. There also seems little doubt that the new foods will continue to be foisted on unwilling consumers, as they already have been in North America, though in the latter case they were unwitting as well as unwilling.

It is possible to imagine a world where biotechnology is utilised to promote sustainable, low-energy, low-waste, low-pollution, labour-intensive, traditional mixed farming. This would however be a world very different from the one we live in now. First, it would require that all food subsidies were directed environmentally at forms of farming which encouraged biodiversity, which had lower energy requirements and which operated as far as possible a closed energy and waste cycle. Second, since the subsidies were all in the direction of sustainable agriculture, those involved in biotechnology research would find it commercially attractive to seek to service this form of agriculture by developing seeds which were designed for minimal chemical inputs, which could be inter-cropped to take advantage of natural cycles for replenishing the soil between plantings, and which had a hardy resistance to the vagaries of climate and pests. The focus of research would shift from high-yield, chemical dependency to hardy, low-input seeds. Similarly it would be possible to breed animals which had low requirements for drugs and special mechanical care systems, which could live in the open air for most of the year while still producing high-quality meat. Genetic engineering would be used to enhance the sustainability and lower intensity of agriculture, to reduce soil erosion, enhance biodiversity, increase tree cover in arable farming regions, reduce water usage and eliminate chemical dependence.

The principal reason why this scenario is more fantasy than reality is the control exercised over global agriculture by seed

corporations and chemical companies. Multinational corporations such as Cargill, Ciba Geigy, Dow, Monsanto and Zeneca
dominate agricultural research, and the seed and agricultural
chemical markets into which researched products will be
directed in the future. Their aim is to control patents on
germplasm which can be imposed on every farmer in every
country in the world, thus maximising their profits from
every farming enterprise, from the Chinese peasant small
farmer to the large mechanised farmers of the American
prairies. These companies derive no profits from, and have no
interest in helping, the many millions of self-sufficient
traditional farmers who rely on natural cycles and saved seed to
minimise debt and maximise the security of their family or
smallholding. Multinational agricultural and chemical corporations such as Monsanto are already developing seeds which will
not self-seed, with the intention of enforcing annual payments
for new seed and extracting profit from even the poorest
farmers in the South. The enforcement of property rights and
patents over seeds in the South through agreements policed by
the World Trade Organization is specifically designed to
enhance the profits of Northern-based biotechnology corporations. As Nicholas Riding of Monsanto puts it: 'the major
challenge to genetic engineering scientists and companies as
well as national governments is to support uniform worldwide
property rights'.[28]

The new patents on life-forms which have come about in the
context of genetic engineering give monopoly rights over
germplasm, most of it collected in the South, to Northern
corporations who can then use these rights to extract profit
from the poorest farmer. And these new rights can be very
broad in extent. Thus in the United States the Sungene
Corporation obtained patent rights over a sunflower variety
which its scientists developed with high oleic acid content. The
claim allowed by the US Patent Office was not simply for the
particular seed developed, but for the characteristic of high
oleic acid. Sungene holds that this patent gives it patent rights
over any sunflower breeding development which enhances
oleic acid content. Industrial patents designed to protect inventions are now being used to grant ownership of genetic material

---

[28] Cited in Shiva, *Monocultures of the Mind*, 121.

and seed races, many of them only minimally modified. The next step is for farmers who reuse seed from previous plantings to be fined for violating intellectual property rights. The greatest irony is that while the United States accuses Southern farmers of seed piracy, of using germplasm which seed companies claim patents over, it is of course the United States that is the real pirate. Most of the seeds 'developed' or modified by US seed corporations originated on farms in the South, but no royalties are paid to indigenous farmers in the South, nor are they claimable by their governments.[29]

The Recovery of Stewardship

In his ecological classic *A Sand County Almanac*, Aldo Leopold suggests that

> [w]e abuse land because we regard it as a commodity belonging to us. When we see land as a community to which we belong, we may begin to use it with love and respect. There is no other way for land to survive the impact of mechanised man, nor for us to reap from it the esthetic harvest it is capable, under science, of contributing to culture. That land is a community is the basic concept of ecology, but that land is to be loved and respected is an extension of ethics.[30]

Leopold suggests that it is the desire for too much material security and success which drives the mechanised destruction of the farmlands of the prairies, which ensures their soil is transported in rivers down to the sea bed, and which erases the diverse indigenous flora and fauna from the earth:

> the effort to control the health of land has not been very successful. It is now generally understood that when soil loses fertility, or washes away faster than it forms, and when water systems exhibit abnormal floods and shortages, the land is sick.[31]

To overcome the sickness, Leopold suggested that modern humans need to develop what he called a land ethic which 'enlarges the boundaries of the community to include soils, waters, plants, and animals, or collectively: the land'. Leopold also saw the limitations of an agricultural system based upon

---

[29] Shiva, *Monocultures of the Mind*, 124–7.
[30] Leopold, *Sand County Almanac*, viii.
[31] Leopold, *Sand County Almanac*, 194.

economic self-interest and government regulation and planning. Such a system 'tends to ignore, and thus eventually to eliminate, many elements in the land community that lack commercial value, but that are (as far as we know) essential to its healthy functioning'.[32]

Leopold was a sharp and eloquent observer of the agricultural economy of North America, the first industrial-scale monocrop culture, which was already, in his day, destroying the very soil on which it depended. Leopold was, however, a poor interpreter of the Old Testament when he argued that the Abrahamic concept of land involves the idea of absolute ownership and that Abraham saw the land only as having one function which was 'to trip milk and honey into Abraham's mouth'.[33] Wendel Berry is a much more acute interpreter of the Bible when he argues that the concept of human ownership of land is limited by the belief that 'the earth is the Lord's', and that human ownership of land 'quickly becomes abusive when used to justify large accumulations of real estate'.[34] The Incarnation of God in Christ involves the affirmation that 'God made the world and made it to be good and for his pleasure and that he continues to love it and to find it worthy, despite its reduction and corruption by us'.[35] As Berry puts it, 'belief in Christ is thus dependent on prior belief in the inherent goodness – the lovability – of the world':[36]

> We will discover that for these reasons our destruction of nature is not just bad stewardship, or stupid economics, or a betrayal of family responsibility; it is the most horrid blasphemy. It is flinging God's gifts into His face, as if they were of no worth beyond that assigned to them by our destruction of them.[37]

Berry believes that many modern Christians have misconceived the relationship between God and God's creation because of the concentration of the Christian practice of holiness and worship upon built and consecrated churches, a concentration which for Berry seems to imply that the rest of

[32] Leopold, *Sand County Almanac*, 214.
[33] Leopold, *Sand County Almanac*, 205.
[34] Berry, *Sex, Economy, Freedom and Community*, 97.
[35] Berry, *Sex, Economy, Freedom and Community*, 97.
[36] Berry, *Sex, Economy, Freedom and Community*, 97.
[37] Berry, *Sex, Economy, Freedom and Community*, 98.

the space of creation does not continually participate in that continuous care which is conferred on all by the divine spirit which breathes life into creation:

> By denying spirit and truth to the non-human Creation, modern proponents of religion have legitimized a form of blasphemy without which the nature- and culture-destroying machinery of the industrial economy could not have been built – that is, they have legitimized bad work. Good human work honours God's work. Good work uses no thing without respect both for what it is in itself and for its origin.[38]

Berry sees the deleterious effects of modern industrialised farming on rural communities, wild species and the soil as the product of bad work, work which fails to honour God, work which lacks appreciation of the artistry which the Creator of the universe displayed in God's handiwork, work which lacks awareness of the divine origin and destiny of the cosmos itself and of the extent to which the creatures of God participate by their very being and continued existence in the life of God. Genetically modified foods are the latest example of bad work: they represent the denial of the original goodness and order of the creation, they dishonour the Creator, and like other forms of bad work they make 'shoddy work of the work of God'.[39]

In the first part of this paper we saw that the Old Testament writers believed that there was a connection arising from the wisdom and order of the Creator between human greed and human hunger and between landlordism and environmental degradation and exclusion. The ancients believed that the natural order was also a moral order, and that descriptions of the world interact with human behaviour in the world. Moderns describe the origins of life as inherently competitive, violent and conflictual. The modern enterprise of agriculture is represented as a war against pestilence, disease and famine. In this war, productionist science and technology are the crucial weapons. Ethics and value is for moderns said to be located not in nature but exclusively in human consciousness, purposes and choices. This view of ethics sets humanity at odds with the purposes of the non-human world and constructs agriculture

---

[38] Berry, *Sex, Economy, Freedom and Community*, 104.
[39] Berry, *Sex, Economy, Freedom and Community*, 104.

and the industrial economy as modes of activity which must be pursued against the grain of the economy of nature.

Until the Enlightenment, the Christian tradition sustained the belief in Western culture that God and not humans is the principal locus of consciousness and of moral purposiveness in the cosmos. Similarly, the creation was regarded first and foremost as God's possession, not humanity's. On this traditional view humans dwell in it and experience their own life, and the biophysical cosmos in which they live out their lives, as a gift or, as Karl Barth puts it, a 'loan from God' rather than as their absolute possession.[40] Jesus' parable of the talents, and the Apostle Paul's affirmation that humans are not owners of their own bodies, nor of the mysteries of faith, but rather stewards, that all belongs to God,[41] reaffirmed the ancient Jewish belief that humans enjoy the creation as gift and not possession. In the stewardship tradition, the duty of respect for natural order arises from this recognition that the earth is the Lord's, and that in its design and order it displays not an order of being independent from human being, available for human remaking at will, but a shared realm of created being. And, according to the Psalmists, monks, nuns and hymn writers who gave ritual form to Jewish and Christian prayer and worship over the centuries, this recognition finds its paradigmatic form in the worship through which creation is invited to share in the gracious relational abundance of the being of God from which it is birthed. Christian worship and prayer form 'part of the praise that the whole creation, consciously or unconsciously, offers to its Creator'.[42]

Stewardship alone is not enough, however, without the connection to worship and spirituality that the Christian tradition sustains. For stewardship to be practised aright it requires the recognition of the participation of creation in the life of God which for Christians is definitively displayed in the Incarnation of Jesus Christ. For unless we worship God as creator, sustainer and redeemer of all that is we may imagine

---

[40] See further Karl Barth, *Church Dogmatics III, The Doctrine of Creation*, trs A. T. Mackay, T. H. L. Parker, H. Knight, H. A. Kennedy and J. Marks (Edinburgh: T&T Clark, 1961), Part 4 , 327.

[41] 1 Cor. 6.19.

[42] European Province of the Society of Saint Francis, *Celebrating Common Prayer: A Version of the Daily Office* (London: Mowbray, 1992), 677.

ourselves as stewards and managers of lands belonging to an absentee landlord who is long gone from the creation, and we may further imagine that in God's long absence we are in control of the earth. Apart from the worship of God as sovereign and redeemer of creation – as not only its originator but its incarnate and involved redeemer – humans always stand in danger of turning their ownership and use of the earth into a substitute for God, and worshipping the creature rather than the Creator.

The First Commandment both enjoins the worship of God and prohibits idolatry, or the worship of created things: it involves the recognition that when humans do not worship God with their whole heart, soul and strength, they are in danger already of worshipping that which is not god. Idolatry – of technology, of consumer goods, of human greed and corporate power – is at the heart of the collective and individual sins which constitute the crisis in modern agriculture. Turning back to God, and recovering a sense for the original wisdom of natural order, is the only truthful response to this crisis.

Jesus revisited the command tradition of ethics in his moral teaching and proposed that its essence is discoverable in the experience and expression of love; love of God and love of neighbour. Love between God and the creature involves both in a mutual relation in which the different being and order of both is recognised and affirmed. Created being apart from God stands in need of completion through participation and loving relation with the Creator. The promise of this completion is realised in the resurrection of Christ, and is anticipated and brought near in the power of the Spirit. The Christian tradition for many centuries affirmed that this bringing near, this reconciliation of created life to God, was something which happened to the whole creation. There is no more solemn and morally weighty conception of the moral value of natural order than this incarnational tradition. It means that when Jesus sums up the rest of the law in terms of loving our neighbour as ourselves, we cannot limit the implications of this love to other persons. We are enjoined to love creation, to love nature, and especially to love the places which are near us, which

---

[43] On the significance of the virtue of love for Christian ecological theology and ethics, see further James Nash, *Loving Nature: Ecological Integrity and Christian Responsibility* (Nashville, TN: Abingdon, 1992).

are our neighbours, because we share with nature in the restoration which is promised us in the resurrection of Jesus Christ.[43]

Envisaging the human relation to nature in terms of love has profound implications for the modern economy which has birthed industrial agriculture and its latest manifestation in GM foods. It radically calls into question the cost–benefit calculus which ensures that billions of animals every year are imprisoned in cruel and valueless life to provide cheap protein for humans; which sustains the corporate and inter-governmental calculus that sets as a price for international debt repayment the systematic clear cutting of ancient forests and the environmental exclusion of peasant farmers and tribal peoples from their ancestral lands; and which advances the market ideology that sets imperialist patents and monopoly prices on the modified but ancient gene races of indigenous peoples.

Response to Chapter 4 – Nature to Order: But Which Nature and Whose Order?

Peter Scott

A Disagreement

Michael Northcott's *The Environment and Christian Ethics*[1] is a very important contribution to ethical consideration of the 'environment' from a Christian perspective, and I have learned a lot from it. We need, God knows, interventions such as this. Yet it emerged at the consultation at which an earlier version of this response was read, and in subsequent conversation, that we do not agree on much in his essay ' "Behold I have set the land before you" (Deut. 1.8): Christian Ethics, GM Foods and the Culture of Modern Farming'.

Yet even this statement is not quite right. So let me try again: I agree with much of the paper – with the political diagnosis and aspects of the theological resources on which it draws – yet I wonder if the emergent phenomenon of genetically modified foods raises issues to which Northcott does not attend. Furthermore, I consider that these issues raise some significant questions against the theological response he develops in the final section.

To put the matter more directly: although Northcott develops a theology in support of the notion of stewardship, in my view stewardship is not here recoverable as a way of indicating Christian responsibility. Or to put the matter

---

[1] Michael S. Northcott, *The Environment and Christian Ethics* (Cambridge: Cambridge University Press, 1996).

differently – because I do not want to start a discussion of the merits or otherwise of stewardship *in abstracto* – genetic modification is also the modification of our concepts of nature. And because, in my judgement, nature is *not* creation, the recovery of the notion of *creation* against the horizon of genetic modification is a rather more strenuous and tentative task than is indicated by the conclusion of Northcott's paper.

Undeniably, Northcott's essay offers a comprehensive theological response to the phenomenon of GM foods. Yet that same comprehensiveness leaves Christianity remarkably untouched. In the face of what appears to be a novel phenomenon, appeal is made to what may be regarded as that most traditional of Christian responses, namely, stewardship.[2] There must, I readily agree, be Christian answerability in this situation. But is the call of God in the context of genetic engineering best construed in such received ways?

I hope these comments indicate that there is something important at stake, practically and theoretically, in this disagreement and that there are significant issues here that need to be worked through. To my mind, these issues are the novelty of genetic engineering, the question of the validity of stewardship and our ethical orientation. I am not convinced, finally, that the possibility of a 'Nature-to-go' by which we are now faced through genetic engineering is encountered with sufficient radicality in Northcott's paper. Nor am I persuaded that the turn to the ordering of nature by a steward properly faces the actuality and future of God's ordering of the world. I repeat that it is my hope that these issues are not a distraction born out of an 'academic disagreement' but instead take us further into the consideration of the well-being of the human creature with other creatures before God.

Novelty?

There is some ambiguity in Northcott's paper as to whether processes of the genetic modification of food are novel. On the one hand, we learn that genetic modification is part of a wider

---

[2] How traditional a response stewardship is could be questioned. In the third section of this response, I try to set out what I think is the central reason why stewardship is popular.

set of agricultural practices that are employed in 'the enhancement of farming productivity' (p. 96).[3] Thus Northcott can argue that practices of genetic modification 'seem set merely to enhance existing deleterious tendencies in agriculture' (p. 98). Such language and phrasing suggest continuities in farming traditions to which genetic modification should be referred if it is to be comprehended. On the anthropological–political level, genetically modified foods may represent the intensification of agricultural practices but not their transformation.

In contrast, at the theological level proper, Northcott cites with approval some of Wendell Berry's comments, thus: 'Genetically modified foods are the latest example of bad work: they represent the denial of the original goodness and order of the creation, they dishonour the creator, and like other forms of bad work they make "shoddy work of the work of God" ' (p. 103). Is there an aspect of God's work that is to be respected therefore? It seems that there is: the Christian moral project in the context of modern agriculture should work with 'the grain of the economy of nature' (p. 104).

Is not a large claim about stability and novelty being smuggled in here, however? That the shape and end of the natural order is required by Christian ethics and, by implication at least, the genetic modification of foods is an alteration of that shape and ending. The phrase, 'playing God', may not, as Ted Peters points out, have much cognitive value.[4] Nonetheless, does not genetic modification raise the issue of human creativity, and its use? Peters calls this 'playing human as God intends us to'.[5] However, 'playing human' is now problematic in that the shape of the human – especially the shape of the human as this relates to 'natural' contours – needs to be rethought from the ground up.

Genetic engineering may be characterised as not simply the refusal of the gift of the conditions of creaturely life but also the capacity to amend those very conditions. In the face of such novelty, we are presented with not only the matter of the possibility of moral failure, as Northcott rightly holds, but also the

[3] All references in parentheses are to Northcott's paper.
[4] Ted Peters, *Playing God? Genetic Determinism and Human Freedom* (New York and London: Routledge, 1997), 10–14.
[5] Ted Peters, *Playing God?*, 162.

possibility of a failure of 'world-view', if you like, or of the orientation and direction of a society. So we need to work out over
again what 'human good' might be.

How should these intimations of novelty be interpreted
theologically? Of course, we may begin by noting an important
continuity. In genetic engineering the values of the present
society are manifest: values which emerge in a culture of plenty,
in a surfeit of commodities. But we need also to reckon with the
possibility – a discontinuous possibility – that in the commodification of DNA we are confronted by the completing of the
commodification of the world. In combination with the use of
technologies of data retrieval, one sort of mapping, systematic
and entire, of life is possible.

More than this: we may also say that we have a new
'structure of feeling', to borrow a phrase from Raymond
Williams, out of which a new notion of nature is born. Now
what emerges as discontinuous is our notion of nature.
Technologies and techniques of genetic modification –
whether or not new when taken singly – alter our view of
nature and of ourselves, with the result that we are presented
with the denial of the agency of non-human nature and the
constitution of its otherness by manipulation. To put the
matter the other way round: does the development of
procedures of genetic modification require, as cultural
permission, a new notion of nature?

The emergence of a new notion of nature is not as curious as
it may seem at first sight. Consider two ways in which we might
think about the transformation of nature: as alteration in
the environment and as transformation of the idea itself. In the
sharpest cases, the two senses converge. Transformation of
'environment' may also transform human experience of and
encounter with its environment. Thereby our understanding of
nature as a whole, and human nature, may also change.[6] The
techniques and technologies of genetic modification may
indicate the reported victory of humanity over nature, which in
turn considers humanity as separate from nature and embodiment Is this not the completion of a transformation of our

---

[6] Willis Dulap, 'Two Fragments: Theological Transformations of Law, Technological
Transformations of Nature', in Carl Mitcham and Jim Grote (eds), *Theology and
Technology* (Lanham, MD: University Press of America, 1984), 231–3.

environment *and* the transformation of our understandings of nature, human and other?

Beyond Stewardship?

If this is close to the mark, it should come as no surprise that I am not persuaded by the appeal to stewardship. In a discontinuous situation, stewardship presupposes continuity: the presentation of nature and humanity, and the mediation of nature by humanity to God. But, as Donna Haraway has suggested, perhaps the distinction between humanity and nature in these terms is less easy to make today. Genetic modification is the humanisation of nature which in turn suggests that we should not be thinking of humanity 'and' nature in the way that stewardship invites. Instead, we might adopt a phrase of Haraway's: nature and culture as 'fields of difference'.[7] But we could do so only if we recognise that the humanisation of nature posits nature as *objectified* other; the difference in which is constructed by processes of intervention and manipulation.[8]

Without doubt stewardship remains a popular option in the ecotheology literature. Part of the reason for this popularity is, I think, because stewardship operates as an atonement metaphor, albeit an atonement metaphor on vacation.[9] One of the central difficulties in theological interpretation of the atonement is to avoid subjectivist and exemplarist tendencies. That is, to focus overmuch on the response of believers following after the example of Christ downplays, as Donald MacKinnon has pointed out, the identification of God in Christ and the depth of moral evil.[10]

Yet, of course, given that stewardship is proposed as a Christian way of promoting ecological responsibility, what is rightly stressed is human responsibility and the need for action, indeed conversion. Northcott's paper is no exception

[7] Donna Haraway, *Simians, Cyborgs and Women: The Reinvention of Nature* (London: Free Association Books, 1991), 162.

[8] Stewardship, then, is to be regarded as an *intermediate* notion in that its construal of nature lies between nature humanised and nature as agential other.

[9] For a fuller defence of this claim, see Peter Scott, *A Political Theology of Nature* (Cambridge: Cambridge University Press, 2002), ch. 8.

[10] Donald MacKinnon, 'Objective and Subjective Conceptions of Atonement', in F. G. Healey (ed.), *Prospect for Theology* (Welwyn: James Nisbet, 1966), 167–82.

here. But we should be alert to the fact that the construal of stewardship in voluntaristic ways is eminently *suitable* for our present North Atlantic culture. Stewardship does not deny the reality of nature but neither does it stress the otherness or agency of nature. Thus, as stewards, we seek to steward but there is no genuine other to be stewarded. In my view it is right, as Northcott suggests, to affirm the continuities between the human and the non-human: 'a shared realm of created being' (p. 104). It is right also to refuse the making other of nature as that which is available for manipulation by human activity. Yet a threefold distinction is here required that moves us beyond a simplifying contrast between the human and the non-human. Such a distinction has the following form: (1) nature independent of humanity; (2) the natural conditions of human life; and (3) the cultural or social sphere of human life.[11] Stewardship engages the second and third aspects, of course. The theological issue, however, is that genetic engineering either manipulates independent nature or will have important consequences for that nature (as in the tainting of ordinary crops by varieties of GMOs, for example).

An important question now emerges: Is stewardship a sustainable position in the context of the manipulation of nature in genetic engineering? In other words, does not the notion of stewardship in fact connect with, and support, the concept of nature in genetic engineering? The terminus of both is the same: the denial of the agency and genuine otherness of nature. Put differently, genetic modification operates with a notion of nature as mastered; stewardship with the demand for action in the face of nature. Both support a view of nature as inert, without agency. We travel by two different routes to a single destination: the denial of the agency and genuine otherness of nature.[12]

---

[11] Here I am drawing on John Clark, 'The Dialectical Social Geography of Elisée Reclus', *Philosophy and Geography*, 1, 1997, 117–42 (123).

[12] I remain unconvinced that the Old Testament emphasis on the land meets these objections. However, if it does, then the notion of stewardship is called into question. But in Northcott's presentation, we are still presented with nature in terms of the otherness of organisation, standing reserve: the promotion of otherness but the denial of *extra nos*. This organisation is complicated, but not complex: it seeks to simplify nature and reduce its unruliness.

But then in a curious dialectic, we find ourselves stewarded. Because the notion of nature operative in our genetically modified world is that of nature subjugated, as I have just argued, stewardship deconstructs into mastery. And then the dialectic flexes once more: we who would be 'masters' of nature find ourselves 'mastered'. The dialectical outcome of the 'stewardship of nature' is the 'mastery of humanity'. So although we might hope that stewardship is a way, as Dietrich Bonhoeffer once put it, of speaking of embodiment as one of God's ways to us, instead we now learn that stewardship throws humanity back on to its own resources *etsi deus non daretur*.[13]

Conclusion: After Consequentialism?

Certainly several of the papers collected in this volume, including Northcott's, decry consequentalism. For Northcott, stewardship provides a way of countering the profound moral failings of capitalist agriculture. But if my earlier analysis is correct, will not the concept of nature have to be reconstructed theologically in order to develop an adequate ethics of nature against ecological degradation? Without such reconstruction, how is moralism to be avoided?

How *is* moralism to be avoided? Two ways seem open: a revolution or a strictly circumscribed consequentalism. A revolution could open a way, as Herbert Marcuse once noted, for a new science and a new technology. And working for a revolution would also have the merit of acknowledging that the phenomenon of resistance to genetic engineering has its source in science as a productive force. That is, today the principal objection to scientific 'progress' is being generated by science itself, and not by any social agent; the principal resistances are being generated within capitalism itself.[14]

As for consequentialism, in a situation of confusion and ignorance, what other – less dangerous, more persuasive, more acceptable – moral position is there?[15] Could not a strictly

---

[13] The references are of course to Dietrich Bonhoeffer, *Christology* (London: Collins, 1978), 64–5; *Letters and Papers from Prison* (London: SCM Press, 1971), 360.

[14] Perry Anderson, 'Renewals', *New Left Review*, 1, 1, January–February 2000, 17.

[15] To propose a different moral position is also to be obliged to offer the details of an alternative ethic. Otherwise one offers a moral position, but without any moral resources for practitioners to draw on. It follows that stewardship in Northcott's paper bears a heavy, argumentative, burden.

circumscribed consequentialism offer some moral guidance if the consequences for the marginalised – the poorest, non-human nature – were written into ethical reflection; if, above all, moral consideration were extended to non-human nature?[16]

The possibility of a non-moralistic consequentialism now emerges in which moral discernment resides in the ability to take note of consequences for non-human nature in our analyses of risk and benefit; an ethical theory which is attentive to an abundant nature that is both *pro nobis* and *extra nos*; a consequentalism which thereby questions the hubristic and self-righteous stories we like to tell of ourselves; an ethics of nature for creatures, not stewards.[17]

---

[16] This would be one way of interpreting the quotations from Leopold on pp. 101–2.
[17] Northcott hints at this in his employment of the love ethic: 'It means that when Jesus sums up the rest of the law in terms of loving our neighbour as ourselves, we cannot limit the implications of this love to other persons' (p. 105).

PART II

Reflections from Specific Cases

PART II

Reflections from Specific Cases

Introduction to Part II

The second section of the book invites readers to change gear somewhat from thinking more generally about the social, historical, political and theological significance of genetic engineering to more particular issues associated with it. Arthur Peacocke reminds us in chapter 5 that the world of genetic engineering is located within a certain structure of scientific knowing. Hence, in order to understand more fully its scientific and cultural significance we need to examine issues of epistemology that structure different sciences. Analysis of the philosophy of genetics has tended to portray it in a way that assumes a reductionist method alongside a reductionist philosophy. Peacocke invites us to consider the paradox that is easily missed, that the molecular basis for genetics, DNA, point more to the emergence of new capabilities at higher levels than to a simple reduction of everything else to genetics. Such emergence is not vitalism in a new guise, but rather points to the discovery of new and different functions at different levels of scientific knowing.

Peacocke thus rejects reductionism as a philosophy of science in favour of a critical realism, where the discoveries of science are acknowledged as provisionally given, but always subject to further testing and critical analysis. As we move further up the layers of scientific knowing to the human sciences, including sociobiology, behavioural science and cognitive neuroscience, it becomes increasingly difficult to determine the genetic basis for such activity. Indeed, in contrast to some of the hubris surrounding genetic interpretations, Peacocke roundly rejects the idea that personhood can in any way be explained by our genetic make-up. Religious experience, as one might expect, overarches other experiences, though he detects a significant shift in cognitive science and psychology where subjective inner experience is now valued in a way that was not so apparent in its earlier history. His chapter ends on a somewhat tantalising note, suggesting that the human experience of freedom challenges anyone who dares insist that all humanity is locked up solely in our genes. Given this possibility the claims of some geneticists that they have the tools to reorder who we are as persons, as well as a plethora of other supposed benefits, need to be qualified. Such qualification comes not so much by setting them against sociological interpretations of reality but through recognising the wider map of scientific knowing. In other words, scientists themselves need to recognise from within their own epistemology the limits of scientific knowledge arising from genetics.

Michael Reiss, like many other authors in this volume, resists a simple analysis of new technologies in terms of their likely consequences. In chapter 6 he examines the specific case of the boundaries between species and the legitimacy or otherwise of moving genes across such boundaries, characteristic of at least some genetic manipulations. In particular he seeks to probe more deeply the question of why it is that we might be worried about moving genes between species. He explores the way that boundaries are set up in our earliest beginnings as developing persons, defining our cultural sense of self in categorising what might be food or not, foreigner or not, male and female, culminating in social choices about who might be suitable marriage partners. He suggests that for Christians New Testament teaching on breaking down boundaries supersedes that found in Judaism. Jewish prohibition of certain kinds of foods reflected a wider social exclusion towards those of other cultures and helped to reinforce the boundary between the Jewish State and the Gentiles. The New Testament affirms that there are no foreigners, and that all foods are acceptable. Yet there are some limits to such breaking of boundaries, as for example in the Pauline prohibition against intra-familial sexual relations.

The implication of his analysis might be that attempting to preserve fixed boundaries between species is not in keeping with the radical breakdown of Jewish boundaries in Christianity. However, he resists such an extrapolation for the case of moving genes from humans to animals, implying that this particular boundary might in some sense be different from other boundary considerations and worthy of special treatment. He suggests that recognising the minute percentage of actual human genes involved in this kind of transgenic manipulation misses the theological issue at stake, namely, that a significant boundary has now been crossed. Yet Reiss resists blanket affirmation or rejection of the legitimacy or otherwise of crossing species boundaries; rather we are left with a puzzle that invites further reflection as to how we arrive at our own particular concept of limits.

In chapter 7, Donald Bruce raises the particular question of how far we might go in genetic technology in a rather different way from that encountered in Reiss's analysis. He introduces the theme by suggesting that risk has become not just a part and parcel of human experience, but an alternative way of seeing reality. Moreover, he argues that a growing cultural aversion to risk, both to health and the environment, is a recurrent theme in the genetically modified foods debate. But how precautionary should we be? He suggests that the public perception of risk is associated with value judgements that may either exaggerate or play down the actual risks, depending on particular political presuppositions. He puts forward a theological argument to support the idea that God's creation is an intrinsically risky place, rather than riskiness simply being the result of the fall. Instead, God's involvement in life is necessarily risky, and the gift of human creativity as made in God's image also presupposes uncertain outcomes. One might even surmise that risk is associated with the possible redemptive involvement of human beings in creation through the practice of technology. He suggests, therefore, that Christians should be wary of the cultural aversion to risk and accept that absolute safety is out of step with the way the world is created.

The task of Christian theology for Bruce is to delineate a middle path between those who stress the risks of genetic technology and those who promote it as completely safe, both of which positions are grounded in a futile attempt to deny contingency and uncertainty. Any re-ordering of nature through genetic engineering cannot avoid risk; but it also allows humanity to take responsibility for the gifts that have been given by God. In the light of the unknown nature of many of the risks of genetic modification to human health and the environment he asks how far this is greater or less than other risks humanity has taken in the course of history. Hence, in contrast   to the position taken by Northcott in chapter 4, Bruce rejects the precautionary approach to genetic modification from a theological point of view. The precautionary approach stresses conservation, rather than 'progress'. He believes that if we are wedded too much to keeping nature as originally created we give the natural world a quasi-divine status that is not biblical. At the same time, he also recognises the hubris of some supporters of genetic technology; he acknowledges the ambiguity noted by Brooke in chapter 2, namely, that it is possible to justify new technologies by alignment of human creativity with the action of God. His chapter does not amount to a blanket affirmation of all genetic engineering. Rather, he suggests that genetic risk needs to be evaluated in terms of a contract with society, which requires a responsible sense of stewardship. It is interesting to note the radical divergence between the positions that Bruce and Northcott both use to support the idea of 'stewardship', a divergence on which Scott's response to Northcott's chapter may shed further light.

In chapter 8 Stephen Clark reflects on the specific situation of the treatment of animals that emerges through biotechnological developments, reflections arising from his own involvement in working groups of government advisory bodies. He notes that most ordinary members of the public favour the experimental use of animals for serious purposes, though the extent of harm inflicted and its justification is still open for debate. Hence genetic engineering that is known to inflict lasting pain on animals is rejected as a matter of principle. However, Clark suggests that we need to consider other possible intrinsic wrongs, such as violating the integrity of a living being, extensive mixing of kinds, such as creating chimeras, or reducing sentience of a living being so that it is viewed simply as an artefact. In particular, the crossover into human species is the subject of particular concern, thus echoing the sentiments raised by Michael Reiss in chapter 5. However, Clark takes the view that the actual effect of the human DNA is important; there are no strands of DNA that are only found in the human genome and we need to consider whether the expression of the gene leads to a feature identified as specifically human. Like Reiss he asks what might be behind the aversion to the creation of half-human kinds. The response to genetic modification of animals so that they no longer feel pain may depend on the purpose sought in such modification, but also whether there are any more fundamental reasons to question the use of engineering rather than artificial breeding and selection programmes. Many object to the genetic engineering of primates, though Clark admits that restrictions in this regard are most probably related to the particular identification we feel towards primates over and above other mammals. He also suggests that regardless of the scientific basis for a particular act (even if it might be possible to regard fixed boundaries between species as no longer tenable), the intention of the agent and his or her attitude needs to be taken into account. He suggests that inappropriate motives might include just making the changes 'for fun', commercial goals, academic self-advancement, or sentimental reasons. Treating animals as simply tools for human manipulation shows inappropriate or even dehumanising attitudes. Making a parallel with Just War Theory, Clark concludes with some specific and practical suggestions as to what might constitute Just Experimentation Theory, including a list of procedures involving the genetic manipulation of animals that he suggests ought to be forbidden, whatever their potential benefits. He suggests that while many of these procedures do not yet take place, the issues they raise need to be addressed before they are present realities.

5

Relating Genetics to Theology on the Map of Scientific Knowledge[1]

Arthur Peacocke

There has been considerable confusion in the public mind about the aims of the Human Genome Project – is it to provide the data to enable genetically based diseases simply to be diagnosed and treated, or to enable society to reconstruct humanity in the image of some, presumably widely accepted, ideology? The first aim is unexceptionable and relates to scientifically well-established relations, in certain cases, between gene structure (= Deoxyribonucleic acid (DNA) sequence) and particular diseases or metabolic deficiencies. But the second, more general, aim is based on a presumption about the relation between genes and human behaviour and dispositions, as well as (even more doubtfully) about what is universally desirable in such a relation.

It is with respect to this second, wider aim, usually expressed hopefully and journalistically, that it is important first to examine the relation of any knowledge about human genes to scientific understandings of the many-levelled hierarchy of structure and function that constitutes the individual member of the species *Homo sapiens*. Secondly, there are more general

[1] This contribution is a shortened version of a chapter in Philip R. Sloan (ed.), *Controlling Our Destinies: Historical, Philosophical, Ethical and Theological Perspectives on the Human Genome Project* (Notre Dame: University of Notre Dame Press, 2000), 343–65. The fullest version, with a different focus and in a wider theological context, is to be found as Chapter 12 of my *Theology for a Scientific Age Being and Becoming – Natural, Divine and Human,* 2nd enlarged edition (London: SCM Press, and Minneapolis: Fortress Press, 1993), 213–54.

considerations of the relation of genetic information to the nature of human personhood with which theology is so deeply and directly concerned. This paper, therefore, attempts to relate genetics to theological reflection on humanity by locating more precisely genetics on the map of scientific knowledge of human beings.

I would hazard the guess that one of the most influential catchphrases of our times which has influenced popular perceptions of the implications of biology, especially genetics, is Richard Dawkins's dubbing of genes as 'selfish' in the title of his widely read book, *The Selfish Gene*.[2] Within the general academic community a close runner-up, if not as an influence but rather as a goad, had appeared in the previous year in the first few defining pages of that seminal work of E. O. Wilson which launched the ship of sociobiology:

> Sociobiology is defined as the systematic study of the biological basis of all social behaviour ... One of the functions of sociobiology ... is to reformulate the foundations of the social sciences in a way that draws these subjects into the Modern Synthesis.[3]

But in the scientific world, especially that of molecular biology, which developed with the discovery of the molecular basis of heredity in DNA, much more influential in shaping the stances of many scientists was an earlier remark of Francis Crick. As one of the discoverers of the DNA structure, he had, some ten years before Wilson, thrown down the gauntlet by declaring that 'the ultimate aim of the modern movement in biology is in fact to explain *all* biology in terms of physics and chemistry'.[4] Such a challenge can, in fact, be mounted at many interfaces between the sciences other than that between biology and physics/chemistry. The ploy is called 'reductionism' or, more colloquially, 'nothing-buttery' – 'discipline X (usually meaning yours) is really nothing but discipline Y (which happens to be mine)'.

Before investigating further the whole question of reductionism, there is an even more sweeping claim that is

---

[2] R. Dawkins, *The Selfish Gene* (Oxford: Oxford University Press, 1976).
[3] E. O. Wilson, *Sociobiology – the New Synthesis* (Cambridge, MA: Belknap Press/Harvard University Press, 1975), 4.
[4] F. H. C. Crick, *Of Molecules and Man* (Seattle: University of Washington Press, 1966), 10.

sometimes implicit in the writings of certain scientists, namely, that not only is (scientific) discipline X nothing but (scientific) discipline Y but also that the *only* knowledge worthy of the name is *scientific* knowledge. All else is mere opinion, emotion, subjectivism, etc. This is the belief system called 'scientism' (hence the adjective 'scientistic'), which asserts that the only sure and valid knowledge is that which is found in the natural sciences and is to be obtained by its methods. It is the belief of only some scientists and of very few philosophers. Nevertheless, scientism, together with reductionism, often underlie, as all-pervading assumptions, statements made by a number of influential biologists and geneticists which penetrate into the public consciousness of the Western world.

There has, of course, been a strong and often effectual response to these exaggerated claims – mounted, be it noted, often by scientists as well as by philosophers of science. But their proponents have nevertheless succeeded in conveying to many thinking people in our Western society that those who work on genetics, especially human genetics, share their (apparently)[5] reductionist and scientistic stances. It is this, I would surmise, which often engenders much suspicion of the whole Human Genome Project, which is consequently believed to possess, over and beyond its avowed aims to counter human genetic disease deficiencies, a hidden agenda to control the future of humanity through manipulating its genes.

In order to allay such suspicions it is not enough simply to affirm the integrity and good intentions of the scientists and fund-providers involved. For the suspicion arises from the belief – encouraged by the 'selfish gene' terminology and the philosophical stance of many sociobiologists – that these scientists think that it is the genes alone which are indeed the control centres of human behaviour, and even of human thought. This involves an implicitly reductionist assumption, and the whole question of reduction*ism* as a philosophy of the relation between the sciences therefore needs clarifying.

In order to examine the consequences for theology of genetic research it is, then, necessary to clarify the relation

---

[5] I say 'apparently' because both R. Dawkins and E. O. Wilson, in the appropriate contexts, modify such intentions – in spite of their emphatic statements such as those quoted.

between knowledge about human beings gained from the various sciences. A closer look will, in fact, show a widening horizon of understanding as we move from the physical sciences to the life and social sciences and finally to the realm of human culture with its apprehensions of a transcendent dimension to human experience.

Reductionism, Emergence and Reality

To indicate the kind of issue at stake here, let me recount how the discovery of the structure of the genetic material DNA, led me – as a physical biochemist studying, in the early 1950s, its behaviour in solution – to *anti*-reductionist conclusions, unlike Crick. What was impressive about this development, and it is a clue to many important issues in the epistemology and relationships of the sciences, is that for the first time we were witnessing the existence of a complex macromolecule the *chemical structure* of which had the ability to convey *information*, a program of instructions to the next generation to be like its parent(s). Now, as a chemistry student, I had studied the structure of the purine and pyrimidine 'bases', which are part of the nucleotide units from which DNA is assembled. All that was pure chemistry, with no hint of any particular significance in their internal arrangement of atoms of carbon, nitrogen, phosphorus, etc. Yet here, in DNA, there had been discovered a double string of such units so linked together through the operation of the evolutionary process that each particular DNA macromolecule has the new capacity, when set in the matrix of the particular cytoplasm evolved with it, of being able to convey a program of hereditary instructional *information* – a capacity absent from the component individual nucleotides. Now the *concept* of 'information', originating in the mathematical theory of communication,[6] and indeed that of a *program*, had never been part of the organic chemistry of nucleotides, even of polynucleotides.

Hence in DNA we were witnessing a notable example of what many reflecting on the evolutionary process have called

---

[6] C. E. Shannon and W. Weaver, *The Mathematical Theory of Communication*, 2nd edn (Urbana: University of Illinois Press, 1962).

KEY to Figure 5.1

'Focal levels' correspond to foci of interest and so of analysis (see text). Focal level 4 is meant to give only an indication of the content of human culture.

Solid horizontal arrows represent part-to-whole relationships of structural and/or functional organisation. Dashed boxes represent sub-disciplines in particular levels, which can be coordinated with work at the next focal level in the scheme (the connections are indicated by vertical, dashed, double-headed arrows).

In each of the focal levels 1–3, examples are given of the *systems* studied, which can be classified as being within these levels and also of their corresponding *sciences*. Focal level 2 elaborates additionally the part–whole relation of levels of organisation and analysis in the nervous system (after Fig. 1 of P. Churchland and T. J. Sejnowski, 'Perspectives on Cognitive Neuroscience', *Science*, 242, 1988, 741–5 (742).

In focal level 2, the science of *genetics* has relevance to the whole range of the part–whole hierarchy of living systems and so, if included, would have to be written so as to extend across its entire width.

CNS = central nervous system.

'emergence' – the entirely *neutral* name[7] for that general feature of natural processes wherein complex structures, especially in living organisms, develop distinctively new capabilities and functions at levels of greater complexity. Such emergence is an undoubted, observed feature of the evolutionary process, especially of the biological. It is in this sense that the term 'emergence' is being used here and *not* in the sense that some actual entity has been *added* to the more complex system. There is no justification for making such assertions (as, for example, in the discredited vitalist postulate).

DNA itself proves to be a stimulus to wider reflections, both epistemological, on the relation between the knowledge which different sciences provide, and ontological, on the nature of the realities which the sciences putatively claim to disclose. Figure 5.1 is intended to clarify what I am referring to and, in

---

[7] This term need not (*should* not) be taken to imply the operation of any influences either external in the form of an 'entelechy' or 'life force' or internal in the sense of 'top–down' causative influences. It is, in my usage, a purely descriptive term for the observed phenomenon of the appearance of new capabilities, functions, etc., at greater levels of complexity.

Figure 5.1 *The relation of disciplines (an elaboration of Figure 8.1 of W. Bechtel and A. Abrahamsen, Connectionism and the Mind (Oxford and Cambridge, MA: Blackwells, 1991).*

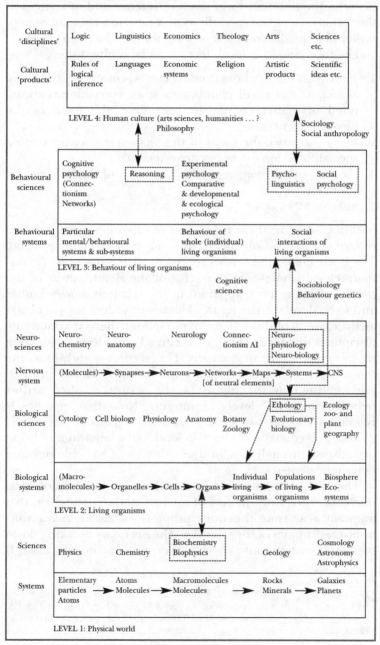

particular, the scope of genetics.[8] It represents the relations between the different focal levels of interest and of analysis of the various sciences, especially as they pertain to human beings, rather like the different levels of resolution of a microscope.

The following four focal 'levels' can be distinguished:

1. *the physical world*, whose domain can be construed, from one aspect, as that of all phenomena since everything is constituted of matter–energy in space–time, the focus of the physical sciences;
2. *living organisms*, the focus of the biological sciences (with a special 'box' for the key neuro-sciences);
3. *the behaviour of living organisms*, the focus of the behavioural sciences;
4. *human culture*.

W*ithin* some of these four levels of interest at least portions of series of part–whole hierarchies of complexity can be found. The horizontal, solid arrows represent such sequences. Yet this hierarchical whole–part character of the relationships of the natural world is more apparent in the relations *between* higher and lower levels in the figure. Moreover, within any particular analytical level of this scheme of disciplines, there are often sub-disciplines that form a bridge with an adjacent level by focusing on the same events or domains. This allows for and shows the significance of interdisciplinary interactions. These 'bridges' are indicated in the figure by the vertical, dashed arrows between the focal levels of interest. Note that genetics is relevant across the whole range of living organisms (focal level 2) and, indeed, has an impact on level 3 (the behaviour of living organisms) through the 'bridge' sciences of sociobiology and behaviour genetics.

The scheme represented in the figure is an epistemological one concerned with the foci of interest, and so of analysis, that naturally arise from the, quite properly, *methodologically* reductionist techniques of the sciences – the necessary breaking down of complex wholes into their smaller units for investigation. It

---

[8] This figure is reproduced from the second, expanded edition of my *Theology for a Scientific Age*, 217. It is an elaboration by me of Figure 8.1 of W. Bechtel and A. Abrahamsen, *Connectionism and the Mind* (Oxford and Cambridge, MA.: Blackwells, 1991), 257.

serves to illustrate 'part–whole' hierarchies of complexity in which a science focusing on a more complex 'whole' is distinct from those focusing on the parts that constitute them.[9] For, going up the figure, one finds the need to deploy distinctively new concepts and theories containing new referential terms in order to represent the observed capacities and functions and to describe accurately the structures, entities and processes which occur at those more complex levels (inevitably 'higher'[10] on the printed page).

The concepts and theories, with their particular referential terms, that constitute the content of the sciences focusing on the more complex levels are often (not always) logically irreducible to those operative in the sciences that focus on their components. This is an epistemological affirmation concerned with the nature of our knowing and knowledge. In particular, and with reference to our concerns in this inquiry, it seems unlikely that the contents of level 3 and, even more so, that of level 4 are likely to be reducible entirely to that of the science of genetics, which is located across the width of level 2.

A variety of independent derivation, identification or measurement procedures for examining the existence and character of a phenomenon, object or result can be directed at a particular complex level. Sometimes such investigations find an invariance in the concepts and referential terms of the theories needed to account for the phenomenon, object or result in question. W. C. Wimsatt[11] has called these concepts and referential terms 'robust'. I would argue that, when this is the case, it indicates that the terms yielded by the procedures appropriate to each level of investigation can be said to have a putative, ontological status. That is, the terms refer to what can be said to be 'real', if we use that term in the admittedly loose, but pragmatic, sense of what we cannot avoid taking into account in our practical and experimental interactions with the

---

[9] Such relations occur both horizontally, within the four broad categories of the boxes, and vertically, though it is these latter which are of most concern to us here.

[10] No evaluative or normative meaning should be attached to the use of 'higher' in this context.

[11] W. C. Wimsatt, 'Robustness, Reliability and Multiple-Determination in Science', in *Knowing and Validating in the Social Sciences: A Tribute to Donald Campbell* (San Francisco: Jossey-Bass, 1981), 124–63.

system at the level in question. That is, when concepts and referential terms in theories applied to a more complex level, higher
in the figure, turn out to be 'robust' in Wimsatt's sense, there is
then a prima facie case that they actually refer to new realities[12]
distinctively emerging at that level of complexity. There are, it
would putatively appear, genuinely new realities to be observed
in the behaviour of living organisms (level 3) and in human
culture (level 4) which are not subsumable under and reducible
to the concepts which refer to the genetic realities observed at
level 2. In particular, human culture includes religious
experience and the theologies that are the intellectual
reflections upon it – and upon all the other levels.

What I am saying here assumes some form of 'critical' realist
philosophy of science. This philosophy continues to commend
itself to me as the appropriate account of the scientific enterprise for many reasons. It also seems to be the working
philosophy of most practising scientists who infer from their
experiments to the best explanation, and thereby to postulated
provisional realities ('candidates for reality'), based on the
normal criteria of reasonableness – fit with the data, internal
coherence, comprehensiveness, fruitfulness and general
cogency.

Such considerations now allow us to infer from the map of
knowledge depicted in the figure a kind of 'scale' of being and
becoming. Science has shown that the natural world is a
hierarchy of levels of complexity, each operating at its own
level, and each requiring its own methods of inquiry and developing its own conceptual framework, in which at least some of
the terms can refer to new non-reducible realities distinctive
of the level in question. Moving up the figure from bottom to
top also corresponds very closely to the sequence of the actual
appearance in time of the entities, structures, processes, etc. on
which the hierarchy of sciences respectively focuses. That is,
there is an emergence in time of new complex entities, etc., so
that the natural world is now perceived as having evolved and as

---

[12] If a concept referring to a 'higher' level of complexity *can* be reduced, one has no
warrant for affirming that the higher level manifests a new *kind* of reality.
Certainly the higher level will still have its distinctive properties as a whole (and
the corresponding *qualia* for the observer) but these will not then be, if the
concept is reducible, pointers to the higher level consisting in a new kind of
reality.

still evolving. The natural world manifests the emergence of new kinds of reality. For, on the basis of our considerations concerning the reality of what is referred to at different levels, one cannot say that atoms and molecules are *more* real than cells, or living organisms, or ecosystems.

Moreover there are *social* and *personal* realities, too. As one moves up the figure, this recognition of the possibility of the emergence of new realities in the natural world gives a recognisable location within the map of knowledge for the emergence of the distinctively human, all that is signalled by the use of the word 'person'. The language of personal experience, especially that of personal relations (including, for theists, relations to God and so the language of theology), thereby acquires a new legitimacy as referring to realities which could be emergent in humanity. Such realities are not prematurely to be reduced to the concepts applicable to the constituents of the evolved human body, in particular, its genes. The higher-level concepts, in this case the personal ones, must be accorded a prima facie status of referring to realities until their respective terms and concepts have been shown unequivocally to be reducible totally to the sciences of the lower levels. So our particular concern in appraising the significance of genetic research, and concomitantly the implications and results of the Human Genome Project, must be to persist in asking whether or not a reduction of the personal to genetics is occurring with the elucidation of the human genome.

Levels in Human Beings

Structures, functions and processes present in human beings are, of course, to be found at all focal levels 1 to 3. No other part of the observed universe appears to include so many levels as do human beings and level 4 is, of course, unique to them. Hence it is imperative that theologians take seriously into account the multi-layered complex entity that the sciences reveal human beings to be with causal influences going both up and down between the levels. In particular, the level of operation of DNA, that of genetics, is certainly – there is no gainsaying – a key and influential one in the microcosm of the macrocosm which human nature transpires to be in this twentieth-century scientific perspective.

It is possible here to comment only on certain key sciences that have been the subject of recent discussion, not to say controversy. The sciences which bridge levels 2 and 3 include, on the one hand, cognitive science (or, 'cognitive neuro-science') and, on the other hand, sociobiology (often now called 'behavioural ecology') together with behaviour genetics.

Cognitive science is concerned with relating to behaviour the different levels of analysis of information processing (roughly, 'cognition'). The detailed ways in which the various levels of analysis are being applied and shaping investigations concerns us less here than the now widespread realisation by cognitive scientists that, in order to understand the relation between the behavioural, at one pole, and the molecular, at the other, understanding of all levels of analysis, organisation and processing is necessary.

This pressure to integrate the study of different levels is, it seems, generated by the very nature of the problems which cognitive scientists address. Moreover, what applies to the operation of the nervous system also applies to the operation of the brain as a whole.[13] This is a clear example from the cognitive sciences, of a general feature of biological systems. Because of their intricate complexity, especially that of nervous systems and a fortiori the human-brain-in-the-human-body, no one description at any one level can ever be adequate and therefore no one level has epistemological priority nor (on a critical-realist reckoning) ontological priority. The emergent properties and functions at the more complex levels of analysis, organisation and processing are emergent *realities* – and those of consciousness and self-consciousness are notably so.

It has, moreover, been proposed[14] by the brain scientist R. W. Sperry that the way the brain acts on the body through the operation of the central nervous system is best conceived as an instance of 'top-down causation' (or, in my terminology, 'whole–part influence'). In his account, the total state of the human brain-as-a-whole, a state describable to our self-consciousness only in mentalistic language, is a constraint

---

[13] P. Churchland and T. J. Sejnowski, 'Perspectives on Cognitive Neuroscience', *Science*, 242, 1988, 741–5 (Fig. 1, 742).
[14] R. W. Sperry, *Science and Moral Priority* (Oxford: Blackwell, 1983), ch. 6, 77–103; R. W. Sperry, 'Psychology's Mentalist Paradigm and the Religion/Science Tension', *American Psychologist*, 43, 1988, 607–13.

upon, and so causally effective on, the firing of individual neurones, or groups of neurones, in such a way as to trigger, and actually be, the specific action intended in the consciousness which was that brain state. This notion of whole–part influence can be regarded as a contemporary exposition of what is happening when human-brains-in-human-bodies are agents. The mechanism through which they act is based on interconnected neuronal connections genetically coded in their original formation in the embryo but modified and elaborated by their subsequent interactions with the world, including people. The actions themselves cannot be accounted for by genetics alone, because total brain states are constraining factors in human actions and are only referable to, and perhaps describable by, mentalistic language, such as that of purposes or intentions. This places a fundamental limit on what we can expect genetics to explain.

Sociobiology may be broadly defined as the systematic study of the biological, especially the genetic, basis of social behaviour and, in relation to human beings, aims even at exploring the relations between biological constraints and cultural change. The purpose of *behaviour genetics* since 1960, when it first came to be recognised as a distinct discipline, has been to examine 'the inheritance of many different behaviours in organisms ranging from bacteria to man'.[15] These studies cannot but influence our general assessment of human nature and, in particular, the degree of responsibility assigned to societies and individuals for their actions. The genetic boundaries that limit what we can do are, from a theistic viewpoint, what God has purposed shall provide the matrix within which freedom shall operate. Furthermore, theologians should acknowledge that it is this kind of *genetically based* creature which God has actually created as a human being through the evolutionary process. That genetic heritage cannot, in advance, however, itself determine the *content* of thinking and reasoning – even if it is the prerequisite of the possession of these capacities.

Some of the principal behavioural sciences and the systems on which they focus are indicated in level 3 of the figure. This includes various forms of psychology, which is, in its usage since the eighteenth century, the study of the phenomena of mental

---

[15] H. A. Hay, *Essentials of Behaviour Genetics* (Oxford: Blackwells, 1985), 1.

life. Recently there has been a 'cognitive', 'consciousness' or 'mentalist' shift of emphasis in psychology that moves its focus of interest towards the content and activities of ordinary consciousness[16] (sometimes neutrally denoted as 'self-modification'). Consciousness is now much more frequently regarded as a theoretical term that refers to realities the existence of which is inferred from observation. How it is to be a thinking and feeling human being has again come on to the agenda of many of the behavioural sciences.

A rehabilitation thus appears to be occurring, from a scientific perspective, of the reality of reference of humanistic studies – in which theology should be included, if only because of its concern with religious experience. It also gives scientific credibility to what had never been doubted in theology, namely, the preeminence of the concept of the personal in the hierarchy of our interpretations of the many-levelled structure of the world of which humanity is an evolved constituent. This has important implications for the relation of science and theology. For instead of a dichotomy between, on the one hand, a dualism of 'body' and 'mind' (a common misapprehension of the Christian view of humanity) and, on the other, a reductive materialism, a new integrated 'view of reality' could emerge. This view of reality, Sperry hopes, 'accepts mental and spiritual qualities as causal realities, but at the same time denies they can exist separately in an unembodied state apart from the functioning brain'.[17] The more the sciences are concerned with the mental life and behaviour of human beings, the more they will impinge on the concerns of the Christian community. Though it is worth noting that the social conditioning of religious beliefs which the social sciences disentangle and reveal does not, of itself, settle any questions as to the *truth* of these beliefs.

Such considerations bring us to the domain of human culture – that of level 4. The 'cultural products' at focal level 4 are embodiments of human creativity in the arts and sciences and in human relations including, theists would add, relations to God.[18] Those patterns of discernible meaning within the

---

[16] Sperry, *Science and Moral Priority*, 608.
[17] Sperry, *Science and Moral Priority*, 609.
[18] I have argued elsewhere (*Theology for a Scientific Age*, 191–212) that relations to God are expressed by their own distinctive means through meaningful patterns created in what is received initially through our senses.

natural nexus of events in the world, which are the means of communication between human beings and between God and humanity, are generated through their historical formation in continuous cultures which invest them with meaning enabling such communication. Thereby they have the unique power of inducting humanity into an encounter with the transcendence in the 'other', whether in the form of another human person or, for theists, of God – the Beyond within our midst. We can expect all such encounters with 'cultural products' to communicate only in their own way, in their own 'language', with an immediacy at their own level which is not reducible to other languages.

This reassertion of the conceptual and experienced autonomy of what is communicated in human culture is reinforced by the rehabilitation of the subjective, of inner experience, in cognitive science and in psychology – in fact, in the recovery of the personal, the recognition of the reality of personhood. We really do seem to be witnessing a major shift in our cultural and intellectual landscape which is opening up the dialogue between the human spiritual enterprise (broadly, 'religion') and that of science in a way long barred by the dominance of a reductionist, mechanistic, materialism, thought erroneously to have been warranted by science itself. The human is undoubtedly biological, but what is distinctively human transcends that out of which and in which it has emerged.

This pressure for a wider perspective on humanity is being generated from within the sciences themselves (if not by all scientists, as such) in attempting to cope with the many levels of the figure. Is it too much to hope that we see here the first glimmerings for some time of a genuine integration between the humanities, including theology, and the sciences? Are we seeing the beginnings of a breakdown of that dichotomy between the 'two cultures' that was engendered by the previous absence of any epistemological map on which their respective endeavours could be meaningfully located?

Conclusions

Even a rapid survey such as this highlights the superficiality of any talk that speaks of there being *particular* genes for *particular*

kinds of human behaviour. For, first, behaviour is nearly always
influenced by complex *sets* of genes and the link between the
immediate output of these genes and human behaviour is
extremely tenuous. This is not least because even the synapsal
linkages in the brain are not exclusively genetically determined,
but depend on the input from learned experiences which
create new ones and which, in the human case, means the input
from the experiences mediated by human culture.

Secondly, the genes operate within the hierarchy of nested
levels shown in the figure. The higher of these are sensitively
dependent on their interactions with the environments specifically operative at those levels – not least that of human culture
(level 4). Thirdly, a human person is not a static entity but is
always in process of becoming – one ought to speak of 'human
becomings', rather than 'human beings'.[19] This dynamic
process has occurred historically, as humanity has evolved out
of the inorganic material of planet Earth, rising from level 1 to
4. It also occurs in the life of each individual since we all begin
as DNA inherited from our parents immersed in the evolved
cytoplasm of a fertilised egg, but gradually emerge as social
beings/becomings interacting personally with other members
of our species. Eventually we are inducted into the world of
culture and into the rich heritage of human concepts and
values. These latter in their multiform aspects and influences
shape our actions continuously within the limitations imposed
by the genes that we possess. In those actions we have the
irrefutable experience of being free to choose within limits (of
which we may not necessarily be conscious) and this
experience is a raw *datum* that even the reductionist cannot
deny. This experience of freedom is acknowledged by all
ethical systems, however differing in particular content, and by
all systems of law in societies that attribute responsibility to
individuals for their actions. These are observable features of
all societies – even our own Western one with its current
loss of nerve concerning the content of law and ethics – and
they are not to be rubbished by the excessive claims of those

[19] 'We are not so much human beings as human becomings' (Peter Morea,
Personality: An Introduction to the Theories of Psychology (London: Penguin Books,
1990), 71).

geneticists who, expressing an unwarrantable reductionist philosophy, give the impression that we human beings are *determined* by our genes.

More generally, I conclude from this survey that – however much might be possible in the future in remedying particular, localisable and identifiable biological deficiencies – it would be unwise to place too much hope on the ability of any directed genetic engineering to ameliorate the general human condition, especially the psychological and spiritual. It would be irresponsible of all those engaged in the Human Genome Project if they ever gave the impression that it could do so.

6

Is It Right to Move Genes between Species? A Theological Perspective

Michael J. Reiss

It is increasingly recognised that many of the ethical analyses of genetic engineering and allied technologies (including cloning), for all that such analyses are of value, have missed what large numbers of people feel to be important for them. This is because such analyses have focused, sometimes exclusively, on the likely consequences of these new technologies. One obvious problem with consequentialism is that accurate predictions of consequences are virtually impossible when we are talking about new technologies – it is for this reason that advocacy of the precautionary principle has become so widespread in recent years. In addition, for all that consequences are important, they may not be enough for ethical conceptualisation in this area. It is, at least in some people's eyes, the nature or essence of things that is of especial import.

There are, of course, plenty of ethical approaches that go beyond consequentialism yet remain entirely secular. However, numerous surveys have now shown that, even in the UK and other Western European countries where some suppose that we live in increasingly secular societies – let alone in many countries where churchgoing or other forms of religious attendance are much more frequent – many people use theological language, even if haltingly, to give voice to their concerns about the new genetics.[1]

---

[1] For a summary of surveys about people's concerns about genetic engineering; see M. J. Reiss, 'What Sort of People Do We Want? The Ethics of Changing People

However, the intention of this chapter is not to look at the issue of the movement of genes between species solely from an overtly religious perspective. I am interested in a diversity of ways of understanding the feelings that may attach to genetic engineering. While there are some who feel optimistic about what genetic engineering may bring, there are many who feel uneasy about what it entails. A considerable amount has been written, much of it by theologians, about the extent to which genetic engineering is 'unnatural' or can be said to involve our 'playing God'.[2] The focus of this chapter, though, is quite specific. It is to look at the significance of the boundaries that exist between species. Since genetic engineering often involves moving genes between species, it is worth investigating the ethical and psychological importance of boundaries in general and species boundaries in particular. After looking at these issues I address one particular question, namely, whether it is wrong to eat animals that have been genetically engineered to contain human genes.

Species Boundaries and Genetic Engineering

Not all genetic engineering entails moving genes between species. For example, the genetic engineering of yeasts to 'improve' breads and beers has involved using the tools of genetic engineering to move genes between strains or varieties of yeast but still within the one species. Here genetic engineering is being used to speed up a process that could equally be carried out by conventional breeding – the essence of a biological species being that within it individuals are able to breed among themselves.

---

through Genetic Engineering', *Notre Dame Journal of Law, Ethics & Public Policy*, 13, 1999, 63–92. More generally, it has been argued that religion is increasingly becoming a means through which identities are articulated on the public stage – see R. Thomson, 'Diversity, Values and Social Change: Renegotiating a Consensus on Sex Education', *Journal of Moral Education*, 26, 1997, 257–71. For the argument that we are now seeing a global resurgence of religion, see S. Thomas, 'The Global Resurgence of Religion and the Role of the Church of England in World Politics', *Crucible*, July–September 2000, 149–60.

[2] See: J. R. Nelson, *On the New Frontiers of Genetics and Religion* (Grand Rapids, MI: William B. Eerdmans Publishing Company, 1994); C. Deane-Drummond, *Theology and Biotechnology: Implications for a New Science* (London: Geoffrey Chapman, 1997); and T. Peters, *Playing God? Genetic Determinism and Human Freedom* (New York: Routledge, 1997).

Another example is provided by the use of antisense technology; for example, in the production of tomatoes whose fruits take longer to go mouldy once picked. The core of this approach is that an artificial gene is made in the laboratory and then inserted into the tomato so as to prevent a normal gene – one that hastens fruit softening – from working.[3]

Nevertheless, most examples of genetic engineering, and certainly those of most concern both to the general public and to members of pressure groups opposed to genetic engineering, involve the movement by scientists of genes between species, often between completely unrelated species. For example, the gene in humans responsible for the production of the hormone insulin has been moved into bacteria or yeast. As a result genetically engineered human insulin is now widely used in the treatment of people suffering from juvenile-onset diabetes. Equally, and notoriously, genes from scorpions have been moved into viruses in an attempt to make such viruses more toxic to insect pests.[4]

In any useful sense, moving genes from humans to bacteria or yeast, and from scorpions to viruses, is unnatural. Although hybridisation between closely related species and so-called 'horizontal gene transfer' does occur in nature – meaning that the genetic boundaries between species are not as absolute as is widely supposed – there is no doubt that genetic engineering has already breached a number of species boundaries in ways that nature has not and almost certainly never would.

The question is, how concerned should we be at this breaching of species boundaries? Does it matter that plant crops contain bacterial or animal genes if the result is that their yields are greater? Does it matter that certain bacteria confined to fermenters in pharmaceutical factories contain human genes if the result is that life-saving and health-restoring medicines are produced? Does it matter that pigs are being genetically

---

[3] G. A. Tucker, 'Improvement of Tomato Fruit Quality and Processing Characteristics by Genetic Engineering', *Food Science and Technology Today*, 7, 2, 1993, 103–8.

[4] See M. J. Reiss and R. Straughan, *Improving Nature? The Science and Ethics of Genetic Engineering* (Cambridge: Cambridge University Press, 1996), 96–102, for the genetically engineered human insulin story, and 111–13, for the scorpion gene story.

engineered with human genes in the hope that their internal organs may be used for human transplants?

One important psychological point is that as we grow up, the boundaries between species help us to organise our understanding of the natural world. Children learn from their infancy about living things in their immediate environment. In particular, they learn about animals, learning both to recognise different types of animals and what their basic names are.[5] It has been argued that the concepts 'animal' and 'plant' are fundamental ontological categories; that is, categories used by children to organise their perceptions of the world in which they live.[6] Certainly for most children, animals form a significant part of the world around them, whether as wildlife, pets or zoomorphic toys. It is therefore unsurprising that names for familiar animals form a large part of the vocabulary of young children. Anglin reorganised the categories of words identified by Rinsland in the early vocabularies of young children.[7] He found that the largest of the resultant semantic categories was that of everyday types of animals (36 words out of a total of 275). The next category was that of people (which contained 35 words).

Individual Boundaries: Learning to be Oneself

Before each of us is born we are, in a sense, not a self. We depend on our mothers for everything. Of course, after birth we continue to depend on others but we are no longer physically a part of another person. Birth, above all, is a detachment. With the arrival of our birth comes the end of the most physically intimate relationship we will ever know.

It takes the new-born baby some considerable time to realise that it is alone. Indeed for some time after birth a new-born, in so far as it is capable of thought, 'thinks' that it and everything

---

[5] E. Rosch and C. B. Mervis, 'Family Resemblances: Studies in the Internal Structures of Categories', *Cognitive Psychology*, 7, 1975, 573–605; M. J. Reiss and S. D. Tunnicliffe, 'Conceptual Development', *Journal of Biological Education*, 34, 1999, 13–16.

[6] F. C. Keil, *Semantic and Conceptual Development: An Ontological Perspective* (London: Harvard University Press, 1979).

[7] J. M. Anglin, *Word, Object, and Conceptual Development* (New York: W. W. Norton, 1977); H. D. Rinsland, *A Basic Vocabulary of Elementary School Children* (New York: Macmillan, 1946).

else are one; that it is the universe and that everything is it. The first great task in conceptual development is, therefore, for a baby to realise the distinction, to effect the boundary, between self and non-self.[8]

As the baby, in her or his mind, begins to emerge as a distinct entity, anything that passes into it or out from it is of significance, especially if the baby has some control over the process. Urination and defecation are both important for this reason. In each case a baby can feel itself filling up and then, as it lets go, that which was inside it leaves, and the accompanying tension dissipates. Skin too plays an important role in the development of self.[9] Our skin does several things. For a start, it marks the physical boundary between inside us and outside us. And it also holds us together.

A baby does not suddenly learn its own boundaries. Such knowledge grows over the first twelve months or so. During this time the baby's brain is growing from only 25 per cent of adult mass at birth (compared to 41 per cent for a chimpanzee) to around 50 per cent at its first birthday. During this first year a baby undoubtedly learns a great deal about its environment, though the fact that it cannot yet speak makes it difficult for another to discern precisely what it has learnt.

By the time a child is three years old its brain is already 75 per cent of adult mass. By now it will normally have a network of social relationships, know whether it is a boy or a girl, have a rapidly growing vocabulary and be learning voraciously as it takes in and gives out information across its boundary.[10]

Other Boundaries

The argument above can be summarised as follows:

1. Genetic engineering often, though not always, involves transgressing species boundaries in a way that is completely unnatural.
2. During our childhood, learning about both species boundaries and the boundaries between ourselves and other people are

[8] E. Rayner, *Human Development: An Introduction to the Psychodynamics of Growth, Maturity and Ageing*, 3rd edn (London: Unwin Hyman, 1986).
[9] R. D. Hinshelwood, *A Dictionary of Kleinian Thought*, 2nd edn (London: Free Association Books, 1991).
[10] P. K. Smith, H. Cowie and M. Blades, *Understanding Children's Development*, 3rd edn (Oxford: Blackwell, 1998).

important ways in which we organise our understanding of ourselves and the natural world.

In addition, there are many other boundaries that people find important. Boundaries serve to divide entities into categories; in this way a boundary enables classification. Important boundaries include four that I shall briefly review here, namely, those that separate (1) food from non-food; (2) foreigner from non-foreigner; (3) male from female; and (4) potential marriage partner from non-potential marriage partner.

The boundary between food and non-food is one that, for any of us, is quite firmly set in place, yet is one that we can often see to be largely culturally determined and of little or no universal ethical significance. When once travel was limited and occasional, people would have almost never realised the cultural specificity of their own food rules. Nowadays, though, the ethnocentrism of our food taboos and likes and dislikes is all too apparent. We all know of cultures where snails are a delicacy, and of cultures where they cannot be eaten; similarly with horse meat, insect grubs, whale meat, pigs, cattle, shellfish and so on. This is not to imply that the boundary between food and non-food is entirely fluid. Aside from ascetics and the occasional exception that proves the rule, no one, for example, drinks urine or eats faeces. Nor is it to imply that the boundary between food and non-food always lacks any health or other functional underpinning – pork may be infected with trichinae and shellfish with disease-causing bacteria. Nevertheless, it is clear that food boundaries serve culturally to help order the near-infiniteness of the natural world. To acknowledge that they may then grow in some societies or for certain individuals into a codified set of regulations of Byzantine complexity is to do no more than to accept that our mental capabilities are such that we can end up over-structuring almost any human activity.[11]

The usefulness of the boundary between foreigner and non-foreigner is obvious. Foreigners, in the original sense of people who live elsewhere, rather than in the sense of immigrants, are

---

[11] For a classic attempt to explain apparently bizarre examples of human culture in functional terms, see M. Harris, *Cows, Pigs, Wars & Witches: The Riddles of Culture* (Glasgow: Fontana/Collins, 1974/1977).

people with whom one interacts only rarely if at all. A foreigner may be useful for trade (including trade in people, whether as slaves or potential sexual partners) but a foreigner is also a potential adversary in war. With non-foreigners, of course, contact is more frequent and the variety of possible types of interactions far greater. As a rule of thumb, an individual is a foreigner if there is no possibility of a significant personal relationship with them.[12]

Divisions by gender occur in every society. This is not the place to enter into a substantial review of the extent to which gender-specific patterns of behaviour – for example, the fact that the fastest athletes and the world's best chess players are male – are innate or culturally determined. Here all that needs to be pointed out is the extent to which gender and sex are used as structuring agents of classification. That is why activities such as cross-dressing makes so little sense to some people and are so deeply disturbing to others. As anthropologists inform us, societies differ in the extent to which certain activities, for example, weaving or bingo playing, are regarded as activities suitable for women or for men. As all of us also know, even when individuals strive consciously, purposively and consistently to eradicate gender-specific routines in a family or larger organisation, let alone in the wider society, such sex equality remains very difficult to achieve.

A marriage is a formalised long-lasting relationship between a human female and a human male. It typically occurs between adults (at any rate, between those who will become adults while still married) and grants permission for the couple to enjoy (at least in a legal sense) sexual relationships with one another. In almost every society a huge amount of negotiation, whether tacit or formalised, surrounds the choice of a marriage partner. Beyond the boundaries of negotiation, though, certain categories of people are debarred from being considered even as potential marriage partners. Most notably these include close kin, such as one's brothers and sisters. In fact, almost no one ever wants to marry their brother/sister – for reasons which are understood

---

[12] I trust it is evident that this division between foreigners and non-foreigners would have had its roots in our past when humans spent their lives in small groupings of a few dozen individuals. At that time, individuals living only a few miles away would be foreigners. Nowadays, of course, the word foreigner connotes a member of a different nation-state.

from both a developmental and a functional perspective.[13] We
lose the ability to be sexually attracted to those with whom we
spend a lot of our early years. The evolutionary advantage of this is
that it prevents harmful inbreeding. The point here is that the
boundary between suitable and non-suitable marriage partners is
not so much put in place by societies so as to prevent unsuitable
marriages but rather is acknowledged as a natural boundary
between suitable and non-suitable marriage partners.

New Testament Teaching About Boundaries

So boundaries exist in societies between such things as food and
non-food, foreigners and non-foreigners, males and females
and suitable marriage partners and unsuitable marriage
partners. What theological significance do such boundaries
have? I shall restrict myself to the Judaeo–Christian Scriptures.
In the Hebrew Scriptures, of course, one of the key threads is
the formation and maintenance of the state of Israel. It
is precisely the, at times, rigidity of the boundary between Jews
and non-Jews that leads some of the prophets to remind their
listeners of how they too were once slaves in Egypt and to
encourage them to look forward to a time when Israel's God
will be worshipped throughout the whole world.

For a Christian, this promised time was ushered in by the
life, work, death, resurrection and ascension of Christ. The
deliberations in Acts, with their climax at the Jerusalem
Council, led to an acceptance by the early Church that Gentile
Christians need not be circumcised (if male), need not keep
any of the food laws (beyond abstaining 'from what is strangled
and from blood'),[14] indeed need not keep much of the Torah
at all. It was precisely this licence, backed up by such Pauline
rhetorical questions as 'Did you receive the Spirit by works of
the law, or by hearing with faith?'[15] and injunctions as 'There is
neither Jew nor Greek, there is neither slave nor free, there is
neither male nor female'[16] that led to debates about the need
to keep the Sabbath[17] and other aspects of the Jewish law.

[13] M. J. Reiss, 'Human Sociobiology', *Zygon*, 19, 1984, 117–40.
[14] Acts 15.20b.
[15] Galatians 3.2b.
[16] Galatians 3.28a.
[17] Colossians 2.16.

It is widely supposed that it was the whole-hearted acceptance of this feature of Paul's teaching that lead to the situation described in 1 Corinthians 5:

> It is actually reported that there is immorality among you, and of a kind that is not found even among pagans; for a man is living with his father's wife. And you are arrogant! Ought you not rather to mourn? Let him who has done this be removed from among you.[18]

There are several features of note in this passage: (1) the 'immorality' is of a kind not even found among pagans – in other words, Paul's message about the breakdown of divisions between people and boundaries in society has been so taken to heart/over-interpreted that even universal norms are being eroded; (2) the activity in question is not a transient sin entered into secretly but an ongoing state of living that is being openly – arrogantly – celebrated; (3) to define acceptable and unacceptable behaviour, Paul firmly reimposes boundaries – 'Let him who has done this be removed from among you'; and (4) no further reason for Paul's decision is given. As is typically the case with moral absolutes, they are asserted not explicated.

The Significance of the Human–Animal Boundary

For a particular issue raised as a result of the movement of genes between species in genetic engineering, consider the question: Is it wrong to eat animals that have been genetically engineered to contain human genes? This question may soon become pressing as the number of animals with human genes continues to increase. In the UK alone, the delayed but soon-to-be published figures for the number, in 1999, of transgenic animals used in animal experiments – and most of these are mice genetically engineered to carry human genes – are likely to show that over half a million such animals were used. While most of these, being rodents, are never likely to end up as human food, an increasing number of farm animals, such as sheep and pigs, are being genetically engineered for research into the production of human proteins in milk or for xenotransplantation.

At one pole are those who argue that eating an animal, or a plant, into which a human gene has been inserted has nothing

---

[18] 1 Corinthians 5.1–2.

whatever to do with cannibalism. Cannibalism is about eating human flesh, not eating minute amounts of DNA that once came from just one of the 80 000 or so human genes and is now merely a copy of that original human gene. In any case the human genes that are likely to be inserted into animals are almost bound to be more than 90 per cent the same as animal genes there already – we share a very high proportion of our DNA with other mammals. Further, every baby who breast-feeds eats large amount's of another human's (i.e. its mother's) DNA.

Those who object to inserting human genes into animals that are subsequently used for human consumption may argue that the parallels with cannibalism cannot so lightly be dismissed. Although Imutran, one of the companies actively engaged in xenotransplantation research, has argued that '[t]his involves changing only 0.001 per cent of the genetic make-up of the pig',[19] it could be argued that the actual percentage of change is not of prime importance. After all, if I am unfaithful to my spouse on only 0.5 per cent of nights, is this ten times better than if I am unfaithful on 5 per cent of nights?[20] Reverting to traditional theological concepts, one either exists in a state of purity or impurity; one is either sinful or righteous – there are no half-way positions, no inter-boundary no-man's-lands gradually to be traversed.[21]

Similarly, just because a baby less than a year or so old does certain things with its mother doesn't make it right for the rest of us to do those same things with its mother. Further, the argument, expounded in some detail in Annex G of the Polkinghorne Committee Report,[22] that there would be virtually no chance of people eating original human genes in instances of people eating animals genetically engineered with human genes, but merely copies of them, can be criticised on

[19] Novartis Imutran, *Animal Welfare: Xenotransplantation – Helping to Solve the Global Organ Shortage* (Cambridge: Imutran Ltd, 1999).

[20] M. J. Reiss, 'The Ethics of Xenotransplantation', *Journal of Applied Philosophy* (in press).

[21] See also my other contribution in this book on pp. 77–84 for a brief discussion of the extent to which genetic engineering threatens to blur the dividing line between humans and the rest of the created order. A fuller analysis would profit from a review of cyborgs in science fiction.

[22] Ministry of Agriculture, Fisheries and Food, *Report of the Committee on the Ethics of Genetic Modification and Food Use* (London: HMSO, 1993).

two grounds.[23] First, in some people's eyes, a minute probability, even one as vanishingly small as the 1 in 10^{55} suggested in Annex G of the Polkinghorne Committee Report, is still non-zero. Secondly, does the fact that only copies of human genes are eaten make it any better? A copy of a human gene is chemically identical to it in terms both of chemistry and information. If I attempt to publish and sell the text of one of the Harry Potter books, on the grounds that this is only a copy of the original, J. K. Rowling, her publisher and the courts are unlikely to be convinced by my reasoning.

Perhaps inevitably, given the diversity of views on the acceptability of allowing human genes to be incorporated into animals that are subsequently eaten, the Polkinghorne Committee fell back on labelling as the solution:

> We recognise that many groups or individuals within the population object on ethical grounds to the consumption of organisms containing copy genes of human origin. We therefore *recommend* that food products containing such organisms should be labelled accordingly to allow consumers to exercise choice.[24]

The suggestion that labelling can solve the problem relies on the presumption that there is nothing definitely wrong about eating food with human genes but that people should, if they so wish, be able to choose either to avoid such food or actively to seek it out. Mandatory labelling is inappropriate either where one of the alternatives is certainly wrong – it's no good shops or manufacturers labelling goods 'Made using slave labour' – or where insufficient public good would result from the labelling – I don't have a right to argue that milk must be labelled according to the county from which it comes merely because I would like to be able to choose to buy milk from Cornwall.

Concluding Thoughts

Most of us now need fewer boundaries than our ancestors did. Just as symbols (e.g. blood) can be, in different contexts, either defiling or sanctifying, so a boundary can serve either to maintain order and strengthen that which it encloses or to

---

[23] Reiss and Straughan, *Improving Nature?*, 186–90.
[24] Ministry of Agriculture, Fisheries and Food, *Report of the Committee on the Ethics of Genetic Modification and Food Use*, 23.

lead to disunity.[25] Increasingly we find ourselves uncomfortable with boundaries that seem to lack a rational basis. Why shouldn't women be ordained? Why shouldn't people of the same sex be able to get married if they want to? And yet, are all boundaries to be crossed, all divisions eroded if they cannot be defended on consequentialist grounds? Is incest between freely consenting adults to be permitted if they use reliable contraceptives? Is it right to move genes between species?

I wish to close with a shaggy dog story. I won't attempt to explain its relevance to the issues addressed in this paper for, as Tangwa reminds us, 'it is the fool who says a proverb and then proceeds to interpret it himself/herself'.[26]

Simon had led a fairly uneventful childhood until, at the age of twelve, he asked his parents at dinner one day 'Why are sausages slightly curved?' Both his mother and father put down their knives and forks and looked ashen-faced. 'Son,' his father said, 'you should never have asked that question. You can no longer remain in this house.' Thus it was that, within the hour, Simon, to his amazement, found himself evicted from his home, never again to see his family.

The years passed and Simon eventually started to work as an assistant for a plumber and joiner called Ted. Ted was somewhat taciturn but Simon and he got on very well together. Eventually, as they ate their sandwiches one day, Simon plucked up the courage to ask the question he had for years wanted to have answered. 'Ted,' he said, 'I realise this may be a difficult question for you, but why are sausages slightly curved?' Ted put down his sandwich, went rather white and after a pause said, 'Simon, you shouldn't have asked that. Nevertheless, though I myself cannot tell you the answer, if you go across the road to the baker's, you'll find the person serving in there will tell you what you want to know.'

---

[25] It was Mary Douglas who most prominently suggested that taboos have as their main function the imposition of order on inherently untidy experiences. See: M. Douglas, *Purity and Danger* (Harmondsworth: Penguin, 1966/1970); B. Morris, *Anthropological Studies of Religion: An Introductory Text* (Cambridge: Cambridge University Press, 1987); and C. J. E. Moody, 'Drawing Near', *Theology*, 103, 2000, 243–50.

[26] G. B. Tangwa, 'Globalisation or Westernisation? Ethical Concerns in the Whole Bio-Business', *Bioethics*, 13, 1999, 218–26 (219).

Relieved and excited that he was going, at last, to find out just what it was that was so very significant about the shape of sausages, Simon immediately headed off across the road, only to be run over and killed.

7

Playing Dice with Creation: How Risky Should the New Genetics Be?

Donald M. Bruce

Introduction: the Nature of Risk

Today when we think about re-ordering nature, we do not go very far without encountering the notion of risk. Humans have always sought to reorder the natural world in some measure; it is intrinsic to the human condition. From primitive tools, the cultivation of grasses and domestication of animals, our humanity is characterised in part by what we call technology. What were once 'the practical arts' are now primarily the applications of science. As our knowledge of the living world has gone deeper, so have our interventions, and with them the challenges to basic norms and values. The ability to switch genes, now more or less at will, across all species of life has brought to the surface a number of underlying questions about how far and how fundamentally we ought to reorder nature. In the forefront of these is risk. How risky is it to utilise our new-found genetic skills?

Changed perceptions of risk

A shift has occurred in UK society from the notion of risk as a part and parcel of human experience to risk as an alternative way of interpreting reality. In the period of post-war recovery, technology was the vehicle of progress, convenience and affluence. Fifty years on, there is a trend in European society to see technology increasingly in terms of its risks. The industrial

151

systems created to overcome very real threats from natural
hazards and to harness the forces of creation to human ends
have, in turn, generated new systems of risk.[1] The confidence in
what science and technology would deliver has been undermined by a growing awareness of disadvantages and unintended
consequences. A progression of events including DDT,
thalidomide, nuclear waste, the ozone hole, Chernobyl, global
warming and, perhaps above all, BSE, has eroded the public
trust formerly put in science in the UK. New technology may be
viewed as danger or as possibility. In a post-modern context, an
emphasis on 'risk-to-me' as a way of framing life is emerging in
many walks of life.

Bewildering new interventions and past scientific failures
have together generated a more risk-averse society. The precautionary principle is often cited as though this occupied the
moral high ground. Has this aversion lost sight of the role risk
plays in human life, both practically and spiritually? To answer
this would need a book to itself, but this chapter seeks to
provide some basic insights.

The nature of risk

To engage with risk and uncertainty is part of being human. We
are aware from experience and observation that certain
phenomena and actions are potentially hazardous or unknown in
outcome. We proceed or refrain, depending on whether we judge
the risk worthwhile. Risk can be thought of as having three aspects:
magnitude, frequency and weighting. First, how big is the hazard?
How large would the consequences be, if the event did happen?
Secondly, how probable is it that it would happen? Probabilistic
safety analysis attempts to calculate these scientifically, on the
basis of past knowledge, to varying degrees of accuracy. This
numerical expression of the risk, say, of aircraft safety can then be
compared with values calculated for other, broadly accepted
technologies. When applied to nuclear power, a third factor was
highlighted, namely, that people often perceive risks quite differently from the evaluations given by scientific risk analysis.

In ordinary life we normally assess risk in a complex, qualitative way. We put weightings on different types of risk

[1] U. Beck, *Risk Society* (London: Sage, 1986).

according to our perceptions of them, based in turn on a wide range of individual and social values. For instance, people tend to be more averse to large rare accidents than smaller ones that happen more often. Insidious risks are also more feared than ones we can see. We distinguish between voluntary risks, like rock-climbing, driving a car or smoking; risks imposed by others, like passive smoking or other people's driving; and those arising from society as a whole, like global warming. Some suggest that we tend to revert to a preferred level of risk. If life is too risky we take more precautions; but if it gets too predictable, we look for new risks to take.[2] Risk perception is qualitative, subjective and often quirky. We can fool ourselves about our ability to drive while using a mobile phone, while fearing much lower risks of phone-mast irradiation. The human imagination can equally fail to see risks that are serious, and exaggerate risks that are trivial.

Risk in its social context

Risk involves an invisible social contract. Society is prepared to embrace technology to deliver certain benefits, and will accept a certain degree of risk and adaptation, provided certain basic factors are not infringed. These include:

- the realistic provision of tangible benefits to the consumer
- how familiar the activity is to our own experience; how much we understand it
- whether it threatens something deeply cherished
- its basis within the structures of the society
- our sense of control over the forces involved
- how much we trust those responsible; whether we share their aims and motives
- how much say we have in the decision
- whether something like it has gone wrong before, or has proved reliable
- the relative rarity of the accidents
- the scale of the consequences
- a fair distribution of risks and benefits.

[2] J. Adams, *Risk* (London: University College London Press, 1995).

A social limit of technology arises if a number of these factors are challenged. Thus the public reaction against GM food was hardly surprising because it failed so many conditions.[3] It challenged value norms about genes and nature, but the particular applications offered no tangible benefits to the average person, compared say with producing medicines in GM sheep. Whether in technical terms GM risks are especially high is a moot point, but the technology is unfamiliar and is less socially embedded than other risky technologies like coal. GM crops are perceived to pose a much greater threat to wildlife, biodiversity and human safety than selective breeding. GM has had no Chernobyl, but some see as almost inevitable that invisible genetic effects will spawn another BSE/CJD event or run haywire with the environment. People feel no control over the decisions and, after BSE, do not trust the scientists and regulators involved to have taken all eventualities into account.

In general, genetic risks are outwith most people's immediate knowledge. Perceptions of a case like GM food risk are therefore much influenced by what different groups express about it in the media. Each of these is shaped by particular underlying values about re-ordering nature, variously reflecting environmental, organic, commercial, scientific, overseas development and other perspectives.[4] On the one hand, if one believes in the importance of scientific advance or commercial potential, the risks will be evaluated against a prior assumption of going ahead while reducing the risk. If, on the other hand, the greatest concern is the inexorable progress of technological reshaping of the natural world without apparent bounds, environmental risks will appear paramount. In a country where food was scarce for many people, environmental risks might be less significant than securing enough food. Some committed to justice to the poor argue that genetic modification is too wedded to the unjust corporate power structures and global inequities to risk being countenanced as a solution to poverty and hunger.[5] Each of these is a partial insight on a

---

[3] D. M. Bruce and A. Bruce, *Engineering Genesis: The Ethics of Genetic Engineering in Non-Human Species* (London: Earthscan, 1998), 178–80.

[4] D. M. Bruce and J. T. Eldridge, 'The Role of Values in Risk Perception in the GM Debate', in M. P. Cottam, D. W. Harvey, R. P. Pape and J. E. Tait (eds), *Foresight and Precaution* (Rotterdam: Balkema, 2000).

[5] Christian Aid, *Selling Suicide* (London: Christian Aid, 1999).

complex problem. To help see them in perspective, the next section offers some theological reflections on risk and the nature of human existence.

The Risk of Nature: God's Risky Creation?

The universe is God's creation, not merely nature. Its forces and natural phenomena obey God's laws. The created order abounds in God's providence yet the same forces also constitute many things which are hazardous to humankind and other life forms. God has ordained our existence within certain physical and biological bounds. For the human body to live and flourish, it must be kept within these bounds. We are not designed to withstand certain forces, chemical environments and temperatures. We cannot fly or spend indefinite periods under water. Consequently many common features of our environment present potential risks to humans, such as cliffs, lakes, seas, rivers, deserts, glaciers, ice fields, high mountains. There are also risks from external physical events, such as being overwhelmed by the effects of an earthquake, hurricane, lightning, flood or a volcanic eruption. These are also risks which arise from other human beings and from other living organisms, for instance wild animals, fungi and bacteria.

It has been traditional to regard the creation itself as being in some measure fallen as a consequence of the rebellion of humankind portrayed in Genesis 3, and reflected in Romans 8. It is very difficult from the biblical data, however, to be specific, or to attribute the existence of the above hazards to the fall. Indeed, at the very heart of the story, God creates a physical object of risk, in the 'the tree of the knowledge of good and evil'. In creating a tree the fruit of which Adam and Eve are forbidden to eat, God has also created the condition of the risk that they might disobey. A moral and spiritual risk follows directly from the gift of free will to humans, but symbolised in a concrete physical act. Rowan Williams suggests that a God who speaks must also be a God who takes risks, because the very nature of communication implies the risk of being misunderstood and misrepresented in idolatry.[6]

---

[6] R. Williams 'God and Risk', in R. Holloway (ed.), *The Divine Risk* (London: DLT, 1990), 11–23.

The very notion of creating living organisms implies a sense of openness about the created order, because God gives all living things lives of their own.[7] Within God's universal call to all creatures to 'be fruitful and multiply' lies indeterminacy, in choices of mates and in the genetic outcome of the fusion of male and female zygotes. Genetic randomness is intrinsic to sexual reproduction, and incidentally represents a key moral objection to cloning human beings. The complete genetic composition of human offspring should not be predetermined by human agency, by copying that of another person who already exists.[8]

It seems reasonable to conclude that, for humans, both uncertainty and risk are intrinsic aspects of living in God's creation, because of the way God has made not only us but also the created order as a whole. The context we see for risk is one disfigured by our broken relationship with God, and by the spoiled relationships in every other sphere of life. But it seems that in some degree risk was present already.

Human creativity and risk

If this is the case, then risk is not something thrust upon us rudely by scientists, politicians or others outside our immediate control, to disrupt our Arcadian existence, because our existence was already risky. Indeed, it can be argued that risk is also part of all human activity *in* creation. The assertion that human beings are 'made in God's image'[9] is a source of much theological speculation.[10] Without going into its complexity, we may be said to be bearers of something God-like in our nature, and also of a calling towards the rest of God's creation. One aspect of this is that human beings have been made creative

---

[7] This discussion is primarily concerned here with events that are risky or random to human agency rather than to God's omniscience. The author is not, for example, advocating a process-theological interpretation at this point. The wider theological debate over whether anything that is unknown to creatures may ever be also unknown to the Creator, or whether all such outcomes are foreknown by God, lies beyond the scope of this paper.

[8] D. M. Bruce, 'Ethics Keeping Pace with Technology', in R. Cole-Turner (ed.), *Beyond Cloning: Religion and the Remaking of Humanity* (Harrisburg, USA: Trinity Press International, 2001), 34–49.

[9] Gen. 1.26–8.

[10] See, for example, the discussion in G. Wenham, 'Genesis 1–15', *Word Biblical Commentary*, Vol. 1 (Milton Keynes: Word (UK), 1991), 33.

under God within creation. The popular expression 'playing God' usually denotes human beings overreaching their due sphere of activity, but in a sense we *are* called to play God, by acting 'as God would' towards the creation, on God's behalf.

Humans have marred this calling, amongst other things, in running risks they ought not to have undertaken and subjecting others to their consequences. Just as pain in childbirth was *increased* rather than created as a consequence of human rebellion,[11] we may fall into new and greater areas of risk by the disrupted patterns of life we pursue in rebellion against our Creator. In the Incarnation, death and resurrection of Jesus Christ, however, God reaffirms the value of the whole created order, and points it to a final goal in which it will be 'liberated from its bondage to decay'.[12] An outworking of the restoration of human fellowship with God and the gift of the Spirit is that we should show the first fruits of the eventual 'glorious freedom of the children of God' in our handling of God's creation. There can now be a redemptive role towards the creation in our creativity.

God made humans creative but not omniscient. In our human condition we are both creatures and creators. Because we are finite and time bound, it is not given to us to know all the outcomes and their possible ramifications, intended or unintended. It would have taken remarkable foresight to have foreseen that the creation and widespread use of especially inert chlorofluorocarbon solvents would, because of their inertness, lead to catastrophic ozone depletion in the stratosphere. Often we see such an evolution of ideas, innovations and outcomes, in the arts and sciences alike, only in retrospect. Since God does not expect us to act as though we could predict the entire outcome of our actions, it implies that God intends that uncertainty and risk taking is part of our creativity. The mere existence of uncertainty is not a sufficient reason to refrain.

If technology is a creative outworking of God's image and calling, this implies that technological risk is generally to be managed rather than avoided. Relatively seldom is a technology so misconceived in terms of risk that there is no way to redeem

[11] Gen. 3.16.
[12] Rom. 8.19–22.

it. The Old Testament laws include some careful risk-management systems over such things as digging holes, putting parapets on flat roofs and warning people about dangerous bulls. Our fallen nature distorts our creativity. This should lead to a healthy scepticism of motives and human capacity for self-deception. A Christian response would challenge claims of human mastery to which some scientists have been prone. Deception can work both ways, however. Proponents of genetic intervention can be so bound up with promoting the technology that they overlook side effects which carry a substantial risk. Opponents can be so committed to their cause, however, that they are convinced that something carries a substantial risk when it does not.

To conclude that if a technological hazard is at all conceivable, then that is unacceptable, regardless of its improbability, is out of step with how God has made the world. That level of certainty is not how life, as given by God, is to be lived. This challenges the contemporary trend to demand assurances of scientists, politicians, corporations, hospitals, schools or other public authorities, assurances that are tantamount to guarantees of absolute safety, and also challenges the emerging culture of blame. This presumes a human capacity to know with more certainty than God has allowed to be possible. Human beings have to operate on the basis not of absolute certainty but of degrees of trust.

Reversibility and risk

Creative uncertainty also queries the assertion that only reversible risks should be undertaken. A frequent argument against releasing genetically modified organisms to the wider environment is that any unintended gene flow would be irreversible. Humans cannot take reversible risks, because all human acts happen in time and cannot be unacted. In many cases there is a very considerable absorptive capacity of the systems of the planet, to anneal out the cracks which humans often cause, but this is not the same thing as reversibility. Global warming and ozone depletion occurred when the capacity was exceeded by the nature and scale of particular activities. In genetics the issue is often proliferation not irreversibility. The important question is therefore to ask if a particular activity goes beyond the capacity of the systems to correct, were something to go wrong, including the likely extent of proliferation. The gene-flow question changes to whether the existence, say, of a new, unintended weedy transgenic variety of oil-seed rape would be a minor perturbation to the local ecology or a serious force for adverse change.

Risk and social justice

A redemptive approach to risk seeks social justice and fair dealing. In the politicised climate of the GM debate, fairness is called for in critical analysis. The risks of organic agriculture or conventional breeding must be examined with no less rigour and relentlessness than that applied to GM crops. Risks and benefits of technologies are also often unevenly distributed. Injustice occurs if one community carries most of the risk and another the main benefits, as with the importing of US GM soya and maize. It is more complex where a benefit is shared nationwide but the technology is situated only in certain locations. Some communities inevitably shoulder a relatively greater share of the risk than others, such as those living downstream from a hydroelectric dam or next to an airport runway. Society can expect that only a certain level of risk should be borne locally for the common good.

In contrast, only a certain level of local objection can be justified. NIMBY ('Not In My Back Yard') is ethically problematic. Its justification is in response to the failure of bureaucracy to take account of local concerns, or undue power residing in large corporations which operate hazardous technologies. It can incline to mere selfishness, however, if it becomes a tool to avoid bearing any local risk for a common good. In a context where it is impossible to share all risks equally across society, love for one's neighbour looks out for the victims of society's maldistribution of risk. But it also calls each person to take a due share in society's risks for the sake of all.

Risk and the Christian

Christians of all people, living by the daily 'risk' of our faith, should beware of encouraging an aversion to risk that demands minimising every conceivable hazard, no matter how tiny its probability. Following the pattern of Christ, a preparedness to bear risk for the sake of others might be a more Christian virtue than to take the law into one's own hands to avoid risk. Many of the redemptive acts of God's people in history, like the heroes of faith of Hebrews 11 or Paul and the apostles, have involved very great risk. To demand 'absolute safety' could be seen as a form of idolatry, putting our external material security in the place of trusting in God, as in the parable of the rich fool.[13] To reject anything because there is a finite element of uncertainty is altogether misleading, not just because it conflicts with reality. It also distracts us from the very basis of life, which is not in externalities like peace and material well-being but a relationship of trust with God. We are to seek first God's kingdom and righteousness, and not make an absolute even out of such essentials as food security.[14] Seeking first God's kingdom does not necessarily equate to avoiding risk.

These perspectives on risk in a theological context offer a corrective to the current cultural trend of risk aversion, and its corollary that risk avoidance is morally better than risk taking. Neither an attitude of risk aversion nor one of carefree risk taking represent responsible action in God's universe. On the one hand, God's calling to humans to intervene in creation suggests a somewhat adventurous approach. On the other, the responsibility to care for creation and fellow humans sets limits. The conclusion is not, if in doubt, always to take the 'safer' option, but rather to find a balance in this tension. This leads us to consider risk regulation and precaution.

Risk, Regulation and Precaution

There are two forms of risk regulation, known as reactive and precautionary.[15] The reactive approach considers that the only risks a society should have to regulate are those it can reasonably foresee and calculate from past experience. Risk management is rational and evidentially based, using scientific risk assessment. We should respond only to that for which there is good scientific data, not to merely speculative risks. Ethically,

[13] Luke 12.16–21.
[14] Matt. 6.31–3.
[15] Bruce and Bruce, *Engineering Genesis*.

it is utilitarian with an implicit stress on progress with technology. The greater good of the many justifies the risks that the few may have to bear. Human intervention is encouraged. We should not hold back human benefits by unnecessary fears, provided we act in the light of the knowledge that we have.

The precautionary approach asserts that where insufficient data exist to assess potential risks with large consequences and a fair probability, it may be appropriate to take counter-measures in advance of the data. Proponents of a new technology have only a limited right to subject society to unknown, or ill-defined, risks. It is not enough to leave it up to the market. Ethically, this stresses value rationality. Particular values lead to the need to protect certain things, often of wider scope than are amenable to scientific risk analysis. It highlights the plight of the human groups and ecosystems most vulnerable to the particular risks, against the utilitarian norm. The precautionary principle has, however, become widely reinterpreted by the agendas of different groups – environmental, industrial and governmental alike. It is apt to mean whatever the speaker wants it to mean. The question is therefore what *level* of precaution is appropriate, and according to whose values? We examine below some interpretations.

At one end of the spectrum, precaution has become the flagship of the environmental lobby, which interprets it as a reversal of the burden of proof. Before technology can proceed it must show the absence of harm, instead of presuming to go ahead unless intervenors can demonstrate harm. While this expresses the philosophical root of the Green movement, it does not reverse the burden but overbalances it, because a scientist can never prove the absence of risk. Taken literally, this would mean that all innovation would cease if anyone once postulated the slightest doubt. As we have seen, nothing in God's creation is free from risk in that sense. Therefore precaution cannot be considered absolute.

At the other extreme, North American risk analysts tend to regard the precautionary principle as an unnecessary and irrational approach, since it is not based on scientific data. This fails to recognise that, whatever the final number, the decision whether or not it constitutes too big a risk is not scientific but ethical. Ironically, both extremes make equal and opposite misjudgements about how much humans can and should know.

Since God has not given humans to be omniscient, we will always have to make decisions on data that will be to a greater or lesser extent inadequate.

A more moderate interpretation is that the precautionary principle is applied only in cases of a reasonable measure of probability of a major event. Here the precautionary principle is a corrective to the assumption of automatic progress, rather than a non-interventionist manifesto. The presumption is still that biotechnology is a good thing. Precaution is value laden. This is also illustrated by the Soil Association's view that making individual genetic changes at the molecular level changes the nature of nature, and cannot but lead to more risks than selective breeding.[16] To return to more natural methods takes us back to safer ground, less fraught with uncertainties and unsuspected dangers. The association's belief that nature is safer than GM technology is based more on the principle of the organic system, however, than of strict comparative evidence. This is problematical from a biblical viewpoint, where nature is at best ambiguous in beneficence. It is not something morally pure, pristine or even quasi-divine, to be touched minimally and with great fear lest we disturb its balance and it hits back at us. It is God's creation, and God calls humans to intervene and to an extent to change. Thus to present the escape of one GM pollen grain as something morally outrageous, whether or not it led to a serious environmental disruption, suggests a neo-pagan view, rather than a Christian one.

GM field trials present two views of precaution. For some these trials, despite their shortcomings, are a classic case of the precautionary principle, seeking to discover whether such risks are acceptable or serious enough to refrain. For others, precaution demands that even the smallest risk that the trial will itself cause environmental effects means that we should not do uncontained trials at all, and thus not have GM crops. This goes beyond the strict precautionary principle, because it takes no account of probability and treats the results as a foregone conclusion.

Many feel we have rushed into developing novel GM technologies whose far-reaching safety and environmental implications we do not sufficiently understand. There should

[16] Soil Association, *Contrasting the Use of Genetic Engineering in Medicine and Agriculture*, Soil Association Briefing Paper (Bristol: Soil Association, 1999).

thus be a moratorium while risks are reviewed in a wider frame of reference. A moratorium certainly represents a breathing space within which to get used to the idea of an unfamiliar and possibly threatening technology, and to assess at a more leisurely pace whether we want it or not. The value judgement is that such precaution is more important than pressing ahead to stake a claim in a competitive commercial market. This illustrates a problem. What benefits will be forgone in the meantime? There is a perceived urgency in medical genetics but not in agricultural GM because benefits are less clear. The Church of Scotland advocated a precautionary approach, but rejected a complete moratorium as too blunt an instrument. It recognised many current applications as misconceived, but a complete moratorium could unreasonably hold back GM uses that are not especially risky. It called for a focus on less risky and more obviously beneficial applications.[17]

A moratorium also needs to specify clearly what conditions need to be satisfied to make a decision, one way or the other, at the end of the relevant period. This offsets its potential for political abuse by groups opposed in principle to GM, whom no amount of data would ever satisfy. But in the nature of ecological or safety risks, at the end there could still be substantial uncertainty. Therefore at some point a value judgement will have to be made on inadequate data, and therefore to asking what, and whose, precaution is enough.

Conclusions – Risk and Reordering Nature

In the light of a theological analysis of risk, we should be cautious about accepting the picture of risk as presented by some perspectives in the GM food debate, either way. To reorder nature at the level of genes is to handle powerful forces, and this carries a heavy responsibility. A Christian view of risk recognises human finiteness, fallibility and the hubris, which can mislead those motivated by progress. Things can go wrong not only because of our calculations, but also in not even seeing the question. Commercial, scientific or other pressures can

---

[17] Church of Scotland, 'The Society, Religion and Technology Project Report on Genetically Modified Food', *Reports to the General Assembly and Deliverances of the General Assembly 1999*, 20/93–20/103, and Board of National Mission Deliverances 42–5, 20/4 (Edinburgh: Church of Scotland, 1999).

distort the broader perspective on risk so that the people involved may see only the outcomes they are looking for, or address only the risks that are convenient or affordable, and cross their fingers over the others. We should set more value in the longer future than the short term.

We must, however, challenge the view that any aspect of the new genetics must be rejected if it bears any finite environmental or health risks, because nothing in God's creation is risk free. We are justified in demanding that society avoids a particular risk if we have good reason to evaluate it as so catastrophic and so likely to occur that it is untenable. It may also be that the risks were so small that we were mistaken to have avoided them. A rigorous scientific risk assessment will take us some distance, provided it is independent enough to merit society's trust, but the final decision is based on a complex array of ethical and social factors.

It is argued that a theological understanding of risk in the human condition should make us think twice before saying GM crops in particular are inherently too risky. God calls humans to intervene in creation, despite the fact that our creativity involves risk and that we are finite and not omniscient. The notion of precaution needs to be seen in this perspective, and that of the risky nature of creation. It is misleading to interpret precaution with neo-pagan notions of a pristine or even divine nature. Our fallen state can incline us equally to presume we are in control when we were not, or to avoid risk when we should have had faith. A responsible stewardship of God's creation means that there will indeed be some genetic risks humans should not take. There are other occasions when it would have been unreasonable, at least on risk grounds, not to take them. Each must be worked out in its context. Such is part of the complexity of our calling to bear God's image.

8

Thinking about Biotechnology: Towards a Theory of Just Experimentation

Stephen R. L. Clark

The Background

I have recently been involved in three distinct working groups of governmental advisory bodies (the Banner Committee on the ethical implications of new technologies in the breeding of farm animals, a Farm Animal Welfare Council (FAWC) working group on the cloning of farm animals, and an Animal Procedures Committee working group on biotechnology). All three groups consulted widely, debated fiercely and reached some conclusions. So far two reports have been published, and their recommendations broadly accepted by government. What follows are my *own* thoughts on the matters discussed, and should not be taken to represent any committee view.

The Banner Principles

In the most recent consultation, a letter asking for advice about the likely impact of emergent technologies on the welfare of laboratory animals was sent to a considerable number of individuals and organisations. There were fewer replies from church bodies or philosophers than might have been expected. Most replies made familiar points, ranging from complaints about bureaucratic delays in the granting of licences under the Animal (Scientific Procedures) Act of 1986 to pleas to refuse all such licences in the future. The Banner Committee principles were widely accepted:

1. Harms of a certain degree and kind ought under no circumstances to be inflicted upon an animal.
2. Any harm to an animal, even if not absolutely impermissible, nonetheless requires justification, and must be outweighed by the good which is realistically sought in so treating it.
3. Any harm which is justified by the second principle ought, however, to be minimised as far as it is reasonably possible.[1]

Some commentators – though none of those who responded directly to the working group's letter – have argued against these rules, and against the long-standing principles of Replacement, Refinement and Reduction proposed by Russell and Burch,[2] urging that *all* bars on invasive experimentation be removed, on the plea either that animals have no moral weight at all, or that scientific experimentation is so important that no obstacles should be placed in the path of experimenters.[3] Others, in contrast, have argued that *no* invasive experimentation can be justified, on the plea that no sentient individual should be used merely as a means to the profit of another, supposedly superior class of individuals (a rule which would also prohibit the farming of such animals for their meat or milk). Both such extreme positions are, at the moment, favoured only by minorities.[4] The majority of the population, and of our correspondents, favour the *regulated use of animals for serious purposes*. Non-human animals have been protected, in law, since the early nineteenth century, and many formerly acceptable uses forbidden, but their use on or in farms,

---

[1] Ministry of Agriculture, Fisheries and Food, *Report of the Committee to Consider the Ethical Implications of Emerging Technologies in the Breeding of Farm Animals* (London: HMSO, 1995).

[2] W. M. S. Russell and R. L. Burch, *The Principles of Humane Experimental Technique* (London: Methuen, 1951): these were long supported by the Universities Federation for Animal Welfare, and are now embedded in Home Office practice.

[3] See, for example, Stuart Darbyshire, 'In Defence of Animal Experimentation' (http://www.informinc.co.uk/LM/LM115/LM115_Futures.html), originally published in *Living Marxism*, 115, November 1998.

[4] Both these camps agree that, in Darbyshire's words, 'animal researchers and their advocates cannot have it both ways. Professed concern for the welfare of laboratory animals is simply inconsistent with the reality of laboratory experiments that almost invariably result in distress and death for the animal. Medical research is not concerned with the welfare of animals and nor should it be: its aim is to get answers about diseases and problems that afflict humanity.' Our correspondents generally thought it possible to care about the animals' welfare while continuing to use them in ways that do them some harm.

racecourses, circuses, laboratories, zoos and domestic households has continued.

So the realistic questions for present-day practical politics concern the *nature* of those harms that should not be inflicted on any animal, and the *justification* for such harms as seem, in principle, excusable. Popular, professional and philosophical judgements vary widely. The most serious divisions between those identified as 'animal welfarists' and 'animal rightists' are that the former do not consider an animal's violent death an especially serious issue, nor do they give any weight to the need for an experimental subject to give 'informed consent' (or for that consent to be given on its behalf, with a view to its own good) if its use is to be justified. Few experimentalists would think it reasonable or right to operate on orphaned human neonates, on the excuse that such work would help other people, and that the neonate would of course be 'euthanised' at the first sign of distress. Some experimentalists have defended the use of human embryos (for example, to obtain stem cells), but few recommend that human beings be genetically engineered, at least in our present state of knowledge. Being *human* is still, for most people, to have a status utterly different from that accorded even to our closest relatives – but it is not clear what reasons can be given for the distinction now that 'species boundaries' are permeable. Animal welfarism is, so far, the compromise position (reckoning that animals can be killed, but should not be hurt unbearably, nor treated *only* as means). Some commentators – but not all – think that this approach may need to be modified to deal with the possibilities created by modern biotechnology.

Intrinsically Objectionable Procedures

The most obvious example of an 'intrinsically objectionable procedure' is that provided in the Animals (Scientific Procedures) Act 1986: experimental animals which are, in the judgement of the Home Office Inspector responsible for that laboratory, suffering severe or lasting pain must be killed, whether or not the experiment has been successfully concluded. That is, no individual animal should be required to bear severe or irremediable pain, and no experiment the object of which was to *produce* such pain (and track, perhaps, its course over several months) would be given a licence. Correspondingly, no licence should be given for the production of any genetically modified organism which could be *expected* to suffer such severe or lasting penalties. Since all genetic engineering is hit-and-miss, and the failure rate considerable, this *might* be held to exclude *all* such experiments. But most of the failures occur early on in the intra-uterine development of a genetically modified organism, and – so long as care is taken to watch out for the unexpected consequences of gene modification as they affect animal welfare – welfarists are likely to permit at any rate the modification of genetic sequences the function of which is already suspected. An absolute use of the precautionary principle (to forbid anything that has any likelihood of producing disastrous consequences for the animal thereby created) would slow scientific progress more than the majority opinion would allow.[5]

Correspondents, published articles, and the FAWC *Report on the Implications of Cloning for the Farming of Livestock*, also identified other intrinsic wrongs, in addition to severe or lasting pain. 'Anxiety, distaste or even revulsion, may be expressed about the 'unnatural' mixing of kinds – about creating chimeras, about altering the 'telos' of species (so as to interfere with a pig's 'pigness', for example), about crossing the species barrier, and about the mixing of genes between humans and other animals.'[6] The FAWC summary of what may be considered 'intrinsically objectionable' is as follows:

1. inflicting very severe or lasting pain on the animals concerned;
2. violating the integrity of a living being;
3. mixing of kinds to 'an extent which is unacceptable'; and
4. generating living beings whose sentience has been reduced to the extent that they may be considered mere instruments or artefacts.[7]

---

[5] So would any strict 'act-utilitarian' assessment of the justification for any *particular* invasive experiment: any such invasion is bound to impose some costs on the animal and is – statistically – very unlikely to lead to any substantial benefit: see Hugh LaFollette and Niall Shanks, *Brute Science: Dilemmas of Animal Experimentation* (London: Routledge, 1996).

[6] Boyd Group Draft Discussion Paper on *Genetic Engineering: Animal Welfare and Ethics*, 7, cited with the authors' permission.

[7] *Report on the Implications of Cloning for the Welfare of Farmed Livestock* (FAWC: December 1998), 4.

These are – perhaps – absolute wrongs, in the sense of Banner's First Law. At least they are reckoned *intrinsic* wrongs – wrongs in themselves, whether or not they have further drawbacks. The first is also an *absolute* wrong: no animal is to be used in such a way even if there might be a scientific advantage. The last three are less clearly specified: deciding whether they are to be regarded as *absolute* wrongs or only as *intrinsically undesirable acts* which might still be excused under particular circumstances, is more debatable. The notion that there are *intrinsic* wrongs other than the infliction of severe pain has sometimes been disputed, as though the only intrinsically bad thing is pain (and the only intrinsically good thing is pleasure). This doctrine has little to support it, and issues in counter-intuitive conclusions. Many supporters of animal experimentation, for example, point to the *intrinsic* value of scientific knowledge, irrespective of any further pleasures it may make possible or any pains it may alleviate, and to the *intrinsic* (indeed the *absolute*) wrongness of falsifying one's data. There seems no good reason to exclude the possibility that there are other intrinsic wrongs, like those listed above. But whether they are *absolute* wrongs is a question that can only be approached when we understand more clearly what they are, and what it is that is felt to be wrong about them.

The violation of a living being's integrity, or perhaps of its 'species-specific life', or its *telos* was identified by some correspondents in terms drawn from Bernard Rollin's development of an Aristotelian ethics.[8] Examples might include: dressing chimpanzees in flowery hats, making a dog walk on its hind legs, declawing cats, rearing monkeys with deliberately unresponsive or hostile imitation mothers, breeding animals that cannot mate or give birth without surgical assistance, creating hybrids or chimeras without a consistent 'biogram'. It is assumed, by those who identify this sort of harm (which can be, of course, of very different weights), that animals do indeed normally have a coherent biogram, an inherited pattern of growth and behaviour against which deviations can be tracked. The Fourth Freedom identified by the Brambell Committee (and since made central to much animal welfare

[8] See Bernard Rollin, *Animal Rights and Human Morality* (Buffalo, NY: Prometheus Books, 1981).

literature and legislation) is 'freedom to express normal behaviour'.[9] Whether an individual animal finds it *painful* to be so frustrated is not the only issue: the frustration is an objective wrong, whether it is an external constraint or a deliberate confusion of the genetic basis for normal behaviour.[10] Slight changes in the genome need not always make normal behaviour (which is not just 'usual' behaviour) of the ancestral kind impossible; major or exploratory changes may. The claim, widely supported, must be that such major changes should not be planned because they make it – at least – very unlikely that the animals will have any chance of 'flourishing according to their kind'.

Hybridisation may be disliked for just those reasons – but some correspondents expressed a particular concern about 'humanisation'. Although sheep engineered to secrete alpha-1-antitrypsin, or the recent (at the time of writing) clutch of pigs intended as eventual sources of xenotransplants,[11] may, technically, be 'humanised', in that they produce 'human' proteins rather than ovine or porcine equivalents, the true worry is about the production of creatures with overtly human properties – or conversely the production of human-born entities with 'animal' properties. It may be that these worries are for the future: genetic modification is not yet as fully developed as the dreams of its more extreme advocates, or the nightmares of its opponents, might suggest. It is also true that talk of 'human genes' may be misleading: there are no strands of DNA found only in the human genome, and the insertion or excision of DNA so as to replicate a human gene may not involve any actual transfer of human material, any more than it encourages the

---

[9] F. W. Rogers Brambell, *Report of the Technical Committee to Enquire into the Welfare of Animals Kept under Intensive Livestock Husbandry Systems* (London: HMSO, 1965). The other Five Freedoms are: (1) freedom from hunger and thirst, (2) freedom from discomfort, (3) freedom from pain, injury and disease, and (5) freedom from fear and distress.

[10] All objective wrongs are intrinsic wrongs; not all intrinsic wrongs are objective wrongs.

[11] Xenotransplants are unlikely to be given clinical trials for many more years: at present it seems that recipients of such organs – and their intimates – would have to be subjected to intolerable restraints to avoid infecting the population with porcine retroviruses. Our fear of such infections may stem partly from realistic assessments of the danger – but may also simply be the mode in which a deeper revulsion is expressed. 'Hygienic' categories are now widely used to give a respectable gloss to what would once have been obviously fear of 'pollution'.

expression of a *significantly* human feature. Polly is no more *human* than Dolly.[12] It may also be that many things which *could* be done never actually will be – even if the relevant authorities make no attempt to prevent them. But popular feeling is perhaps more realistic in suspecting that what *can* be done often *will* be done unless we take serious steps to make it much less likely. Once again: to know whether we should take those steps depends on trying to understand what would be objectionable about them.

The concern may be partly for the likely fate of such hybrids. One correspondent claimed that the use of non-human ova for the receipt of human nuclear DNA would make 'therapeutic cloning' ethically easier, apparently because any putative organism thus cloned into being could be regarded, without qualms, as a collection of spare parts whereas one cloned into a *human* ovum would have greater moral standing.[13] Others might reasonably *not* agree that humanity (and 'human rights') depends on the source only of the ovum. Demands that human – and primate – genomes should not be tinkered with are, in this context, understandable. But there may be a deeper repugnance at the thought of cross-breeds and half-human hybrids: the wrong may not be in how we would treat them if they did exist, but in their existing at all. They would be badly treated partly because many people would deny them any right to exist. 'Confusion of kinds' is something that many cultures and ages have deplored, even if – to our eyes – they were unduly rigid in identifying 'kinds'.[14]

---

[12] On which see the account of work done at the Roslin Institute, in Donald M. and Ann Bruce (eds), *Engineering Genesis: The Ethics of Genetic Engineering* (London: Earthscan, 1998). Both are cloned sheep, but only Polly is transgenic.

[13] In such 'therapeutic cloning' the object is not the production of a new individual, the sort-of-twin of the donor, but rather the production of particular organs which would not trigger an immune response in the donor.

[14] Paradoxically, the standard answer (that there are no such real *kinds*, but only varying populations of organisms between which genetic information flows) makes it still more difficult to insist that human beings are so radically different *in kind* from the non-human as to deserve wholly different treatment. 'Animal rightists' are actually less likely to be perturbed by the mere creation of hybrids, while still denying that we have any right to treat other animals as means. The main opposition to hybridisation probably comes from those who wish to maintain real boundaries between human and non-human.

The deliberate production of insentient 'artefacts' might even, as Rollin has pointed out,[15] have welfare advantages – but the usual response to the suggestion that we deliberately breed them is very strong disapproval. This is partly the same response as the one concerned with species-integrity. An animal thus decerebrated would have suffered an assault, even if it never guessed, and even if the assault was genetic rather than chemical or mechanical. Such a creature cannot live a decent life according to its kind, because it has been deprived of the ability to live that life. Other possible research projects might excite less disapproval: breeding or engineering sheep resistant to sheep scab, flystrike, lice and ticks, for example. That sort of alteration, it seems plausible to suggest, would actually make it *easier* for sheep to live a decent life – and without recourse to dangerous organo-phosphorous dips.[16] But once again, there may be a deeper repugnance: are *engineered* alterations, even ones that do the creatures *good*, always as acceptable as the familiar techniques of artificial selection?

Finally, several correspondents objected especially to the use of primates. It may be that what they chiefly had in mind were the Great Apes, but there may also be an issue about Old World or even New World Monkeys. There are at least three gradients of concern about non-human animals. First, they may be more or less 'historically involved' with us: on this gradient, horses, dogs and cats are of more concern to us than pigs or chimpanzees (other cultures may order the list differently, and place pigs well above pariah dogs). Second, they may be more or less closely *related* to us: chimpanzees are a great deal closer than dogs, and Old World Monkeys closer than New World Monkeys. Third, they may display more or less personality, or individual awareness: marmosets are probably more like mice than they are like macaques or baboons. All three gradients come into play in deciding on the justifications for particular procedures. At the time of writing, the UK Government has

---

[15] B. E. Rollin, *The Frankenstein Syndrome: Ethical and Social Issues in the Genetic Engineering of Animals* (Cambridge: Cambridge University Press, 1995), 172; cf. M. J. Reiss and R. Straughan, *Improving Nature? The Science and Ethics of Genetic Engineering* (Cambridge: Cambridge University Press, 1996), 183, 193. See M. C. Appleby, 'Tower of Babel: Variation in Ethical Approaches, Concepts of Welfare and Attitudes to Genetic Manipulation', *Animal Welfare*, 8, 1999, 381–90.

[16] Which are currently banned because of their very bad effect on *human* health, but with considerable damage to sheep.

already decreed that licences will not be issued for any invasive experimentation on any of the Great Apes. They cannot therefore be subjected to genetic experimentation, whatever the temptations, any more than members of our own particular hominoid species. Other primates are only to be used when no other animal species would be suitable, and particular care is to be taken to minimise distress and provide suitably enriched habitats. Whether macaques *really* need to be treated more carefully than dogs or pigs is uncertain: there is evidence that they are indeed social and intelligent creatures – but so are dogs and pigs. The probability is that we feel guiltier about using them simply because we know that we are primates too, or feel that identity more clearly than our identity as mammals or as higher vertebrates.

The Importance of Attitudes

The mere fact that people *are* troubled by what they see as violations of 'species-integrity' may be enough to identify this as a matter of concern.[17] The *benefits* of biotechnology are themselves identified by referring to widespread desires for improved health or safety: if people *also* wish to preserve the supposed integrity of animal kinds, this must be taken into account. This is true even if, as some have suggested, the notion of 'species-integrity' (and associated condemnation of genetic engineering, hybridisation and humanisation) is obscure or even unreasonable. Some forms of that belief may indeed be founded upon error (or at least on unfashionable or unscientific views about the nature of living creatures). But it is possible to see a different and more plausible foundation for public disapproval of such supposed 'violations': namely, the belief that *attitude* matters as well as outcomes. Maybe such actions do

---

[17] See P. Devlin, *The Enforcement of Morals* (Oxford: Oxford University Press, 1965), 17: 'I do not think that one can ignore disgust if it is deeply felt and not manufactured. Its presence is a good indication that the bounds of toleration are being reached. Not everything is to be tolerated. No society can exist without intolerance, indignation and disgust; they are the forces behind the moral law.' Some moralists have urged us to ignore disgust unless it is directed at identifiable 'harms', but it is not clear how those 'really objectionable' harms are in fact identified except by the force of indignation. Nor is it clear why people who have decided to tolerate *some* practices that they had hitherto found disgusting should also be expected to fund them.

not do *the individual animal* any harm at all – and yet are objectionable. Mainstream philosophical discussion of moral reasoning nowadays includes the agent's motives and characters as well as the nature or consequences of the act.[18] We judge what is done not only by the immediate or foreseeable outcome, but also by the motive and goal. In identifying an error in the *attitude* taken by some experimentalists (and others), we may note that the *wrongness* of some procedures may not lie in what is, straightforwardly, accomplished, but in what is intended, and how. The use of material from aborted human embryos does the dead embryo no further harm (and it is unlikely that the embryo was aborted simply to provide the material): but it is not obvious that we should applaud such uses, or relish a society in which this was common practice. Even if invasive experimentation can be allowed for what seem to be serious ends, we might still forbid it to be undertaken with an inappropriate motive (and so not license experimenters with those motives, or experiments that seem to embody the offensive attitude). Such motives might include:

1. doing it for fun – either to enjoy the exercise of a craft or to generate some sort of toy-organism;
2. doing it for purely commercial goals – for example, to provide leaner meat;
3. doing it just to earn a doctorate, or otherwise improve the experimenter's portfolio;
4. doing it for 'sentimental' reasons – for example, to retrieve a version of a supposedly 'much-loved pet', at whatever cost to other creatures of the kind.

In every case the proposed goal *might*, in itself, be acceptable under the Act, and yet the motivation of the experimenters or their patrons be inappropriate. This point is paralleled in standard Just War Theory. Even if a war has to be fought (for good and sufficient reason, having exhausted alternative courses of action, and with the approval of a legitimate authority), it must be fought only with appropriate means, when there is hope of a successful outcome, and *with the proper*

---

[18] See Michael A. Slote and Roger Crisp (eds), *Virtue Ethics* (Oxford: Clarendon Press, 1997) for a collection of recent papers on the subject. Virtue ethics provide a context for concerns about ways in which animals can be recognised as 'flourishing' and – as here – for concerns about motivation.

attitude. Even an originally 'just' cause is contaminated if the agents are moved by pride, hatred, boredom or blood-lust, and fight not to secure an honourable peace but to *destroy* or utterly humiliate their enemies. It is also contaminated if they use inappropriate or excessive means: aiming to kill civilians, or letting them perish through culpable inattention; using more lethal force even against combatants than is required to halt them. Once again, we condemn the *attitude* partly because it may so easily have bad effects, but also because it is itself deplorable.

This is not to say or suggest that laboratory scientists are any likelier to have such attitudes or temptations than anyone else: the discovery that any one did would be an immediate cause for dismissal in any decent institution. But overt sadism or active dislike of animals are not the only failings. Looking on an animal as no more than a *tool* or a *toy* or a 'mini-factory' or a 'bioreactor' is likely to lead to actions injuring that animal, but it may also constitute an intrinsic error of judgement and feeling. Some correspondents reckoned that animal experimentation always involved this faulty mindset – a claim made more plausible by the language of some other correspondents, who could find nothing else to say of biotechnological inventions than that they provided valuable new *tools* – that is, new sorts of animal – for scientific work. Thinking of other living creatures only as our tools, critics would say, is not only damaging to animals, but 'demeaning to humanity'. Others claim, also with some justice, that experimentalists and technicians are often very attached to their animals, and struggle to provide as good an environment as possible.[19] The general attitude of experimenters has certainly changed over the last few decades: training programmes and ethical review committees are as much symptoms of that change as a continuing cause of it. We should continue to require that those we trust to do, under the Act, what would otherwise be forbidden, do have the proper attitude to their task.

---

[19] Anti-sentimentalists hurriedly add that it is important that laboratory animals aren't 'stressed', and that gentle handling pays. Why we should need an *excuse* to be gentle is a serious question.

What Should be Forbidden

Just War Theory was devised, by moral theologians, diplomats and mercenary soldiers, to provide a framework within which decisions about the use and limits of military violence could be rationally debated. Some commentators have always held that the theory is only an excuse for something that cannot be justified. Others have argued that there should be no limits on available means to victory. Most people, however, have denied both that *victory* (even in a good cause) is all that matters and that military violence can always be avoided. Just Experimentation Theory (so to call it) may have to tread a similarly narrow path. On the one hand, some commentators reckon that the costs (to animals or to ourselves) are insignificant when placed against the intended benefits of invasive experimentation. On the other, some commentators think such intended benefits can never excuse the use of sentient beings as mere tools. The majority – at present – prefer (as above) a *regulated* use of animals, on condition that no single animal is required to endure severe or lasting pain, and that those who carry out the work display a proper *attitude* (both because this will lead to a greater concern for animal welfare, and because that attitude is intrinsically better).

It seems appropriate (and not unduly difficult) to forbid the following:

1. invasive experimentation on the genome or the persons of any of the Great Apes;
2. the creation of human–animal hybrids;
3. any work which can be expected to produce creatures who would suffer severe or lasting distress (including animals to be created as disease models unless there is clear evidence that the problems could be handled humanely);
4. the production at least of chimeras and of those hybrids which involve hybridisation outside closely related taxa;
5. the creation or reduplication of toys, favourite 'pets', or fashion accessories;
6. any work intended to strip organisms of their species-specific biograms, or render them incurably insentient;
7. any *unguided* genetic modification that runs ahead of reasonable guesses about the function of particular genes, and the chance of managing any damaging effects.

Many of these procedures, it may be said, are unlikely, in any case, to find backers or scientists interested in performing them. Alternatively (and inconsistently), if we forbid them in the UK, they will nonetheless be carried out in other countries. Neither claim is altogether convincing – any more than parallel arguments against banning or regulating child-labour, slavery and the free movement of capital. Public tolerance or support of animal experimentation of any kind, and especially of modern biotechnology, will not be secured merely by insisting on the *benefits* to be won. It also requires that experimentalists demonstrate that they themselves acknowledge real limits to their actions by proving that there are *some* things that they would not do, and that they share public respect for the individual animals in their charge.

Biotechnologists may reasonably say that many of our fears depend on fantasy. There is no immediate prospect of a world entirely without limits, where organisms can be produced at will with whatever properties are required, as mere tools. The problem is that unless we recognise and understand those fears, the fantasy may actually, in the end, be realised. When changes are distant and hardly imaginable it is too soon to take action to prevent them. When they are present realities it is far too late. We live in one of those rare moments when we can just imagine what might develop, and might perhaps avoid it. Let us place limits on what we are prepared to tolerate or fund, so as to preserve that proper attitude of love and respect for all things living.

Part III

Public Voices and Genetic Technologies

Introduction to Part III

The third section of this book engages in deeper sociological analysis of public attitudes to genetic technologies. The public do not have vested interests in drawing lines between what is acceptable or not, so might be expected to take a more open-minded approach to ethical issues in genetic engineering. In chapter 9 Mairi Levitt begins the discussion by her survey of young people from four European countries and a range of ability groupings. While some of the questionnaires asked for the religious affiliation of the children, this was not always included because of the fear that this might seem to be a church- or religious-sponsored survey. The use of genetic technology in human health programmes assumes that individuals will be able to make a choice as long as they receive the correct technical information in terms of risks and benefits. However, the discourses that surfaced in the children's responses showed a much richer variety of concerns other than simple risk/benefit analysis. There were, broadly, three different approaches adopted by different young people. The first was human-centred, in other words, the main concern was with the particular value to humans, and reflected a largely positive attitude to genetic engineering. The second was more naturalistic and combined interest in nature/God/biosphere, where nature was seen as having almost sacred qualities and a real concern was the abuse of that nature by human beings. It is of interest that there were approximately eight times more respondents in this second category. The third minority group (all male) took an indifferent attitude to the new technologies; it represented a laissez-faire approach where there was no concern either way with genetic engineering.

Another interesting aspect of Levitt's research was that it showed the real concern of many children that not enough was being done to look at alternative approaches to the problem. For example, what other measures could be taken to improve transplant rates, other than a 'technical fix' through xenotransplantation. Genetic engineering also threatened the variety and diversity of life, and this was more important than perfecting the species. Even those who took a more humanistic approach were concerned about issues of social responsibility and the need to set particular limits. Those in the second group believed that the future was far less certain and tended to be highly critical of the new technologies. While the responses of the children were not overtly religious, Levitt suggests that the kind of questions that children asked, such as the place of humans in the world, human nature and good and evil resonated with the concerns of theologians. In this respect her study complements the suggestion made in chapter 1 that there is an implicit public religious response.

In chapter 10 Bronislaw Szerszynski returns to the focus group discussions on agricultural biotechnology analysed in chapter 1, this time using them as the basis for a rather different analysis, suggesting provocatively that lay risk talk might be regarded as a post-traditional liturgy for the risk society. His argument first starts with a critical analysis of the contrasts often made between liturgical and everyday speech, presenting the latter as prosaic and narrowly referential. He points out that careful analysis shows that everyday conversation such as that occurring in focus groups can be seen as a collaborative interactive ritual that has many of the attributes displayed by liturgical language. Szerszynski goes on to set out more formally the nature of liturgy in the Christian tradition – formalised, collective acts of worship carried out repeatedly by a specific faith community. He acknowledges that a focus group discussion – an exchange of private opinions amongst an ad hoc group of strangers in a once-off, improvised conversation – seems far away from this definition of liturgy. However, he suggests that such a discussion *can* bear the weight of being analysed in liturgical terms, and when it does so it reveals much about the withdrawal of the transcendent in modern life, and the affinity between the contemporary spiritual desert with a theology emphasising divine mystery.

He then uses Ulrich Beck's analysis of the different qualitative nature of contemporary technological risks, and his argument for the increasing importance of non-knowledge in contemporary experience, to support the notion that the implicit theology of a risk society is one not of the *beautiful*, of order and *ratio*, but one of the *sublime*, of incalculability and ungraspability. Having made these connections between risk society, the sublime and negative theology such as that developed in *The Cloud of Unknowing*, he argues that lay risk talk as evidenced in the focus group discussions shows many of the characteristics that one would expect of a liturgy of the sublime – an analysis of utterances radically different to that proposed by Wynne in the next chapter, by which they are regarded as judgements about public institutions. He closes by focusing on a kind of utterance found repeatedly in the focus groups, the rhetorical question. By breaking down this category of utterance further and further, he settles on a specific kind of rhetorical question asked by the participants – one that expresses human solidarity under conditions of non-knowledge and 'organised irresponsibility', yet the almost impossibility of concerted action – as a key speech act of risk liturgy.

In chapter 11 Brian Wynne takes a different approach again to understanding public concerns, suggesting that there are not just opportunities but also dangers in the use of social scientific research methods to try to understand public responses to agricultural biotechnology. Drawing on examples from a number of major recent British and European studies, he argues that there is a growing consensus among social scientists about the nature of public concern, a consensus that he argues is preventing an adequate comprehension of what it is that the public are actually saying. He identifies four main assumptions made uncritically by these studies. First, the studies start from a position that 'it is only public concerns, and not institutional presumptions in favour of biotechnology, that are unthinkingly held and cry out for ethical reflection and rational scrutiny'. According to this assumption, the advance of biotechnology is naturalised as a kind of inevitable, desirable development, and public attitudes are constructed as a kind of barrier to such an advance. Wynne points out that the asymmetry in the treatment of expert and lay thinking means that deep-rooted assumptions in favour of biotechnology within scientific and regulatory cultures are not subjected to the same critical examination as the more cautious attitudes of the public. Secondly, Wynne argues, the studies assumed – assume, that is, rather than demonstrate – 'that the public is only concerned about specific consequences of biotechnology, rather than also about the wider consequences of the endemic institutional denial of uncertainty'. In contrast to Donald Bruce's claim in chapter 7 that the public are prone to make unrealistic demands of absolute safety in relation to technologies like GM, Wynne argues that in fact the public often appear more realistic than scientists and regulators about the limits of scientific knowledge in relation to the possible consequences of such technologies.

The third assumption that Wynne identifies in the studies is 'that cognitive content and emotional affect are not only categorically separable, but are in some sense mutually inimical'. Accordingly, it is assumed that the more that people are formally educated, and the more they are informed about the technical 'facts' of genetic manipulation, the more they will be able to rise above contextual factors such as the media, and above emotion, thus arriving at an informed acceptance of official assurances of acceptability. Such a framing invisibly reproduces the idea that the issue is fundamentally a scientific, technical one, rather than one about social relations, accountability and democratic control. Finally, Wynne identifies a fourth problematic assumption made by these studies – that any non-utilitarian objections that people may hold to crop biotechnology, such as worrying that scientists are 'playing God', or seeing the technology as involving an 'unnatural' interference with Nature, can be understood as private preferences held by individual consumers. This assumption, he suggests, delimits the significance of such worries, which ought not unreflectively to be seen simply as bilateral attitudes held by individual persons about individual technologies, but more the expression of '*social sensibilities*, about the ways in which dominant institutions are seen as exaggerating the adequacy of existing knowledge and obliterating fundamental questions about the quality of that knowledge itself' (p. 242). Through social scientific studies which uncritically reproduce – rather than empirically test – these assumptions, Wynne is saying, social institutions 'tacitly embody and project into society powerful models of the human as prescriptive potential ontologies of human relations, human subjects and social order (p. 248). He concludes with a call for the authors of studies such as those he discusses to recognise their own responsibility for making such a projection, and the need for wider public deliberation about the meaning-frame within which contemporary risk debates ought to be conducted.

9

'Just because we can do something doesn't mean we should': Young People's Responses to Biotechnology

Mairi Levitt

Introduction

Developments in biotechnology will have most impact on those still at school rather than today's adults. Research with teenagers has found that they have limited understanding of genetics and DNA technology, as do the general public.[1] However, at the same time it has been shown that when young people and adults are asked about particular applications of genetic technology they raise issues about their ethical, social and political and practical implications, and discuss them in a sophisticated way.[2] Detailed knowledge of genetics is not necessarily relevant to understanding the practical, ethical and social implications of, say, xenotransplantation or bringing up a

[1] R. Lock, C. Miles and S. Hughes, 'The Influence of Teaching on Knowledge and Attitudes in Biotechnology and Genetic Engineering Contexts', *School Science Review*, 76, 276, 1995, 47–59; M. Bauer, G. Gaskell and J. Durant, 'Europe Ambivalent on Biotechnology', *Nature*, 387, 1997, 345–7; J. Lewis, R. Driver, J. Leach and C. Wood-Robinson, *Understanding of Basic Genetics and DNA Technology*, Working Paper 2 (Leeds: CSSME, University of Leeds, 1997).

[2] J. Leach, J. Lewis, R. Driver and C. Wood-Robinson, *Opinions on and Attitudes towards Genetic Screening: A, Pre-Natal Screening (Cystic Fibrosis)*, Working Paper 5 (Leeds: CSSME, University of Leeds, 1996); The Wellcome Trust Medicine in Society Programme, *Public Perspectives on Human Cloning* (London: The Wellcome Trust, 1998). For a fuller account of young people's attitudes to the 'anti-obesity' gene, see M. Levitt, 'Natural Ways Are Better: Adolescents and the "Anti-Obesity" Gene', *Science and Engineering Ethics*, 3, 3, 1997, 305–15.

child with a genetic disorder. When the questions are set by experts the public will generally be judged to be 'ignorant': however, when asked to discuss the new genetics in a more open way the public can display a greater sophistication than the official and professional policy documents.[3] Unlike the experts the public do not have a vested interest in drawing a clear and simple line between acceptable and unacceptable research and practice. While Kerr, Cunningham-Burley and Amos found that geneticists distance modern genetics from past abuses which they define as 'bad science', the public recognises the existence of the large 'grey area' around research and practice.[4] This lack of certainty can be difficult for those with scientific and professional expertise who prefer to control the discussion around areas in which they have technical knowledge. Studies of genetics health professionals have found that doctors and counsellors tend to adopt a technical role when faced with the personal and social implications of a genetic test result or a genetic condition; for example, explaining the genetics of the condition rather than what it would be like to care for a child with that condition.[5] Similarly science teachers can be uncomfortable asking students to discuss social and ethical aspects of science because 'you don't know what they're going to say'.[6]

When 'non-experts' discuss applications of biotechnology they may stray outside the boundaries of a technical assessment of risk and safety and introduce issues or perspectives which experts see as irrelevant, subjective or idiosyncratic. A presentation of young people's views on biotechnology was

[3] A. Kerr, S. Cunningham-Burley and A. Amos, 'Drawing the Line: An Analysis of Lay People's Discussions about the New Genetics', *Public Understanding of Science*, 7, 1998, 113–33.
[4] A. Kerr, S. Cunningham-Burley and A. Amos, 'The New Genetics: Professionals' Boundaries', *Sociological Review*, 45, 1997, 279–303 (288); A. Kerr et al., 'Drawing the Line', 117.
[5] J. A. Smith, 'Beyond the Divide between Cognition and Discourse: Using Interpretative Phenomenological Analysis in Health Psychology', *Psychology and Health*, 11, 1996, 261–71; D. Layton, E. Jenkins, S. Macgill and A. Davey, *Inarticulate Science? Perspectives on the Public Understanding of Science and Some Implications for Science Education* (East Yorkshire: Studies in Education Ltd, 1993), 36–58.
[6] M. Ratcliffe, 'Teaching Ethical Aspects of Science: Evaluation of Case Studies' (unpublished paper). This paper evaluates the case studies published in P. Fullick and M. Ratcliffe (eds), *Teaching Ethical Aspects of Science* (Southampton: Bassett Press, 1996), 3.

greeted with the comment 'why ask young people about xenotransplantation when the health profession have already agreed that transplants will not begin until they are safe?' The obvious answer is because for the public, including young people, safety may not be the only or even the most important issue, and the question takes a human-centred view of the procedure which cannot be assumed to be universal.

This chapter focuses on the responses of 956 young people, aged eleven to eighteen, in five different countries to different applications of biotechnology. It was the language in which young people expressed their views and the ethical frameworks they employed that were of interest; for example, the invoking of moral categories: 'this goes too far'; 'we are playing God'); the weighing up of risks and benefits, and perceptions of the relationship between nature, animals and human beings. The research was carried out in 1996–7, before media interest (at the time of writing) in genetics, and many of the young people would have been assessed by scientists as ignorant about its applications. Nevertheless, it will be argued that many of their responses take a broader and more sophisticated understanding of risks and benefits than those of a traditional technical risk assessment while others rejected a simple consequentialist approach to ask deeper moral questions about human rights and duties in the area of biotechnology – thus corroborating the findings of the research reported by Deane-Drummond, Grove-White and Szerszynski in chapter 1 of the present book. The chapter examines young people's perspectives and considers the ways in which they understand their place in the world, their rights and responsibilities and the nature of moral authority.

Research Method

Young people's views were gathered as part of a one-year project funded by the European Commission to investigate ideas of risk and safety in relation to biotechnology, with particular reference to the ideas of young people.[7] Young

[7] The project report, containing material on the four European countries only, has been published by the E. C. R. Chadwick, M. Levitt, M. Whitelegg, H. Häyry, M. Häyry and J. Lunshof, *Cultural and Social Attitudes to Biotechnology: Analysis of the Arguments, with Special Reference to the Views of Young People* (European Commission: Directorate-General Science, Research and Development, EUR 18491 EN, 1998).

people were chosen as the decision-makers of the future who are growing up with biotechnology and who might have different approaches to thinking about risks and benefits than those who are currently adult. The research instrument was inevitably a questionnaire since the research involved four European countries, four languages and ten schools/colleges. All the questionnaire responses were translated into English and coded for consistency. The main part of the question-naire used stimulus passages on applications of biotechnology taken from UK newspapers and the *New Scientist* and rewritten to be accessible to the youngest children. The questions that followed each passage were mainly open-ended, asking 'what do you think?', 'should this research go on?', which allowed the young people to use their own words and give varying types of response according to age and ability. Two questions invited both drawn and written answers. General questions on attitudes to science and technology and to nature, sources of information on biotechnology and their trustworthiness, preceded the material on specific applications. In addition there were questions to gather basic information on age, sex, career plans, parental occupations and, where possible, religious practice. The question on religious practice was rejected in Germany as intrusive, and in Finland because it was felt that young people would assume the survey was sponsored by a church organisation and this could affect their answers. There was no correlation between those claiming to practise a religion (one-third overall, a fifth in Britain) and particular points of view, except in one instance. In Spain, practising Roman Catholics were much more enthu-siastic about using pig's hearts for human transplants than the rest of the sample, including those at a Roman Catholic school.

Project members in each country were asked to select two or three secondary schools covering rural and urban areas, including a selective and non-selective school if the system was not comprehensive. According to the child's reporting of father's occupations the sample was split fairly evenly between middle class, intermediate and working class with 10 per cent not employed, absent or retired. Overall, 26 per cent of mothers were not in employment. Teachers were asked to give out the questionnaires to one or two classes in the three age groups 11–12, 14–15 and 17–18 (post compulsory schooling in all countries, and so to some extent selective). Children of all abilities within mainstream education were included. In Britain this was achieved by using mixed-ability tutor groups in each school. Questionnaires were to be completed in lesson or tutorial time, but not in a science lesson or with a science teacher, so in practice all children present took part. Only around 1 per cent were discarded because they were largely incomplete. The sample of 956 young people is not claimed to be representative of the countries as a whole; nevertheless the sorts of country differences found in the literature were evident in the results. In particular, German children had a high level of concern about biotechnology and its dangers, and a high level of environmental awareness.

The questionnaire was administered without prior discussion and with the emphasis that 'there are no right or wrong answers. We want to know what you think.'[8] The introduction explained the term biotechnology using an adapted version of Macer's definition:

> Through biotechnology we can make or change living things. In agriculture, industry and medicine we can make use of living things; bacteria/microbes, plants, animals or parts of living things, a cell, to create new products.[9]

Some examples of applications were then listed. There was no mention of whether the procedures were either safe or risky but it was pointed out that they could be invisible. Before examining the young people's responses it is useful to consider expert discourses around genetic technology.

Professional and Expert Discourse in the New Genetics

The rhetoric surrounding the use of genetic technology in health is that of individual choice or consent from an informed position. It is the individual who has to decide whether to take part in a screening programme, particularly during pregnancy or when there is a family history of a disorder. Genetic counsellors have been trained in the

---

[8] The full questionnaire is in appendix 1 of the report, R. Chadwick et al., *Cultural and Social Attitudes to Biotechnology*, 133–40.

[9] D. Macer, *Shaping Genes* (New Zealand: Eubios Institute, 1990).

ideology of 'non-directiveness'.[10] Individuals can also choose to purchase an increasing number of over-the-counter and mail-order gene tests.[11] For those having genetic testing for themselves the relevant questions are seen to be on the lines of 'Should I take the test?' 'How will it affect my family, health or life insurance or employment?' 'What benefits could the result bring?' For pregnant women attention in the health education literature is focused on having a healthy baby and using tests to assess 'risk'. These questions centre on the individual and family, including unborn and even as yet unconceived children. Women in particular are expected to weigh up the risks and benefits of tests thereby taking personal responsibility for their health. However, the public have not necessarily confined themselves to these issues. Broader questions include where to draw the line in genetic testing, what constitutes 'normality' and suffering, how the availability of a test for a condition might affect those who have it and how far people can be said to make a choice when they are dependent on expert information and subject to social pressures.[12]

In the area of GM food the public were similarly expected to have individualistic concerns about choice and safety. The supermarket information about GM tomato purée assured the public about safety and explained the energy savings in production in California which allowed lower prices.[13] When the public debate became hostile and the biotechnology industry was accused of promoting GM for profits without consumer benefit the pro-GM lobby emphasised the benefits

[10] The standard view is that genetic counselling should be non-directive. D. Wertz and J. C. Fletcher, 'Attitudes of Genetic Counsellors: A Multinational Survey', *American Journal of Human Genetics*, 45, 1988, 592–600. Clarke provoked controversy when he argued that non-directiveness is 'inevitably a sham' in pre-natal counselling: A. Clarke, 'Is Non-Directive Genetic Counselling Possible?', *Lancet*, 338, 1991, 998–1001.

[11] Mail order genetic tests include those for cystic fibrosis carrier status and a paternity test. US-based websites offer tests for susceptibility genes for breast and ovarian cancer and for genetic predisposition to cardiovascular disease – see http://www.homeaccess.com/; http://www.myriad.com/gt.html.

[12] A. Kerr et al., 'Drawing the Line'.

[13] Safeway, *A Guide to Safeway Double Concentrated Tomato Purée Produced from Genetically Modified Tomatoes* (London: Safeway, undated, c.1997). As it is pointed out in D. Bruce and A. Bruce, *Engineering Genesis*, 176, if energy saving was the driving concern, local tomatoes would be preferable to those transported from California.

for poorer countries in terms of increased production and nutritionally enriched crops. The argument was that farmers in the Third World should be free to 'choose' to grow GM crops rather than have decisions made for them by the affluent countries. As the Nuffield report put it 'we should give more weight to the life-and-death concerns of the hungry, than to the less pressing concerns of the well-fed'.[14] An African plant geneticist made a similar point: 'You in Europe are entitled to your own opinion. But I think it is dangerous when you tell everyone else what to do.'[15] Non-individualistic concerns about long-term consequences and the effects on developing countries can be made to appear self-centred because of the exploitative relationships there have been between these countries and Western Europe.

Thus those promoting biotechnological applications prefer to centre the public debate around the technical assessment of risk and benefit in which they have expert knowledge and defend themselves from critics by saying it is the choice of patients or consumers to use the technology.[16] Attempts by the public to widen the debate can appear to be subjective and relying on anecdote as opposed to the apparently objective evidence of those with scientific and technical expertise. The young people drew on two main discourses, neither of which shared the individualistic rhetoric of genetics in health but one of which did share other human-centred concerns of risk and safety.

Discourses

Young people employed a variety of justifications for their answers rather than applying a consistent set of principles. Looking at the responses as a whole they drew on two main discourses; one was human centred and the other focused on something wider than the needs and wants of human beings;

---

[14] Nuffield Council on Bioethics, *Genetically Modified Crops: The Ethical and Social Issues* (London: Nuffield Foundation, 1999), 4.1. Available on their website: http://www.nuffield.org.

[15] F. Pearce, 'Opinion Interview: Feeding Africa', *New Scientist*, 2240, 27 May 2000, 40–3.

[16] I. Barns, 'Manufacturing Consensus: Reflections on the UK National Consensus Conference on Plant Biotechnology', *Science as Culture*, 5, 2, 1996, 119–216.

for example, on nature, God or the biosphere, which they endowed with sacred qualities and moral authority (in what is called here 'super/natural discourse'). The third perspective that emerged from the responses could be termed 'self-centred' and consisted of an indifferent attitude to the consequences of actions and to other people. Only a few of the young people thought of applications only in terms of individual or human choice without justifying it in some way; for example, by considering the benefits of the choice. Around 7 per cent, all male, consistently gave responses which could be termed self-centred or laissez-faire and displayed an indifferent attitude to the consequences of actions and to other people. For example, in response to the statement 'Human beings can use science and technology to do what they want', a boy from Finland answered, 'Why not? We can do anything we want and if we make a few mistakes, so what?'

The humanistic discourse manifested a confidence about the ability of human beings to exercise their knowledge and to use the power gained from science and technology; there was no need for anything extra or superhuman. Those who made room for the sacred emphasised the fragility of nature, the dangers of technology getting out of hand and the possibility that human beings would harm or even destroy the world. The difference between these two discourses can be seen in the contrast between:

> Scientists have invented more and more modernised and comput-erised ideas so we can do anything (girl, age 12, UK).

and

> the principle of 'we will do what we want' can destroy the world. Morals should come before science (boy, age 14, Finland).

In the super/natural discourse human beings are charac-terised as over-confident, careless, destructive and unwise in their use of science and technology:

> we might destroy important things without even noticing (girl, age 15, Finland).

> Human beings can't estimate today the danger which might arise tomorrow. Men may play God but they shouldn't. Tomorrow they may regret it (boy, age 18, Germany).

We are far too self-confident and have too much trust in our abilities to be given the right to conduct nuclear tests or genetic manipulation. We should not imagine that we have sufficient knowledge about anything at all (girl, age 18, Finland).

Only a few young people referred specifically to God as having rights and powers which human beings lacked; more imbued nature with sacred qualities, particularly when asked to describe 'something natural'.[17]

Something Natural

Students were asked to choose up to six adjectives from a list of twelve to describe nature and then to complete the sentence: 'I think something natural is ...' In the humanistic discourse there was an instrumental view of nature. Nature is there to be used by human beings. In all these quotations something natural is something which is unaltered by humans but only in the natural discourse is it equated with special qualities such as purity, perfection, goodness, as something to be valued and as wonderful.

Something natural is ... something that hasn't been touched by men yet, it comes from nature as it is (boy, age 16, Spain).

In the humanistic discourse people touch or use nature, whereas in the naturalistic discourse people tamper with and destroy natural things, they pollute and spoil nature:

Something natural is ... not interfered with by man's destructive hand. There are very few natural things left (boy, age 14, Spain).

Natural things have a sacred quality, which sets them apart from things made by humans:

Something natural is ... something true, the truth in life. Not superficial like society (girl, age 11, Spain).

Something natural is ... how it should be (girl, age 15, Finland).

The majority of young people gave a non-utilitarian view of nature in their answers but this did not mean that they were

[17] Russell argues that the countryside and nature have 'become one of the principal vehicles of the sacred' and 'imbued with a quasi-religious significance'. E. Bailey (ed.), *A Workbook in Popular Religion* (Dorchester: Partners Publications, 1986), 45.

opposed to specific biotechnological applications that could be seen as using nature for human benefit. Only 3 per cent of the sample wrote that something natural is for people to use whereas around a quarter imbued it with god-like qualities. Although when it came to specific applications young people would move between humanistic and naturalistic discourses depending on the case, most were opposed to an unfettered use of biotechnology.[18] The lack of correlation between reported religious practice in Spain, Britain and New Zealand and particular views on biotechnology has already been noted. However, this did not mean that young people were consistently secular in their responses.

More Than a Question of Risk and Benefit

At the moment, as is so often the case with technology, we seem to spend most of our time establishing what is technically possible, and then a little time trying to establish whether or not it is likely to be safe, without ever stopping to ask whether it is something we should be doing in the first place.

For this young German, innovations are technologically rather than ethically driven. The weighing up of risks and benefits was not always seen by young people as the relevant way to think about the issues; it depended on the application and the circumstances in which it was to be used. For example, when thinking about the idea of genetically modifying pig hearts to transplant into humans, weighing up the benefits to humans and the effects on pigs was one level of argument. There were at least four alternative ones. First, some questioned the use of biotechnology in this area and argued that more could be done to prevent heart disease through diet and exercise, and to increase the human organs available by improving the donor system and by more people carrying donor cards. Secondly, others wrote about the crossing of species boundaries and speculated about the effects without necessarily being able to label them as risks or benefits: 'What if the whole thing is developed so far that something happens to the pig; e.g. a thinking pig or something equally astonishing?' (girl, age 17,

---

[18] M. Levitt, 'Drawing Limits: Contemporary Views on Biotechnology', *Journal of Beliefs and Values*, 20, 1, 1999, 41–50.

Finland). Thirdly, some dismissed the further development of this technology because it relied on the implicit belief that humans are more important than pigs and have a right to use animals to benefit themselves:

> No!!!! It is not ethical and we should not have the right to engineer such things. Humans should not have the right to use their knowledge and genetically mutate other animals (girl, age 17, New Zealand).

> Pigs and any animals are part of nature and should not be taken advantage of. It is cruel to use them because they also have a life and do not want to lose it (boy, age 13, New Zealand).

One boy neatly reversed the situation to make his point:

> I think we should stop this because people wouldn't like it if we used a person's heart for a pig (girl, age 15, UK).

Fourthly, some went straight to the purpose of the technology, that is the prolonging of human life, and thought about the future:

> It is not good to prolong life so artificially using medicine. We can see the consequences. The earth is already overpopulated and already exploited to its limits. If we go on like this it will end in disaster (boy, age 18, Germany).

An 11-year-old put it more simply: 'people are meant to die otherwise there would be too many'. A Finnish girl brought in the common idea of a point at which genetic technology should stop:

> This research goes over a barrier, why do we want to live forever? Death is normal (girl, age 18, Finland).

In contrast, the biotechnology companies have, understandably, focused the debate on the shortage of organs for transplant and on safety, in particular the prospect of animal viruses being introduced to the human population. The desirability of prolonging human life is taken for granted.

Interests and Values

Tait, in her discussion of European regulations of GM crops, distinguishes between interest-based responses and responses based on 'fundamental values or ethical judgements'.[19] Both the humanistic and natural discourses made value-based arguments which were not simply to do with a personal or group interest. Only the small number of self-centred made comments on the lines of 'I do not need this application of biotechnology so further research should not be carried out'. However, the human-centred arguments could more often be countered by scientific or technical information or reforms to practice. A German boy recommended that 'a sort of commission should be installed to supervise and control all scientists dealing with these matters'. The technical conception of risk is designed to address concerns about safety, effectiveness and choice. In the technical view of risk 'the decision whether or not to re-engineer nature is one made by a rational exercise in balancing benefit against risk' in a 'cool, rational analysis of all the issues'.[20] Using this model Sir Ian Lloyd, who was the first chair of the Parliamentary Office of Science and Technology, could assert that 'ordinary people do not understand risk analysis and probability'.[21] In practice such an analysis focuses on the risks and benefits which can be calculated. Young people refer to unknowable risks, to incalculable effects, to concepts of 'balance' and 'a force outside ourselves', the need for variety and diversity rather than perfection. These are not open to 'cool, rational analysis' and calculation.

When young people were asked to advise a friend of their own age who was taking the 'anti-obesity' gene in order to lose weight, some of the concerns they identified could be countered by legal controls. For example, the concern that the technology should only be used to save life and not for cosmetic purposes could be addressed by the 'anti-obesity gene' being available only on prescription for the clinically obese. Other risks could not be addressed so easily. One was the risk of having an easy solution to a problem, in this case, controlling your own weight:

[19] Tait, *More Faust than Frankenstein: The European Debate about Risk Regulation for Genetically Modified Crops*, SUPRA Paper No. 6, (Edinburgh: University of Edinburgh, 1999), 6.

[20] 'The Green Man', editorial, *New Scientist*, 2240, 27 May, 2000, 3.

[21] I. Lloyd, 'The Tyranny of the L-shaped Curve', *Science and Public Affairs*, February 2000, 14–15.

If we had a solution to every problem our life would be less difficult and we wouldn't have the will to improve things and that would be a great loss to human beings' (boy, age 16, Spain).

For him the availability of a genetic solution would contribute to a weakening of our sense of social and ethical responsibility.

Another risk was that of the reduction of diversity among human beings. The friend was advised that s/he should resist the pressures to conform:

In this world there's everything and there should be everything (fat, thin, ugly, beautiful, intelligent, less intelligent) (boy, age 16, Spain).

This is the perfect case of a sad person who has been influenced by the stereotypical image projected by the media of the perfect body (boy, age 16, UK).

[I]t is an attempt on our freedom. As we start there, what other things could be manipulated genetically? We would end up being clones (boy, age 16, Spain).

All these young people used a humanistic discourse to raise ethical issues beyond a rational risk/benefit analysis. From a super/natural discourse a girl also argued that human beings should not use genetic technology to reduce diversity but wrote about a power outside ourselves which has given us the means of coping for ourselves:

You have been made by a power which wants you the way you are. You have a soul and energy in you. That's enough to deal with your problems. It does not matter whether you are fat or thin, disabled or healthy. We don't have the right to change our own organs just as we don't have the right to change others (girl, age 18, Germany).

Younger children, age 11–12, were found in the pilot study not to be interested in or not to understand the idea of a gene for slimming, so answered an alternative question on applying genetic modification to their favourite fruit or vegetable. They also raised issues that fell outside a risk/benefit analysis. For the following two 11-year-old children the safety of GM food or the effect on the environment was not the prime issue:

I don't think you should change fruit or vegetables because they don't need it, you should concentrate on the things that need changing.

A straight banana would fit in a lunch box. But God made bananas and he likes them like that.

The last child was unusual in explicitly mentioning God; most young people spontaneously brought in the idea that there should be limits to human action in the field of biotechnology. Like the focus groups described in *Uncertain World* the young people distinguished between different applications in terms of their use.[22] Thus over half supported xenotransplantation, whether unreservedly or 'even if I don't agree with it that much', because it saved human life, but most rejected the 'anti-obesity' gene where the alternatives were easier to find and it was not usually an irresolvable medical problem. When considering uses of biotechnology to clean up the environment most rejected it not because of concerns over safety but because there were simpler methods. When asked to think about something that needed cleaning up in their local area or somewhere they had visited, the most common problems were litter and polluted beaches and sea. Even though the example given in the question was of GM bacteria cleaning up oil on a beach, young people suggested that rather than use genetic technology people could pick up litter or not pollute in the first place and behaviour could be changed by regulations and fines.

Conclusion

When a controversial issue is to be discussed on radio or television the producers will want to know 'which side' each prospective speaker is on. Those who do not have a clear 'side' are unlikely to be invited to take part. In the area of GM, public educators still write about the need to simplify the issues for the public but this sample of young people had a more complex model of the issues than could be contained in a scientific risk/benefit analysis. Many of the schoolchildren were capable of considering the purpose, value and effects of different applications as well as placing them in context. Three-quarters of the sample argued that human beings should not use science and technology to do what they want, usually because of unforeseen

[22] R. Grove-White, P. Macnaghten, S. Mayer and B. Wynne *Uncertain World: Genetically Modified Organisms and Public Attitudes in Britain* (Lancaster: Centre for the Study of Environmental Change, Lancaster University, 1997).

consequences and/or a need for limits to be drawn on ethical grounds. The remainder either argued that science brought benefits which would make the world better in some way or that science is all powerful and cannot be stopped. Without a vested interest in drawing clear boundaries in which GM is either good or bad, they wrestled with the complexities in the 'grey' area. Thus those who agreed that 'human beings can use science to do what they want' did not necessarily agree with specific applications of genetic technology.

Long live science but it should watch where it goes (boy, age 16, Spain).

What do the young people's responses tell us about the way that they think about nature, technology and the sacred? In the super/natural discourse nature is sacred, in the Durkheimian sense of 'things set apart and forbidden' and endowed with special qualities. Young people using the super/natural discourse recognise the tensions between being human and considering nature as a whole, but when they make exceptions they feel uneasy about them: like the 11-year-old girl who wrote clearly that using pigs' organs for humans is wrong and then added 'but what if it was your mum'. In the humanistic discourse humans are supreme and there is no need to look beyond them. While the super/natural discourse is cautious the humanistic is confident; while the super/natural discourse sees humans as rash, overconfident of their abilities and irresponsible, the humanistic sees them as clever, capable and able to use science and technology for their own ends. Overall, one discourse has people in control of the world and their future:

With the high degree of technology anything is now possible and in later years more knowledge will make even greater things possible (boy, age 16, UK).

No one can tell us what to do (girl, age 11, New Zealand).

The other discourse recognises superhuman powers that may not be specifically located or may reside in nature, an ethical code or, less often, in a personal God. The recognition of these powers makes the future less certain and human responsibilities more extensive:

Everyone has to answer to someone (girl, age 18, UK).

Life cannot be controlled through technology (boy, age 14, Spain).

Those who used the humanistic discourse tended to sometimes slide into the self-centred one without a comment, whereas those who used the super/natural acknowledged that it was not always easy to maintain.

They [humans] can discover many things but they can't do as they please. Nature always comes first ...

[I]f we don't make a sacrifice we will destroy the Earth (girl, age 11, Spain).

The ideas of restraint and sacrifice do not come into the humanistic discourse which is 'in favour of what is best for man' (boy, age 16, Finland).

Young people in full-time education at the end of the twentieth century rarely refer overtly to their religion as a source of guidance on what should be done in relation to biotechnology. Only a handful mentioned their faith or God and only one mentioned Jesus when he wrote 'It is against what Jesus told us to do' (boy, age 14, Spain). However, when asked to think about biotechnology and its potential many more of them were asking theological questions about the place of humans in the world, their status and responsibilities, about human nature, good and evil. Their ability to step outside the conventional risk/benefit analysis and think about the wider implications of genetic technology for the world in which they live, bodes well for future public debate in this area.

Acknowledgements

I am grateful to the Commission of the European Communities for funding the BIOCULT project, which investigated cultural and social attitudes to biotechnology. I am also grateful to Professor Darryl Macer, Tsukuba University, Japan, who organised the use of the questionnaire with a sample of young people in New Zealand.

10

At Reason's End: The Inoperative Liturgy of Risk Society[1]

Bronislaw Szerszynski

Introduction

In this chapter I want to argue that lay speech about risk issues such as genetically modified organisms can be understood as an apophatic neo-liturgy of abandonment. In pursuing this argument I will draw once again on the nine focus groups that were held in late 1996 in the Lancaster study published as *Uncertain World*.[2] Although Deane-Drummond, Grove-White and myself have already used these focus groups as the basis of our analysis in chapter 1 of this volume, the approach I take in the present chapter is rather different. Rather than asking, 'what do people say about GMOs', I want to ask, 'what are people doing when they talk about GMOs?' Broadly speaking, the social scientific study of language can take one of two forms. The first takes its focus as the *content* of what is said, pursuing question such as: What words and phrases do people use when talking about this issue? How do they negotiate the different dilemmas involved? How do they talk about the actors involved? What does this tell us about how they frame and understand the

[1] I want to thank Greg Myers, Paul Fletcher, Karin Tusting and Peter Scott for extremely helpful comments on early drafts of this chapter, and Phil Macnaghten for permission to use the focus group transcripts.
[2] Nine focus groups were held in November and December of 1996. Four of these were held in North London, the other five in Lancashire. For more details, see R. Grove-White, P. Macnaghten, S. Mayer and B. Wynne, *Uncertain World: Genetically Modified Organisms, Food and Public Attitudes in Britain* (Lancaster: Centre for the Study of Environmental Change, Lancaster University, 1997).

issue? Alternatively, studies of language can choose to focus more on speaking as an *activity*, as part of social life. Such studies treat spoken language as a kind of action that takes place in certain social situations, and that serves particular social functions.[3] Taking this latter approach, I will argue that, when people talk in groups about risk issues such as genetic modification, their speech organises itself into liturgical expressions which thematise the self-undermining of instrumental reason and the irruption of the sublime in late modern experience.

Lay Speech as Eventful

In what way is focus group talk like or unlike liturgical language? To begin to address this quesion, I want to address a number of analyses that directly contrast ordinary, secular speech with liturgical language. My approach here draws on J. L. Austin's notion of speech acts and the performative dimension of language – the way that we use words not just to state facts but also to do things.[4] Austin developed this largely as a reaction against logical positivists such as A. J. Ayer, who insisted that for an utterance to be meaningful it must be capable of verification.[5] Austin pointed out that many sentences, which he called performatives, are not used in order to make statements which might be true or false, but actually to *do* things – naming, betting and so on. Such speech acts might have certain 'felicity conditions', without which the procedure cannot be said to have really taken place – such as the existence of such a conventional procedure, its correct execution in appropriate circumstances, and in some cases the having of appropriate feelings, intentions and follow-up behaviour – but they cannot really be said to be true or false in the way that statements can.[6]

---

[3] R. Bauman and J. Sherzer (eds), *Explorations in the Ethnography of Speaking* (London: Cambridge University Press, 1974); J. J. Gumperz and D. Hymes (eds), *Directions in Sociolinguistics: The Ethnography of Communication* (New York: Holt, Rinehart and Winston, 1972).

[4] J. L. Austin, *How to Do Things with Words* (Oxford: Oxford University Press, 1975); J. R. Searle, *Speech Acts: An Essay in the Philosophy of Language* (Cambridge: Cambridge University Press, 1969).

[5] A. J. Ayer, *Language, Truth and Logic* (London: Gollancz, 1936).

[6] Austin, *How to Do Things with Words*, 14–15.

Austin later abandoned his initial distinction between statements and performatives in a more general theory of
illocutionary force, in which statements themselves are seen as
a particular kind of performative. He did this by distinguishing:
(1) the *locutionary* act of uttering a given sentence; (2) the *illocutionary* act that the speaker is performing in using that locution
– for example, describing, offering, promising, naming; and
finally (3) the *perlocutionary* act that may be being attempted of
bringing about effects in the addressed party – persuading,
alarming and so on.[7]

Operative, eventful or serious speech, then, is speech that is
not 'just talk', speech in which things happen. The sort of
things that might happen in serious speech would typically be
changes in people's statuses, identities or relationships,
generally in ceremonial settings such as marriage, baptism and
excommunication. So would it be right to see our focus group
talk as serious speech of this kind? Nothing 'happens' in these
groups. It is hard to discern the creation of any new identities
or relationships, or any alteration in the status of present or
absent persons.[8] Is this because modern everyday speech has
been stripped of its performative power?

Both Northrop Frye and Catherine Pickstock suggest such a
diagnosis, arguing that modern speech has become dominated
by a narrowly descriptive understanding and usage of language.
Frye, following Giambattista Vico, argues that language has
passed through three main historical stages. The first, pre-
socratic stage he terms *hieroglyphic*. The dominant form taken by
language in this era was characterised by poetry and metaphor,
and by a quasi-magical belief in a connection between sign or
word and thing. Frye's second stage he terms the *hieratic*,
characterised by the use of continuous prose and logical
syllogism, the key trope being analogy or simile, as words are
taken to *stand* for things. Finally, in the modern period, we
move to what Frye calls *demotic* language – dominated by purely
descriptive statements. Frye suggests that this latter kind
of language always characterised the 'ordinary' language of
'vulgar' activities such as buying and selling, even in earlier

---

[7] Austin, *How to Do Things with Words*, 98–102.
[8] As Pickstock points out, from a secular point of view it is liturgical rather than
secular speech in which nothing really happens (C. Pickstock, *After Writing: On the
Liturgical Consummation of Philosophy* (Oxford: Blackwell, 1998), 244).

periods, but has only become culturally ascendant since the scientific revolution.[9]

Pickstock argues in a similar way that the modern era has seen a decline in a liturgical notion of language and meaning – an understanding of language as always grounded in the act of praise of the divine – and the rise of a form of discourse dominated by one kind of speech act, the unpoetic *constative* or statement of fact. Knowledge thus becomes conceived as a spatialised grid of names and statements in possession of seductive clarity and order. Nominalisations prevail, both in the form of the brute object, stripped of relational meaning, and in that of abstract nouns such as 'information', and 'the market'. The characteristic trope of this era is *asyndeton*, structured as a linear, informational sequence, a mere list of propositions, without linking explanatory conjunctions or reference to the responsibility of the speaking or writing subject.[10]

A rather different, extended attempt to contrast liturgical and secular speech is supplied in the work of Richard K. Fenn.[11] As his main example of modern, secular speech, Fenn uses 'seminar talk', as transcribed from an academic seminar. This kind of speech manifests a sharp separation between speakers and their utterances (through conventions of the neutral, objective voice), and an ostensive separation of different classes of speech act (with speakers making it clear, for example, when they are stating facts and when opinion; when they are making their own 'point' and when they are referring or assenting to someone else's).

While of great value, such accounts needlessly derogate ordinary speech. Frye neglects the Arendtian distinction between private and public – the instrumental, constative mode of accountancy and contract is characteristic of the realm of necessity, of meeting basic human needs, but not of the public sphere of politics, civic life and public interaction.[12] Pickstock, for her part, underestimates the differences between expert and lay discourses, exaggerating the extent to which a nominalised, constative style has spread from elite forms of

[9] N. Frye, *The Great Code: The Bible and Literature* (London: Ark, 1983).
[10] Pickstock, *After Writing.*
[11] R. K. Fenn, *Liturgies and Trials* (Oxford: Blackwell, 1982).
[12] H. Arendt, *The Human Condition* (Chicago: University of Chicago Press, 1958).

discourse such as natural science and accountancy to everyday speech. Finally, Fenn's analysis of secular speech is compromised by his use of academic seminar talk as his example of ordinary conversation.

In contrast to such accounts, ethnographic studies of spoken language tend to problematise any simple opposition between everyday conversation and either poetic or liturgical speech. For example, many studies have revealed the essential rhythmicity of everyday conversation.[13] Speakers have to grasp the underlying rhythm and shape of the conversation if they are to take part. In the following example, taken from another focus group study,[14] a group of women known to each other are asked why they get involved in local voluntary work (the symbol / is used to indicate simultaneous moments in overlapping speech).

Mod:	I mean, why don't you just not say, 'no', you know? I mean …
Woman 1:	But you can't because of the children.
Woman 2:	Yeah.
Woman 1:	Because they would lose out if there wasn't a / Playgroup, or a Toddlers / …
Woman 3:	/ Mmm … / or Cubs or / …
Woman 1:	/ or money to raise things / for the schools for computers and things.
Woman 3:	/ Mmm.
Woman 3:	Mmm.
Mod:	Yeah.
Woman 4:	If you won't do it then – and you've got children – who else is there to do it?

Conversations can best be understood as ensemble performances, where synchrony of speakers and hearers is achieved.[15] Conversations also use situational formulae, such as greetings and farewells, and manifest high levels of repetition, either

[13] See, for example, A. Kendon, R. M. Harris and M. R. Key (eds), *Organization of Behavior in Face-to-face Interaction* (The Hague: Mouton, 1975).

[14] *Global Citizenship and the Environment*, which was funded by the Economic and Social Research Council (ESRC), award number R000236768. For more about the project, see B. Szerszynski, J. Urry and G. Myers, 'Mediating Global Citizenship', in J. Smith (ed.), *The Daily Globe: Environmental Change, the Public and the Media* (London: Earthscan, 2000), 97–114.

[15] D. Tannen, *Talking Voices: Repetition, Dialogue, and Imagery in Conversational Discourse* (Cambridge: Cambridge University Press, 1989), 18–19.

exact or varied, of oneself or someone else.[16] This repetition can serve a number of functions: to help render a series of utterances into a unified discourse; to indicate that the speaker is a participant in the speech situation; to ratify an earlier speaker; to bound episodes.[17] Group talk such as that in focus groups often comes close to what Pickstock describes in her analysis of the Latin Rite – a gloriously ordered disordering of voices, roles and positions.

It is not insignificant that I am talking about focus group talk in this way, rather than talk that takes place in another kind of public forum, such as a public inquiry or a citizen's jury. The focus group as a 'speech situation' is halfway between everyday conversation and the kind of public debate theorised as deliberative democracy by writers such as Jürgen Habermas.[18] The focus groups analysed here, like most such groups, consist of people who are strangers to each other, discussing issues of public concern. Yet the focus group setting typically encourages what might be called 'thicker' discourse than the conventionally public forum. First, there is a sense in which it is clearly *not* public, but closed to the scrutiny of non-participants, and anonymised when transcribed. Secondly, whereas fora like citizen's juries are entrusted with delivering a verdict, of which some institutional body has agreed to take account, focus group talk is typically more like conversation than debate. As speech situations, focus groups are designed to encourage a stream of interaction where the aim is not to persuade or to agree, but simply to take up one's part in the flow of conversation.[19]

Of course, focus groups in this regard must also be divided. Some topics elicit little passion or 'heat'. The conventional use of focus groups in the market research context is designed to elicit inconsequential – but indirectly revealing – talk. But other focus groups are more 'charged' in their subject matter. Of such charged topics, some have been talked about greatly; conversations about these tend to follow the grooves of the commonplace. Others, such as those discussed here have not – they have remained latent for various reasons, and take

[16] Tannen, *Talking Voices*, 38–44.
[17] Tannen, *Talking Voices*, ch. 3.
[18] J. Habermas, *The Theory of Communicative Action*, Vol. 1, *Reason and the Rationalization of Society*, tr. Thomas McCarthy (London: Heinemann, 1984).
[19] M. Oakeshott, *Rationalism in Politics and Other Essays* (London: Methuen, 1962).

surprising routes as people struggle to verbalise inchoate feelings. Pleonasm is exhibited as people pass the topic one to another in collaborative conversation, as people struggle to construct fitting speech.

Lay Risk Talk as Liturgy

I have suggested, then, that writers who have dismissed lay speech as demotic and uneventful have done so without sufficient consideration of its actual character. Everyday conversation does indeed have the kind of qualities possessed by liturgical speech – poetry, rhythmicity, repetition, imitation of other speakers and so on. Focus group talk has those qualities of everyday conversation, and thus should be seen as a collaborative ritual, where meanings and speech acts are not just created *de novo* by participants, but are elements of a collective composition, within which participants take up shifting roles. But is this enough to make it reasonable to analyse focus group talk as 'liturgy'?

The word 'liturgy' derives from the Greek *leitourgos*, meaning public (*leitos*) work (*ergon*). In classical Greece it was used to refer to works performed for the public good. Greek translations of the Old Testament used the same word to describe the official services of priests and Levites, and from the New Testament onwards 'liturgy' was used within Christianity to refer to the prescribed, collective services of the Church, as contrasted with private devotion.[20] Geoffrey Wainwright distinguishes six 'registers' in liturgical language.[21] For our purposes, we can regard them as different classes of speech act, addressed to divine, saintly or human addressees. First and foremost, liturgy incorporates *adoration* – the praise of the divine, often performed through reference to the divine attributes.[22] Second, liturgy can contain acts of *thanksgiving*. These are related to adoration but differ by making reference to specific past (or

---

[20] G. Wainwright, *Doxology: The Praise of God in Worship, Doctrine and Life – A Systematic Theology* (London: Epworth Press, 1980), 8; G. Abbott-Smith, *A Manual Greek Lexicon of the New Testament* (Edinburgh: T&T Clark, 1937). I am grateful to Paul Fletcher for helping me with this derivation.

[21] G. Wainwright, 'The Language of Worship', in C. Jones, G. Wainwright, E. Yarnold and P. Bradshaw (eds), *The Study of Liturgy* (London: SPCK, 1992), 521–2.

[22] For Pickstock this is the central speech act not only of liturgy but also of language itself.

future) events or states of affairs for which thanks are expressed. Third, liturgy includes passages of *proclamation* or *kerygma*. Here the addressee is not God, as with the first two 'registers', but human beings, whether members or non-members of the faith community, to whom articles of faith are announced. Proclamation is not argument – no supporting clauses are given or deemed necessary; but neither is it mere statement, nor even a series of statements. By proclaiming their faith, Christians affirm and perform their membership of the faith community.[23]

Wainwright then highlights a number of speech acts that are future-oriented. Fourth, then, liturgy contains expressions of *expectation*, particularly organised around the Eucharist. Fifth, there are moments of *petition*, again mentioning specific historical events and states of affairs, but this time as a context for requests for intercession. Sixth, there are liturgical expressions of *commitment*, as members of the faith community bind themselves into future forms of action through acts of repentance.

There are a number of obvious objections to regarding the focus group talk about genetic engineering as liturgy. First, whereas liturgy is grounded in a community of faith, focus group talk typically takes place outside such a context. Liturgy's grounding in the life of a worshipping community and its authoritative myth ensures that the meaning of utterances are anchored. Within liturgy, there is no ambiguity about the kind of speech act being made. The same congregation meets week after week to perform the same patterns of speaking, and, by taking up the pre-determined roles within the ceremony, speakers and listeners are authorised and sanctioned. By contrast, focus groups are typically one-off assemblies of strangers who improvise their own collaborative speech anew every time.

Secondly, the *kind* of talk that goes on in focus groups is very different from that in conventional liturgy. Liturgy can be seen as that speech that we collectively enter into in a context where individual thought, opinion and speech fails, in the face of the absolute; focus group talk, by contrast, is characterised by the easy giving of individual opinion about mundane

[23] Pickstock, *After Writing*, 207.

affairs.[24] Liturgy is also characterised by eventful, serious speech, which affirms and establishes identities. By contrast, the shifting 'chatter' of focus group talk seems not operative or eventful. The secular speech of focus groups is relatively unsecured in its meaning, and rarely changes the situation of speaker and hearer, or even defines it in unambiguous ways.[25]

Thirdly, it is hard to find Wainwright's liturgical speech acts – praise, thanksgiving, proclamation, expectation, petition and commitment – in the talk of the participants. Depending on the topic being discussed, we may see statements proclaimed, and future events anticipated or promised, but these are likely to be individuals' private thoughts that have been shared, rather than a shared confession of faith or relationship to the future that is entered into by individuals. And where, in focus group talk, is the God that is praised, thanked or petitioned in liturgy?

In advancing the counterintuitive suggestion that we look at lay risk speech as a kind of liturgy, I am making a double claim.[26] First, I want to suggest that the inoperative speech of focus group talk is a fitting, post-traditional, liturgical expression of contemporary life – that its very inoperativeness is expressive of our current condition. At the end of the chapter I will qualify this theological defence of lay talk; for now, though, I want to present it in an unequivocal way. As Louis Dupré has argued, the felt absence of sacred significance in everyday life shades almost imperceptibly into an experience of God's utter transcendence. Modern existence thus lends support to a negative theology – one that emphasises divine mystery.[27] The spirituality of the desert thus moves from the margins to the centre of society, finding a natural home in the modern city. The 'work of the public' that is the shared talk of strangers

[24] One way of capturing this contrast is through Roy Rappaport's distinction between canonical and indexical rituals – see R. A. Rappaport, 'Veracity, Verity and *Verum* in Liturgy', *Studia Liturgica*, 23, 1, 1993, 35–50.

[25] Fenn, *Liturgies and Trials*, 85.

[26] Of course, if rather than arguing *for* one started *from* a position that saw liturgy as the ground of language (Pickstock, *After Writing*), the question would not be 'can it be shown that focus group talk is liturgy?', but one more like 'what traces of liturgy underpin the meaning of focus group talk?', or more specifically 'traces of *what* liturgy underpin the meaning of focus group talk?'.

[27] L. Dupré, 'Spiritual Life in a Secular Age', in M. Douglas and S. Tipton (eds), *Religion and America: Spiritual Life in a Secular Age* (Boston: Beacon Press, 1983), 3–13; cf. K. Flanagan, *Sociology and Liturgy: Re-Presentations of the Holy* (Houndmills, Basingstoke: Macmillan, 1991).

within focus groups is more than simply the mundane sharing of individual opinion or belief, but also a fitting – if not fulfilling – liturgical expression of this apophatic[28] experience of modern life. The descending moment in Christian experience, the condescension of God in the Incarnation, is attenuated to the edge of silence; the ascending moment, the capacity of the human mind to reach upwards to God, fails in its motion, returning to itself as its unwitting object in a parabolic fall.

Secondly, I want to make a more specific claim about focus group talk about *risk* – that living in an era pervaded by techno-logical risks such as those presented by genetic technology gives rise to certain patterns of speech, patterns which are best understood as elements of a neo-liturgy of a risk society, a sublime liturgy not of expectation and plenitude but of abandonment and the void. The next section of the chapter will set out this part of the argument in some detail, through a consideration of the work of the German sociologist Ulrich Beck.

Invisible Risks, Impossible Liturgy

Ulrich Beck first introduced the concept of 'risk society' in *Risikogesellschaft*, published in German in 1986 and in English as *Risk Society* in 1992.[29] Beck's thesis – developed in a host of other publications since, and much debated in wider society – is that contemporary technological risks have become the key organ-ising factor in contemporary society. Where earlier, industrial society was organised around the problem of the distribution of goods, in contemporary society the key question is that posed by the distribution and avoidance of risks or 'bads'. Whereas in times of scarcity the problem was that of hunger, with scarcity now largely replaced by risk, the main problem is that of fear. For Beck the effects of such risks stretch far beyond the physical realm; they impact on society (in terms of the capacity of the major institutions of society to proceed with business as usual), but also on the everyday lifeworld and human consciousness

---

[28] Apophatic theology is one of the three strands of Dionysius the Areopagite's mystical theology of the early fifth century. *Symbolic* theology regards the word as bearing divine meaning to us; *cataphatic* theology concerns the returning movement of giving praise to God; *apophatic* theology starts where both senses and concepts fail, and the mind is reduced to speechlessness, unknowing and submission to God.

[29] U. Beck, *Risk Society: Towards a New Modernity*, tr. Mark Ritter (London: Sage, 1992).

itself. Indeed, so pervasive are the effects of risk that Beck suggests we should see ourselves as living in a distinct kind of society, one that he calls a 'risk society'. Although it is far from Beck's project to speculate about the effects of risk on liturgy, it is this claim – that risk is such a central organising principle in contemporary society that perhaps no area of human experience is left unaltered – that gives us licence to ask such questions.

However, what complicates this picture further is that, for Beck, contemporary risks have a particular character, making them qualitatively distinct from those familiar to earlier forms of society, in a number of respects. First, because of techno-logical advances the potential impact of contemporary risks can be massive and widespread. The hazards generated by many technologies are potentially unlimited in space and time; the effects of global nuclear war, climate change, or the escape of nano- or genetic technologies, for example, could in theory be global in scale and catastrophically irreversible in nature, rendering compensation and remediation all but impossible. Contemporary risks can also be 'socially' unlimited, in that the capacity for sections of the population to avoid them either through geography or affluence are greatly reduced. This *quantitatively* different potential impact and pattern of distri-bution of contemporary risks, Beck argues, is itself sufficient to propel us into a *qualitatively* different order of risk, one where the cultural salience and meaning of risk takes a quite different character.

Secondly, our experience of contemporary risks is far more indirect than was the case with those of earlier epochs, reliant on processes of representation and mediation rather than on direct sense perception. Many potentially risky substances and processes, such as ionising radiation or modified genes, are invisible to the senses, and are only rendered visible through technical and scientific instruments, procedures and discourses. Many, such as those faced by distant environments like the Amazon rainforest or the Antarctic ice shelf, are for most of us only experienced indirectly, through the media. Even those risk effects which might be available to the senses, such as those of acid rain on native forests, can only be perceived as such when we are given a particular interpretative framework for the actual phenomena, such as brown leaves, that we can actually perceive. This mediated character of contemporary risks has a number of effects. It makes individuals more reliant on the representational practices of others, whether scientific experts, media organisations and professionals, or pressure groups. And it makes them more contested, as different evaluations of risk – made by industry, government, pressure groups – compete for social authority and legitimacy, with no higher court to arbitrate between them.

Thirdly, whereas responses to earlier risks were focused on knowledge, the management of contemporary risks is dominated by the task of coping with what Beck calls 'non-knowledge' – uncertainty, indeterminacy and ignorance. Many risks have an intrinsically probabilistic character, and are impossible to eliminate entirely, and all estimates of their magnitude and even their provenance are simply that. Such is the potential impact of contemporary risks that, combined with their mediated, contested nature, the insurance principle, so central to the birth of the modern era in mercantile capitalism, is rendered inoperative. Although contemporary risks like ionising radiation are predominantly anthropogenic, they are characteristically difficult or even impossible to attribute. Due to their mediated character, to their capacity to cross geographical boundaries, to their capacity to generate wholly unanticipated consequences, and above all to the complex scientific, technical, managerial and regulatory matrix in which their production and management is embedded (what Beck calls 'organised irres-ponsibility'), it becomes almost impossible to attribute responsibility or blame for many hazards and accidents.

If Beck is right – that we are now in a very different kind of society, one where power and agency clusters less around knowledge and more around non-knowledge – then perhaps a distinctive kind of theology could be seen as called for. A clue as to what the nature of this theology might be lies in the concept of the sublime. The culture of risk society is one where an aesthetic of beauty is displaced as the key ordering principle by an aesthetic of the sublime.[30] If the experience of the beautiful is characterised by proportion and harmony, that of the sublime is engendered by situations which exceed the

---

[30] S. Lash, 'Risk Culture', in B. Adam, U. Beck and J. van Loon (eds), *The Risk Society and Beyond: Critical Issues for Social Theory* (London: Sage, 2000), 47–62.

capacity of reason to find any proportion or harmony. Beauty has its *ratio*, whereas the incalculability of the sublime exceeds reason. The beautiful is homely, commodious to human dwelling, as if the thing of beauty was made for our pleasure and appreciation. By contrast, the sublime exceeds the human, our capacity to comprehend and absorb it into an ordered world. Risk society has an elective affinity with the aesthetic of the sublime, and through that with apophatic, negative theology. A theology of the sublime thus emphasises the absolute transcendence of God, approaching his utter absence.

If risk society implies a turn to a theology of the sublime, and thus deepening and radicalising what Dupré pointed out is industrial society's affinity with negative theology, what happens to liturgy under these conditions? Returning to Wainwright's six liturgical speech acts, we can see how a liturgy of the sublime affects each in turn. First, liturgical speech acts organised around propositional expressions of the faith are rendered dumb, as the emphasis moves from divine reason to divine omnipotence, and thus eludes the grasp of both reason and revelation. Praise, normally organised around the *cataphatic* listing of divine attributes, turns *apophatic*, focusing on what God is *not*. Proclamation, the confession of the truths that bind a faith community together, is replaced by a confession that no such truth can be secured; what we know is displaced by what we do *not* know.

Secondly, those speech acts bound most closely to historical events, thanks and expectation, are replaced by relief and dread. It might be thought that expectation in risk society would be that of apocalypse, and thus result in verbalised anticipation of a genetic catastrophe as yet unrealised; something to be predicted and anticipated. However, the domination of contemporary risk politics by *non*-knowledge tends to flatten out the timeframe of such speech acts. Prediction is rendered insecure by uncertainty, collapsing expectation talk into precautionary judgement on the present. Rather like the biblical prophets, then, speakers in risk society typically refrain from concrete predictions, rather using 'future talk' as a way of bringing out the urgent demands of and judgements on the present, even in the face of non-knowledge. The temporalities of risk society thus turn what might have been apocalyptic into prophetic talk, as in the case of the second male in the following extract, where participants have been asked to pick an image that captures the way they feel about the GM issue:[31]

Man 1:   Number 7 because time never stands still and it's the way forward.

Mod: This is the way forward, so this is what's going to be the future.

Man 1:   Yes, that's right.

Mod: And what do you think about that future, do you feel good, bad, happy, resigned?

Man 1:   Well, resigned really, I mean, go with it.

Mod: Go with it, OK. Yes, that's very good, OK. Who's going to go next?

Man 2:   I'll go for that one as well. Time is at hand.

Mod: Time is at hand?

Man 2:   Through the world yes.

Mod: So what does that say . . . ?

Man 2:   It's now, the time is now for the world to make a decision.

Mod: So it's not a resign thing, you need to make choices?

Man 2:   We need to make a choice.

Fathers, London

Third, and despite the seeming resolve of the above extract, the liturgical speech acts that are action oriented – petition and commitment – are characteristically replaced by speech acts of inaction. With classical liturgy, expressions of commitment turn ~~membership of the faith community into promises. In the litur~~gical setting we know what to do.[32] In the neo-liturgy of the sublime, by contrast, there is no formula for action. What is expressed is solidaristic *in*action. Apostrophic petition is replaced by a rhetorical question that fails to find its addressee and turns in on itself.

In the last section of this chapter I want to focus on this last move in order to illustrate the general negative theological

---

[31] On this distinction between prophecy and apocalyptic, see, for example, C. H. Dodd, *The Parables of the Kingdom* (Welwyn, Hertfordshire: Nisbet, 1961), and G. E. Ladd, *Jesus and the Kingdom: The Eschatology of Biblical Realism* (London: SPCK, 1966). In many ways, the presence of prophecy in focus group talk is the least contentious of the claims made in this chapter. As Fenn points out, a characteristic of prophetic talk is that it is serious, operative speech that has in some sense 'leaked out' from liturgical settings (*Liturgies and Trials*, 104).

[32] Cf. B. Szerszynski, 'On Knowing What to Do: Environmentalism and the Modern Problematic', in S. Lash, B. Szerszynski and B. Wynne (eds), *Risk, Environment and Modernity: Towards a New Ecology* (London: Sage, 1996), 104–37.

character of the liturgical speech of our focus group talk. A striking feature of the focus groups was the frequent use of rhetorical questions. According to the analysis of language offered by Fenn, such questions could be seen as examples of 'autistic' language. Fenn suggests that, at the extreme latter end of the spectrum of language between the liturgical and the secular, there are

> utterances for which there are not events either before, during or after their utterance. These are autistic utterances that do not require to be heard or read to be completed or valid. Nothing happens when they are spoken because nothing is intended to happen.[33]

Rhetorical questions, for which no answer is either required or expected, seem likely candidates for being classed as autistic, as 'mankind . . . speaking only to and for itself'. However, I want to suggest that despite – and indeed *because* – of their very muteness, such utterances are profoundly expressive of life in risk society, and form a core speech act of what I am calling the neo-liturgy of risk society. In order to understand this claim, it is necessary to distinguish between different kinds of rhetorical questions.

Unanswerable Questions, Uninhabitable Positions

Questions, as ethnographers of language point out, can have both instrumental and expressive uses. They can be used to seek information from the addressee, but they can also be used to communicate, and specifically to be expressive of wider cultural models that are being indirectly communicated to the addressee by the nature of the question.[34] The rhetorical question, a question that is not to be answered, is clearly not instrumental in this sense, since it cannot be used to gain knowledge. But if it is expressive, what does it express? In order to answer this question, we will first have to distinguish between

---

[33] Fenn, *Liturgies and Trials*, 90.
[34] See, for example, J. M. Roberts and M. J. Forman, 'Riddles: Expressive Models of Interrogation', in J. J. Gumperz and D. Hymes (eds), *Directions in Sociolinguistics: The Ethnography of Communication* (New York: Holt, Rinehart and Winston, 1972), 180–209.

two kinds of rhetorical questions, which I want to term positive and negative.

The conventional rhetorical question is one that does not expect a reply because it is assumed that both the speaker and the addressee already know the answer. The question is used to express and affirm the shared knowledge and understanding of the situation, and to mark this sharedness out as relevant. This I want to refer to as a 'positive rhetorical question'. The negative rhetorical question, by contrast, is an expressive question that does not expect a reply because it is taken for granted that *neither* the speaker nor the addressee knows the answer.

But the negative rhetorical question itself can be seen as having two variants, depending on whether it is implied that the question *can* be answered or not. The *relative* negative rhetorical question is one that is used to point out that, while speaker and addressee do not know the answer, someone else probably does. What is being communicated and performed here is the existence of social boundaries between those who know and those who do not. There were many examples of these in the focus group discussions about genetically modified food:

Man: I'd want them to say what they're up to really with that. I mean, why do they want to change it in the first place? I'd want to know what's behind it.

                                                              Fathers, London

Woman: It still doesn't say why they're modifying the yeast, why can't they use yeast? What are they doing to the yeast?
                                                      Working Mothers, London

Man: I do have definite reservations about that. What are they messing around with? What are they doing with it? What are they adding?

                                                              Fathers, London

The above questioners seem to assume that no one present can answer their questions. But at the same time they seem to assume – or, one might say, hope – that someone somewhere *can* answer them. The condition they thus express is one of secrecy and unaccountability, and thus one of a lack of solidarity, of a polity divided into agents with knowledge and patients without.

With what I want to call *absolute* negative rhetorical questions, however, we move more deeply into what I am suggesting is the neo-liturgy of risk society. The assumption being communicated by questioners such as the woman quoted below seems rather to be that *no one* could answer her question:

> F: Maybe if you can give like some, if you can do it and it's going to improve and you can give cold hard evidence that it's not going to harm you, there's no funny drugs been put in it, there's nothing that's going to cause some disease or something twenty years down the line, then yeah. But how can they ... how can they say what's going to happen twenty years down the line?
>
> Mod: And how can they say that?
>
> F: Well, they can't, can they?
>
> Working Women, Lancashire

'How can they say what's going to happen twenty years down the line?' The moderator tries to turn the question back to the speaker, to force her to answer it. Instead, she insists on its unanswerability; at the same time, she almost chides the moderator for misrecognising her speech act: 'Well, they can't, can they?' Rather than being expressive of social boundaries between knowledge and ignorance, the first question is an expression of social solidarity under conditions of *agnosis*, of non-knowledge. The ignorance being thematised here is not relative to social position, but made absolute by the epistemological conditions predominating in risk society. None of us can ever know. Human beings are once again all in the same boat: that of uncertainty. In an era of organised irresponsibility, there are no social actors who, whether of goodwill or ill will, can really know.

The neo-liturgy of risk, then, is universal. It thematises the common fate of those inhabiting the risk society, a fate of *agnosis*. But while this is a liturgy which is expressive of solidarity, this is solidarity of a very particular kind. While solidaristic discourse usually points to particular courses of action, this is one that presumes and expresses the *impossibility* of grounded action. Even the boundary-performing discourse of the relative negative rhetorical question presumes some possible action, some desired state of affairs other than that which is currently the case. To ask, 'what are they doing to the yeast?' is to express a desire for the sharing of knowledge, openness and transparency. But as we move to the absolute negative rhetorical question, and we enter into the domain of agnosis, what is being expressed is our common fate. We have moved from the theology of the beautiful to that of the sublime – from the possibility of order and desired harmony to that of the irrational, the ungraspable, the scatteredness of being in risk society. Modernity offered the promise of a securing of language outside liturgy, through the notion of its referentiality to a world of objects.[35] Knowledge became conceived not as temporal and performed, but as a timeless, spatialised grid of true propositions. With risk society, the promise of being held firm by that grid has been resoundingly shaken. What we perform in our speech with others becomes our incapacity to know what to do.

Conclusion

I have argued here for an approach to lay talk about risk issues such as genetic modification that treats it as liturgical speech. In order to defend this approach, and at the same time better to understand what this talk, when treated as liturgy, then reveals about our contemporary spiritual predicament, I made a number of steps. First, whereas many scholars have argued that the everyday speech of the modern era is resolutely secular and deracinated, in stark contrast to liturgy's rhetorical richness, I pointed out that studies of everyday spoken language have revealed it to be a richly poetic, collaborative ritual. Secondly, I argued that the very 'inoperative' character of focus group talk, rather than disqualifying it as liturgy, is liturgically expressive of the withdrawal of the transcendent from modern life. Thirdly, I suggested that the self-exceeding of modern reason through technologies such as genetic modification radicalises this emphasis on a negative theology of the sublime, so that the collaborative exploration of contemporary risk issues produces liturgical formulae that are expressive of the cultural character of 'risk society'. Just as liturgy normally secures the stability of meaning and intention, the very instability of meaning in risk society produces a certain kind of liturgy.

But it is not my intention to imply that the inoperative speech of public risk talk is the *only* liturgy possible in our time. The

---

[35] Szerszynski, 'On Knowing What to Do'.

exhaustion of modern reason which risk society represents does indeed threaten to jettison us into a void of unknowing, the void against which reason insisted it was the only bulwark. If this was the only reading of reason's end, then an inoperative liturgy that could never reach beyond itself to – or itself be reached by – a transcendent ground would indeed be all we could hope for. And yet this empty void was always a fiction, a 'back-projection' of modern reason itself, a consequence of its insistence that knowledge consisted in and only in reference between words and things. Ironically, the modern attempt to erase the sublime from both language and experience has resulted in its very intensification, in the form of the empty void that is all that seems to be left when reason overreaches itself and stutters to a halt. Risk society is thus the return and revenge on human hubris not of nature but of the sublime.

Our focus group talk may not give us the shape of a viable liturgy, but it points towards its possibility. The shrinking back of reason's hubris creates an opening for a renewed sense of the divine. Sublimity, experienced in the limitedness of creaturely, human capacities before the limitlessness of God, can serve as an opening for the experience of transcendence. The sublime can thus be an event through which a sense of God, the very ground of the beautiful, is made possible.[36] The temptation for religious institutions faced by issues such as the genetic modification of food is to mimic the regulatory institutions by denying uncertainty and non-knowledge, by insisting that technical *or* ethical reason can still know and measure the consequences of such technological interventions, and thus silence the sublime. The public voices quoted here insist that we should not be led into this temptation.

---

[36] J. Milbank, 'Sublimity: The Modern Transcendent', in Paul Heelas (ed.), *Religion, Modernity and Postmodernity* (Oxford: Blackwell, 1998), 258–84.

11

Interpreting Public Concerns about GMOs – Questions of Meaning[1]

Brian Wynne

Introduction

In the fevered public policy controversy over the acceptability of commercialised genetically manipulated (GM) crops and foods, public attitudes towards the technology and its risks have become a focus of intense interest. The nature and causes of those attitudes have been extensively examined and judged by a huge variety of social scientists, government officials, scientists, industrial analysts, consultants and media commentators. This general activity has involved the creation of representations of the public, resulting from the way in which the nature and causes of their attitudes and concerns have been described. This has formed part of a cluster of public policy questions: Is the widespread public opposition justifiable? On what factors is it based, and how might these be addressed by governments,

[1] I would like to thank all my colleagues in the EU PABE project for their invaluable contributions to the sustained intellectual discussions that informed both the project and my thinking on this chapter. Earlier versions greatly benefited from presentation and discussion at the Society for the Social Studies of Science (4S) and European Association for the Study of Science and Technology (EASST) joint annual meeting in Vienna, September 2000. They also benefited from seminars at *Politeia*, Milan, October 2000, and the University of Trieste, October 2000. The further inputs of Ulrike Felt, Tina Thiel, Sheila Jasanoff, Ruth Chadwick, Robin Grove-White and Sarah Franklin were especially helpful. Any remaining problems are of course my own responsibility. An earlier version appeared as B. Wynne, 'Expert Discourses of Risk and Ethics on Genetically Manipulated Organisms: The Weaving of Public Alienation', *Politeia*, 17, 62, 2001, 51–76.

scientific bodies and industrial innovators? Nearly all of these actors continue to share the absolutely firm conviction that GM crops and foods are of immense social value and remain a vital innovation that should be established without undue delay. Indeed, these claimed benefits are often asserted by scientists to be as much a part of the factual domain over which science claims sovereignty as are questions of risk.[2]

Social scientific representations of 'the public', its multiple forms of reasoning and its ways of shaping reactions to such innovations have thus become an important public-policy actor. I wish to suggest, however, that this knowledge and its tacit, largely unexamined assumptions play a fundamentally different – and more problematic – policy role from that which is conventionally understood.

It was widely accepted that a major factor in the UK public rejection of GMOs in the late 1990s was public perception (influenced by others, of course) of the inadequacy of regulatory frameworks – in particular the narrow reductionism of institutionalised risk assessment. This led to significant changes in the UK regulatory framework when in late 1999 and early 2000 two new government 'super-committees' were established, the Human Genetics Commission, HGC, and the Agriculture and Environment Biotechnology Commission, AEBC. The hope and expectation of policy authorities was that these changes would change public perceptions for the better by alleviating their concerns that existing regulations did not provide adequate safeguards, did not address all the relevant questions, and did not reflect broader inputs.

In this sense the mainly social-science-generated *intellectual* representations of the public have also become important forms of *political* representation. They are much more than merely academic constructs and questions. Thus it becomes even more important to examine how these understandings of the public and its concerns about GMOs are themselves understood by their authors, communicators and users – and perhaps also by those they are supposed to represent. Just as it has been

---

[2] See, for example, the statement by Patrick Bateson, Vice-President of the London Royal Society, 9 June 2002, about the genetic manipulation of animals, reported in the British press, 10 June 2002.

argued, for example by the new AEBC,[3] that *the quality of environmental scientific knowledge* in the GM crops issue should be more of a subject of explicit public examination and debate so it can also be argued that there is a need for explicit reflection and open deliberation about the quality of those social-scientific and related representations of the public which constitute part of the taken-for-granted culture of modern policy. Here it is important to recognise that in addition to the explicit representations of public perceptions provided by social science, there are significant *implicit* representations of public perceptions and concerns informing scientific and policy discourses of the issues. For example, the common use of the term 'risk perceptions' (and also the form of the title to this chapter) to describe public perceptions and responses repro-duces the taken-for-granted assumption that the object of public attention is indeed either 'risk' (as defined by insti-tutional science in this field) or 'GMOs' (implying the exclusion of the institutions involved) and nothing else.

In this chapter I offer some reflections on these questions of how we understand both public responses themselves, and our own understandings of them. Moreover I want to explore the subtle ways in which apparently innocent and corrigible *representation* becomes *performative* in a normative and human-ontological sense. With this in mind I focus particularly on the rise of ethical discourses in this field and their relationships with the longer-established discourses of risk. I suggest that the construction and projection of these ethical discourses, as representations of the public in the public policy domain, embody tacit representations of three related key aspects:

• the intrinsic meaning of 'the issue' – the object(s) of concern and attention;
• the quality of prevailing scientific risk knowledge;
• and the public, its meanings, concerns and its forms of judgement.

It is important to underline that the implicit representations which I try to identify and discuss here are not held and disseminated in the form of explicit hypotheses. They are distinctly *cultural* assumptions embodied implicitly and thus

---

[3] AEBC, *Crops on Trial* (London: Department for Agriculture, Food and Rural Affairs, September 2001).

unquestioningly in the existing institutional routine habits of thought, assumptions and commitments. As such I argue they are often exercised without even conscious awareness on the part of their practitioners. Therefore, from within this culture, they are unable to imagine that negative public responses supposedly to GMOs as technically defined may in fact be negative responses to this self-referential institutional culture and its normative projections of the human. I suggest these unspoken cultural presumptions are of crucial significance in the public domain, not only because they generate negative public reactions 'to GMOs' but also because they betray a deep and more general default of democratic principles of accountable human represen- tation in late modern democratic culture.

The intellectual disciplines of the humanities and social sciences are being challenged to provide better resources for the public task of rendering this culture more overt and reflexive, thus more accountable and more adequate as a public culture of human representation, including its instrumental dimensions.

Public Concerns – Emotions Versus Intellect?

Public concerns about the handling of new technologies like GMOs have occasioned influential recognition of a crisis of public confidence in science in late modern society.[4] The long- held belief on the part of promoters of such technologies that the public's unwillingness to comply with scientific prescrip- tions is due to public ignorance and media irresponsibility has been falsified by copious evidence and experience.[5] This is not to say that these unfortunate conditions do not exist, but to say

[4] U. Beck, *Risk Society: Towards a New Morality* (London: Sage, 1992); House of Lords, Select Committee on Science and Technology, *Science and Society* (London: HMSO, March 2000); Commission of the European Communities, *Science and Governance* (Brussels: 2001).

[5] E.g., S. Martin and J. Tait, *Public Perceptions of Genetically Modified Organisms* (London: Department of Trade and Industry, 1992); EPCAG (European Public and Concerted Action Group: (J. Durant, coordinator), 'Europe Ambivalent on Biotechnology', *Nature*, 387, 26 June 1997, 845–7; R. Grove-White, P. Macnaghten, S. Mayer and B. Wynne (eds), *Uncertain World: Genetically Modified Organisms, Food and Public Attitudes in Britain* (Lancaster: Centre for the Study of Environmental Change, Lancaster University, 1997); Eurobarometer, 'The Europeans and Biotechnology', report by INRA(Europe)-ECOSA, for EU, DG Research, Brussels, 15 March 2000; PABE, *Public Attitudes towards Agricultural Biotechnologies in Europe*, final report of project with five partner country teams

that they do not play the role assigned to them. A key argument against such beliefs has been that sceptical public reactions are not reactions to (supposedly misperceived) risks as such, nor to media representations of these, but reflect public judgements of dominant scientific and policy institutions and their behaviours, including their (mis)representations of the public.[6]

This alternative understanding of the basic forces and responsibilities underlying public responses recognises that they have (of course, always fallible and arguable) intellectual substance, but an intellectual substance which does not even correspond with institutional expert categories, which goes much deeper than simply 'disagreeing with' or 'rejecting' expert views. Conventional approaches, in contrast, reproduce long-standing, deeply cultural presumptions of a categorical divide between factual, objective and real knowledge on the one hand and cognitively empty emotion or values on the other, and assume that, while science looks after the former, lay publics are only capable of taking sentimental, emotional and intellectually vacuous positions. This basic structure was evinced by the statement of UK Prime Minister Blair[7] in a high-profile speech at the London Royal Society in May 2002, in which he demanded that protesters destroying the controversial GM crop-trials should allow 'the facts' to be revealed by observations first, and only then to allow judgement and values into play once open to discipline by the revealed facts.

According to this modern cultural world-view, therefore, insofar as the lay public does get on proper terms with rational scientific views, this results from recognising its proper dependency on and trust in science. This general approach is expressed in the phrase of a team of leading social scientists of biotechnology risk perceptions that 'trust is a functional

(Spain, Italy, Germany, France and UK), funded by EU, DG Research, Brussels, December 2000, coordinated by B. Wynne and P. Simmons, Centre for the Study of Environmental Change, CSEC, Lancaster University – also in special issue of *Politeia*, 16, 60, 3–29. The PABE final report is published on the web at: www.pabe.com.

[6] B. Wynne, 'Risk, Technology and Trust: On the Social Treatment of Uncertainty', in J. Conrad (ed.), *Society, Technology and Risk* (London: Arnold, 1980), 83–117; B. Wynne, 'Frameworks of Rationality in Risk Management: Towards the Testing of Naïve Sociology', in J. Brown (ed.), *Environmental Threats* (London: Frances Pinter, 1989), 93–110.

[7] Rt Hon. T. Blair, UK Prime Minister, speech at the London Royal Society, 6 June 2002.

substitute for knowledge',[8] which suggests that trust or mistrust is not even an issue when adequate knowledge prevails, since knowledge preempts the very need for trust, or mistrust. This therefore implies that mistrust and opposition must be founded on ignorance.

The idea that public responses to modern technologies and their risks are founded essentially on emotion not intellectual substance originated in the 1960s and 1970s with the first significant modern forms of public opposition, in the nuclear controversy. Research in the social sciences was funded on a major scale at this time in order to explain why it was that the public responded so 'irrationally' to the objective risks of nuclear power which were, in existing scientific terms, demonstrably lower than various risks accepted in everyday life. The psychometrics programme of Fischoff, Slovic and colleagues[9] that developed during this early period became the dominant perspective on the perception of risk by the public, in the fields of social science and policy formation.[10] It did this by building its highly productive and influential theoretical framework on an absolute conceptual separation of the emotional and cognitive dimensions of public reactions, which could be represented as orthogonal axes of a graph, thus independent of one another.

This work valuably demonstrated that public reactions 'to risks' were based not only upon quantitative (mis)understandings of relative risk but also on salient qualitative attributes of those risk activities, such as their voluntariness, unit-concentration, trend over time, anonymity of victims, and regulatory trustworthiness. However, this did nothing to question the fundamental cultural assumptions, institutionalised in risk management and policy, of: (1) a categorical divide in principle between facts and values, cognition and emotion, objective and subjective; and (2) that there is universal, objective meaning to such issues, thus also of an object of public attitudes, namely, 'risk', even if this now includes its qualitative attributes as well as its (selected) quantitative magnitudes.

---

[8] EPCAG, 'Europe Ambivalent on Biotechnology'.

[9] P. Slovic, *The Perception of Risk* (London: Earthscan, 2000).

[10] P. Slovic, 'Reflections on the Psychometric Paradigm', in S. Krimsky and D. Golding (eds), *Social Theories of Risk* (New York: Praeger, 1992), 78–92.

The psychometric paradigm thus provided important insight into the more complex foundations of the reasons behind the public's perception of risks, and of their frequently observed divergence from scientific expert perceptions. It highlighted that these public responses went beyond scientific normative assumptions that they should be based only on scientific estimates and comparisons of averaged magnitudes of risk of death (from what were anyway artificially reduced representations of the supposed risk-generating units).[11] Some of this psychometric work, especially later research, provided ample grounds for contradicting the initial framing of the intellectual and emotional dimensions of public responses as if categorically separate. This question was never explicitly addressed, however, and this assumption thus remained substantially unchallenged. In addition the suggestion in the psychometric research findings of some substantial (if largely implicit) intellectual as well as emotional content to public responses was never explicitly recognised and compared with conventional expert views.

For all its valuable elements, however, the psychometric paradigm's leading influence in social science and policy more broadly consolidated the basic taken-for-granted cultural assumption that the object of universal meaning is indeed only 'risk' and moreover risk as defined by institutional science. This presumptive risk-centred meaning completely exempted the relevant institutions from the frame of attention.

Thus even though psychometrics did assert the legitimacy of public perceptions, this was advanced on the familiar but dubious grounds that perceptions create their own reality. The psychometric paradigm remained at-best ambiguous on the question of whether public responses were founded in substantively grounded intellectual as well as emotional dimensions; that is, whether they involved reference to material reality, in the form of institutional behaviour at the very least. This not only left intact and unchallenged the initial categorical divorce of the emotional from the cognitive, but allowed it to be regularly reinforced and extended into the new era of biotechnology, GMOs and their associated newly ascendant 1990s discourse of ethical issues and concerns.

---

[11] Wynne, 'Frameworks of Rationality in Risk Management'.

The research and policy culture which has continued into the GMO era was founded and has remained within this frame, in which public deviance from 'true' expert knowledge has been deemed to require explanation in psychological or social terms, as a form of 'pathology', while what has been deemed to be the objective truth of risks as provided by scientific institutions has been assumed to require no such questioning of its underlying foundations and qualifications, and indeed no qualification as the assumed objective universal meaning of the issues.

Levidow and Carr have criticised the form of the institutionalised policy discourse of ethics in the case of GM crops and foods.[12] Anticipating some elements of my critique, they noted the way in which the split into 'risk' and 'ethics', as if they were distinct dimensions, unduly reduces the recognised ethical dimensions. They identified an implicit unacknowledged set of ethical choices – a hidden ethical agenda beyond the explicit ethical issues – which are embodied in regulatory processes. However, as their focus was the discursive constructions involved in the regulation of GMOs, they did not identify the implicit constructions of the public, its capacities and its forms of judgement both embodied and reproduced in those dominant discourses. In this chapter, therefore, I go beyond Levidow and Carr to focus on leading discussions and analyses – representations – of the ethical dimensions of public concerns; and I seek to expose the implicit, unquestioned assumptions about the public, the issues and the knowledge which supposedly enlightens the policy-handling of them, which are being imposed upon the field.

It is important to emphasise that the critical focus of this chapter is not GMOs as such, but the impoverished mode of policy culture, especially the linked aspects of: (1) how science has become the unreflexive policy *culture* rather than its key intellectual resource; (2) the corresponding implicit and unaccountable public representations which this policy culture imposes; and (3) the way this institutional framing seamlessly exempts those institutions themselves from being part of the issue. As already noted this criticism partly includes the current

---

[12] L. Levidow and S. Carr, 'How Biotechnology Regulation Sets a Risk/Ethics Boundary', *Agriculture and Human Values*, 14, 1997, 29–43.

culture of mainstream social scientific research, in addition to the scientific and policy institutional culture (which is the patron and reference point for that social science).

Nucleation – Myths of 'Real Versus Perceived' Risks

The early expressions of public concern about new technologies in the post-war era – the most dramatic case being nuclear power – were met with a monumental wall of expert puzzlement at the irrationality of such widespread primitive reflexes which could recognise neither the huge benefits assumed to accompany these enterprises nor the trustworthiness and presumed credibility of the scientific and technical experts in charge of them. With hindsight we can now see that a major factor in converting what was, even in the 1950s, widespread but localised and largely unmobilised public concern into public protest and overt opposition to nuclear power by the 1970s was not only the escalation of risk and of risk perceptions as the programmes and associated accidents grew but also, more fundamentally, the wholly inadequate, unaccountable and provocative ways in which those expert discourses and behaviours represented the public and its concerns.[13]

Although the nuclear issue may have taken the lead in this characterisation of the public perceptions issue, and was arguably the first and still most prominent victim of its own institutional delusions in this respect, this 'real, objective risk versus subjective, perceived risk' framing was more deeply and pervasively institutionalised in modern risk management culture across the whole of policy thinking and practice. In this sense it represented the pervasive modern societal model of the relationship between scientific knowledge and popular culture, between the worlds of 'facts' and 'values' (or emotions).

This same basic dichotomy between objective and subjective – the factual and the emotional – is reproduced and sustained in the current GM crops and foods issue. In this manner expert discourses of the issue are unquestioningly taken to be grounded in reality, even if this may sometimes be – temporarily

[13] E.g., S. Krimsky, S. Golding and D. Golding (eds), *Social Theories of Risk* (New York: Praeger, 1992).

– only 'imprecisely' grasped; whereas public discourses are seen as essentially groundless and only emotionally based. This typical view was expressed in a UK Biotechnology and Biological Research Council report, that: 'Many people know little about biotechnology. This may make them frightened about its implications for our lives.'[14]

The same basic view was expressed by the UK Prime Minister in 2002, when he lamented that public refusal of support for GM technology was due to their 'fear of the unknown'. The apparent unfalsifiability of this assumption that opposition is caused by ignorance, despite counter-evidence since at least the early 1990s, lends it the identity of institutional myth, affecting scientists as much as political leaders, rather than reasoned standpoint.[15]

This self-justifying character of expert representations of the public – that expert knowledge is grounded in reality whereas lay knowledge and attitudes are politically real but intellectually unreal – may seem far-fetched in the face of the mushrooming official enthusiasm for public involvement in expert deliberations about GM risk and regulation and the manifestly more transparent, more participatory climate of expert advice and decision-making in the GM era compared to the nuclear heyday of twenty-five years earlier.[16] However, although it was eventually recognised and 'accommodated' as 'political fact' by the experts – for example, in stricter regulatory standards – this accommodation rested on the same basic grounds: that the public's attitudes were not rooted in real intellectual substance deriving from objective reality itself, but merely in emotion.

Thus the accommodation of the political fact of public opposition was always grudging, condescending and strictly in terms dictated by the experts' still-unquestioned basic

---

[14] R. Straughan and M. Reiss, *Ethics, Morality and Crop Biotechnology* (London: Biotechnology and Biosciences Research Council (BBSRC), Department of Trade and Industry, 1996), 2.

[15] B. Wynne, *Risk Management and Hazardous Wastes: Implementation and the Dialectics of Credibility* (London and Berlin: Springer, 1987), especially ch. 11; Martin and Tait, *Public Perceptions of Genetically Modified Organisms*, note ii; A. Irwin and B. Wynne (eds), *Misunderstanding Science* (Cambridge and New York: Cambridge University Press, 1996); EPCAG, 'Europe Ambivalent on Biotechnology'.

[16] E.g., UK Office of Science and Technology, *Guidelines for the Procurement of Scientific Advice for Policy*, update (London: UK Department of Trade and Industry, 2000); R. May, *Scientific Advice to Government* (London: Department of Trade and Industry, 2000).

assumptions: (scientists') knowledge which reflected reality versus public 'knowledge' which, as was sarcastically put by the radiation expert J. H. Fremlin, advising Cumbria County Council at the 1997 Windscale nuclear inquiry, reflected 'how many people would be frightened rather than how many would be killed'. This political accommodation thus did nothing to dent or question the continuing conviction that this was an objective issue, in relation to which the public was not only wrong but also congenitally incompetent to play a role.

The new and high-profile ethical agenda for GMOs also reflects these fundamental and deeply problematic commitments. Indeed, it has in some ways allowed their further intensification, because it has provided an outlet for public concerns which can give them legitimacy and public policy standing, while defining them as emotionally based thus intellectually vacuous and, in real terms, irrelevant. A key corollary of this is that, in dividing scientific matters and ethical concerns so absolutely, then using the 'ethical' as a catch-all residual category for everything that cannot be corralled by scientific risk discourse, institutional culture of scientific knowledge, commitments and assumptions is wholly protected from critical collective public examination, including critical self-reflection on the part of those constituent institutions defining and dominating the policy agenda. To this culture it is simply unimaginable that risk concerns as defined by science, and ethical concerns as defined by institutional ethical experts, might have different meanings to those assumed. It is thus unimaginable that those public ethical concerns might *interweave* moral judgement with intellectual judgement of the risk knowledge being given institutional authority. It is thus also inconceivable to this institutional culture that these public judgements might be intellectually substantive and amenable to rational debate, even if they are not deterministically resolvable.

Thus the key aspect of the GMOs public responses issue is not just the apparent status given to 'ethical concerns', as reflected in the high density and status of bioethics committees, ethical discourse generally about genetic manipulation, and the apparent respect given to public concerns defined as 'ethical'. It is, I argue, that this shift, and the related move towards wider public involvement, is seriously compromised by the inadequate way in which it is still framed in subordination to the false 'objective-versus-perceived' risk dichotomy, and within the misconceived facts *or* emotions dichotomy which informs that classification.

Boundary Work – Ethical and Trust Concerns

When I first proposed the idea that public reactions to risky technologies were not just reactions to (their understanding of) the risks involved, but also to the behaviour, track-record and trustworthiness of the institutions in charge, my argument envisaged this element of public reaction as an essentially instrumental form of reasoning.[17]

The logic was as follows:

> Responses to new technologies are based not only on the question which science addresses, namely, 'what are the risks?' They are also based on the further recognition that the risks as known to science exclude the important category of 'unknown' and unanticipated effects. Historical experience shows these to be at least as important as known risks, the domain of scientific risk assessment. Given that the focus of public concern is thus justifiably on surprise and how it may be handled, it is logical for people to ask, 'who will be in charge of the necessary adaptive responses to such unknowns when they occur? And given that we inevitably depend on them, and their responses will control society's fate, what is their track-record and their trustworthiness?'

Thus I suggested that the previously unrecognised public focus on the issue of *trust* could be seen not as a purely emotion-based response but as one combining emotional orientations with a rational calculative one deriving from public awareness of both inevitable ignorance behind science, and inevitable dependency on the institutions using that science. It was not a naïve – and, of course, insatiable – demand for certainty, as this 'mistrust' is often represented, but a recognition of the inevitability of uncertainty; thus a demand for the implications of this endemic predicament of science and its public dependants to be taken seriously. One consequence, again found in public responses, would be to have proper debate about whether the human purposes of the

[17] B. Wynne, 'Risk, Technology and Trust: On the Social Treatment of Uncertainty', in J. Conrad (ed.), *Society, Technology and Risk* (London, Arnold, 1980), 83–117.

innovation in question were sufficiently important to justify taking on such unpredictable possible effects, and about whether the institutions responsible for innovation, promotion and regulation were sufficiently trustworthy to defend the public interest.

Nevertheless, despite my initial characterisation of public mistrust as founded in (fallible) reason and judgement of the unacknowledged limits of dominant legitimatory scientific discourses, it has typically been completely misunderstood and patronised, being misrepresented as a 'touchy-feely', emotionally based concern, with no intellectual substance at all. Thus the key point, about the difference between (known) uncertainties and ignorance (unpredictable consequences) was also neglected. I have already referred to the bald assertion by one of the most influential social science teams concerned with public perceptions of GMOs, responsible for the four Eurobarometer surveys of public attitudes towards GMOs in 1991, 1993, 1996 and 1999, that 'trust is a functional substitute for knowledge'.[18] In an identical representation, another prominent US analyst of public attitudes to risk asserts that 'the less comfortable we are with assessing the technological evidence, the more stock we must put in evaluating the social evidence (for example of trust)'.[19]

This framing of the issue of public trust or mistrust in risk and regulatory science thus again represents it as intellectually vacuous, trust being thought to be necessary only when we are ignorant. This also reflects the mistaken assumption that trust is only a necessary question when technical expertise is lacking – as if scientific knowledge is not also pervaded by the need for trust, emotion and faith just because they are not spoken.

In both policy circles and academic research, public perceptions, responses and acceptance issues are typically seen as arising from emotionally inspired and essentially intellectually vacuous ethical and trust concerns. They are therefore not recognised to be *what they are*, which is (of course questionable)

---

[18] EPCAG, 'Europe Ambivalent on Biotechnology', note ii.

[19] S. Hornig Priest, 'Popular Beliefs, Media and Biotechnology', in S. Freidmann, S. Dunwoody and C. Rogers (eds), *Communicating Uncertainty: Media Coverage of New and Controversial Science* (Mahwah, NJ, and London: Lawrence Erlbaum, 1999), 95–112.

public judgements of the quality of existing knowledge and of the exaggerated claims made for it by scientists and the policy bodies they advise. Instead they are subtly reconstructed so as to delete these questions from attention. The problematic nature of the *ethical dimensions of the culture of scientific knowledge itself* are thus conveniently ignored. These dimensions include its own self-delusions and its lack of reflexivity about the quality of knowledge it provides and of its own organisational forms of ownership, control and direction as public issues requiring public deliberation.

Expert Ethical Reports – Framing the Public and Scientific Culture

I now examine the reports of some leading expert bodies about the ethical issues that are taken to underlie public concerns about GMOs. As described below, these indicate several implicit framing assumptions and understandings which are utterly unexamined and thus uncritically reproduced, yet which crucially shape their 'findings'.

The first assumption in this literature is that it is only public concerns, and not institutional presumptions in favour of biotechnology, that are unthinkingly held and cry out for ethical reflection and rational scrutiny. For example, the UK BBSRC Report on *Ethics, Morality and Crop Biotechnology* makes some distinctions between moral and ethical concerns before turning its attention to how to evaluate moral concerns about GM crops by the stricter forms of reasoning which they call ethics.[20] The discussion centres on the oft-dissected and criticised claims of opponents that GM crops are uniquely a case of humans 'tampering with nature', and the distinction offered between 'intrinsic' and 'extrinsic' ethical concerns. Yet although it starts from some sound premises – for example, that 'science cannot be pursued in an ethical and moral vacuum' – the discussion reproduces others that are more problematic. These include the fundamental meanings given to 'risk' and 'ethics' concerns, and the expression of these meanings as if they were purely natural, objective and thus given – as if they were not themselves a cultural construct embodying human

[20] Straughan and Reiss, *Ethics, Morality and Crop Biotechnology.*

agency and responsibility. Therefore it is important to identify the report's implicit framing of the questions and issues as ethical and scientific.

It states that 'worries are being increasingly expressed that the potential benefits of biotechnology may be lost if the new processes and products fail to gain "consumer acceptance" because of moral concerns'.[21] This again suggests that public concerns are only moral and not intellectual, and that they need more disciplined ethical scrutiny because 'we all probably hold some moral views unthinkingly', having failed to subject these to rational deliberation and conscious analysis of an ethical kind. The suggestion is then that public moral concerns about GM crops tend towards their rejection, and that such concerns are 'unthinking' and need disciplining. It is relevant to ask why this argument was phrased in this way – that ethical concerns, if not properly scrutinised, might get in the way of GM exploitation – and not in the alternative way, which would have been to ask whether existing narrow understandings of the ethical and scientific issues are not encouraging an irresponsibly precipitous rush into GM commercial exploitation, which is responsible for generating public ethical concerns? The alternative would have been to ask why it is that ethical considerations are not seen to apply to scientific research, only to its 'applications', when this boundary has been so severely and deliberately eroded in just the same period when GM science and technology has developed. Part of such a concentration on the ethics of scientific knowledge and culture itself would have meant asking why it is that public ethical concerns are not recognised as being focused on the issue of the quality of the scientific knowledge which, it is claimed, justifies promotional commitments. Further questions would arise over the repeated denial of the limitations of scientific knowledge as causes of public concern and the lack of transparency of this whole intellectual culture. These questions cross the artificial boundary between the ethical and the scientific which is constructed and defended as inviolate in the dominant discourse, because they are (of course fallible) intellectually based ethical judgements of that knowledge authority.

---

[21] Straughan and Reiss, *Ethics, Morality and Crop Biotechnology*, 3.

Qualitative research going back at least four years in several projects on public perceptions of GMOs[22] shows these kinds of judgement to be incessantly expressed as central elements of public concern – yet they have no place in the existing framing of the issues. Indeed, in this respect the recent apparent accommodation of the 'ethical dimensions' makes the situation worse since it appears to address a fundamental issue only to misconstrue and conceal it.

A second assumption often made in recent reports is that the public is only concerned about specific consequences of biotechnology, rather than also about the wider consequences of the endemic institutional denial of uncertainty. The BBSRC report describes one of its aims as being 'to identify the range of moral concerns felt about the consequences of crop biotechnology and to analyse the logic of these concerns'.[23] Yet again, this is framed as the exercise of 'value judgements' about *consequences, good and bad*. Nowhere is the more reflexive and essentially relational dimension of public concerns and responses even fleetingly aired, *that people might also be responding to how the scientists are characterising not only those consequences but also their scientific knowledge of them – and also, further, the public itself*. The report briefly recognises the issue of the unpredictability of consequences from GM crops, but dismisses them on the – pedantically correct – grounds that this is a universal problem not peculiar to GMOs. 'History has demonstrated how all new technologies inevitably have far-reaching effects. Crop biotechnology cannot then be singled out as the sole target for moral censure on these grounds, any more than can information technology or the steam-engine.' 'Far-reaching effects' here means lack of intellectual control by science over future consequences. The syndrome of institutional denial of this lack of control, of dismissing unpredictability, is simply not addressed as an ethical issue which might be fuelling public concerns and mistrust, and which scientific and policy bodies may have some responsibility to address in those terms rather than in the mistaken terms of patronising definitions of public mistrust and ethical concerns as essentially emotional and intellectually vacuous. One logic of the admission of unpredictable consequences is to focus questions

---

[22] Grove-White et al., *Uncertain World*.
[23] Straughan and Reiss, *Ethics, Morality and Crop Biotechnology*, 17.

on the human purposes for the actions which will release such uncontrolled consequences. This is a typical public response; but it meets with denial and neglect from the institutional authorities, as well as from many who are supposed to be understanding and explaining public attitudes.

For its part, the Nuffield Council on Bioethics report on *Genetically Modified Crops* noted that the ethical issues raised by global GM crops commercialisation ranged from the security of the food chain for all people including future generations, to food safety and environmental sustainability; it assumed that all of these could be dealt with in broadly utilitarian terms; that is, by assessing likely consequences.[24] This way of defining these issues as utilitarian *by definition* implicitly assumes that the consequences can be confidently identified so as to be weighed as 'costs' and 'benefits'. This ignores the very issue raised by typical public concerns, however, which is whether we should assume that science can indeed reliably identify future consequences, or whether, on the contrary, there are going to be consequences of which current knowledge is ignorant. Such consequences are contingent on so many independent conditions that we can only say they are conceivable but that their probability is unknown and so also (like the unknowns) uncontrollable. Both kinds of consequence lie outside the boundaries of intellectual – let alone practical – control offered by current scientific knowledge. Yet the report nowhere recognises that this is an issue in the ethical and social aspects of GM crops and public attitudes towards them. Indeed, this is underlined by the report's overall ethical conclusion about the question of consequences: 'the working party does not believe there is enough evidence of actual or potential harm to justify a moratorium on either GM crop research, field trials or limited release into the environment at this stage'.[25]

As Gaskell and Allum have observed,[26] the dominant institutional paradigm of 'risk' admits for recognition as legitimate objects of scientific and policy responsibility only that range of possible consequences which are under predictive control and

---

[24] Nuffield Council on Bioethics, *Genetically Modified Crops: The Ethical and Social Issues* (London: Nuffield, 1999).

[25] Nuffield Council on Bioethics, note xxvii, 7.

[26] G. Gaskell and N. Allum, 'Sound Science; Problematic Publics? Contrasting Representations of Risk and Uncertainty', *Politeia*, 17, 63, 2001, 13–25.

probabilistic quantification. Any other possibilities are dismissed as mere 'speculation' or 'theoretical risk'. Grove-White[27] reports an exchange with a UK GM crops regulatory scientist who condemned talk of such unknown consequences as the illegitimate fulminations of a 'fevered brow'.

As field work has shown,[28] the public's awareness of the scientific ignorance which science itself routinely denies does not lead them to the conclusion that innovation should therefore be stopped. People are not endemically anti-uncertainty: indeed, they take its existence, and the lack of control it signifies, for granted. On the contrary, what they seem to be saying is that the issue of unanticipated consequences should first be acknowledged as a responsibility of those institutions supposedly in charge; and should then also be explicitly connected with the presently-foreclosed question of purposes – 'why are we doing this?' Such a question is asked incessantly by the public in fieldwork situations, and goes beyond unqualified claims of 'benefits'. If the purposes driving research and innovation are sound then uncertainties will probably be tolerated; but if they are not sound, or are simply so unaccountable that no one can even tell whether they are, then why should gratuitous uncertainty be tolerated?

Thus in all the influential treatments of the ethical issues of GM crops, the ethical and risk dimensions are categorically divided, and the ethical aspects of risk are assumed in a utilitarian manner to be only about their scale and distribution, which are regarded as known. The crucial further issues about whether we can or do reliably know enough, and what we should do about inevitable ignorance, are not even recognised as questions. Even when consequences are recognised as part of the ethical domain, the two crucial issues of public concern, where the questions of ethics and consequences combine, are yet again not even hinted at. These two dimensions of public concern are the inherent inability of even the best scientific knowledge to identify all the consequences, but crucially also the effective *denial* of this predicament by the institutional powers-that-be, in their routine exaggeration of the power of

---

[27] R. Grove-White, 'New Wine, Old Bottles? Personal Reflections on the New Biotechnology Commissions', *Political Quarterly*, 72, 4, 2001, 466–72.
[28] PABE project, *Public Attitudes towards Agricultural Biotechnologies in Europe*.

risk assessment, as if it covers all consequences when it cannot do so. Again, these are concerns rooted not in objective independent reality (or its misunderstanding) but in the institutional behaviour of those sitting in judgement on those same public reactions.

A third assumption made in this literature is that cognitive content and emotional affect are not only categorically separable but also in some sense mutually inimical. The Eurobarometer studies already referred to reproduce this basic framing.[29] As already noted, they assume a categorical distinction between risk and ethical or moral concerns about GMOs. They allow this problematic framing assumption, and the researchers' assumed meanings of 'ethical' and 'risk', to be reproduced without anywhere being tested. As a leading practitioner of public attitude survey methods like Eurobarometer on biotechnology, Gaskell has acknowledged that this issue, of the meanings of key terms such as 'risk', 'ethical concern' and 'uncertainty' which survey methods have to impose (sometimes after limited pilot-testing) on respondents as if they have universal objective public meanings, is an open question. Qualitative methods are essential for exploring open-mindedly just those questions about the variety and complexity of such crucial meanings in the social world.

Thus the category of 'knowledge' in the Eurobarometer biotechnology study is constructed as a single-dimension measure of public knowledge of GMOs, so as to see if levels of knowledge correlate with attitudes. However there is rank confusion about what 'knowledge' is in this context, a problem which may relate to the neglect of explicit reflection upon the quality of the knowledge in play when the risk and ethical issues are framed as if they could be cleanly separated into cognitive (risk) and emotional (ethics) dimensions. The issues ignored by the dominant institutions, over the quality of the knowledge in play, and over the exaggerated claims being made for it, are at one-and-the-same-time, issues about risk and ethics together. The artificially purified classifications, of one *or* the other, as reproduced unexamined in surveys like Eurobarometer, fail to see this subtlety in public responses. Here, unfortunately, social

---

[29] EPCAG, 'Europe Ambivalent on Biotechnology'; Eurobarometer, *Europeans and Biotechnology*.

science research has inadvertently reinforced dominant institutional myths rather than challenged them. Those same
discursive constructions seamlessly but erroneously deflect the
critical force of public disaffection away from the responsible
institutions and on to the public itself, the media, NGOs or
anyone else who could be deemed responsible for public
'misperceptions'.

Although the Eurobarometer study team recognises that
attitudes 'consist of both cognitive factors and emotions', they
assume a one-dimensional hierarchy of possible 'knowledge'
about GMOs, which means that:

> Knowledge may increase the individual's capacity to understand
> new information and arguments, and personal involvement may
> lead to a more critical consideration of the arguments. Lack of
> knowledge or interest, on the other hand, usually means that an
> attitude is based less on the contents and more on the context of
> the information, e.g., the media. Lack of awareness can lead to
> diffuse and unstable attitudes ... Higher education can lead
> to more cognitive-based attitudes. This is the basis for a relatively
> stable and cognitively based attitude.[30]

In effect this definition of the relationship between emotions
and cognition in attitudes treats them as mutually contrary, so
that more cognitive content means less emotion in attitudes,
less 'context', e.g., media, and more 'content'. Note also that
the distinction between 'context' (influenced by the media, for
example) and 'content' (influenced by higher education,
for example) reflects an assumed hierarchy in which content is
'real' and 'context' is something else. Yet as research into the
public understanding of science has underlined for at least a
decade,[31] it is just as much a *content*-based dimension of public
understanding of and response to 'science' to give salience to
its institutional forms of ownership, control, direction and
regulation, as it is to give salience to its cognitive contents such
as whether antibiotics kill bacteria or viruses. To define
these other dimensions as 'context' and relegate them to

---

[30] A. Olofson, member of EPCAG team, 'Public Attitudes and Biotechnology', paper
to European Sociological Association, workshop on Social Theory, Risk and
Environment: Istanbul, Turkey, September 2000.
[31] E.g., B. Wynne 'Knowledges in Context', *Science Technology and Human Values*, 16,
1, 1–21.

media-propagated dimensions is to reproduce and impose an assumed definition of the sovereign *meaning* of the public issue as a *science-centred* meaning, when public responses are saying it is not just a scientific issue but it is also *centrally* about the social relations involved – about accountability, control, direction, the representation of science as a creator of innovations, and a culture of public policy: in short, about the undemocratic control of public meanings.

It could be thought that this issue had been addressed by the Eurobarometer team, since despite its use of distinct risk-ethics categories the 1997 *Nature* paper does conclude with an overall recognition that the risk and ethical dimensions of modern science and technologies are converging – that 'risks are fundamentally moral and political'.[32] Unfortunately, however, as we shall see with another treatment of the ethical and social dimensions of GM crops below, this alone does not address the basic issue. The ethical dimensions can still be, and are thought to be, about consequences without also addressing how we should deal with the unpredictability of these. Nor do they address the questions about the reliability of our knowledge more generally as justification for commitments which will generate unanticipated effects for which no one will admit responsibility. This implicit definition of responsibility by limiting it to the scope of prediction and control and externalising any other possible consequences without any accountability for this societal commitment is itself a huge ethical issue yet to be acknowledged and dealt with as such by the institutional culture which performs it.

A fourth assumption underlying these expert reports is that non-utilitarian ethical objections to crop biotechnology can be understood as individual, private preferences. For example, the 1999 report *Ethical Aspects of Agricultural Biotechnology* by the European Federation of Biotechnology's Task Group on Public Perceptions of Biotechnology recognises that there are non-utilitarian public concerns about agricultural biotechnology, specifically, those of 'playing God' and 'unnatural' interference with Nature.[33] But these are then problematised by

---

[32] EPCAG, 'Europe Ambivalent on Biotechnology'.

[33] European Federation of Biotechnology, *Ethical Aspects of Agricultural Biotechnology*, report to Task Group on Public Perceptions (The Hague: EFB, 1999). The EFB task group is drawn from a wide-ranging mixed academic, industry, NGO and

being taken without question to be literal expressions of a 'real' attitude which can be judged at face value, as an attitudinal 'object', referring to an object-practice, namely, GM technology. The possibility is not even recognised that the expression may be an oblique reference to the experience and judgement of the dominant institutional actors, their alleged hubris, haste and irresponsibility. The public ethical attitude about GMOs being unnatural is framed as a literal statement, within the observation that humankind has long interfered with nature, thus some objective discontinuity in this historical process needs to be identified for GMOs in order for this ethical objection to be valid. The 'playing God' objection is simply counterposed with the equally defensible religious position that GM technology represents a responsible partnership with God in developing his creation.

Both the 'unnatural interference with Nature' and the 'playing God' ethical objections are thus constructed as individual private emotional responses to technology as object. Public meaning is constructed as the aggregate of such private bilateral relationships between individuals and the technology alone. That these responses might be derived from *essentially relational, thus also endemically social sensibilities,* about the ways in which dominant institutions are seen as exaggerating the adequacy of existing knowledge and obliterating fundamental questions about the quality of that knowledge itself, and thus about societal responsibility for unpredictable consequences of human choices, is totally obliterated even as a question. The systematic avoidance – by a self-consciously rational culture – of this more reflexive and relational collective question allows public meanings to be imposed which may be doing violence to the meanings which people themselves invest in the issue. That these constructed institutional meanings may be seamlessly, if not deliberately, excluding their originating institutional culture from accountability and responsibility may not be entirely accidental.

---

media-communications industry membership from European and Scandinavian countries. It has been funded for over ten years by the European Commission, and has close contact with Commission policy-makers and advisers on biotechnology. This report can therefore be taken to reflect commonly held assumptions across a large international sector of specialist understanding on the issues of public concerns and responses to GM agriculture and food.

Thus the EFB report reproduces a framing of how public concerns are to be understood which is identical in key respects with those other influential approaches already examined here. A further aspect of this typical framing of what the public's 'real concerns' are also illustrates how these discourses project constructions of the public which are not only unreflected upon and unaccountable but are also, nevertheless, deeply normative. This is the delimitation of 'the public' as '(individual) consumer', rather than the more complex, relational and comprehensive notion, of 'citizen'. Thus once science has been left to take care of consequences under the discourse of risk, with the ignorance issue seamlessly deleted, leaving the utilitarian ethical issue of weighing costs against benefits as if these can be unproblematically identified, the remaining ethical issues are reduced to those private ones of giving consumers choice, thus providing labelling and 'playing God'. However, the latter is then effectively reduced to the former, labelling–consumer choice issue, by asserting that people who have legitimate moral or ethical concerns on the 'playing God' issue have the right to choose not to consume GM foods if they wish, hence the need for labelling – but this is defined as a private, individual matter, not even conceivably a public issue of collective institutional behaviour. A major, unacknowledged ethical issue stalks this discursive-normative reduction of collective relations to individual consumer identities.

In this way, crucially, I would suggest that *the collective dimension* of the 'playing God' issue is also deleted; that is, the possibility that public concerns of the 'playing God' kind may be an expression of concern about the institutional culture of public policy issue-definition, promotion and 'regulation' of GMOs, including its systematic institutional exaggeration of how much 'we scientists and rational beings know', is nowhere recognised. This cultural condition of exaggeration, if it is judged by citizens to be that, is a material form of idolatry, or hubris. It can therefore be understood as a form of 'playing God'. So too can the presumptive commitment, powerfully embodied in the institutional culture's reaction to public concerns, that science does not just *identify* the risks and consequences of GM crops and foods but gives the issue its very meaning – on behalf of the public. Instead, however, this putative *citizen* concern about the institutional culture's presumption of its own quasi-divine status – a concern which, we note again, combines ethical with intellectual judgement – is translated into the completely different issue of *private consumer* moral rights to choice in the marketplace alone.

Who will take responsibility for these specific and powerful, if tacit, representations of the public, when 'representation' is not even recognised as being performed? The result of this multi-layered discursive construction is that the whole institutional culture, with its culturally embodied denial of ignorance, and its associated hubris, is protected from being problematised as a central object of public questioning.

Conclusion

It is important to emphasise that although this chapter can be seen as deeply critical of the ways in which contemporary policy culture imagines and handles public policy on GMOs, the main point of the chapter is not at all against GMO technologies. It is certainly against the current ways of promoting and regulating them; but its critical focus is the mode of contemporary policy culture, especially the linked aspects of: (1) the ways in which science has become the culture of policy rather than its key intellectual resource; and (2) the corresponding implicit yet unaccountably normative representations of the public, and the profound denials of responsibility, which this political culture involves.

It is imaginable that commercial GM technologies – of a correspondingly different kind perhaps – could be developed under a different culture. Indeed I suggest that their future viability would require it, since the deeper cultural fabric of social relations in and around the current science and technology of GMOs which my analysis here indicates is profoundly inadequate and unsustainable.

I have argued at two distinct levels: first, more generally, that the discourses about risk and ethics of GMOs which frame the policy debate and policy-making embody a raft of prior unacknowledged and thus unaccountable yet arbitrary human values and ethical commitments which have to be recognised as contingent human commitments, not revealed truths that any rational person should automatically respect. These human commitments are not deliberately concealed, but are culturally embodied, taken-for-granted habits and routines of thought and practice, the *constitutive framework* of deliberate analytical thinking rather than the focal objects of such rational examination. They need to be rendered more explicit, and more open to public deliberation, as a democratic principle, and in order to save the prevailing scientific culture from itself. Recognising such buried and powerful values and ethical commitments does not have to abandon the processes of their public resolution to subjective anarchy. As various authors have argued, values issues can be rationally debated even if they cannot be reduced to deterministic singular resolution.[34]

Secondly, at a more specific level, I have argued that the particular discourses of risk and ethics on GMOs which policy experts, including some social scientists, claim accurately and objectively represent public concerns, themselves suffer from the unrecognised cultural syndrome referred to above, and tacitly represent the public in a way that depends upon prior cultural presumptions about scientific knowledge and about the public as human subjects. These presumptions are taken for granted, unaccountable, protected from falsification; and are wholly inadequate. Moreover these tacit representations protect scientific institutions from critical attention to the unrecognised cultural biases which they embody, project and reproduce in the name of a non-negotiable rationality. Inevitably this gives science and rationality a bad name, because they are thus sensed by a wider society to be concealing (and attempting to control) an extensive but inaccessible human political agenda. Thus even when they are, as in this case, explicitly referring to ethical concerns, they appear to be acting unethically.

According to my analysis the dominant discourse of public concerns, including the recently more influential ethical dimensions, habitually projects the public and its concerns in ways which tacitly portray them as epistemically vacuous, and incapable of relevant inputs based on any recognisable form of reason. This in turn defines the strictly controlled freedoms

---

[34] J. Dryzek, *Discursive Democracy: Politics, Policy, and Political Science* (Cambridge: Cambridge University Press, 1990); M. Jacobs, 'Environmental Valuation, Deliberative Democracy and Public Decision-Making Institutions', in J. Foster (ed.), *Valuing Nature? Economics, Ethics and Environment* (London: Routledge, 1997), 211–31.

of the public's proper role. Since risk-assessment scientific knowledge is assumed to identify all the significant consequences, even if imprecisely , and this is assumed objectively to frame the utilitarian element of ethical concerns, only the deontological ethical questions are left to be disposed of. Since the public scientific culture itself is taken to be a culture of 'no-culture', the only deontological ethical questions left are assumed to be those private emotional ones resolvable by purely individual choices that can be freely made (with labelling the only condition for *informed* choice) in the marketplace. Thus: risk and ethical concerns are absolutely differentiated; risk knowledge is assumed to be unproblematic, apart from known uncertainties; and exaggerated claims which are made for its authority and reach in terms of control over consequences, and the attendant denial of unpredictable consequences and responsibility for them, are assumed to bear no *collective* public ethical implications. The only ethical questions left are private ones. No ethical questions are recognised relating to questionable official institutional claims about the quality of that scientific knowledge, nor about the tacit representations of the public projected in these claims. Yet this ill-defined but intensely-experienced terrain is precisely where public concern appears to bite most intensely. It could be better described as intellectually founded moral outrage at these implicit misrepresentations, rather than the (misplaced) 'fear' that it is often said to be.

My emphasis on the unrecognised pervasive importance of the unknowns which always lurk beneath any commitment, and behind any scientific risk assessment, can of course be countered by the response that there is nothing special about GMOs in this respect. All innovation involves future unpredicted consequences. But this easy dismissal avoids the basic point, which is that the public's typical concerns *combine the common predicament of unpredictable consequences with the crucial further elements:*

- a judgement of the institutional scientific denial of this endemic limitation of scientific knowledge; with
- a judgement of the available science as 'culturally-captured' by commercial and other politically-'interested' forces and expectations; a sense which has been dramatically exacerbated by the deliberately cultivated commercialisation

culture which has pervaded even academic science in the last decade or more; and

- a concern that the correspondingly greater need for public accountability and debate over the human purposes, aspirations and forces driving scientific research for innovation in this domain is prevented by the focus of the dominant discourse only on 'objective' consequences – risks and benefits – and now ethics (as constructed in the false way described above).

In the supposedly 'reflexive' analyses of the ethical and risk issues of GMOs analysed in this chapter, there is a total absence of any recognition of the crucial need for open inclusive reflection and deliberation on the quality of the knowledge on which we rely for policy commitment. In this respect, these analyses and their patrons are part of the same institutional culture that is at least as much the cause of public concerns as the 'risks' or the 'playing God' dimensions themselves. Indeed this could be redefined as an existential human risk which arises from the public's sense of its unavoidable dependency on such a dogmatically insensitive, unaccountable and alienating institutional culture.

Official institutions continue to blame public opposition to GMOs on a new version of the public ignorance of science narrative. Where the older version asserted that the public objected to such things as nuclear power because they did not understand nuclear physics (reactors cannot suffer a nuclear weapons explosion) and radioactivity (its invisibility and penetrability must be hyper-dangerous), the new version is based on the claim that the public craves certainty in these matters and does not understand that science cannot provide it.[35] My understanding of public experience of these issues, based on extensive research and research literature as cited in this paper, is almost diametrically opposite – that the public sees science expressing only denial of its intrinsic lack of control as manifested in the endemic predicament of unanticipated consequences; a predicament which the public typically takes for granted. Thus public opposition and mistrust is encouraged by the routine cultural habit of institutional

---

[35] R. May, then UK government chief scientific adviser, 'Science and Public Policy', lecture to EXPO, Hanover, Germany, July 2000.

science of exaggerating its intellectual control, and denying moral or practical responsibility for its lack.

Ultimately the failure of scientifically enculturated policy institutions to command public confidence and trust is based on their inability to recognise either their own cultural commitments or their own imposition of the debatable but in practice unaccountable normative human visions involved, as if these were non-negotiable declamatory revelations. This crippling of a more mature and expansive political and cultural – and scientific – agenda is most stark where it is observable that dominant institutional presumptions about the meaning of the issues – about risk and about ethics, as these terms are defined by the prevailing institutions – are simply imposed as if universal and objective. Moreover, and even more perversely, these self-referential parochial cultural circuits are then reinforced when the public tries to challenge those presumed and imposed meanings, because that public divergence is assumed to be a misunderstanding of factors from within this institutionally assumed meaning-frame, rather than being understood as an attempt to express and establish different frames of public meaning.

Thus the final and most important conclusion I wish to suggest is that public concerns and what are misleadingly called 'risk-perceptions' – whether of GMOs or of any other technological domain – cannot be objectified and studied as if they are distinct from the ways in which relevant scientific and policy institutions behave, including how these bodies articulate dominant discourses of the issues. These 'rational' discourses tacitly embody and project into society powerful models of the human as prescriptive potential ontologies of human relations, human subjects and social order. Therefore their authors and others who pretend to analyse these have a so-far unrecognised responsibility to become aware of these (by definition not sensible to solely evidence-based observation) unstated dimensions of both scientific discourses of the issues and public expressions of concern. After this responsibility goes the further one of making sure that these deeply embedded and denied human commitments, especially the human driving forces and commitments which shape innovation trajectories, are rendered more accountable to wider deliberation, and shared responsibility.

PART IV

Technology, Theology and Society

Introduction to Part IV

In chapter 12, Jacqui Stewart invites us to revisit the work of Jacques Ellul, as a theologically grounded discussion of broader questions about the effects of technology on contemporary society. His work is significant in that it offers a critical appraisal of modern technology, as involving a particular kind of rationality, which he terms 'Technique'. Technique manifests itself: as an emphasis on artificiality and the subordination of nature; as a social dynamic where the logic of efficiency results in technical development becoming an autonomous process beyond individual control; as the constant extension and mutation of technologies through endless small alterations; as a shared set of values embedded in particular technologies which exclude moral questioning; as relations of interdependence between different technologies which result in further extending the effects of technological change; and as an irresistible globalising tendency, whereby technical logics spread and threaten indigenous cultures elsewhere in the world. Technological rationality thus expresses a desire for control, evacuates moral choice and leads to a diminishment of human responsibility.

Ellul draws on Pauline theology in order to portray the resistance to technological culture in terms of a cosmic spiritual battle. Christians become a sign, witnessing to the ordering in nature as given by God in a way that aligns with moral principles of truth and justice. The ends of God's work is communal and Christological, rather than individualistic and a matter of

Technique. The means of any process must be tested in relation to the eschatological end, thus limiting the powers of technology. Christians must strive to prefigure the Kingdom in this world, without themselves falling into the revolutionary or reformist trap of simply advocating technical fixes in the realm of politics.

Stewart then argues that 'the rhetoric surrounding the promotion of GM technology has many of the characteristics Ellul ascribes to Technique' (p. 273). The development and adoption of GM products is presented as inevitable, and GM crops are marketed around the world as part of a package which includes both other technologies (such as the use of certain pesticides) and industrial values (such as productivism and efficiency). She points out that in arguments for GM, the undeniable need of people for food is translated as the need for genetic modification. From Ellul's point of view, however, it is only an appropriate *end*, such as the feeding of the world, that can belong to the Kingdom, and not any particular *means*. Given this, the principal debates should be political and social, not scientific and commercial. Indeed, Stewart argues, given the complex social and political reasons for famine in the contemporary world, the potential benefits of GM as a means to eliminate famine are not at all clear. Stewart highlights the need to resist the further instrumentalisation of nature, and calls for more resources to be put into research on safety. She concludes by cautioning against the way that the churches' contributions to the GM debate tend to be in the form of ethical prescriptions, since these can be dismissed as 'matters of private morality', and calls for them to engage in the technical and political arguments.

In chapter 13, Peter Scott also focuses his attention on eschatology, the doctrine of the end of things, distinguishing three different versions underpinning the various positions taken in debates about genetic technology. The first – his main target – he calls an eschatology of *correction*, one where the Creator – and indeed his created co-creator, humanity – is seen as intervening in order to correct nature for human benefit. Scott goes on to suggest that this often taken-for-granted eschatology reproduces the typically modern reading of technology as a mere instrument for manipulation, and nature as the mere object of that manipulation.

Environmentalist critics of this view, Scott suggests, tend to rely on a second implicit eschatology, one of *closing down*, where humanity's overreaching of itself through genetic technologies brings down God's judgement in the form of an ecological apocalypse. Against both of these, Scott suggests that a fully Christian eschatology has to be one where God rather *closes in*. His elucidation of this point also serves as a general argument for the centrality of eschatology in the theology of genetic modification. A properly Christian eschatology looks to the future transformation and fulfilment of the cosmos as the glorification of God, making it uniquely equal to the task of reflecting on a nature that is no longer understood as unchanging or as simply for human purposes. Furthermore, by thematising God's final ordering of the world, eschatology rightly emphasises the normative character of divine goodness – that it involves the judgement, not merely the sanctification, of what is.

Scott then explores how specific technologies, whether genetic or otherwise, might be judged against the coming rule of God. He does this through a discussion of two different understandings of technology in contemporary society. In an analysis that echoes that of Ellul, Albert Borgmann suggests that modern technology is so pervasive that technological thinking has invaded much of everyday life, damaging our relationships with nature and with other human beings. For Borgmann, resistance to technology can thus only be grounded *outside* it, in 'focal things' such as wilderness, and non-commodified 'focal practices' such as music-making or gardening. According to Andrew Feenberg, though, this approach neglects the way that technology is itself shaped by wider norms and values. For Feenberg, technologies such as genetic engineering are not intrinsically damaging but simply need to be re-embedded within democratic rather than efficiency-led social norms and institutions. Scott leaves the choice between these two paths unresolved, but suggests that on either route a key reference point for judging technologies must be the quality of our relations with the natural world as well as with each other, as the primary anticipatory mediators of divine goodness.

In chapter 14, Celia Deane-Drummond argues that ethical consideration of genetic engineering has failed in the past because it has become too narrowly defined in terms of consequences. She argues for a recovery of virtue ethics in relation to the new technologies, as suggested by Stephen Clark in chapter 8. Nonetheless, the particular virtues that she suggests are most relevant are prudence (practical wisdom) and wisdom, taking her cue here from the work of Thomas Aquinas.

While contemporary literature has tended to read Aquinas either as a philosopher or a theologian, she suggests that the richness of his analysis is lost unless both aspects are considered together. In particular, his idea of wisdom is both that which is learned and is one of the intellectual virtues, and also that which is revealed and given as a gift of the Holy Spirit. His understanding of prudence draws on the philosophy of Aristotle, yet it seeks to direct all the other virtues and so has a central place in a virtue ethic. Aquinas is realistic about the possibility of prudence to work effectively when difficult individual cases are considered, though he is keen to point out that prudence may also be either 'sham', or 'incomplete'. Complete prudence comes when the particular ends of an action are aligned with the goodness of God. Such a task is only possible when God's wisdom is given by grace, allowing wisdom to be expressed and deepened by charity. Aquinas's notion of natural law is also significant in that it shows how he viewed the particular ordering of nature under God. Contrary to expectations, such ordering is not so much a simple naturalism; rather it springs from the twin command to love God and neighbour as expressed in the fundamental principle to seek good and resist evil.

Aquinas is also aware of the importance of the virtue of justice, arising from a consideration of natural law. This opens up a link with the more political aspects of Aquinas's thinking in relation to political prudence. Deane-Drummond suggests that Aquinas's thought is particularly relevant to issues in genetic engineering as not only does it offer a critique of science but also it includes teleology, deontology and virtue in a holistic synthesis. Furthermore, in an age when knowledge seems to be getting less certain Aquinas's virtue ethics makes possible a move away from the current emphasis on known consequences and towards the consideration of the character and attitudes of the individuals and organisations who have to act in the face of such uncertainty. She suggests that Aquinas's ethic is relevant to particular practical cases to hand, such as the recent move towards the use of human embryonic stem cells in medical research. Moreover, the social justice questions aired in relation to agricultural genetics by Northcott in chapter 4 come under particular scrutiny. While Aquinas's particular political stance needs some adjustment today, she suggests that his ethics offers a challenge to the various facets of the new genetics, both at the level of particular examples as well as wider social and political concerns.

Finally, in chapter 15, Bronislaw Szerszynski and Celia Deane-Drummond close the book with a postscript which provides a critical discussion of some of the main motifs running through the various contributions, while at the same time setting an agenda for further theological reflection and intervention. The key theme for their discussion is that of *uncertainty*, which, they suggest, has emerged in recent years as a significant frame in debates about nature, technology and risk such as those concerning genetic modification, threatening the hegemony of the 'sound science' frame. The increasing recognition of the indeterminacy of natural processes, of the provisionality of human knowledge, and of the inevitability of unanticipated consequences of new technologies may be contributing to the emergence of a radically new situation, one that is both a challenge and an opportunity for religion. They suggest that, with the shaking of the settled division of labour that saw science as producing value-free, objective knowledge and religion concerned with merely private meaning and morality, there is an opportunity for religion to claim a wider space of action than has generally been the case in modern societies. They also suggest that the irruption of uncertainty into the modern world can be understood theologically, as a return of repressed transcendent mystery.

Developing their suggestion in chapter 1 that the biotechnology revolution might serve to reveal timeless theological truths that have been neglected or forgotten, they suggest that the increasing recognition of uncertainty and the humbling of hubristic modernist reason may remind Christianity of its rightful calling in the world. Rather than presenting itself as a source of secure moral principles, against which individual technological developments can be judged, they argue that Christian ethics should be conceived as a nomadic, restless engagement 'that seeks to discern which path ahead most fully anticipates and prefigures the eschatological morning' (p. 320).

They also suggest that virtue ethics can play a key role in an uncertain world. The public are right to make judgements about technological developments by reference to the character of the institutions that are responsible, that will have to deal with the unanticipated consequences that are bound to arise. And on an uncertain journey, where certain knowledge is in short supply, individuals need not rules nor calculations of outcomes but dispositions to seek the good, courage and fortitude to weather the storms, and skills of discernment and wisdom to choose which path to take.

They conclude by setting an agenda for theologians and religious institutions. First, they contend that theologians need to engage more closely with science and technology, not just 'black boxing' it as a different way of knowing, to which religion has to defer in an increasing number of domains. Secondly, theologians should be helping to develop a better understanding of ethics as a process of discernment, rather than as a fixed set of rules or moral prescriptions. Thirdly, theologians and religious institutions should be playing an active role in the task of devising new deliberative spaces for the disclosure of human values in this and cognate areas. Fourthly, they argue, religious institutions should not shrink from using theological language in public debate, in the mistaken belief that the wider public thinks in an entirely secular and pragmatic way about technological change.

12

Re-Ordering Means and Ends: Ellul and the New Genetics

Jacqui Stewart

Introduction: Underlying Anthropologies and Constructions of Nature

All discussions of ethics have underlying them, whether acknowledged or not, frameworks of assumptions and values which guide the participants, affecting the kinds of arguments chosen as well as the outcomes. In chapter 1 of this volume, Celia Deane-Drummond, Robin Grove-White and Bronislaw Szerszynski demonstrate the clash between the frameworks commonly used by the 'experts' in the GM debate and those of the concerned general public in this area. It is therefore of practical and theological importance to have a clearer under-standing of what may be implied by current world-views of nature and humanity. Christian ideas are distinctive, centring on an understanding of the universe and humanity as created, dependent, having a purpose, and, being fallen, in need of redemption. Theologically, these concepts are dealt with in theologies of creation and theological anthropologies.

Since before the nineteenth century, science and technology have been seen as positive aids in the war waged by Enlightenment reason against poverty, ill health and other perceived consequences of human ignorance. Christians often supported this optimistic position, although Christianity has been ambivalent in its attitude to nature. John Hedley Brooke's historical analysis in chapter 2 notes that, on the one hand, nature may be seen theologically as something to be harnessed for the improvement of humanity's situation and, on the other, it may be a direct source of revelation.[1] Peter Scott in this volume adverts to an analysis of a more recent dichotomy, between this common view of nature as a passive object for technological domination (the modern tendency) and nature as redemptive and a source of salvation. The latter emerges from Heidegger's critique of technology and his characterisation of nature as discloser of truth as gift, *poesis*. This position has been rightly critiqued for the absence of *phronesis* or truth as value, and the consequent downplaying of its social and political implications.[2] In this chapter, I wish to concentrate further on the critique of the modern tendency. The GM crisis, and the clash of cultural values reflected in it, shows that technology has not been merely a passive servant of modernity, dominating nature at the behest of rationality. Rather, features of technological thinking have themselves modified the rationality of modernity, and have altered the framework of values underlying it. This charge has been most energetically made by the French theologian, Jacques Ellul, who is better known for his work in sociology, history and law. Interestingly, he also allied himself with the French environmentalist Bernard Charbonneau and campaigned vigorously for many years against the destruction of the coastal regions of France south of Bordeaux.[3] Ellul's work has been acknowledged as anticipating much postmodern critique, and is therefore doubly appropriate as an aid in the theological analysis of the issues raised by the potential of GM technology.[4] However, Ellul is difficult to read, and is often misunderstood. This arises in

---

[1] For example, Michael Banner, in ch. 3 of this volume, gives a classic account of creation theology as celebration of nature as gift. The ambivalence of theology towards nature is discussed by D. J. Hall in *Imaging God: Dominion as Stewardship* (Grand Rapids: W. B. Eerdmans, 1986).

[2] R. J. Bernstein, 'Heidegger's Silence? Ethos and Technology', *The New Constellation: The Ethical–Political Horizons of Modernity/Postmodernity*, 1st MIT edn (Cambridge MA: MIT Press, 1992), 79–141. I am grateful to Peter Scott for drawing this work to my attention. A similar concern is also behind Gadamer's recovery of *phronesis* for hermeneutics.

[3] A valuable introduction to Ellul is given by Andrew Goddard, 'Obituary: Jacques Ellul 1912–1994', *Studies in Christian Ethics*, 9, 1996, 140–53. Ellul's relationship with Charbonneau is discussed by D. Cerezuelle, 'La critique de la modernité chez Charbonneau', in P. Troude-Chastenet (ed.), *Sur Jacques Ellul* (Bordeaux: L'esprit du Temps, 1994), 61–74.

[4] For example, Patrick Troude-Chastenet claims that he anticipates Barthes, Baudrillard, Bourdieu and Debray; see *Sur Jacques Ellul*, 7.

part from his use of a dialectical approach. He presents his arguments in a series of parallel works, sketching out socio-political issues in one series and their theological dimensions in another.[5] Understanding can only emerge in the reader who holds these two approaches together in necessary tension. Therefore, I shall present first the arguments from two particular sociological contributions, written more than thirty years apart, for a phenomenological description of the problems, before I turn to Ellul's theological analysis and its implications.

The Sociology of Technique, Early and Late

Ellul's first major work on the sociology, politics, philosophy and cultural role of technology, *The Technological Society*, was written in 1950, appearing first in French, followed by the English translation in 1964. In this dense and difficult book, Ellul laid out the foundations of his analysis of the transformation in cultural thinking caused by the rise of technology in the West in the last two hundred years. He refers to 'La Technique',[6] by which he means not technology itself but a technological approach to thinking, a techno-logical world-view. It is important to note at the outset that Ellul does not deny the effectiveness of actual technological means,[7] but he questions the consequences of thinking that does not go beyond their immediate effects. He is concerned that technology has provided a plethora of instruments or means by which humans exercise power in the universe, to such an extent that questions of purpose, goal or ends are suppressed. In the thinking, which he describes as Technique, the means have actually become the ends. It is also important to be clear that Ellul is not objecting to the use of technology in itself, but to the distortion in public thinking and discourse

---

[5] See the excellent essay on Ellul by Daniel B. Clendenin in the 1989 edition of J. Ellul, *The Presence of the Kingdom* (Colorado Springs: Helmers & Howard, 1989), xxi–xlii.

[6] I use capitalisation to distinguish Ellul's term from the ordinary meaning in English.

[7] 'It is not my intention to show that technique will end in disaster. On the contrary, technique has only one principle: efficient ordering. Everything, for technique, is centred on the concept of order' (J. Ellul, *The Technological Society* (New York: Alfred A. Knopf and Random House, 1964), 110.

caused by its annexation of technological rationality and evaluative criteria.[8]

Ellul characterises Technique by a *rationality* which includes systematisation, division of labour, standardisation and exclusion of individual creativity. This rationality brings its own discourse, suppressing anything external to it – and it is interesting to note that John Brooke observes this problem of the limiting nature of scientific language.[9] Ellul describes six additional features of Technique, as follows. First, *artificiality* – the creation of an artificial world by the accumulation of technical means. This involves the elimination, absorption, or subordination of nature, and reflects the total opposition of the values underlying Technique to nature manifest in and of itself. For example, Ellul refers to the problems caused by the destruction of parts of the South American rain forest to permit the growing of cash crops and industrialised agriculture. The negative ecological consequences were not foreseen. Ellul argues that blaming such ecological disasters on inherent selfishness in some aspect of human organisation (e.g., capitalist economics or communist politics) is too superficial an explanation.

Secondly, Ellul asserts that the priority given to efficiency removes any actual choice; the biggest or fastest option must be selected, and he terms this *automatism*. This has a secondary consequence in that it leads to the use of means simply because they become possible. This is most tragically seen in the results of the 'arms race'. Ellul's third characteristic of Technique focuses on the way technical progress comes to be identified as inevitably good. This causes technical processes to be gradually extended by numerous small alterations, refining and expanding them. Ellul calls this *self-augmentation*. It is collective and anonymous; not visionary and individual. Further, each set of technical solutions generates a further set of technical

---

[8] Such a misunderstanding informs the treatment of Ellul in, for instance, M. Tiles and H. Oberdiek, *Living in a Technological Culture* (London: Routledge, 1995). I would also contend that his account of Technique is mistakenly bracketed with Heidegger's account of technology by Andrew Feenberg, e.g., in *Questioning Technology* (London: Routledge, 1999), as I argue elsewhere.

[9] John Brooke in this volume; his point is that policy-makers insist on non-religious language, but the reductionist, scientistic language actually used has its own, different bias.

problems, so there is a perpetual expansion of technical solutions. But this results in an endless series of technical fixes.

A fourth feature of Technique is the interconnectedness of technical means. Ellul criticises Mumford for regarding the printing press as a neutral technology being put to an inappropriate purpose in producing poor-quality newspapers. Ellul argues that the content of the papers is a consequence of the same thinking which produced the presses. This interconnectedness or shared set of values he terms *monism* (in French, *unicité*). Partly because of this, and paradoxically, the technological approach, although it requires peace and order to develop, makes war much easier. Weapons technology allows more people to be killed at less pain and expense to the killers. There is no predictive factor that allows advance knowledge about which aspects of technology being developed in one area will be applicable to another, so that anything may turn out to be applicable to military issues, or to environmental ones, good or bad. Ellul is hostile to the concept of neutral technology – the idea that a moral dimension inheres only in the use to which the technology is put – because technological thinking specifically excludes consideration of the moral.

Related to *monism* is a further feature that results from the normative, systematising tendency of the rationality employed – *technological integration*. Ellul gives the example of the introduction of the flying shuttle in weaving; this increased the speed of the process so much that the supply of thread became limiting. The technological rationality which governed the devising of the flying shuttle also required a search for a technical way of increasing the supply of yarn, and the introduction of the Spinning Jenny resulted. The requirement for efficiency makes succeeding developments necessary within that logic.

The last significant feature of Technique is *technological universalism* – the technological approach does not require any given set of cultural values for its implementation, and has therefore a global implementation. Ellul cites the spread of industrial agriculture into the most remote and rural economies in the developing world. He argues that the desire for the outcome – large-scale production of food for undernourished populations – has blinded people to the other consequences of technological agriculture. Ellul argues that the thinking of Technique is destroying cultures all over the world, since it appears to render their systems of belief and value superfluous, replacing all with a commitment to technical logic and efficiency.

He notes the increasing desire for order and control originating with the Enlightenment, and, recalling the shock of the Lisbon earthquake, the problematic status ascribed to nature. This lead to the imposition of human order on to nature, a process that has so accelerated that, in our time, it is seen as the defining characteristic of humanity. Ellul asserts that in our time, 'domination of the irrational is a fulfilment of the very being of humanity'.[10] This is a total inversion of Christian theological anthropologies that see humanity as created by, and therefore dependent on, a God whose mystery and being cannot be objectified. It should be noted that Ellul is not arguing for a Romantic position that glorifies the irrational, and even less does he deny the necessity for human action. Rather, humanity should be engaged in enabling God's order to be reflected in nature, and human activity should be organised to this end.

Ellul describes the developing rationality of Technique which has led to this as 'unreason', and protests that as rational systems increase in human society social maladjustment and marginalisation also increase. Technique justifies and encourages instrumentalisation at all levels. This is the rationality which justified the concentration camps as economic enterprises, using not only the labour of the inmates but also their body parts as industrial resources.[11] In this later work, Ellul describes technological rationality in more detail than previously. He notes the importance of *normalisation* or standardisation, which is necessary, if a wide variety of means is to be employed together. The pressure for *change* derives from the argument that, in competition with others or nature, to stand still is to go backwards. Change becomes a good in itself. Similarly, *growth*, the extension of power, becomes an ultimate necessity because efficiency requires always the greatest exercise

---

[10] J. Ellul, *The Technological Bluff* (Grand Rapids: Eerdmans, 1990), 162.
[11] Ellul, *Technological Bluff* (1990), 170; Zygmunt Bauman arrives at similar conclusions about rationality and modernity in his study on social causes of the Holocaust – see Z. Bauman, *Modernity and the Holocaust* (Cambridge: Polity Press; and Oxford: Basil Blackwell, 1989).

of power for the least effort. *Speed* also becomes desirable in its own right – this arises because as the speed of technology in one area increases all other areas have to increase speed to maintain technological integration. The most devastating aspect of this kind of rationality is the evacuation of moral choice – only technological rationality can be employed in the evaluation of alternatives.[12]

Ellul points to the problems when this kind of thinking is applied to agriculture. Increased productivity becomes a good in itself and there is a carry-over of industrial values. (And the justification for GM crops is enhanced productivity, as I shall discuss further.) Ellul summarises the basic issue – for the 'modern' secularist, the re-ordering of nature has only secondary, consequentialist or aesthetic value implications. In this volume, Michael Northcott demonstrates that, for the Christian, the ordering of nature has moral dimensions. It involves the maintenance of relationships within creation as well as the provision of shelter, etc.: mere nutrition is not the only point. Industrial agriculture leads to the demise of stewardship, the loss of rural communities and the loss of their relationships with nature as creation. Instead, the 'consumer' is constructed and distanced from production, so we have famine at the feast, inappropriate diets of processed and contaminated food, particularly for the poor.

There are also costs to the Technique. Ellul argues that the responses of technological rationality to pollution have been ineffective, whether small technical fixes (car catalysers), clean up attempts (Lake Michigan) or legislative control (the twenty-year delay in cleaning up the Rhine).[13] More technology is clearly not the answer; Ellul gives the example of the Acquitaine coast, where attempts at creating artificial resorts failed because new sea defences were technical failures, where deliberately increased tourism lead to large-scale failure of sewage systems, with consequent pollution, and where a major technical fix involving a new outfall also failed, with further extensive pollution of the Arcachon basin. He notes that a significant feature of Technique is that no one is responsible for these failures. No one is in charge. The experts only advise the

---

[12] Ellul, *Technological Bluff* (1990), 223–8.
[13] Ellul, *Technological Bluff* (1990), 229–32.

politicians, the politicians aren't experts; the technicians and contractors only do what they are told. Polemically, Ellul recalls the same problem being voiced at the Nuremberg trials, but his point is that the rationality involved is the same.[14]

Ellul's Theological Understanding of Nature

The principle statement of Ellul's theological foundations is made in the book first published in French in 1948 as *Présence au monde moderne: Problèmes de la civilisation post-chrétienne* and translated as *The Presence of the Kingdom*.[15] In the first ten pages, Ellul sets out his vision of the relation between humanity, creation and God. It is a vision influenced especially by the theology of Paul, which is an underlying theme of the whole book and Ellul's theological position as a whole. The Christian is inseparable from the world, as *aion* (meaning the age or epoch) and as *kosmos* (meaning the physical world): to be in the world is fundamental.[16] But this being in the world is an engagement with the total, whole aspect of the world, especially the spiritual. It is to be a struggle against the powers that are in conflict with God (Eph. 6.10–20). This is therefore different from, and more than, engagement in good works. Christians are to be the 'light of the world', because in itself, the world, particularly as *aion*, does not disclose truth about itself. Here is the theological correlative of Ellul's socio-political suspicions about human knowledge and rationality. Christians are not 'of' this 'world', nor to be complicit with it, but they are enlivened by the Spirit, and the texts he returns to throughout the book reinforce this view. Christians are not so much to do this or that, but to be, 'to be a sign'.[17] The fundamental problem of the world is that, on the one hand, it is corrupted; sin is a collective issue (Ellul anticipates increasing globalisation and the implications it has for collective human responsibility) and we are all guilty by association. Throughout

[14] Ellul, *Technological Bluff* (1990), 300.

[15] J. Ellul, *Présence au monde modern: Problèmes de la civilisation post-chrétienne* (Geneva: Roulet, 1948); J. Ellul, *The Presence of the Kingdom* (London: SCM Press, 1951). In this chapter, I will cite from the 1989 edition of *The Presence of the Kingdom.*

[16] See discussion of the confusion caused by New Testament words translated as 'world' in Hall, *Imaging God*, 43–6.

[17] Ellul, *Presence of the Kingdom*, 3–4 ; throughout his work he cites 1 Cor. 1.20 and 7.23, Rom. 12.2, Heb. 11.13 and 1 Cor. 6.19 in support of being 'not of this world'.

his work, Ellul acknowledges the essentially problematic dimension of humanity. On the other hand, the Christian is called to resist this destructive propensity, in that Christians are called to work for the redemption of the world. Ellul's recognition of sin is not an ultimate pessimism, as he makes clear in other writings.[18]

So the Christian has to live out a position of impossible tension, knowing both the impossibility and the imperative of realising the Kingdom now. But the Christian does not avoid the practical and technical work that is needed to make the world a better place; rather, both that and more is required. Thus Ellul spells out the role of human action –

> For the world ought to be preserved by God's methods, not by man's technical work (which can, however, be used by God and form part of his activity, on condition that men bring the whole sphere of technics under his judgement and his control). Further, the world ought to be preserved in a certain *order*, willed by God, and not according to the plan that men make of this order (a plan, however, which *may* be accepted by God on condition that men are genuinely concerned for truth and justice).[19]

Here we see clearly the theological foundations for the sociological analysis later presented by Ellul in works such as *The Technological Society* and *The Technological Bluff*. The Christian has a spiritual as well as a practical engagement in the struggle for the world. Ellul stresses the importance of prayer, and the realness and relevance of understanding the power of the Holy Spirit. But he does not paint a picture typical of so-called charismatic churches. Instead, he stresses the contrast between on the one hand a secular, historical, factual account of humanity and its relation to the universe and on the other hand a Christian, open and apocalyptic account of God and his creation. He argues that the politics of revolution, so common in the twentieth century, are actually politics of determinism or

---

[18] Ellul, *Presence of the Kingdom*, 9–12; he cites Rom. 3.10 (there is no one who is righteous) and similarly Gal. 3.22, but Christians are to act against sin; he cites Col. 4.5–6 (conduct yourselves wisely) and similarly Eph. 5.15–17 and 2 Cor. 5.20. See also J. Ellul, 'Chronicle of the Problems of Civilization', in M. Dawn (ed.), *Sources and Trajectories* (Grand Rapids: Eerdmans, 1997), 13–22. (This is a translation of an early article, 'Chronique des problèmes de civilisation', *Foi et Vie*, 44, 6, 1946, 678–87.)

[19] Ellul, *Presence of the Kingdom*, 16.

inevitability, because they have become scientific.[20] Elsewhere, he sees the desire for a 'technical fix' in politics issuing in the demonising of others. The assumption is that if we protest against inequality, slavery, etc., then civilisation can be stable and make steady progress to well-being. When this does not work out, the technical fix is the rational demonstration of the inadequacy of this or that easily marginalised group (the Jews, the Bolsheviks). This is often built in to the large-scale technical solution – for example, the Third Reich, communism. Ellul does not expect the sum of technical solutions or the thinking of Technique to be the source of salvation: only God can be that.[21]

By contrast with such politics, Christians are called to be properly revolutionary, to expect the genuinely unpredictable, and be prepared for the truly new, because they are open to the action of God in the Holy Spirit.[22] This revolutionary attitude calls for the constant restatement of the claims of God and the constant rediscovery of what the world would look like if it reflected the order and harmony willed for it by God. Hence Ellul's stress on the necessity for Christians to evaluate worldly knowledge.[23] This is always to be done in expectation, in hope, illuminated by the anticipation of the eschaton. But this does not give any certain, logical knowledge of how God's response to the world will develop, only that God is always present and waiting for humanity's engagement. Hence Ellul argues that the construction of ethical systems of fixed principles and guaranteed procedures is impossible for Christianity. Ellul redefines Christian ethics as the constant revisioning by the Christian community of its ways of responding to God's call to the world. This is very much in line with Barth's conception of ethics,[24] and is a rejection of ethical systemisation. This is not to

---

[20] '[S]ocialism, in becoming scientific – that is to say, in submitting to fact, and in following the development of facts – has become anti-revolutionary' (Ellul, *Presence of the Kingdom*, 29).

[21] Ellul, 'Chronicle of the Problems of Civilization', 14–15.

[22] 'For the intervention of the Holy Spirit is not dependent on man and his choice, any more than the revolutionary character of the Christian situation depends on man. It is not because people choose Christ that they become Christian, it is because Christ has chosen them' (Ellul, *Presence of the Kingdom*, 32).

[23] He cites 1 Thess. 5.21 (test everything) and similarly, 1 Cor. 6.3.

[24] For a careful and critical discussion of this, see Nigel Biggar, *The Hastening That Waits: Karl Barth's Ethics* (Oxford: Clarendon Press, 1993).

say that Ellul is suggesting some kind of situationist free-for-all. He calls for Christian judgement to be exercised upon the claims of the world, and such judgement must use a theological framework founded on criteria derived from the reappropriation of the New Testament by each age and culture. In the last section of this chapter, I will present some of the empirical consequences of such an evaluation of the GM debate, showing that Ellul's position does not imply any evasion of responsibility for concrete ethical decisions.

We have seen that much of Ellul's sociological and political analysis of Technique is occupied with the issue of purpose and value. In his explicit theology, Ellul argues that while the ancient philosophical questions about the values implicit in the relation of ends and means are apparently not discussed today they underlie the urgent problem that technology presents for contemporary society. Technologies are means, ways of producing effects, exercising power. Ellul argues that modern society has become so concerned with technological means that it has forgotten ends in the sense of the ultimate values known to the old philosophers. Instead, short-term results of technology are accepted as ends themselves, and this has been extended to an instrumentalisation of humanity itself.[25]

He suggests that the pursuit of ends has been replaced with the concept of progress, an endless process of change, which, Ellul argues, has no real direction. Happiness, justice and liberty have become 'empty phrases' as an individual becomes like a cog in a machine, in the service of struggles that are not his own. The end result of wars or strikes does not bring happiness or justice, but only more of the same.[26] This replacement of implicit ends by technological means itself makes evaluation of those means difficult; the technological multiplication of means cannot be questioned without recognition of ends. The means, in replacing an end, have become their own justification. Again, Ellul draws the theological consequences from the sociological arguments he

---

[25] 'Thus *man* – who used to be the end of this whole humanist system of means – *man*, who is still proclaimed as an "end" in political speeches, has in reality himself become the "means" of the very means which ought to serve him: as, for instance, in economics or the State'. (Ellul, *Presence of the Kingdom*, 51.)

[26] Ellul, *Presence of the Kingdom*, 54.

presents elsewhere. The concept of efficiency is crucial for the justification of means. The means applied must produce an effect and the greater the effect, whether faster, larger, or some other type of more of the same, the 'better' the means is. This can apply to politics – the communist economy, the Russian army, etc. Because it is technical, moral evaluation cannot take place. In his sociological analysis of the Holocaust, Zygmunt Baumann makes a similar objection to the technological replacement of ends by means.[27]

Ellul fears the loss of control, or the evasion of responsibility, consequent on this technological transformation of society. He sees the extension of the technical paradigm to all areas of life, because extension of human power is regarded as a basic good.[28] This desire for unlimited power leads ultimately to a usurpation of the position of the Creator. Ellul cites Genesis 3.6; the fact that the tree was there and offered power to Eve and Adam was enough for them to abandon their relation with God. They would not accept dependence on God. Ellul sees it as essential for Christianity to resist this tendency for totalising technical means to substitute themselves for ends in present societies. He sees it as a conflict with the Pauline powers, which can only be waged with the weapon of Christ, which is love. Ellul understands the powers as manifestations of human collectivity, rather than as Gnostic forces or Marxist ideological superstructures.[29] It is interesting to note that the contemporary social theorist Slavoj Žižek analyses the suppression of value involved in public discourse in terms of Lacanian psychoanalysis, and not only comes to the same conclusion about the inversion of 'you can because you must' into 'you must because you can', but also

---

[27] Ellul says 'sometimes, technical results, like concentration camps, make the majority of men shudder with horror, but that is simply because these people were outside this sphere of technical means: a Russian communist does not shudder over the camps in Siberia, nor was a National Socialist in Germany horrified at the extermination camps. When these practices have become general, and we have all become used to the mechanism of these "means", no one will be surprised by them any longer' (*Presence of the Kingdom*, 58). See also Z. Bauman, *Modernity and the Holocaust*, 116.

[28] Ellul, *Presence of the Kingdom*, 59.

[29] See the discussion by Marva Dawn, 'Chronicles of the Problems of Civilization', in Dawn, *Sources and Trajectories*, 25.

to the same conclusion that the Pauline understanding of love is the appropriate solution.[30]

For the Christian, the ends of God's work are present in Christ who is also the means. Hence Christians should not regard their communities and institutions in any instrumental light; they are not means to an end, but instead, in themselves, are the partial realisation of the end, the anticipatory presence of the Kingdom. For Ellul, the intention of God as ends has precedence over considerations of means. His view of Christian living follows this: 'we do not have to strive and struggle in order that righteousness may reign upon the earth. We have to be "just" or "righteous" ourselves, bearers of righteousness.'[31] Again, this represents the freedom from law and the gift of grace as witnessed by Paul, and Žižek gives voice to it in our contemporary situation.[32] So Ellul reconceptualizes ethics as a manifestation of the love of God, not a means of obtaining it. He asserts that this is a feature of community, rather than a collection of individual acts, because the manifestation of love is the creation of community, and rationalistic Technique is ultimately individualistic.[33]

The implications of this for the relation of Christians to nature are uncomfortable; it will not be enough for churches to put up the odd Green poster or circulate improving documents. They are called to manifest, in all of their aspects, the love of God for the created world, animate or not. This will include the unfashionable recognition, in an era of inspectors and task forces, that Technique is a temptation to be resisted. An efficient church risks being not a church at all, since the Christian community is asked to be the Body of Christ, and this is different from the maximising of its own power implicit in the concept of efficiency. Human means and mechanisms should be employed by Christians to enable the embodiment of Christ in their communities, and the realisation of this is the criterion by which means are chosen or rejected. Unless human power is exercised under the rule of God, its fruits decay.[34] Christianity differs from contemporary politics in that Christian realism

---

[30] S. Žižek, *The Fragile Absolute* (London: Verso, 2000), 130–5, 145–7, 157–60.
[31] Ellul, *Presence of the Kingdom*, 64–6.
[32] Žižek, *Fragile Absolute*, 143–7.
[33] Ellul, *Presence of the Kingdom*, 67–8.
[34] Ellul, *Presence of the Kingdom*, 71.

gives rise to partial, fragmentary and temporary or evolving
solutions, because it is in dialogue with the Spirit in a changing
world. The politics of modernity depend on systematisation and
Technique, and look for guaranteed, secure results.[35] Ellul says
of the right ordering of technological means:

> If these means are really to be ordered in the light of this eschato-
> logical event, they must cease to be limitless in their demands, and
> subject to no authority higher than themselves. They must be
> judged, accepted, or rejected. It is not their intrinsic virtue, their
> quality as means, that counts; it is their eschatological content,
> their faculty of being integrated under the lordship of Jesus Christ.
> They are not good or bad, they are called to enter into the
> Kingdom of love and they are able either to enter it or not.[36]

Ellul's insight will itself degenerate into an ideology if it is not
accompanied by an understanding of the necessity of spiritual
transformation for the perception and experience of the
Kingdom as now, and still not yet. God acts through humans,
and the question for Christians is that of their willingness to be
part of something that is not history but the radical action of
God; that is, their willingness 'to be' in some new way, not to act
in or of themselves. The issue for Christianity is not which forms
of social action to choose, but how to 'live', to participate in life
with the Spirit.[37] Ellul cites the promise made in Matthew 6.33
('Strive first for the kingdom of God and his righteousness and
all these things will be given to you') as a sign of the real
possibilities opened up by God for humanity.

Ellul is not a naive supernaturalist and he is much nearer to
a postmodern rejection of metaphysics than some have
thought.[38] His analysis of the theological weakness of

---

[35] This is discussed in the important essay translated as 'Political Realism (Problems
of Civilisation III)', in Dawn, *Sources and Trajectories*, 51–84, and first published as
'Problèmes de civilisation III: Le realisme politique', *Foi et Vie*, 45, 7, 1947,
698–734.

[36] Ellul, *Presence of the Kingdom*, 71.

[37] Ellul, *Presence of the Kingdom*, 78.

[38] Those French authors who compare him to Heidegger and conclude that Ellul's
arguments are themselves subject to Heidegger's critique of theological ontology
do not examine Ellul's explicit theological work. The comments by M.
Weyembergh, 'J. Ellul et M. Heidegger le prophète et le penseur', 75–100, and
M. Van den Bossche, 'Technique, esthétique et métaphysique', 251–70, in
Troude-Chastenet, *Sur Jacques Ellul*, fall into this category. Ellul differs radically
from Heidegger in that relationship, the relationship of love radically initiated by

Technique and its pervasive influence on public discourse is particularly relevant to the present debate on the environment. Not only does he demonstrate the weakness of much of the argument associated with more powerful vested interests, but also he recalls theology to a more faithful account of creation. It should not be a static account of human origins; God's creative activity is a continuing gift in human affairs. Nor should the purpose of the created universe be subverted for human convenience; it is not a human possession.

How do Ellul's Arguments Apply to the GM Debate?

Ellul's theology of creation, which makes clear the values inherent in the world, alerts him to the suppression of questions of value that is revealed by his sociological investigations into technological discourse and rationality. It also makes him sensitive to the covert substitution of technical means for ends or goods in themselves. What are the implications of this analysis for the GM debate? What are the practical and concrete consequences of Ellul's theology? By way of illustration, it may be interesting to apply some of his key ideas to a discussion of GM technology that has occurred within the scientific community. I will refer particularly to views expressed by professional ecologists, whose scientific concern is most closely focused on the environment.

GM technology is presented principally as the answer to the world's food problems. It will feed the hungry world. In public discussion, this is closely related to the reasons for, and the 'need' for GM technology. Feeding the hungry is a noble purpose, and therefore, it is argued, we 'need' GM technology. But actually, there are alternative means by which the world could be fed. The 'need' can only apply to the feeding of the world, as part of the justice of the Kingdom. It cannot apply to the particular techniques or means by which this end is to be pursued. Two further points can be made in relation to this.

First, if feeding those who have not, and cannot afford, food, is indeed the primary end, then we are dealing with a social and political, not a scientific, problem. The implementation of mechanisms to undertake this should be politically and socially

---

Christ, is central to his conception of the human, in distinction from Heidegger's project of the isolated self.

controlled; it is not a matter for scientists or commerce, as at least one ecologist has pointed out.[39] Western Governments should not be leaving GM to be debated by scientific safety committees, but it should be part of a whole range of considerations undertaken by those responsible for international aid and agricultural planning. Of course, it is not, and this shows how hollow the argument about world hunger is in connection to GM technology. In fact, since the development of GM technology is primarily a commercial matter, it is ludicrous to suppose that firms who exist to make profits should spend their resources on giving food to people who are starving because they have not the financial resources even to preserve their own lives. This is acknowledged by ecologists on both sides of the GM debate.[40] At present GM technology may even be said to be making things worse, since it is associated with the promotion of cash crops and sterile seed, both of which make farmers in the developing world more economically dependent on supplies and knowledge from the West, for which they have to pay disproportionally to the cost of food locally.

Secondly, the usefulness of GM technology in relation to the range of means available to meet world food requirements is not clear. There are a number of reasons for present famines, and inadequate productivity of traditional crops does not seem to be a major one. Instead, war and political instability, the introduction of cash crops for export, and inappropriate land ownership do far more to interrupt the subsistence farming that would otherwise provide people with adequate food. Distribution obstacles related to political and economic factors prevent the proper utilisation of the food and agricultural land that there is. For all of these reasons, it is not possible to support the claim that GM technology is likely to be a primary factor in relieving world hunger.

Ellul would also question the attitude to the global environment underlying much public discussion of these issues.

---

[39] This point is made, for instance, by C. Dormann, following discussion of GM technology in the British Ecological Society, the professional body for ecological scientists in the UK. See C. Dormann, 'BES Lecture at Leeds: An Open Letter to Professor Beringar', *British Ecological Society Bulletin*, 31, 2, 2000, 17–18.

[40] See D. Walton, 'Genetically Modified Futures', *British Ecological Society Bulletin*, 31, 2, 2000,15, and J. Beringar, 'Reply from John Beringar', *British Ecological Society Bulletin*, 31, 2, 2000, 19.

If the environment that supports humanity is God's gift, then it cannot be wagered or staked for profit or political power. This means that safety issues have to be taken seriously. Despite the reassurances offered by those promoting GM technology, it is clear that there is already evidence of problematic effects.[41] A society that valued the environment properly would ensure that appropriate resources were devoted to research on safety and regulation. Instead, the commercial concerns who hope to profit from this technology are also those who test its safety and run the crop trials. This arises because, far from accepting the social significance of GM technology, and providing government resources in the shape of university and state research institutes in which GM techniques could be developed and tested, the British governments of the last twenty-five years have closed down many such facilities and removed funding from others. Again, scientists from both sides recognise the inappropriateness of this situation.[42] The present situation reflects the evaluation of the environment as a disposable human asset available to the strongest and greediest; in Dormann's words, the 'monetary stocktaking of ecological communities'.[43]

The rhetoric surrounding the promotion of GM technology has many of the characteristics Ellul ascribes to Technique. The increased power/productivity of GM products is cited as making them the inevitable, the only seemingly effective, choice, showing the *automatism* and *technological universalism* he describes. The dependence of GM crops on other agricultural technology (for instance, specific herbicides or fertilisation regimes) makes them, as they are at present being marketed, inseparable from a package of Western industrialised agriculture, demonstrating other features of *monism* and *techno-*

---

[41] E.g., M. Crouch , 'Lessons from the Field', *Science and Public Affairs*, October 1999, 19–21; Walton, 'Genetically Modified Futures', 14–16.

[42] Beringar writes acerbically that he 'will never forgive the Conservative Party for selling-off State-owned plant breeding to private industry'. Walton suggests that if GM trials were being done by the UN or government laboratories, the public might believe that 'corners would not be cut to make greater profits, that the objectives were really feeding the hungry and not greater dividends, and that the control and oversight mechanisms were robust enough to ensure that health and the environment would be protected as far as possible'. Walton, 'Genetically Modified Futures', 15.

[43] C. Dormann, 'Lecture at Leeds', 18.

logical integration. I have already discussed Ellul's critique of the
role of technological rationality or *unreason* in forming industrial agriculture, and this critique applies even more strongly to
GM technology, as shown by the comments of the ecologist
themselves. Ellul's exposure of the subversion of values revealed
by an analysis of public discourse and social and political
processes is as revealing when applied to the discussion of GM
technology as it is in the many other areas he has critiqued.

The majority of theological comments on the GM debate so
far have concentrated on ethical questions, and there is a
tendency to preach to science. In fact, it is clearly absurd to
suppose that ethical guidelines for scientists can make any
difference whatever to the promotion of GM technology, since
they are employees in an industry and their work is within the
law. Anyone refusing to do particular experiments would simply
be dismissed. As Ellul has pointed out, the real responsibility for
technology developments is political, and politicians need to be
encouraged to accept that responsibility. In the case of GM
technology, such acceptance would put an end to 'passing the
buck' between politicians and scientific 'experts'. Churches
need to engage with the technical and political arguments, not
to displace their concerns into ethical prescriptions which are
easily neutralised as matters of private morality. The place of
science in the economy and politics of the modern state has to
be recognised for churches to make effective contributions on
the moral issues raised.[44] I believe that Ellul's approach permits
this level of realism and it enables functional analysis and
practical engagement between the Church and the world.

---

[44] Stephen Sykes is a notable exception among theologians. He makes this point in
a recent editorial on science and technology. See Sykes, 'Ethical Reference Points
for Scientific Developments', *Crucible*, 39, 2000, 3–8.

13

Nature, Technology and the Rule of God: (En)countering the Disgracing of Nature

Peter Scott

On Not Beginning from Where We Are

In our image? The 'engineering' of genes suggests an intensification of our capacity to manipulate the environment in ways that suit us. This context includes our own bodies, animals and the agricultural environment: all can now be altered indelibly and more radically than has been possible in the past. The engineering of genes enables the refashioning of a context previously thought to be 'given' or manipulable only within limits. *Anthropos* reigns: nature is to be redirected towards us; what was thought to be radical alterity deconstructs into the human. Our world, including our bodies, is now plastic, to be shaped in our image. Some of us, at least, are *sicut deus*.

The immediate issues are not, in my view, ethical.[1] That most of the theological discussion of 'genetic engineering' concentrates on ethical matters as these engage the human is, I consider, a mistake. My opening question – In our image? – presents a theological invitation: is it possible to consider genetic engineering directly by asking what it means for the human creature to be in the image of God? If we might reframe our thinking and acting by relating genetic manipulation to the

---

[1] The Response of the Church of England Board for Social Responsibility to the Nuffield Council on Bioethics Consultation Document on Genetically Modified Crops (August 1998) concluded that there were no theological or ethical grounds to object to the genetic modification of plants. Implicitly through this chapter I shall be trying to indicate some of the theological mistakes in such a judgement.

understanding of the human before God rather than before the self-images of this postmodern world, what might we learn? It is my hope that in the attempt to answer this question, two secondary questions will also be clarified. These questions are: Who are *we*? And where might wisdom be found in interpreting the realities of genetic engineering?

In working to connect the question 'In our image?' to 'In the image of God?' in the consideration of genetic engineering, I turn to the rule of God (doctrine of eschatology).[2] That is, to speak of the human as in the image of God is also to assert that the human is in the image of the *coming* God. This has immediate consequences: the theological discussion of genetic engineering privileges, as shall be seen in a later section, a *correcting* God. Notions of salvation and redemption (the two are often employed interchangeably) are here reshaped.[3] A millennial tone may be heard in these theological considerations of genetic engineering. Gone is the apocalyptic stress on rupture and judgement; in abundance is the matter of moderate correction of nature towards human benefit. In this essay, I protest against such gradualist notions of social progress. The language of amendment or correction should be resisted.

But the fiercest apocalyptic language which speaks of an ending should also be questioned. On this view, apocalyptic rupture suggests a God who is *closing down*: by its hubristic tendencies genetic engineering prefigures some final overreaching of humanity which can only be corrected by the judgement of God: an apocalypse.[4] Given the largely bourgeois provenance of Christian theology in the academy, such a view is not often heard among theological 'professionals'! But although environmental groups may not be aware that, at its fullest, apocalyptic discourse is always a *theo*logical discourse, such commitments are present in the environmental

[2] While the phrase 'rule of God' may not be to everyone's taste, I use it in preference to more familiar terms such as 'Kingdom of God' and 'reign of God'. Alternatives such as 'project of God' or 'inheritance of God' are not in every way satisfactory: 'project' lacks a normative aspect; 'inheritance' suggests the passing-on of a fixed entity.

[3] I argue this case in the third section of this chapter, and in Peter Scott, 'The Technological Factor: Nature, Redemption and the Image of God', *Zygon: Journal of Religion and Science*, 35, 2, 2000, 371–84, especially 375–9.

[4] For this interpretation, see Catherine Keller, *Apocalypse Now and Then* (Boston: Beacon Press, 1996), 11.

movement. In an analysis of the Earth First! movement in the US, political scientist Martha F. Lee has highlighted a form of environmentalism in which an apocalypse of nature is posited through which it remains unclear whether or not human beings will survive or should survive.[5]

A strange dialectic joins these two views. The stress on cheap hope or false fears are mirror-images of each other.[6] Both these views, I suggest, begin from where we are and maintain a view of humanity as in its own image. Such an image is, to be sure, restricted and partial: *correction* indicates that the blessing of God is at the bestowal of those who can afford the costs of genetic engineering and *closing down* privileges those actions that will force an ending to the practice of genetic engineering. Whichever view is taken, the goodness of God is restricted: awarded to one group and denied to others, the goodness of God is construed as partial and particular.

The Rule of God: Systematic Considerations

In contrast, Christian eschatology recommends a God who neither corrects nor closes down but rather *closes in*.[7] What is involved in making this claim? I wish here to make three points which are, in my view, central to a systematic treatment of the rule of God in the present discussion.

First, if genetic engineering puts an end to all discourse of nature as unchanging, then the doctrine of eschatology is the principal resource for considering such change. For Christian eschatology is concerned with the glorification of God and the contribution of creation to that glorification.[8] It elaborates on

---

[5] Martha F. Lee, 'Environmental Apocalypse: The Millenial Ideology of "Earth First!"', in Thomas Robbins and Susan J. Palmer (eds), *Millenium, Messiahs and Mayhem: Contemporary Apocalyptic Movements* (New York and London: Routledge, 1997), 119–37. Cf. Martha F. Lee, *Earth First! Environmental Apocalypse* (Syracuse, NY: Syracuse University Press, 1995); Derek Wall, *Earth First and the Anti-Roads Movement* (London and New York: Routledge, 1999), esp. 43–5.

[6] Colin Gunton, 'Dogmatic Theses on Eschatology', in D. Fergusson and M. Sarot (eds), *The Future as God's Gift: Explorations in Christian Eschatology* (Edinburgh: T&T Clark, 2000), 139–43.

[7] Walter Lowe, 'Prospects for a Postmodern Christian Theology: Apocalyptic without Reserve', *Modern Theology*, 15, 1, 1999, 17–24, esp. 20.

[8] In this and the next few paragraphs, I am drawing freely on my 'The Future of Creation: Ecology and Eschatology', in Fergusson and Sarot, *Future as God's Gift*, 89–114, esp. 92–4.

the contribution to be made by the future of creation to the glorification of the God who closes in. Concepts of transformation, consummation and fulfilment are central to eschatological discourse. I am arguing, then, that the perspective of the rule of God best engages the altering of nature and technological transformation implicit in the interpretation of genetic engineering. In this straightforward sense, eschatology seems appropriate for the interrogation of genetic engineering.

Second, the rule of God indicates the unrestricted primacy of the actions of this God in and towards the establishing of goodness. Such goodness engages all creation, not only the human. 'God's future, as the future of the Creator', writes Jürgen Moltmann, 'has to do with the whole creation.'[9] But such a position should not be held abstractly. To argue that eschatology presupposes creation and to imply thereby that the rule of God presupposes a creaturely realm is surely correct. However, to understand the relation between the rule of God and the totality of creatures in such fashion is also to require the expansion of the task of eschatology. For now eschatology must speak of the relations between the human and the 'natural'; eschatology must speak of ecological relations governing human communities. When in eschatological discourse mention is made of completion or fulfilment, the triumph of God's goodness must include the non-human.[10]

Third, the rule of God has the quality of finality. 'Many modern 'apocalypses' are not truly apocalyptic', writes Colin Gunton, ' because they do not envisage some form of divine action that is ontologically final.'[11] That is, the rule of God is concerned with judgement. Because it is concerned with judgement, the rule of God is thereby fundamentally normative. To say that creation has a place in God's purposes is not a descriptive but rather a normative statement. We are referred to how the world will finally be with God. In the

---

[9] Jürgen Moltmann, *The Coming of God: Christian Eschatology* (London: SCM Press, 1996), 21, 132.

[10] In addition to setting out the theo*logic* for this claim in 'The Future of Creation', it should be noted here that the inclusion of the non-human has been present as a theme in Christian theological tradition: see H. Paul Santmire, *The Travail of Nature* (Philadelphia: Fortress Press, 1985).

[11] Colin E. Gunton, *The Triune Creator: Historical and Systematic Considerations* (Edinburgh: Edinburgh University Press, 1998), 219.

consummation of God's ruling, attention is directed not only to transformation by divine agency but also to the normative quality of God's goodness. In eschatology we are not concerned with a description of future states but instead with the final ordering of this world and what the final consummation means for the life of God.[12]

These three points are the 'Full Monty': any attempt to reduce the number of components, deny their interrelation or dilute one of the commitments should be treated with considerable suspicion by Christian theology and Christian communities. Thinking about being in the image of God from the claim of the coming of God thus involves beginning not from where we are but from an imperative to enter the goodness – final and comprehensive – of the rule of God.

What this position means for the theological interpretation of genetic engineering is the subject of this essay. In the next section, the suggestion by some theologians that genetic engineering should be understood as salvific is tested against the interpretation of eschatology just adumbrated. In the section that follows, I explore how the concept of technology is to be thought in relation to everyday life by offering a reading of technology and nature adapted to the concrete ordering of this world under the rule of God. In the final section, I suggest a rather different theological way of interpreting genetic engineering which conforms to the unrestricted aspect of God's goodness, its apocalyptic finality and the gracing of nature.

The core question posed – What does it mean to speak of the human as in the image of the *coming* God in the context of genetic engineering? – is answered by reference to living in and towards the unrestricted goodness of the rule of God for all creation. Who *we* are is also discovered: *we* cannot be separated from the particular relations in which we are placed with human and other-kind. And whatever wisdom we may discern is to be garnered from learning to live in such a common realm impartially yet militantly.

---

[12] Daniel W. Hardy, 'Eschatology as a Challenge for Theology', in Fergusson and Sarot, *Future as God's Gift*, 151–8.

Theologies of Genetic Engineering

In my view, many theologies of genetic engineering begin from where we are. What goes unnoticed is the notions of technology and nature operative in these theological presentations. Technology is implicitly regarded as instrumentalist, nature as an object for manipulation. I have elsewhere characterised this view of nature and technology as *modern*.[13] Further, the theme of redemption is also instrumentalised: God's redemption is associated with the re-ordering of nature for human benefit; salvation and genetic engineering mysteriously converge.[14] The God of this image is that of the correcting God, and who we are emerges all too clearly as the few who can afford access to the goodness conveyed by such technologies.[15] The rule of God is associated with a providential and thereby benign gradualism: not so much 'social gospel' as 'medical gospel'. A lack of attention to the notions of nature and technology is combined with the redrawing of doctrinal considerations (a revision of the Full Monty) in which the wider anthropology remains understated.

One way of approaching such theologies of genetic engineering is to note that such optimistic assessments of genetic manipulation draw heavily – if implicitly – on a theological reading of temporality.[16] The drive towards the instrumentalisation of nature, technology and, finally, Christian commitments, draws on gradualist notions of the unfolding of medical therapies as part of the co-creative work of human beings in relation to God. The actions of technological humanity or created co-creator

---

[13] Scott, 'Technological Factor'.

[14] Scott, 'Technological Factor', 375–9.

[15] Writes Ted Peters: 'At the frame and easily missing from our visionary picture will be those who do not benefit. Due perhaps to their suffering from a disease yet without a cure, or due perhaps to their socioeconomic class that prevents them access [*sic*] to the new health care, many among us will wander our streets with disabilities. Children born the old-fashioned way, without benefit of genetic engineering or selection, will live among us for the foreseeable future... It would be a grave injustice indeed if the shadow side of genetic science and medical technology created new forms of neglect, injustice and marginalization. Proleptic ethics keeps our eyes directed toward the shadows as well as the brightly lit possibilities' (Ted Peters, *Playing God? Genetic Determinism and Human Freedom* (New York and London: Routledge, 1997), 176.

[16] Here, I am thinking of the work of Ronald Cole-Turner, *The New Genesis: Theology and Genetic Revolution* (Louisville, KY: Westminster/John Knox Press, 1993), and Peters, *Playing God?*

follow God's redeeming actions towards creation and thereby contribute to the fulfilment of the purposes of the redeeming God.[17] For example, Ronald Cole-Turner makes his case primarily in relation to Christology, Ted Peters concentrates more fully on eschatological themes. As this chapter is concerned with the rule of God, through this section I shall concentrate on the work of Ted Peters. I hope to show that Peters does not operate with a systematically comprehensive eschatology and that his attendant interpretations of the concepts of nature and technology are inadequate.

At the heart of Peters's argument is a double claim, anthropological and theological. Although run together, and without a clear account of how they relate, it is possible to distinguish these two aspects. The anthropological line has the following sequence: creative, future-oriented humanity seeks to overcome human suffering and thereby develops therapies based on genetic engineering. The theological line has the following sequence: humanity is the created co-creator in the image of God, redeemed in the cross and resurrection of Jesus Christ; the latter is proleptic anticipation of the Kingdom; the practice of advent ethics is the way in which the *imago dei* anticipates the Kingdom and participates in the creative activity of God. These two lines of argument overlap to provide a theological legitimation – albeit only partial – of genetic engineering. What unites both is a commitment to temporality, understood eschatologically, as the indirect mediation of God's goodness.[18]

Deferring for a moment a discussion of the notions of nature and technology operative through the argument, what eschatological commitments in connection to transformation and goodness are in evidence? Although Peters prefers the language of creativity, he is right, I am convinced, to relate the possibilities of change given in the techniques of genetic engineering to eschatology. By the rule of God creation is to be brought to a new, transformed, ordering. And the clue to this ordering, here again I agree with Peters, is the cross and resurrection of Jesus Christ. Nevertheless, against Peters, I wish to argue that the content of the future is Jesus Christ, and thereby this future

---

[17] The concept of created co-creator is to be found in Philip J. Hefner, *The Human Factor: Evolution, Culture, and Religion* (Minneapolis: Fortress Press, 1993).

[18] I would cite the following sections in support of this reading: Peters, *Playing God?*, 11–26, 58–62, 167–78.

is also a judgement. In restricting his eschatological considerations to temporality, Peters loses sight of the claim that the resurrection of Jesus Christ is a revolution not in some abstract 'history' but in human embodiment.[19] Such a revolution in embodiment is always a social revolution and the goodness which the rule of God displays is a goodness that engages the social life of humanity.

In one sense, the reference to the raising of social forms to their goodness under the rule of God is present in Peters's argument. 'The future of God', he writes, 'will include a divinely established justice and the elimination of pain.' And, later, 'We can set our sights toward a divine future. The value of this vision is that it provides an image of the good accompanied by the hope that energises work to embody part of that vision ahead of time.'[20] But, in my view, such an image of the good cannot be separated from Jesus Christ and means that the establishment of justice and the elimination of pain must be placed in their full anthropological setting which is the life of humanity as social. Theological discussion of genetic engineering should not then proceed without an account of the system of health care by which advances in medical science are delivered and the ways in which such advances are funded and marketed. *Imago dei* is always also *imago civitatis*.[21]

And what of the relation between humanity and nature of which eschatology speaks? How does the *imago dei* in Peters's rendering relate to nature? The most extended discussion of nature in *Playing God?* occurs in the consideration of the 'sacralisation of nature', a line of argument that Peters rightly rejects.[22] Now is not the occasion for exploring the relation between the modern and countermodern, the secularisation and resacralisation of nature in contemporary discourses on nature.[23] We may note, however, that the stress on nature as sacred – in itself false (for, as created, no part of the world can be treated as

[19] An argument for resurrection as a revolution in human embodiment may be found in Peter Scott, *Theology, Ideology and Liberation: Towards a Liberative Theology* (Cambridge: Cambridge University Press, 1994), 184–8.

[20] Peters, *Playing God?*, 174, 178.

[21] For more on humanity as *imago civitatis*, see my 'Beyond Stewardship? Dietrich Bonhoeffer on Nature', *Journal of Beliefs and Values*, 18, 2, 1997, 193–202.

[22] Peters, *Playing God?*, 14–16, 117, 121–6, 161–3, 175.

[23] For further discussion, see Peter Scott, 'Imaging God: Creatureliness and Technology', *New Blackfriars*, 79, 928, 1998, 260–74.

sacred) – tries to hold to an important truth: the agency of nature. That is, the relations between humanity and nature are to be understood in terms of mutual dependency.

Rightly rejecting the sacralisation of nature, Peters falls into the trap of affirming the manipulation of nature. Consider the following statement: 'nature is far more than just a tool to be used, far more than merely an object of instrumental value'.[24] Yet this curiously phrased view suggests that nature is at least a tool, an instrument. We may agree with Peters that nature is not sacred but nothing follows as a matter of logic from this judgement. Certainly, the rejection of the sacralisation of nature does not require that we affirm the modernisation and instrumentalisation of nature.

Mixed with this discourse on nature is the claim that nature, considered in eschatological perspective, is not fixed.[25] Yet for Peters this position is interpreted in two ways. That nature is not static seems to be employed as a reinforcement for the view that nature should be the site of the exercise of human creativity. That is, this nature is both other and open for manipulation. With this view, however, comes a second, rather different, interpretation: that nature can only be understood as good when grasped as open for an Other: 'To see the lure of nature toward what is good requires discernment; it requires a vision of divinely promised redemption.'[26] But this matter of the redemption of nature is not pursued. Or, more precisely, it is subsumed under the earlier view of the openness of nature: as temporal and thereby to be manipulated by the created co-creator towards the enhancement of human life.

To summarise, the relation between humanity and nature is interpreted in instrumentalist fashion. While I may agree with Peters that nature is not sacred, a permission for the modernisation of nature does not follow. What is lacking is a clear sense of how the *imago dei* is always also *imago mundi*.[27] With this comes a lack of clarity on the criteria for the identification of goodness: is goodness somehow mediated by nature, or by the

[24] Peters, *Playing God?*, 175, cf. 117.
[25] Peters, *Playing God?*, 162, 175.
[26] Peters, *Playing God?*, 20.
[27] The phrase *imago mundi* is from Jürgen Moltmann, *God in Creation: An Ecological Doctrine of Creation* (London: SCM Press, 1985), 51.

manipulation of nature or by the orientation of nature on its final goal in God? The answer to this question is not clear.

And, lastly, to technology: what view of technology emerges in Peters's argument? The discussion of technology is brief, and that genetic engineering is always already a technology is overlooked. The fullest comment on technology occurs early in the argument when its context in human creativity is noted. More than this, creativity and technology are conflated: we cannot be creative except by being technological. I presume here that Peters is making a general anthropological point: 'We cannot be human without being technological . . .'[28] From here Peters argues that technology can be put in the service of many interests, for good or ill. In putting the matter thus, Peters appears to be accepting that technology is neutral and a 'natural' feature of human life.

By such commitments Peters's argument betrays its complicity in the much-announced promise of technology in which technology itself is regarded 'as an essentially uninteresting if powerful tool, neutral in its relation to cultural values and subservient to political goals'.[29] Furthermore, this view of technology is deeply consonant with a liberal democratic polity in which the principle of self-realisation, understood as a certain equality of all individuals in the development of their talents, requires the 'neutral' instrument of technology to secure this self-realisation.[30] In such fashion, rudimentary attention is paid to how technology should be understood, whether there is any difference between modern technology and the technology of the past and how technology shapes life today.

Yet if the rule of God encourages us to think in terms of the finality of goodness, and the orientation of human social life on that goodness, we need some account of technology in order to test whether technological practices mediate this goodness indirectly or – as evil or wicked – should be understood as in contradiction to that goodness. Interpreting genetic

---

[28] Peters, *Playing God?*, 15.

[29] Albert Borgmann, *Technology and the Character of Contemporary Life: A Philosophical Inquiry* (Chicago: University of Chicago Press, 1984), 35. Although at this point in the argument he appears to accept it, at other times, for example, *Playing God?*, 26, Peters rejects for theology the connection between technology and progress.

[30] Borgmann, *Technology and the Character of Contemporary Life*, 85–101.

engineering theologically thereby requires a theological concept of technology as well as a theological concept of nature as creation.

We may now note that there is a conservatism to the argument promoted by Peters. This is not without some irony for, drawing on Karl Rahner, Peters argues that those Christians who set their faces against genetic engineering are themselves hiding behind a conservative construal of Christian values which recommends that we do not interfere in God's creation. Peters calls such a position conservative or reactionary. Yet although Peters supports genetic engineering he begins from where we are and thereby holds to a type of conservative position. Such conservatism will not face the radicality of the goodness of God manifested in God's rule in Jesus Christ. And because such goodness is not faced, hard questions – who benefits from genetic engineering, whether human life as social is enhanced and if our relations with nature may be understood as liberatory – are avoided.

The association of genetic healing with healing and the overcoming of suffering is, we may conclude, in line in a general way with eschatological commitments. The stubborn hope that presses forwards through adversity and suffering is an eschatological principle. Yet is access to God's goodness restricted to the instrumentalisation of technology? Is the sustained attempt to anticipate the rule of God to be conducted through the manipulation of nature, human and non-human?

Technology and Nature in Eschatological Perspective

One feature that recommends the theological stance criticised in the previous section is its 'obviousness'. In the association of redemption and a particular technology the providential ordering of the world under the rule of God is tangible. Behold: a technology that drips goodness, a technology that provides access to God's goodness. Do you need reassurance of the efficacy of God's rule? Well, comes the reply, look no further than this technology. How do I participate in such goodness? Well, comes the reply, support this technology. The circle is complete: God, genetic engineering and the medical well-being of Western humanity are linked together in a seamless loop.

However, through this section I want to explore a different way of thinking about technology and nature. Especially, I wish to place technology in the context of the practice of everyday life. Technology, after all, is ordinary. How can technology be thought in ways that are not modern and instrumentalist but rather refer us always to participation in a concrete social order (both human and natural) that presses towards God's goodness?

Considering technology in non-instrumentalist ways and rejecting the view that nature is an object for manipulation is difficult because in rejecting instrumentalist versions we are usually required to accept what Albert Borgmann calls a substantive account or Andrew Feenberg dubs a substantivist reading of technology.[31] The work of the later Heidegger and of Jacques Ellul are good examples of this tendency. Overcoming technology construed substantively usually requires in some fashion the rejection of technology. Or, more precisely, what is to be rejected is the technological mindset.

In a highly interesting analysis, Borgmann takes a different route from substantive and instrumentalist readings of technology. As ordinary, Borgmann contends, we should expect to find technological devices omnipresent through our contemporary life.[32] And Borgmann conducts his analysis at this ordinary level: playing a musical instrument is contrasted with the commodification of music produced by modern electronic reproduction, walking and running with travelling by car, preparing a table meal to snacking on fast food and microwaved meals. From this position it comes as no surprise that the reform of technology from within technology is held not to be possible. Borgmann denies the usual way of redeeming technology: one cannot begin from an instrumentalist reading of technology and within the technological operation of the causality of means–ends seek to substitute new ends. Such a view is mistaken, Borgmann reasons, because technology has become the dominant pattern of contemporary life. Aspects of that dominant pattern include: the strict separation of means and ends, the separating out of actions and

[31] Borgmann, *Technology and the Character of Contemporary Life*, 9–10, etc.; Andrew Feenberg, *Questioning Technology* (New York and London: Routledge, 1999), 1–3.
[32] Cf. Borgmann, 'The Moral Significance of the Material Culture', in Andrew Feenberg and Alistair Hannay, *Technology and the Politics of Knowledge* (Bloomington and Indianapolis: Indiana University Press, 1995), 85–93.

contexts and the thinning of our affective relationships with nature and others. Technology is thereby intimately related to the commodification of everyday life.

How should we then found, develop and maintain counter-practices to technology? Here Borgmann recommends that focal things and practices should be understood as sites of resistance to and reform of technology. Focal things: what are these? 'Wilderness on this continent,' writes Borgmann, 'is a focal thing.' And he continues:

> It [wilderness] provides a center of orientation; when we bring the surrounding technology into it, our relations to technology become clarified and well-defined ... And surely there will be other focal things and practices: music, gardening, the culture of the table, or running.[33]

On account of the relationship between the notion of wilderness and concepts of nature, it is of particular interest that Borgmann should identify the former as a focal thing.[34] Wilderness, as pristine nature, is that which is untouched by technology. In its greatness, it may encounter us from beyond the world of technology. This is not, Borgmann hastens to add, the resacralisation of nature. Rather, Borgmann proposes 'learning again from the ground up what it is to recognize something as other and greater than ourselves and to let something be in its own splendor rather than procuring it for our use. Nor do I claim that pristine nature is the only or final realm where we can again encounter the divine and learn reverence.'[35]

How convincing is Borgmann's presentation? Any answer depends in part on an evaluation of his theological commitments. The discourse built on the notions of focal things and practices draws on Paul Tillich's discussion of ultimate concern or significance.[36] Much of the cogency of this argument would further depend on the relation between the sacred and the

---

[33] Borgmann, *Technology and the Character of Contemporary Life*, 197. Cf. Albert Borgmann, 'Prospects for a Theology of Technology', in Carl Mitcham and Jim Grote (eds), *Theology and Technology: Essays in Christian Analysis and Exegesis* (Lanham and London: University Press of America, 1984), 305–22 (315).

[34] Borgmann, *Technology and the Character of Contemporary Life*, 182–96.

[35] Borgmann, *Technology and the Character of Contemporary Life*, 190.

[36] Borgmann's theological interests are evident in the essay, 'Prospects for a Theology of Technology'.

profane at which Borgmann, drawing on Eliade, hints.[37] Can
these theoretical resources truly sustain a reform of technology
from 'beyond' technology in ways that are socially engaged and
politically sophisticated?

According to Andrew Feenberg, the answer to this question
is no.[38] The attempt by Borgmann somehow to constrain the
activities of technology is, first, to essentialise technology and,
second, to try to perform the impossible task of separating
technology from culture.[39] The two points when combined
enjoy a certain cogency: if technology is always associated with
domination – the creating of 'technological norms of comfort
and security,' as Borgmann notes elsewhere[40] – then the
circumscription of the rule of technological cause and effect
makes sense. Such an approach, which for Feenberg joins the
prime weakness in Heidegger's philosophy of technology to
what is most problematic in Jürgen Habermas's critique of the
colonisation of the life-world, is unable to theorise how
technology is in fact reshaped by social factors and social
agents. For Feenberg, in this approach technology and society
are reified.

Feenberg's alternative, called in his earlier work 'subversive
rationalization' and more recently 'democratic rationalization,'
turns upon the rejection of substantivist and essentialist
critiques of technology. Or, to put the matter positively, it is not
constitutive of the meaning or practice of technology that it
operates undemocratically. Technology does not oppose
democracy but rather blocks it. Thus technology must be disem-
bedded from the norms in which it usually operates – norms of
mechanisation and efficiency – and be recontextualised in
democratic imperatives.[41] Technology is not thereby to be

---

[37] For example, could this notion of focal things and practices be a profane
analogue of postliberal presentations of the Church and its practices as a
community of resistance? Cf. on Christian counter-practice, Borgmann,
'Prospects for a Theology of Technology', 320.

[38] Feenberg, *Questioning Technology*, 187–93.

[39] An essentialist account of technology is one in which the substantive view is
associated with domination by technology. Thus, according to Feenberg,
Borgmann falls into the very trap of substantivism that he is seeking to avoid.

[40] Borgmann, 'Prospects for the Theology of Technology', 311.

[41] Feenberg takes his examples from the spheres of medicine and computerisation.
In the area of energy production, perhaps it will be politician Tony Benn's
enduring legacy to have highlighted the democratic deficit in the development of
nuclear power in Britain.

restrained by the building up of focal things and practices but is rather a realm of contested meanings and a site of intervention and struggle.[42]

Important differences emerge between the philosophical perspectives of Borgmann and Feenberg. But now at least we have on the theological agenda in the interpretation of genetic engineering that, first, technology should not be construed as instrumentalist and, second, the study of technology cannot be narrowed to the treatment of a single technological development or innovation. Technologies are ordinary, non-instrumentalist and support particular political formations. A theology of the technology of genetic engineering cannot fall behind these insights.

Encountering Eschatological Goodness: The Gracing of Nature

We are trying here to identify theologically how technology contributes to human and natural well-being and how, if evil or wicked, it must be rejected. We are faced by a difficult problem: should we see God's goodness as mediated more fully by way of focal things and practices in which the reform of – and not merely in – technology is envisaged? Or should we rather hold that the meanings of technology are various and can be shaped in ways often unknown to the controllers and producers of the technology and thereby bestow the goodness of God? Which may be understood as the principal modality of participating in the goodness of God?

I am not convinced that a theological answer *simpliciter* can be given to these questions. That is, the systematic account of eschatology proposed earlier does not, I consider, provide theoretical resources in support of a definitive answer. However, those same systematic considerations suggest a way forward. Note that whether nature is to be treated as a focal power or whether the democratising of technology is the best way forward, from an eschatological perspective all creatures, the human and the non-human, are understood as having

---

[42] See Andrew Feenberg, *Critical Theory of Technology* (New York and Oxford: Oxford University Press, 1991); Feenberg, 'Subversive Rationalization: Technology, Power and Democracy', in Feenberg and Hannay, *Technology and the Politics of Knowledge*, 3–22; Feenberg, *Questioning Technology*.

access to God's goodness. We humans are co-participants in a common realm that encompasses non-human nature also. What are the implications of this view? Whichever route is taken – the reform or the democratising of technology – no purchase, theoretical or practical, may be had on the promise of technology except by reference to non-human nature.

By Borgmann's route, nature as wilderness becomes that which is not technologically mediated and thereby might in some way both exceed us and yet be oriented on us. By Feenberg's route, nature becomes the test of the democratising of technology for without democratic reference to the non-human, the hold of technology as promising the liberation of the human from its natural conditions will never be adequately challenged. Such a theological development of these two philo-sophical positions requires an account of the otherness of nature. An account of such otherness is a key aspect of eschato-logical thinking: the holding together of nature and humanity, as was presented in the second section above, in their common, but not identical, ending in God. Critical purchase is secured by reference to a common yet different ending: the criticism of technology is only by way of the gracing of nature.

How does the gracing of nature engage genetic engin-eering as a technology? To answer, I return to the subsidiary questions posed earlier: Who are we? And where might wisdom be found in interpreting the realities of genetic engin-eering? Identifying who *we* are cannot be achieved except by reference to non-human nature. But we are obliged immedi-ately to note that there is no single way or set of ways in which human beings interact with non-human nature. For example, James O'Connor suggests three basic ecological conditions of capitalist production: 'external physical conditions', 'labour power' and 'communal conditions'. By such terms, O'Connor refers to, respectively: 'the viability of ecosystems', etc.; 'the physical and mental well-being of workers ... human beings as social productive forces and biological organisms generally'; and 'social capital', 'infrastructure', including access to transport, education and so on.[43] If these are among the principal means of access to social goods, such ways are

[43] James O'Connor, 'The Second Contradiction of Capital', *Natural Causes: Essays in Ecological Marxism* (New York: Guilford Press, 1998), 160–1.

modulated by class, race and gender. Relations to nature therefore always involve social relations. Identifying who *we* are emerges as problematic and requires attention to the distribution of social and natural goods.

Furthermore, because identifying who we are is problematic, identifying the benefits that might flow from technological advance is problematic also. To identify technology, including genetic engineering, as a principal way of participation in society would be a mistake, for in such privileging, the wider – usually dominant – social relations are occluded. Furthermore, the status of technology as the agent of social division is overlooked. On these grounds alone, technology is not to be understood as the privileged mode of participation in God's goodness.

And where shall wisdom be found? Already noted is that identifying who *we* are cannot be achieved except by reference to non-human nature. By this reference, the unity of the human race is established: all of humanity relates to non-human nature. Impartiality is thereby introduced into our theory of human–nature interaction. Part of what 'common good' will mean is just this impartiality. That is, the common good can only be served by means of the testing required by the switching of perspectives which the notion of impartiality invites. Such switching indicates self-judgement and the requirement of conversion. This impartiality would be very hard to practise, for habitually we side with ourselves against non-human nature. Impartiality here means the criticism of dominant 'narratives' we tell about ourselves in relation to nature; this, then, is a militant impartiality.

Yet such a stance is only part of the demand: if, as suggested earlier, natural relations involve social relations, then the requirement to side impartially with non-human nature may also mean entering into relations of solidarity with those whose modes of access to nature are different from our own, who, on account of their position in a society, suffer restrictive relations with nature and thereby impoverished social relations.[44]

---

[44] Lack of space forbids an exploration of the thorny problem as to whether inter-human relations or human–nature relations are the site of the emergence of domination.

To put the matter in this way is neither to rule out nor to promote genetic engineering. It is rather to try to find a way of referring a technological discourse and practice of change to the God who closes in. Such closing in requires attention to natural and social relations as the primary context for the consideration of God's blessing. So considerable caution is an appropriate Christian response to genetic engineering. This is not conservatism, neither the sort of conservatism rightly criticised by Peters in which Christians hide behind a static view of creation,[45] nor an appeal to traditions of 'custom and practice' to which technological innovation is alien.

Instead, it is to argue the *radical* case that developments in genetic engineering must be tested not narrowly against the laudable desire to overcome human suffering but more widely by the 'social' and 'natural' goods secured by technologies of genetic engineering and by technologies in general. For technology is neither solely an instrument nor a reified force but instead should be interpreted as ordinary, located in the practices of contemporary life. The goodness of God's rule is present in anticipatory form in the political discourse that draws the human into relation to the non-human and in the democratic practice of militant impartiality. The technology of genetic engineering requires the testing of the quality of social and natural relations, for these are the principal mediators of God's goodness.

[45] Peters, *Playing God?*, 156

14

Aquinas, Wisdom Ethics and the New Genetics

Celia Deane-Drummond

Introduction

As presented in the media, public debates over genetic engineering, where they extend beyond scientific questions, raise
issues of particular ethical and social concern. Theologians may
worry that specific religious questions are not taken into
account sufficiently in such debates. However, even within the
ethical debates themselves the approach most often used
emphasises consequences, inspired by the utilitarianism of J. S.
Mill or Jeremy Bentham, or, in some cases, rules or duties,
inspired by the ethics of Immanuel Kant. Hence, the choice in
ethical deliberations over genetic engineering follows a utilitarian or deontological framework, with the former taking
precedence.[1] This may seem somewhat surprising given the
strong move in contemporary philosophy to recover an
alternative approach to ethics that stresses moral character,
namely, virtue ethics.[2] Moreover, I suggest that due consideration of virtue ethics offers a highly constructive approach in
the fraught debates over genetic engineering. A purely utilitarian framework tends to polarise into discussion about risks
and benefits of genetic engineering, with both areas
inadequately characterised, often coloured by particular

---

[1] For further discussion, see ch. 1 of this volume.
[2] See, for example, R. Crisp and M. Slote, *Virtue Ethics* (Oxford: Oxford University
Press, 1998), and R. Hursthouse, *On Virtue Ethics* (Oxford: Oxford University Press,
1999).

political or social presuppositions.[3] In contrast, a deontological approach that frames particular issues from theological norms may seem out of touch with the secular ethical debates.[4] Theologians may respond by rejecting serious ethical inquiry altogether in favour of theological reflection detached from ethical concern. I will argue in this paper that taking serious account of virtue ethics not only brings a fresh approach to the debates over genetics, but also an ethic of wisdom in particular is rooted in theology in such a way that theology can make an active contribution to the debates. Furthermore, a virtue ethic, by focusing on the agent first, rather than the possible outcomes of specific ethical dilemmas, encourages ongoing moral attention that serves not only to sustain human resilience in times when decision-making is difficult but also to challenge all parties involved to re-examine their attitudes.

By definition, virtue ethics is characterised by being agent centred, rather than act centred, putting emphasis on goodness, rather than rights, duties or obligations, even positively rejecting the idea that ethics can be codified in rules. Virtue ethics has been criticised for not defining itself adequately in relation to alternative bases for ethics.[5] Moreover, questions are being asked as to the criteria used to choose some virtues over others, especially in those cases where virtue ethics is used in a non-teleological way.[6] However, the strength of the shift in the last thirty years is such that even those who are basically utilitarian, such as Peter Singer, or Kantian, such as Onora O'Neill, are now taking into account virtue ethics.[7] With respect to genetic engineering relatively few authors have taken up this theme though some have indicated that differences in attitude are crucial to ethical considerations about difficult decisions in the new genetic technologies. David Cooper, for example, suggests that in complex ethical issues over the treatment of animals the character of the agent needs to be

---

[3] For further discussion, see C. Deane-Drummond, *Genetic Engineering for a New Earth* (Cambridge: Grove Books, 1999), and Donald Bruce's paper, in this volume.

[4] See ch. 1 by Deane-Drummond, Grove-White and Szerszynski, in this volume.

[5] See R. Crisp and M. Slote, 'Introduction', in Crisp and Slote, *Virtue Ethics*, 24.

[6] See D. Statman, *Virtue Ethics: A Critical Reader* (Edinburgh: Edinburgh University Press, 1997), 11.

[7] P. Singer, *How Are We to Live?* (Oxford: Oxford University Press, 1997); O. O'Neill, 'Kant after Virtue', *Inquiry*, 26, 1984, 387–405.

taken into account. In particular, he suggests that the virtue of humility needs to be recovered in consideration of the ethics of genetic intervention on animals.[8]

Is there a theological basis for establishing a virtue ethic? John Barton suggests that the particular way that virtue ethics is characterised today cannot be read directly from biblical texts.[9] The Old Testament presents us with the stark contrast of the wise or foolish, the righteous or sinners. Characters seem to be fixed and unchanging, ethical choice seems to be once and for all, where 'the subtlety which sees everyone as a mix of the two, or as living a life in which virtue is cultivated and vice therefore rooted out seems largely lacking'.[10] He suggests that the emphasis in the biblical account is on *conversion* rather than growth in the moral life. One possible interpretation might be that the biblical account actually opposes a virtue ethic, relying instead simply on justification by faith. However, he resists such an interpretation, as it is largely dependent on a particular interpretation of Pauline texts. Certainly moral goodness in the Old Testament is that defined by the Torah, and thus indicates a deontological approach to ethics. Judaism subjected the Torah to detailed *Mishnah* in order for it to be applicable to particular practical situations. Barton also suggests, somewhat strangely perhaps, that wisdom in the Old Testament is orientated towards success, rather than virtue, and is therefore consequentialist in orientation.[11] There are, nonetheless, three important caveats in Barton's critical analysis. The first is that while the ideal of the righteous may have been held up in a literal reading of the text, it is possible that this served as a goal to be aimed at in the context of a more realistic approach to education in the moral life. The second is that the narrative accounts of the Bible, which tell the particular messy and very human stories of the lives of specific individuals chosen by God, such as David or Jacob, demonstrate that human lives are still *examined lives* and are subject to change and growth. Finally, he

---

[8] D. E. Cooper, 'Intervention, Humility and Animal Integrity', in A. Holland and A. Johnson (eds), *Animal Biotechnology and Ethics* (London: Chapman and Hall, 1998), 145–55. See also Clark's paper, in this volume, for further discussion.

[9] J. Barton, 'Virtue in the Bible', *Studies in Christian Ethics*, 12, 1, 1999, 12–22.

[10] Barton, 'Virtue in the Bible', 14.

[11] Barton, 'Virtue in the Bible', 17. In this he follows E. W. Heaton, *Solomon's New Man* (London: Thames and Hudson, 1974).

implies that while the Bible may not spell out a virtue ethic as such, it could be used constructively to achieve good moral character, which is the aim of virtue ethics. In the end he refuses to come to a decision either way as to whether the Bible does or does not support virtue ethics.

I suggest that one of the difficulties with Barton's appraisal of virtue ethics in the Bible is that he seems to assume that the contemporary philosophical approach to virtue ethics sets criteria on which to judge the biblical accounts. Might there be *another* way of defining virtue so that it took into account the particular biblical emphasis, for example, on humility or charity, that we find in the letters to the Hebrews and the Corinthians? Furthermore, the wisdom literature is often not quite as cut and dried as he implies, presenting a certain measure of fluidity in the moral life. Qoheleth and Job are both excellent examples of those who challenged the presumed wisdom of their contemporaries, arriving at more open-ended accounts of the way God works in the world.[12] I have suggested elsewhere that one of the strands in the theological and biblical tradition that needs to be highlighted is the wisdom tradition.[13] I also suggested that Thomas Aquinas provides a useful starting point for thinking ethically about wisdom as a virtue and how this might relate to issues in the new biology. Clearly, Aquinas viewed his own ethical stance as being rooted firmly in the biblical account, as well as drawing significantly from Aristotle and Augustine. The way Aquinas develops and expands his idea of wisdom in the context of his particular understanding of virtue ethics is therefore highly significant for the present discussion.

The preliminary question we need to ask concerns the validity of different particular interpretations of Thomistic literature. Alastair MacIntyre believed that, by going back to Aristotle and Thomas Aquinas, philosophical reflection could avoid some of the pitfalls encountered since the Enlightenment that had led to the neglect of virtue ethics.[14] I am not going to make any attempt

---

[12] See C. Deane-Drummond, *Creation through Wisdom* (Edinburgh: T&T Clark, 2000). My commentary on Aquinas is necessarily brief and I expand and elaborate the arguments further in this chapter, especially in relation to virtue ethics.

[13] This applies to both the Old Testament and New Testament understanding of wisdom: see Deane-Drummond, *Creation through Wisdom*.

[14] A. MacIntyre, *After Virtue: A Study in Moral Theory*, Second edn (London: Duckworth, 1985), 181–203.

to undertake an overview of different possible interpretations of Aquinas in history. The main question that is of relevance here is the alternative contemporary re-appropriations of Aquinas's ethics. MacIntyre's account stresses the Aristotelian nature of Aquinas's works. However, while he is aware of the varieties of definitions of the virtues in different traditions, his focus on tradition *as such* opens up the possibility of a specifically Christian virtue ethic.[15]

Some scholars, such as Anthony Lisska, have recovered Aquinas's understanding of natural law as a basis for both meta-ethics and jurisprudence. He suggests, in particular, that the concept of God is not essential for Aquinas's understanding of natural law.[16] Other scholars, such as Servais Pinckaers, insist that the separation of the philosophical from the theological in Aquinas's account of ethics is artificial. Rather, his writings have to be considered as a whole, including his work in the third part of *Summa Theologiae* on the New Law that is explicitly evangelical.[17]

Alternatively, Aquinas may be read primarily as a theologian, rather than as a philosopher. Catherine Pickstock, one of the supporters of a trend in theology known as Radical Orthodoxy, argues that Aquinas provides an important resource for Christian orthodoxy, but within a literal reading of his writing understood in terms of postmodern performance.[18] Her approach may not be satisfying theologically, as she seems to isolate particular themes in Aquinas's work, reading them in a way that not only ignores the historical issues but, more important for the present context, seems to split apart his theological from his philosophical analysis. More significant, perhaps, the philosophical seems to be evacuated in favour of a re-appropriation of the theological.[19] Jean Porter takes an

---

[15] N. Murphy, B. J. Kellenberg and M. T. Nation, *Virtues and Practices in the Christian Tradition: Christian Ethics after MacIntyre* (Harrisburg: Trinity Press International, 1977).

[16] See A. J. Lisska, *Aquinas's Theory of Natural Law: An Analytic Reconstruction* (Oxford: Clarendon Press, 1997), 117–38.

[17] S. Pinckaers, *The Sources of Christian Ethics*, tr Sr Mary Thomas Noble, 3rd edn (Edinburgh: T&T Clark, 1995), 168–90.

[18] C. Pickstock, *After Writing: On the Liturgical Consummation of Philosophy* (Oxford: Blackwell, 1998).

[19] L. P. Hemming, 'Quod Impossible Est! Aquinas and Radical Orthodoxy', in L. P. Hemming (ed.) *Radical Orthodoxy: A Catholic Enquiry* (Aldershot: Ashgate, 2000), 76–93.

intermediate view, in that while she recognises the importance of Aristotle in Aquinas's concept of prudence, she also gives due consideration to his treatment of the theological virtues.[20] By considering the significance of Aquinas's unified theory of morality, Porter flies in the face of dominant deconstructive tenets in postmodernity. Detailed consideration of the challenge of postmodernity to Christian ethics is outside the scope of this chapter. Suffice it is to argue that a recovery of virtue understood both philosophically and theologically remains a valid *option* even following postmodern critique. Moreover, as I indicate below, the apophatic elements in the notion of wisdom itself means that it is not 'foundationalist' in the philosophical sense.

In the following section I will argue that Aquinas needs to be read *both* as a philosopher and as a theologian in order to appreciate his virtue ethics. I will be focusing in particular on his understanding of *wisdom* and how this relates to prudence and natural law in order to provide a framework for subsequent reflection on current issues in genetics. I will also suggest that it is possible to interpret Aquinas in such a way so as to develop a *wisdom ethic*; one that is sensitive to the discoveries of science but provides a framework for critical reflection on scientific practice.

A Recovery of Wisdom

Wisdom as learned and revealed

Aquinas viewed wisdom as one of the three intellectual virtues: the other two are 'understanding' and 'science'.[21] Science consisted of knowledge arising from a demonstrated conclusion and in one sense is therefore more restricted in its use compared with its definition today.[22] The habit that perfects the intellect in consideration of the truth is known as 'understanding'. However, of all the intellectual virtues wisdom takes priority in Aquinas's scheme, hence: 'What comes last with respect to all human knowledge is what in reality is the

---

[20] J. Porter, *The Recovery of Virtue* (London: SPCK, 1994), 155–171.
[21] Aquinas, *Summa Theologiae*, Vol. 23, *Virtue*, tr W. D. Hughes (London: Blackfriars, 1969), 1a2ae Qu.57.2, 43.
[22] Aquinas, *Summa Theologiae*, *Virtue*, 1a2ae Qu. 57.2, translators note a, 42–3.

principle and most evident truth. Here is wisdom, which considers the highest and deepest causes.'[23] What is the relationship between wisdom and science? Here Aquinas seems to see wisdom as related to science, yet acting as its judge at the same time. Hence wisdom: 'has something proper to itself above the other sciences inasmuch as it judges them all, with respect not only to their conclusions, but also to their premises, and accordingly more completely than science fulfils the nature of virtue'.[24]

Nonetheless, Aquinas's concept of wisdom is more sophisticated than this account suggests so far, in that he recognises not only wisdom that springs from philosophical inquiry but also wisdom from divine revelation through the work of the Holy Spirit. For example, on the one hand, he states that 'The wisdom which Aristotle lists as an intellectual virtue considers the divine in so far as this is open to the investigation of human reason.'[25] On the other hand, at the start of his *Summa Theologiae*, he makes it clear that wisdom is 'received from the outpouring of the Holy Spirit, and as such is numbered among one of the seven gifts of the Holy Spirit.'[26] He agrees with Augustine that wisdom is 'knowledge of divine things'; it is about God as 'deepest origin and highest end', but in a sense this is still shrouded in some mystery as it is only that which God chooses to disclose. Jean Porter defends Aquinas's theological stance in this respect, arguing that his unified account is qualified by the fact that some things are only properly known to God. In this way, 'whatever one thinks of this project, it is not the equivalent of modern philosophical foundationalism'.[27]

Yet for all Aquinas's attraction to philosophical notions of wisdom, he is clear about which must take priority, for 'we do not look upon wisdom as merely yielding knowledge about God (as do the philosophers), but even as directing human life, and in fact, not only according to human standards, but also in

---

[23] Aquinas, *Summa Theologiae*, *Virtue*, 1a2ae Qu. 57.2, 45.

[24] Aquinas, *Summa Theologiae*, *Virtue*, 1a2ae Qu. 57.2, 45.

[25] Aquinas, *Summa Theologiae*, *Virtue*, 1a2ae Qu. 62.2, 141.

[26] Aquinas, *Summa Theologiae*, Vol. 1, *Christian Theology*, translated by Thomas Gilby (London: Blackfriars, 1964), 1a Qu. 1.6, 21.

[27] J. Porter, *Moral Action and Christian Ethics* (Cambridge: Cambridge University Press, 1995), 90.

accord with divine norms, as Augustine observes'.[28] I suggest
that his more philosophical reflections on prudence make most
sense in the context of the *theological* priority that Aquinas gives
wisdom.

Aquinas's understanding of prudence

Prudence, or 'practical wisdom', is one of the cardinal virtues in
Aquinas's scheme, along with temperance, fortitude and
justice. Both wisdom and prudence are virtues and both are
related to each other. Prudence could even be considered an
aspect of wisdom. However, as Aquinas understands the terms,
prudence is more closely aligned to the philosophy of Aristotle,
while wisdom is more closely aligned to theology, especially that
of Augustine of Hippo. The way prudence acts on the moral
virtues is subject to some scholarly debate. A common interpretation is that prudence suggests the particular *means* for gaining a
particular *end* of the virtue in question. However, Jean Porter
presents a more sophisticated and possibly more accurate
interpretation, namely, that prudence sets the particular way a
virtue should be expressed in particular circumstances, or the
'mean' of the virtue.[29] This mean varies with different circumstances and it is the task of prudence to decide, through the use
of reason, the 'rational' mean. Justice is the only exception
where the mean of the virtue is also the 'real' mean, since in this
case justice is always characterised by preservation of mutual
equality.[30]

An important characteristic of prudence is that it is highly
practical in nature. It is not just a quality of mind, but involves
the particular application to a deed or action.[31] Prudence
engages in what Aquinas terms 'commanding', or 'bringing into
execution what has been thought out and decided upon'.[32] In
this prudence is different from art, where the critical faculties

---

[28] Aquinas, *Summa Theologiae*, Vol. 33, *Hope*, translated by W. J. Hill (London: Blackfriars, 1966), 2a2ae Qu. 19.7, 65.

[29] Porter, *Recovery of Virtue*, 155–9.

[30] I will be returning to consider the issue of justice in more detail in the section below on natural law.

[31] Aquinas, *Summa Theologiae*, Vol. 36, *Prudence*, translated by T. Gilby (London: Blackfriars, 1974), 2a2ae Qu. 47.1, 47.2, 5–9.

[32] Aquinas, *Summa Theologiae*, *Prudence*, 2a2ae Qu. 47.7, 27.

are used in judgement, but there is no definite obligation to act. The combination of knowledge of principles with the particular situation in hand is important for the functioning of prudence, hence 'the prudent character, then, must needs know both the general moral principles of reason and the individual situation in which human actions take place'.[33] Here we arrive at a dilemma, namely, that human reason cannot grasp the infinity of possible circumstances. Yet human reason in this situation, through experience and memory, 'can resolve them into some definition according to what happens in the majority of cases'.[34] Prudence, then, involves the use of the memory, present experience and foresight. However, the contingency of the situations in which prudence acts remains so that prudence does not remove 'all uneasiness of mind'.[35] Aquinas is following Aristotle here and shows the distinction between the kind of certainty that is possible with theological truths and that coming from prudence.

Aquinas is also aware that there may be instances where prudence may not be acting correctly, either through striving for a wrong end, or 'sham prudence', or through the good being partial and exclusive to a particular situation, or 'incomplete prudence'.[36] It is only when prudence is directed to the universal end for the whole of human life, or ultimate goodness, that prudence can be regarded as genuine and 'complete'. Such an ideal would seem humanly impossible to achieve and it is here that Aquinas introduces the notion of divine grace. The prudence that comes from God's grace is infused directly by God. He also suggests that prudence can be marred by sin, especially misdirected passions, which distort the use of reason and effectively block the practice of prudence expressed in right action.[37]

Aquinas follows Aristotle in his characterisation of prudence, but he also takes up ideas from other philosophers, such as Macrobius and Cicero. He identifies eight characteristics of prudence.[38] Five are related to knowing; namely, memory,

---

[33] Aquinas, *Summa Theologiae, Prudence*, 2a2ae Qu. 47.3, 13.
[34] Aquinas, *Summa Theologiae, Prudence*, 2a2ae Qu. 47.3, 13.
[35] Aquinas, *Summa Theologiae, Prudence*, 2a2ae Qu. 47.9, 31.
[36] Aquinas, *Summa Theologiae, Prudence*, 2a2ae Qu. 47.13, 41–3.
[37] Aquinas, *Summa Theologiae, Prudence*, 2a2ae Qu. 47.16, 51–3.
[38] Aquinas, *Summa Theologiae, Prudence*, 2a2ae Qu. 48, 53–7.

reason, understanding, aptness to being taught and ingenuity. Three apply knowing to doing; namely, foresight, circumspection (attending to circumstances) and caution (avoiding obstacles). Hence the idea of taking precaution is closely related to prudence. Other related virtues include the ability to be well advised or take counsel, *euboulia*, soundness of judgement, *synesis*, and the wit to judge when departure from rules is called for, *gnome*.

Relating wisdom and prudence

Those who truly express the virtue of prudence will have a settled commitment to live a good life, rather than just show sporadic instances of prudent behaviour. This springs from the unity of the virtues, so that those who have one virtue necessarily have them all.[39] Yet it would seem that wisdom, as given by grace, is needed in order to approach such a high ideal. Hence, 'In the field of human acts the ultimate cause is the common end of the whole of the human life, and it is to this end that prudence reaches out.' In this way prudence is 'wisdom in human affairs', but it is not 'wisdom pure and simple, because it is not about the utterly ultimate, but about good for man, which is not the most ultimate and best of goods that exists'.[40] This reinforces the point that I made earlier, namely, that while Aquinas respects and values the use of reason in prudence, the gift of wisdom that comes from the Spirit transcends rational deliberations and reaches into more mystical and contemplative categories. Hence wisdom moves in the same domain as prudence, but the goal of the activity is subtly different: for prudence the goal is based on human reason alone, while for wisdom the goal becomes aligned with the beatific vision of God. This needs to be qualified by the fact that according to Aquinas, rather oddly perhaps, prudence must also be infused by God's grace in order to be 'complete'. For Aquinas the pervasiveness of sin is such that God's grace is needed to overcome human frailty expressed as deficiency in human reasoning. Wisdom, moreover, as one of the intellectual virtues, can be learned and is also a rational activity. Wisdom and

---

[39] Aquinas, *Summa Theologiae*, *Prudence*, 2a2ae Qu. 47.14, 45.
[40] Aquinas, *Summa Theologiae*, *Prudence*, 2a2ae Qu. 47.2, 11.

prudence need, therefore, to be considered together, rather than separately. Given that wisdom is given priority over prudence in Aquinas's scheme, this is highly suggestive of an ethic of wisdom. Wisdom, in defining the relationship between God, humanity and creation, seems to function as a transcendent theological category in which practical prudence is situated. However, at the same time, wisdom is not separated from the material world, for it expresses the action of God immanent in creation.[41]

Aquinas identifies the theological virtues as faith, hope and charity, and it is above all charity that acts as an organising principle in the personality of those with faith, rather than prudence as such.[42] However, wisdom in its task to judge according to divine truth is aligned with prudence and is distinct from faith, for 'faith assents to divine truth for itself; the gift of wisdom judges things according to divine truth'.[43] It is in *piety* that wisdom becomes most manifest, hence the gift of wisdom is to faith in much the same way that the virtue of wisdom is to the intuitive habit of grasping first principles of thought. Aquinas also distinguishes wisdom as gift in that it always flows from charity and hence is caused by the activity of the will, while rooted essentially in the intellect.[44] Wisdom as gift presupposes charity to the extent that it colours its operation in a way that distinguishes it from the use of reason in prudence.

Aquinas's reflection on the nature of folly is also of interest in helping to distinguish prudence and the gift of wisdom. For Aquinas folly is a 'blunted sense of judgement', rather than total loss of the ability to judge correctly.[45] Folly is a defect in the ability to decide the highest cause, though the 'worldly wisdom' that takes for its goal anything other than God as ultimate cause stands opposed to 'divine folly'. He suggests that folly coming from a natural inability to reason is no sin; rather the sin is in the loss of the spiritual to alternative earthly causes.[46] Such alternatives are fostered through evil desires and

---

[41] See Deane-Drummond, *Creation through Wisdom.*
[42] Porter, *Recovery of Virtue*, 169.
[43] Aquinas, *Summa Theologiae*, Vol. 35, *Consequences of Charity*, translated by T. R. Heath (London: Blackfriars, 1972), 2a2ae Qu. 45.1, 165.
[44] Aquinas, *Summa Theologiae, Consequences of Charity*, 2a2ae Qu. 45.2, 167–9.
[45] Aquinas, *Summa Theologiae, Consequences of Charity*, 2a2ae Qu. 46.1, 181.
[46] Aquinas, *Summa Theologiae, Consequences of Charity*, 2a2ae Qu. 46.2, 183.

especially lust, leading to hatred of God, despair of the future
world and anger, all of which block the operation of true
wisdom. Even prudence would not be able to operate within the
context of such earthly passions, though Aquinas insists that
some exercise in the use of reason is able to continue even
within the context of mortal sin.[47] Hence, while Aquinas does
present us with the stark biblical contrast of wisdom and folly
that I raised earlier, he also allows for some gradation in
advancement in the moral life, so that those with true prudence
anticipate those with true wisdom.

Wisdom and Natural Law

At first sight it might seem that the concept of natural law would
be incompatible with a wisdom ethic. Certainly, Aquinas characterised as one who supports a virtue ethic would seem counter
to the more legalistic framework implied by the idea of natural
law. I shall suggest in the section that follows that his understanding of natural law complements the wisdom themes in
important ways in order to decipher the place of human
ordering in nature.

Natural law, for Aquinas, is 'participation in the eternal
law' through use of our reason. In particular, certain axioms
are generally known to all people. He argues that everyone
acts with a particular purpose in mind and as such this
purpose 'carries the meaning of to be good'. The fundamental principle of natural law is that good be sought and
evil avoided and this is known through reason given in
human nature.[48] He also suggests that there is a *correspondence*
between our natural inclinations and the commands of
natural law. In this I concur with Jean Porter's interpretation
of Aquinas, when she suggests that the primary norms of
natural law are not so much *derived* from natural inclinations,
rather norms come primarily from the twin injunction to love
God and one's neighbour.[49] Such a distinction is important as
it resists alternative interpretations of natural law, which imply

---

[47] Aquinas, *Summa Theologiae, Consequences of Charity*, 2a2ae Qu. 45.3, 171.
[48] Aquinas, *Summa Theologiae*, Vol. 28, *Law and Political Theory*, translated by T. Gilby
(London: Blackfriars, 1966), 1a2ae Qu. 94.2, 81.
[49] Porter, *Moral Action*, 108.

that it is simply a form of naturalism or even biologism. Moreover, while Aquinas does take into account a certain gradient of perfection from non-human creatures to humanity, this does not mean that the inclinations associated with the sustenance of life are 'lower' in the moral scale. For example, in his scheme the tendency for self-preservation is a basic instinct to all life; copulation and the rearing of young shares commonality with the animals, while the search for the rational is unique to human beings.

Some virtues flow directly from natural law, but others require a much more sophisticated use of reason.[50] The natural use of reason in natural law or *synderesis* sets the particular goals of the moral virtues. However, as stated earlier, the exercise of prudence is still essential in discerning the particular mean of each virtue in given circumstances.[51] While we may *begin* with natural knowledge of good and evil, deliberative prudence works to *further* that knowledge by a process of careful deliberation.[52] As Pamela Hall points out 'no rule, let alone those of the natural law, can be applied or constituted without an accompanying understanding of the rule's point as understood by prudence'.[53] Aquinas also suggests that natural law is not fixed in its application to particular cases. In common with the exercise of prudence and aligned with it, there is a degree of uncertainty when particular cases are considered. Hence, 'the more we get to particular cases the more we can be mistaken'.[54] This allows a degree of flexibility in the concept of natural law, apart from the first principles, so its secondary precepts can be changed where such change would be beneficial to the social life of a community. Like wisdom and prudence, misdirected passions may block the right operation of reason and hence natural law in the human heart.[55]

Contemporary interpretations have tended either to dismiss the place of natural law in Aquinas's ethics or to put it in a

[50] Aquinas, *Summa Theologiae, Law and Political Theory*, 1a2ae Qu. 94.3, 85.
[51] Aquinas, *Summa Theologiae, Prudence*, 2a2ae Qu. 47.3, 23.
[52] P. M. Hall, *Narrative and the Natural Law: An Interpretation of Thomistic Ethics* (Notre Dame and London: University of Notre Dame Press, 1994), 39.
[53] Hall, *Narrative and the Natural Law*, 40.
[54] Aquinas, *Summa Theologiae, Law and Political Theory*, 1a2ae Qu. 94.4, 87.
[55] Aquinas, *Summa Theologiae, Law and Political Theory*, 1a2ae Qu. 94.6, 97.

central position.[56] Porter suggests that such a dichotomy is false in that Aquinas's understanding of the virtues and natural law are integrally connected. The first principle of natural law, to do good, is not simply a matter of following one's inclinations, but of fulfilling them in a certain way through the virtues.[57]

Justice, as a virtue, is also intimately connected with the good of others. Justice relates to natural law in that human reason establishes that which is just through positive law, that is, specific legislation, and this in itself is not in conflict with natural law.[58] Prudence is involved in decisions about what constitutes a just deed. Porter suggests that the link of justice with natural law is important since 'the most fundamental relationships of obligation and forbearance which inform justice do not depend on our rationality, but are rooted in those aspects of nature which we share with the other animals'.[59] Yet rationality is still needed to 'flesh out' obligations. Aquinas's characterisation of justice as one of the virtues is particularly significant given the current split between particularist virtue ethics and more universal deontological approaches that focus on justice and the language of rights. Onora O'Neill has suggested that a modified Kantian version of critical reason can successfully marry virtue ethics with justice.[60] However, her practical reasoning seems to be set by the agents themselves, in that what count as rational principles are those that can be followed by all who are making such decisions and those for whom such decisions apply. Her exclusive elevation of reason seems to be excessively modernist. At the same time, in rejecting all metaphysical certainties, the scope of ethical concern is entirely dependent on the agents' own construction of other subjects deemed to be connected with their own.[61]

---

[56] Compare, for example, D. M. Nelson, *The Priority of Prudence: Virtue and Natural Law in Thomas Aquinas and the Implications for Modern Ethics* (University Park: Pennsylvania State University Press, 1992) with J. Finnis, *Natural Law and Natural Rights* (Oxford: Clarendon Press, 1980).

[57] J. Porter, 'What the Wise Person Knows: Natural Law and Virtue in Aquinas's Summa Theologiae', *Studies in Christian Ethics*, 12, 1, 1999, 57–69, esp. 62.

[58] Aquinas, *Summa Theologiae*, Vol. 37, *Justice*, translated by T. Gilby (London: Blackfriars, 1974), 2a2ae Qu. 57.1, 9.

[59] Porter, 'What the Wise Person Knows', 67–8.

[60] O. O'Neill, *Towards Justice and Virtue: A Constructive Account of Practical Reasoning* (Cambridge: Cambridge University Press, 1996).

[61] O'Neill, *Towards Justice*, 4, 57, 212.

In Aquinas's ethical scheme the virtue of prudence connects with justice in that political prudence is prudence as directed to the common good of a community, as distinguished from domestic prudence directed to the good of the household and simple prudence, as directed to the good of an individual.[62] He also suggests that the individual good needs to be subordinate to the good of the people, yet each person has a share in government through their own decisions, so in this sense political prudence is owned by subjects.[63] While Aquinas's understanding of politics is clearly coloured by his own hierarchical view of the State, it is possible to view his schema as a precursor to full democracy, rather than a simple affirmation of hierarchical medieval political institutions.[64] What is most significant for the present discussion is that Aquinas was unafraid to expand his virtue ethic into the realm of the social and political, rather than restricting virtue ethics to an individual account of moral character.

Wisdom, Natural Law and the New Genetics

How might Aquinas's understanding of wisdom contribute to current debates in the new genetics? More generally, I suggest, first, that the recovery of virtue is particularly significant in instilling a way of thinking about the natural world in those situations where there may not be clearly defined right or wrong answers to particular ethical dilemmas. Hence, at a time when particular knowledge is uncertain, ethical debates need to move away from particular calculations based on consequences or defined by rule-based approaches and move towards consideration of the character and attitudes of the agents themselves. In addition, the priority that Aquinas gives to the virtue of wisdom understood as divine gift, over and above rational discourse, forces us to consider deeper theological issues in consideration of the new genetic

---

[62] Aquinas, *Summa Theologiae, Prudence*, 2a2ae Qu. 47.10, Qu. 47.11; 33–7. Stephen Clark discusses the particular significance of Aristotelian familial virtues in his book, *The Political Animal: Biology, Ethics and Politics* (London: Routledge, 1999).

[63] Aquinas, *Summa Theologiae, Prudence*, 2a2ae Qu. 47.12, 39.

[64] P. E. Sigmund, 'Thomistic Law and Social Theory', in P. E. Sigmund (ed.), *St Thomas Aquinas on Politics and Ethics* (London and New York: W. W. Norton, 1988), 180–8.

technologies that relate to both the nature of human identity and human becoming. In other words, a recovery of virtue is one that encourages a change in attitude, not just about specific highly charged individual cases, but also a shift in moral character so that it becomes part and parcel of everyday experience. It is here that the wisdom ethic finds particular resonance, since it both links with the implicit public response to genetic engineering, and invites further theological definition and reflection.

Secondly, a further advantage of Aquinas's scheme is that his consideration of virtue (probing the character of the agent) is inclusive of some strands of teleology (ultimate purpose) and deontology (appraisal according to natural law and divine norms). Wisdom as a virtue is suggestive of a virtue ethic, but wisdom as a motif also allows for reflection on natural law and ultimate purposes through the gift of wisdom and the Wisdom of God in a way that is highly cogent for present debates. Hence while the wisdom ethic that I have suggested here shows some common ground with elements of a secular virtue ethic approach, it moves beyond this to consider the theological premises for human activity. In much the same way that Aquinas draws on Aristotelian philosophy, but then transforms it for his own purposes, so a wisdom ethic can draw on current philosophical understandings of virtue, but move on towards a critical stance towards this position from a theological perspective. Too narrow a focus on wisdom as virtue understood as an *individual goal* might restrict ethical discussion to a consideration of the character of scientists themselves and lead to a hostility and defensiveness on their part. Alternatively, a simple reiteration of divine law is unlikely to be heard in a secular context.

Thirdly, I suggest that in the context of a recovery of wisdom and prudence, a more realistic appraisal of individual ethical dilemmas in genetics becomes feasible. Hence, such ethical dilemmas are certainly not the starting points for ethical reflection, but are pondered following an overall shift towards an ethic of character that has become part of the pattern of ordinary ethical practice. The advantages of a wisdom ethic as I have developed it so far are that it includes both broader theological concerns as well as reflection on the character of the agents. For example, we might ask what is the 'good' end envisaged by the Donaldson Report on the use of stem cells in research?[65] I suggest that the recovery of a wisdom ethic is relevant in a number of respects. In the first place what might be the ontological status of stem cells, if creation is by God through wisdom?[66] Given that prudence is crucial in delineating the practical expression of all the virtues, it is relevant to ask, in addition, whether there has been sufficient prudence understood as foresight, circumspection and caution. This links in to some extent with the precautionary principle widely used in ethical debates about the new genetics.[67] However, the difference between the precautionary principle as commonly understood and Aquinas's concept of prudence is that the former isolates one aspect, namely, the need for caution. Prudence, by contrast, is not simply caution, but includes two more aspects relating knowing to doing that I discussed earlier, namely, foresight and circumspection (attending to circumstances). Moreover, prudence includes the use of memory, reason, understanding, aptness to being taught and ingenuity. Has sufficient time been taken to 'take counsel'? Is the prudence, where it exists, the kind of holistic prudence that Aquinas suggests, or is it in some sense 'incomplete', isolating the good as defined simply in medical terms? Or even more critical, is such prudence in some sense 'sham', covering up other motives, such as financial gain, so that the good striven towards is not the good it appears to be?

Another difficult question to consider in the new genetics is how far it might be justifiable either to cross particular boundaries between species or to drastically alter the characteristics of a species.[68] From the perspective of Aquinas's understanding

---

[65] L. Donaldson (Chair), *Stem Cell Research: Medical Progress with Responsibility: A Report from the Chief Medical Officer's Expert Group Reviewing the Potential of Developments in Stem Cell Research and Cell Nuclear Replacement to Benefit Human Health* (London: Department of Health, 2000).

[66] This argument avoids the difficult question of the particular moral status of the embryo in terms of human personhood. Aquinas's particular views on the status of early embryos prior to quickening that are based on a medieval understanding of reproduction and human development are not necessarily relevant here. I have discussed briefly the application of Aquinas's understanding of prudence and wisdom to issues in the new genetics in *Biology and Theology Today: Exploring the Boundaries* (London: SCM Press, 2001).

[67] For a discussion of the precautionary principle in genetics, see chapter by D. Bruce in this volume.

[68] See M. Reiss, this volume, for further discussion.

of natural law a relevant question is how far such manipulations are directed to ultimate goodness. The instinct for self-preservation in all living creatures concurs with this aim. More specifically, genetically engineering pigs so that they become more placid in crowded conditions, for example, could be seen as a limited good even for the pigs themselves as it makes their lives more tolerable. Yet, given that this involves a loss of brain function, this would seem to deny the integrity of the creature. Aquinas was mistaken in his particular ethic towards animals, namely, that they are simply 'brute beasts' to be used by humans for their advantage. In this sense the divisions he set between all life forms, animals and humans, seem somewhat naïve. However, his scale of perfection does allow a greater degree of respect to be afforded to those species that are closer to human beings. It is a good example of the way the secondary precepts of natural law may need to be adjusted in the light of new knowledge. Importantly, perhaps, his theory of natural law does *not* support a biological naturalism that leads to a rigid fixity of species boundaries in all circumstances. His views resist a total prohibition of genetic engineering, but any changes need to be set in the context of the particular good of each creature in wider perspective of the ultimate good as given by God.

A further issue of particular relevance to the genetic engineering of crops is that of justice. Given that justice for Aquinas is rooted in our commonality with all animals, this opens the way for consideration of issues in genetic engineering not just in terms of the human community, but the wider community of all life forms. A facile individualism casts a shadow over much of the current vogue for virtue ethics. By including political and social arguments in his ethical account, Aquinas reminds us that prudence is not just a question of virtue for the individual moral agent, but carries a political dimension as well. The particular hierarchical and medieval political context that Aquinas imbibed requires some adjustment today, along with his understanding of biology. However, this need not detract from an openness in his thinking towards democracy that I suggest might be extended to include an ecological understanding of community relationships.[69] This is particularly pertinent in the case of genetic engineering of crops and their

---

[69] See P. Scott, this volume, for further discussion.

introduction into the poorer nations of the world. Do such changes represent a holistic good for that community, under-stood as an ecological community, both now and in the future? In particular, how does the *memory* of Western interventions in the past colour current proposals?

However, as I indicated earlier, much uncertainty exists over the ethical debates in the new genetics. This need not be a cause for alarm, since a measure of uncertainty in ethical debate is to be expected if we follow Aquinas's approach both to prudence and to natural law. An ethics of virtue based on wisdom and prudence is able to encompass such uncertainty and could even be said to sustain human existence in the midst of such uncertainty. In a secular world we cannot expect the gift of wisdom to be operative in formulating particular laws. In allowing for prudence or practical wisdom in the world Aquinas opens up the possibility of a dialogue between theology and science, the Church and the wider secular community. Above all, Aquinas encourages those Christian believers who seek after the gift of wisdom to do so in the spirit of charity, in alignment with the particular beatitude that leads to peacemaking.[70] In facing the possible re-ordering of nature Aquinas's wisdom ethic invites us to consider how such re-ordering challenges our own sense of self as moral agents. In arriving at a theological basis for ethics Aquinas reminds his readers to consider all creatures as under divine providence, hence divine Wisdom. Such Wisdom is always sought after, rather than simply attained. Yet in so far as it concurs with secular prudence it opens the way for a richer and deeper engagement with current issues in the new genetics. For without a fostering of the memory of such wisdom in the human community, all attempts to restructure the world according to human design seem certain to lead to fragmentation, rather than order, since they remain focused on specific and limited human goods, isolated from the wider goods of the human community as embedded in the Community of nature.

---

[70] For further elaboration, see Deane-Drummond, *Creation through Wisdom*.

15

Re-Ordering Nature: A Postscript[1]

Bronislaw Szerszynski
and Celia Deane-Drummond

Introduction

In recent years, uncertainty has emerged as a recurring theme
in debates about environmental problems, signifying the
weakening grip of the framing that dominated such debates
since the 1990s, that of the need for 'sound science'. In that
earlier framing, the ideal of sound science, predicated on scientific procedures of validation, was invoked as a way of
overcoming the continual contestation of claim and counter-
claim that characterises much of environmental politics.
Concerted action, it was assumed, needed a consensus over the
truth, and the way to achieve this consensus was through
the securing of facts upon which all reasonable people would
agree. In this we can see echoes of the origins of the Royal
Society in the seventeenth century, in the midst of religious
wars and conflicts. In that earlier period of cultural upheaval,
the scientific experiment was seen as a new social space in which
assent could be achieved across religious divides.[2] Calls for
'sound science' are still to be heard, not least from the
government at the time of writing in the case of debates about
genetic modification (GM). Nevertheless, there is a growing
acknowledgement that a responsible stance toward new

[1] The authors are grateful for comments from Robin Grove-White, Paul Fletcher
and Brian Wynne on earlier drafts of this chapter.
[2] S. Shapin, *A Social History of Truth: Civility and Science in Seventeenth-Century England*
(Chicago: University of Chicago Press, 1994).

technologies has to involve not the erasure or denial of uncertainty, but the recognition that it is intrinsic to human action, and a fortiori in the case of new technologies.

The uncertainty that characterises such technical interventions has many aspects, criss-crossing received distinctions between nature, technology and society. Scientific knowledge about the way that nature behaves is increasingly seen as provisional, as philosophers of science, and many scientists themselves, recognise the intractability of natural processes to any definitive account of the way they operate. Many processes, indeed, may simply not exhibit lawful, determinate behaviour in the conventional sense. New technologies, for their part, typically produce their most significant long-term side effects in areas completely unanticipated in their early stages, problematising conventional processes of technology assessment. Finally, both the consequences of new technologies and also many of the crucial factors shaping their development are social in character, introducing a further intensification of uncertainty.[3]

In the 'sound science' framing, such uncertainties were presented as peripheral and temporary; as the shrinking, as yet unoccupied territory outside an ever-expanding circle of secured and agreed knowledge. In the 'uncertainty' framing, this spatial metaphor has to be reversed, as uncertainty is increasingly brought into the *centre* of debates. Replacing the notion of certain, scientifically generated facts functioning as a space of (positive) agreement, a new space of (negative) agreement is emerging, one of agreement about the limits of human knowledge, prediction and control.[4] Until very recently genetic modification for geneticists seemed one way that knowledge about nature could be secured, agreed and changed. Or, perhaps more accurately, although genetic change brought with it some imprecision, the aim was still to eliminate variables as far as possible through experimental design. Environmental scientists were generally more

---

[3] On the distinctions between ignorance, uncertainty and indeterminacy, see, for example, M. Smithson, *Ignorance and Uncertainty: Emerging Paradigms* (Berlin: Springer Verlag, 1989), and B. Wynne, 'Uncertainty and Environmental Learning: Reconceiving Science and Policy in the Preventive Paradigm', *Global Environmental Change*, 2, 1, 1992, 1–22.

[4] For a similar argument, see H. Nowotny, P. Scott and M. Gibbons, *Re-Thinking Science: Knowledge and the Public in an Age of Uncertainty* (Cambridge: Polity, 2001).

sceptical, viewing genetic change as a catalyst for subsequent uncontrolled changes in the evolution of modified species. The new shift we have identified is the resistance among genetic scientists to the belief that genetic change could ever be absolutely predicted. Genetic modification has thus been both a further example of this shift towards the recognition of uncertainty, and a catalyst for societal reflection upon it.

It is our contention that this shift is both a problem and an opportunity for religion. It is a problem in the sense that it disrupts the ruling division of labour in post-Reformation theology between religion, science and politics. Broadly speaking, this settlement left nature to science and society to politics, confining religion to personal morality and experience. The problematisation of science's self-image as producing objective knowledge blurs the distinction between science and politics, since politics can no longer hive off questions of knowledge to science, and scientists pass on questions of value to politicians. Similarly, we want to suggest, religion's gilded cage as the institution with primary responsibility for morality and private experience is problematised. As Peacocke points out in chapter 5 of this volume, scientific reductionism as a way of knowing is giving way to a new openness, one that leaves room for the personal and the religious. This then is the opportunity and challenge for religion in general and theology in particular – to operate once more in a much wider cultural space than has been the case for the last few centuries, as the power of scientific reason withdraws back to the human scale.

The ejection of God from the world was inextricably linked up with the emergence of modern ideas of certain knowledge (and thus of uncertainty as its expelled Other). God in medieval thought was understood not just as another existent or agency within the world, but as the very ground and possibility of meaning, language and reason. As such, language did not simply refer, on occasions, to God; it celebrated him at all times as the origin and guarantor of all sense. Modern science, from its origins in the scientific revolution of the early modern period, conceived of true knowledge as being the situation where language, purified of excess, ambiguity and ornamentation, is brought into perfect – and timeless – correspondence

with a reality conceived as brute matter.[5] This reconceptuali-
sation of knowledge in the disembodied terms of proposition
and referentiality left God with no place in modern thought.
God became something not just not required but not permitted
by reason and knowledge.

We are suggesting that uncertainty in issues like GM be
conceived as a manifestation of divine mystery. Divine transcendence is reappearing through the cracks in modern technical
knowledge – not simply as a God of the gaps, to be invoked in
order to fill the lacunae in causal explanations, but as that
which is the limit and the excess of causation itself. In a
technical episteme, transcendence manifests itself as that which
cannot be absorbed and accounted for by that episteme. But at
the same time it points beyond that episteme, to its very
exhaustion. Science as a set of practices is not at an end – far
from it. But what is showing signs of weakening is science's
claim to be *the* master-frame of reality, as providing authoritative and certain knowledge, and as serving as a benchmark
against which all alternative claims to truth must be measured.

It is against the background of this interpretation of our
current predicament that we want to discuss the contributions
to the present volume. In chapter 1 we suggested that the
genetic revolution might usefully be seen as a 'revelation', as
'an event which sharply reveals what must always have been the
case'.[6] We want to return to this thought in this concluding
chapter. It is our contention that uncertainty can be seen as the
return of the repressed of modernity, the place in which divine
mystery reasserts itself against and through the over-extension
of scientific and technical reason.

Christianity, Eschatology and Moral Discernment

Given that the discussion about God becomes possible and
permissible once again in the context of an uncertain world,
what possible role could there be for Christianity in particular,

---

[5] H. Schnädelbach, *Philosophy in Germany 1831–1933* (Cambridge: Cambridge
University Press, 1984). B. Szerszynski, 'On Knowing What to Do:
Environmentalism and the Modern Problematic', in S. Lash, B. Szerszynski and B.
Wynne (eds), *Risk, Environment and Modernity: Towards a New Ecology* (London:
Sage, 1996), 104–37.
[6] Deane-Drummond et al., this volume, p. 37.

as well as religion in general, in debates about biotechnology? It is our contention that, not least given the cultural context of uncertainty, seeing Christianity as providing an ethical code which can be used to ground authoritative ethical pronouncements would be a mistake. First, as we suggested above, Christianity should be prepared to operate in a much wider cultural space, not just as an ethical watchdog pronouncing on individual technological options. In chapter 4 Northcott reminds us that it is the underlying technocratic culture of modern farming that is awry, so that genetic modification of crops is the fruit of an underlying misplaced relationship between people and land. In this scenario a Christian ethical response is a call for a love ethic, stewardship properly understood to mean right relationship rather than management. The stumbling of modernity, as the pretensions of scientific reason are undermined under the weight of its ramifying side effects, means that the carefully delineated boundaries of the curtailed cultural space in which religion has operated in the developed world is no longer so clearly bounded. In this changed context it behoves Christian critical thought to raise its sights higher than ethical judgements about individual technological choices.

Secondly, we would go further, to suggest that a Christian comportment in the world is incompatible with definitive ethical sets of rules or constraints. To imagine oneself finally secured against sin is to lose sight of the incarnational and historical nature of Christianity, to turn it from faith to cult. In chapter 12, Jacqui Stewart's exposition of the theological writings of Ellul develops this interpretation of Christian witnessing. For Ellul, 'Christians are not "of" this "world"'.[7] Stewart suggests that the implication of this is that 'Christians are called to be properly revolutionary, to expect the genuinely unpredictable, and be prepared for the truly new, because they are open to the action of God in the Holy Spirit'.[8]

This constant restlessness makes the Christian a pilgrim, the Christian community a 'nomad city',[9] and the ethical life a journey, echoing the socio-theological ethics of Stanley

[7] Stewart, this volume, p. 264.
[8] Stewart, this volume, p. 266.
[9] J. Milbank, '"Postmodern Critical Augustinianism": A Short *Summa* in Forty-Two Responses to Unasked Questions', *Modern Theology*, 7, 3, 1991, 225–37.

Hauerwas. Hauerwas suggests that to have a knowledge-based or rule-oriented notion of ethics is akin to seeing it as a *trip*, in the sense of 'having a clear idea of where you want to go and working out the means to get there'. By contrast, Hauerwas suggests that we should picture life as a *journey*, as a process of discovery and self-development the goals of which can only emerge in the process, and become clear at its end.[10]

But is this end one that will be achieved at some actual point on the timeline of this world? As Stewart points out, 'Ellul argues that the construction of ethical systems of fixed principles and guaranteed procedures is impossible for Christianity'.[11] This is consistent with Peter Scott's advocacy in chapter 13 of a shift from doctrines of creation to those of eschatology for a foundation of a Christian response to biotechnology. Scott invites us to see the God in whose image we are made as the *coming* God, the God that will fulfil but also judge his creation. In this at least he echoes Jürgen Moltmann, for whom 'the true likeness to God is to be found, not at the beginning of God's history with mankind, but at its end'.[12] That creatureliness is good does not point to an original, but a *final* righteousness. In elucidating what he means by this, Scott suggests that a genuinely Christian attitude to GM would neither be one of wholesale endorsement nor one of wholesale rejection. But he also affirms a particular kind of judgement between particular uses, one that seems to be based neither on consequentialist calculation nor on abstract principles, but an eschatologically grounded discernment, in which existence in this world is seen as prefatory, as prefiguring the time when God will be all in all.

Scott's approach is one that orients itself *forward* in eschatological time, to a nature that is unfixed, unsettled, open to change. In chapter 3, by contrast, Banner looks *back*, to the original Sabbath, for the model of our relationship with nature. He suggests that 'our proper and authentic engagement with the created order is that which is learnt by our responding to

---

[10] S. Hauerwas, 'Happiness, the Life of Virtue and Friendship: Theological Reflections on Aristotelian Themes', *Asbury Theological Journal*, 45, 1, 1990, 5–48.

[11] Stewart, this volume, p. 266.

[12] J. Moltmann, *God in Creation: An Ecological Doctrine of Creation* (London: SCM Press, 1985), 225.

God's invitation to share in his Sabbath rest'.[13] In this he seems
to indicate a view of a determinate nature, whose purposes are
not only intrinsically knowable, but are also in fact aligned with
our own. As 'an order which' exists 'for our good', nature is
something we should 'first of all love and cherish'. This is a
Christianity of the *morning*, one that points back to an originary
peace, and seeks to ground our relationship with nature in that
peace. However, we want to suggest that the rise of uncertainty
points us towards a Christianity of the *evening*, one which can
only point forward imperfectly to the eschatological daybreak.[14]
The 'time' in which we live, suspended between the Incarnation
and the Eschaton, is one that can only press forward in anticipation, rather than rest sabbatically in its own self-completion.

The implications of this for the Christian could be seen as
uncomfortable, as they point towards an unsettled, nomadic
ethics, one which prepares to deal with coming surprises by
travelling light, rather than by building deeper foundations.
But we want to suggest that the genetic technology revolution,
along with many other risk issues thrown up by modern
technology, necessitates such an ethics. Indeed, this is one of
the ways, we suggest, in which this technological revolution can
also be seen as a revelation. What is being revealed in new ways,
ways that were impossible before the arrival of modern science
and technology, is the always already true ethical comportment
of Christianity, the precedence of love over law.

One aspect of this is the importance of faith. Donald Bruce,
in chapter 7, recognises this characteristic of Christian
existence when he writes of 'living by the daily "risk" of our
faith'.[15] However, he takes this in a direction we could not
wholly endorse when he seems to imply that this recognition of
uncertainty means that the Christian should not worry too
much about risk. 'Our fallen state can incline us', he writes,
'. . . to avoid risk when we should have had faith'.[16] But trust in
the coming God should surely not be confused with trust in
earthly powers. '[P]utting our external material security in the

[13] Banner, this volume, p. 75.
[14] On the 'prefatory', crepuscular character of Christian anticipation, see C.
Pickstock, *After Writing: On the Liturgical Consummation of Philosophy* (Oxford:
Blackwell, 1998).
[15] Bruce, this volume, p. 159.
[16] Bruce, this volume, p. 164.

place of trusting in God'[17] may be idolatrous, but no more so than putting too much faith in industry and regulators. Furthermore, as Wynne points out in chapter 11, hostile public reactions to new technologies such as biotechnology can be seen, not as grounded in a naïve belief in the possibility of absolute certainty and safety as Bruce suggests, but rather as a realistic recognition of inescapable uncertainty.[18] Under such conditions trust is not so much invested as hazarded – as given to institutions not as a reward for their trustworthiness, but in the hope that such a hazarding will *evince* trustworthiness.[19]

Another aspect is the need to construe ethics in terms of discernment – of skilled habits of paying moral attention to the particularities of a situation, and the moral demands that these place on us. As Iris Murdoch argues, this attention is not just something we switch on at moments of moral decision or crisis, but a continuous, cumulative process whereby we fashion and hone our moral sense:

> [I]f we consider what the work of attention is like, how continu-
> ously it goes on, and how imperceptibly it builds up structures of
> value around us, we shall not be surprised that at crucial moments
> of choice most of the business of choosing is already over ... The
> moral life, on this view, is something that goes on continually, not
> something that is switched off between the occurrence of explicit
> moral choices.[20]

We have suggested in this section, then, that the rise of uncertainty in contemporary technological debates such as those around genetic modification can serve to remind Christian thought of what we consider to be its rightful calling in the world. This, we have argued, is one that should not simply be confined to narrowly ethical prescriptions on individual

---

[17] Bruce, this volume, p. 160.
[18] See also R. Grove-White, P. Macnaghten and B. Wynne, *Wising Up: The Public and New Technologies* (Lancaster: Centre for the Study of Environmental Change, Lancaster University, 2000). Studies of lay knowledge find it to be far more aware of uncertainty and unpredictability – see, for example, B. Wynne, 'May the Sheep Safely Graze? A Reflexive View of the Expert–Lay Knowledge Divide', in S. Lash, B. Szerszynski and B. Wynne (eds), *Risk, Environment and Modernity: Towards a New Ecology* (London: Sage, 1996), 44–83.
[19] B. Szerszynski, 'Risk and Trust – the Performative Dimension', *Environmental Values*, 8, 2, 1999, 239–52.
[20] I. Murdoch, *The Sovereignty of Good* (London: Routledge and Kegan Paul, 1970), p. 37.

developments in biotechnology, but should seek critically to explore the deeper issues that may be at stake. We went on to suggest that what is needed in terms of ethical engagement is less an authoritative set of moral principles about what is and is not acceptable, and more an open-ended, restless engagement that seeks to discern which path ahead most fully anticipates and prefigures the eschatological morning.

Wisdom and Virtue

The notion of discernment leads naturally to a consideration of prudence, wisdom and virtue. If the ethical life should be construed as a journey, as Hauerwas argues, then the ethics of biotechnology, as we will be called upon to inhabit and enact it in the next few decades, is likely to be an eventful, heady journey indeed. What resources will we need to sustain us on this journey? As Michael Reiss points out in chapter 6, consequential reasoning is problematic in relation to new technologies where we can not be certain about what the consequences are, let alone how great they might be. In a situation where consequences are unmeasurable or even unknowable, we can turn in at least two directions. One is to the deontological ethics of commandment; but the other is towards an ethics of virtue, as discussed by Deane-Drummond in chapter 14. She suggests in particular that wisdom is the virtue that needs to be recovered in the context of uncertainty that surround genetic engineering. Post-Enlightenment ethical theory has typically concentrated its attention on individual human actions, inquiring into how we can morally assess them by reference to rational moral principles. Consequentialists such as John Stuart Mill focus their assessment of actions on their consequences – in his case, on their tendency to increase or decrease the general level of human happiness. Deontologists such as Kant have focused on the possibility of generating universally valid rules by which any individual action can be judged as right or wrong. By contrast, for virtue ethics it is moral character itself that is seen as the more fundamental arena for moral assessment and attention.

There are a number of ways, we would suggest, that virtue theory represents an important resource for thinking about genetic technology, not least in consideration of the other contributions to this volume. First, it helps in thinking about the importance of judgements about the character of individuals and institutions in thinking about risk issues such as genetics. As reported elsewhere, the public ask 'What might be the unanticipated effects? Who will be in charge of, and take responsibility for, the responses to such surprises? And can we trust them?'.[21] So the kinds of questions asked by the public also move towards consideration of the judgement of character. The rhetorical 'why?' questions explored as liturgy by Szerszynski in chapter 10 are in part a recognition of the moral significance of motive. Clark suggests further, 'the *wrongness* of some procedures may not lie in what is, straightforwardly, accomplished, but in what is intended'.[22]

Secondly, what kind of character do we need in the biotechnological age? As Deane-Drummond points out, 'a virtue ethic, by focusing on the agent first, rather than . . . specific ethical dilemmas, encourages ongoing moral attention that serves . . . to sustain human resilience in times when decision-making is difficult'.[23] Rather than attempt to give here a list of the virtues needed in an age of technological uncertainty, we would rather simply point out it *is* virtues, more so than rules, that we need. Given the uncertainties about what will happen to us, the resources we need for such a journey – the virtues of willpower and of the intellect, but also the more substantive ones such as kindness as well as wisdom noted above – must necessarily have the character of enduring dispositions and orientations, rather than being the result simply of individual decisions. But such resources must also have the character of craft skills, in that they have to be acquired through example and through personal experience, rather than through the learning of abstract rules. Just as a woodcarver has to learn to negotiate the peculiarities of the grain and knots of each piece of wood, so too does the human being have to navigate and make some kind of coherence out of the contingent and unanticipated details of their own life journey. Moral judgement involves the slow, steady development of craft skills

---

[21] Grove-White, Macnaghten and Wynne, *Wising Up*, 29.
[22] Clark, this volume, p. 174.
[23] Deane-Drummond, this volume, p. 294.

and tacit knowledge, rather than the learning of rules or procedures.[24]

Ways Forward

At the start of this postscript we suggested that the uncertainty facing us in the new genetic technologies offered a way forward for religion, a space in which God may be seen as filling the lacuna of mystery left open by such debates. Moreover, we argued that God is revealed from ahead of us in the midst of uncertainty, in an unfinished creation. The re-ordering of nature turns out to be one where humanity no longer can assume a positive outcome for its own devices and technology. While we recognise that this shift is taking place in the public and political debates about genetic technology, in some quarters at least, applied genetic science is still heavily influenced by a fundamentally Newtonian framework. As Northcott implies, the culture of modern farming is certainly not ethically neutral, rather the means becomes the ends – though this is spelt out more clearly in Ellul's analysis of technology. This becomes the challenge to genetics: to acknowledge more fully perhaps than it has before the nature of the risks undertaken at the boundary of this area of knowledge. In this sense the public, political and religious appraisal of genetic technologies might seem to represent a type of coherence, though it is a coherence that acknowledges the unknown rather than the known. To this extent we are all in agreement. But does theology have anything more to say than simply to acknowledge the uncertain world in which we find ourselves? What does theology need to do?

First, we need a theology of science, rather than simply to accept an implicit division of labour between science and religion which leaves facts to science and values to religion.[25] As John Brooke pointed out in chapter 2, the history of science shows clearly that religious inclinations and scientific practice are not mutually exclusive. Brooke's paper is also significant in

[24] H. L. Dreyfus and S. E. Dreyfus, 'What Is Morality? A Phenomenological Account of the Development of Ethical Expertise', in D. M. Rasmussen (ed.), *Universalism vs. Communitarianism: Contemporary Debates in Ethics* (Cambridge, MA: MIT Press, 1990), 237–64.

[25] R. Grove-White and B. Szerszynski, 'Getting Behind Environmental Ethics', *Environmental Values*, 1, 4, 1992, 285–96.

that he suggests that the ambiguity of theological response does not amount to saying that religion has nothing of interest to contribute to the debates. Those who claim total neutrality today may hide a particular agenda that assumes a scientific reductionism that is equally problematic.

Secondly, theology should be providing not just moral prescriptions but engagement with process. By taking the form of a mix of consequentialist reasoning within certain deonto-logical limits, religious reasoning has failed to realise its own potential. More important perhaps, moral pronouncements are vulnerable to semantic redescription as simple subjective preferences.[26] Instead we argue that we need to understand ethics as representing a process of discernment or wisdom. Ethical reflection becomes in this scenario an unfolding on a pilgrim journey, rather than emerging from pre-set conditions. In this context, the ethical debate draws on an ethic of virtue, rather than rule-based deontological forms.

Thirdly, we suggest that we require not just theology *in* debate but theology *of* debate. In this context theology needs to be involved in designing and creating spaces for disclosure through its challenge to the particular design of institutions. The new strategic commissions such as the Agriculture and Environment Biotechnology Commission and the Human Genetics Commission are a start. But we would suggest that there is a role for a religious contribution here, to try to devise imaginative new spaces for interaction. Christianity's capacity to act as a musical, harmonising context for the interaction between radically different voices may mean it has a particularly important role to play.[27]

Fourthly, religious bodies should not shrink from using theological language. There is a dominant assumption that the public sphere is *not* the place for committed speech, that the public finds deontological language alienating. This enhances the pressure to adopt consequentialism. But as Mairi Levitt shows in chapter 9 in relation to young people, people *do* often reach for religious language in this area.[28] Not only is consequentialism ill fitted to deal with issues of uncertainty, but

---

[26] Stewart, this volume, p. 274.
[27] J. Milbank, 'Postmodern Critical Augustinianism'.
[28] See also chs 1 and 8.

also it is a thin currency which seems to offer nothing substantive by way of hope. Religion, and theology in particular, is missing an opportunity to take a new role in giving voice to wider lay concerns. We suggest that the need to speak out is not necessarily contradictory to the reconceived task of theology away from an authoritarian certainty that we have identified. Rather, boldness in speech may be anticipated as a fostering of conversation between parties, and may play a vital role in assisting people to articulate responses to technology that they feel deeply but may nevertheless lack an adequate vocabulary to express.

At the end of *After Virtue*, Alasdair MacIntyre calls for the creation of small communities 'within which civility and the intellectual and moral life can be sustained'.[29] The religious life can represent a model of such a community as a form of witness to the world. Yet Christian witness can move beyond such limited boundaries. One of the stated intentions of this book was to engage in a genuinely multidisciplinary approach to issues in the new genetics, set in motion initially by the multi-faceted public response to the issues. The first section of this book on current debates in theology properly thus begins with this public response as a way of fostering a richer theological engagement, not only with the scientific facts as they seem to be presented and associated problems defined in terms of risk and benefits, but also through deeper reflection on human identity and our relationship with the natural world.

This book is hopefully a start in the necessary process of giving theology a voice in wider debates about genetic technology. Our own intention in editing it has been for it to be a collection of voices coming not so much from behind the closed doors of institutionalised faith, as one that is open to the implicit theology emerging in the public response. In the light of such response, theological conceptions, such as those of the Eschaton, the place of humanity and our relationship with the natural world, take on a new and urgent role. Such reconceptions begin to offer the space where dialogue in the midst of uncertainty replaces mistrust and unwarranted certainty.

[29] A. MacIntyre, *After Virtue: A Study in Moral Theory* (London: Duckworth, 1985), p. 263.

Bibliography

Abbott-Smith, G., *A Manual Greek Lexicon of the New Testament* (Edinburgh: T&T Clark, 1937).

Abrecht, Paul (ed.), *Faith and Science in an Unjust World*, vol. 2 (Geneva: WCC, 1980). *Manipulating Life* (Geneva: WCC, 1982).

Adams, J., *Risk* (London: University College London Press, 1995).

AEBC, *Crops on Trial* (London: Department for Agriculture, Food and Rural Affairs, September 2001).

Ancora, G., E. Benvenuto, G. Bertoni, V. Buonomo, B. Hoinings, A. Lauria, F. Lucchini, P. A. Marson, V. Mele, A. Pessina and E. Sgeccia, *Biotechnologie, Animali e Vegetali; Nuove Fontiere e Nuove Responabilita* (Vatican City: Libreria Editrice Vaticana, 1999).

Anderson, Perry, 'Renewals', *New Left Review*, 1, 1, January–February 2000, 17.

Anglin, J. M., *Word, Object, and Conceptual Development* (New York: W. W. Norton, 1977).

Appleby, M. C., 'Tower of Babel: Variation in Ethical Approaches, Concepts of Welfare and Attitudes to Genetic Manipulation', *Animal Welfare*, 8, 1999, 381–90.

Appleby, Michael, David Atkinson et al., 'Developing Country Issues', in Bruce and Bruce, *Engineering Genesis*.

Aquinas, *Summa Theologiae*, Vol. 1, *Christian Theology*, tr Thomas Gilby (London; Blackfriars, 1964).

Aquinas, *Summa Theologiae*, Vol. 23, *Virtue*, tr W. D. Hughes (London: Blackfriars, 1969).

Aquinas, *Summa Theologiae*, Vol. 28, *Law and Political Theory*, tr T. Gilby (London: Blackfriars, 1966).

Aquinas, *Summa Theologiae*, Vol. 33, *Hope*, tr W. J. Hill (London: Blackfriars, 1966).

Aquinas, *Summa Theologiae*, Vol. 35, *Consequences of Charity*, tr T. R. Heath (London: Blackfriars, 1972).

Aquinas, *Summa Theologiae*, Vol. 36, *Prudence*, tr T. Gilby (London: Blackfriars, 1974).

Aquinas, *Summa Theologiae*, Vol. 37, *Justice*, tr T. Gilby (London: Blackfriars, 1974).

Arendt, H., *The Human Condition* (Chicago: University of Chicago Press, 1958).

Austin, J. L., *How to Do Things with Words* (Oxford: Oxford University Press, 1975).

Ayer, A. J., *Language, Truth and Logic* (London: Gollancz, 1936).

Bailey, E. (ed.), *A Workbook in Popular Religion* (Dorchester: Partners Publications, 1986).

Baldwin, M., 'Alchemy and the Society of Jesus in the Seventeenth Century', *Ambix*, 40, 1993, 41–64.

Banner, Michael, 'Ethics, Society and Policy: A Way Forward', in Holland and Johnson, *Animal Biotechnology*, 325–39.

Banner, Michael, 'Why and How Not to Value the Environment', *Christian Ethics and Contemporary Moral Problems* (Cambridge, Cambridge University Press, 1999).

Barnes, B., *About Science* (Oxford: Blackwell, 1985).

Barns, I., 'Manufacturing Consensus: Reflections on the UK National Consensus Conference on Plant Biotechnology', *Science as Culture*, 5, 2, 1996, 119–216.

Barth, Karl, *Church Dogmatics III, The Doctrine of Creation*, trs A. T. Mackay, T. H. L. Parker, H. Knight, H. A. Kennedy and J. Marks (Edinburgh: T&T Clark, 1961).

Barth, K., *Church Dogmatics*, Vol. III/2, tr. H. Knight et al. (Edinburgh, T&T Clark, 1960).

Barton, J., 'Virtue in the Bible', *Studies in Christian Ethics*, 12, 1, 1999, 12–22.

Bauer, M., G. Gaskell and J. Durant, 'Europe Ambivalent on Biotechnology', *Nature*, 387, 1997, 345–7.

Bauman, R. and J. Sherzer (eds), *Explorations in the Ethnography of Speaking* (London: Cambridge University Press, 1974).

Bauman, Z., *Modernity and the Holocaust* (Cambridge: Polity Press; and Oxford: Basil Blackwell, 1989).

Bechtel, W. and A. Abrahamsen, *Connectionism and the Mind* (Oxford and Cambridge, MA: Blackwells, 1991).

Beck, U., *Risk Society* (London: Sage, 1986).

Beck, U., *Risk Society: Towards a New Modernity*, tr Mark Ritter (London: Sage, 1992).

Beck, U., A. Giddens and S. Lash, *Reflexive Modernization: Politics, Tradition and Aesthetics in the Modern Social Order* (Cambridge: Polity Press, 1994).

Beringar, J., 'Reply from John Beringar', *British Ecological Society Bulletin*, 31, 2, 2000, 19.

Berkovitz, E., *Faith after the Holocaust* (New York: Ktav), 1973.

Berman, M., *Social Change and Scientific Organization: The Royal Institution, 1799–1844* (Ithaca, NY: Cornell University Press, 1978).

Bernstein, R. J., 'Heidegger's Silence?: Ethos and Technology', *The New Constellation: The Ethical–Political Horizons of Modernity/Postmodernity*, 1st MIT edn (Cambridge MA: MIT Press, 1992), 79–141.

Berry, Wendel, *Sex, Economy, Freedom and Community* (New York: Pantheon Books, 1992).

Biggar, Nigel, *The Hastening That Waits: Karl Barth's Ethics* (Oxford: Clarendon Press, 1993).

Birren, J. E. and L. M. Fisher, 'The Elements of Wisdom; Overview and Integration', in R. J. Sternberg (ed.), *Wisdom: Its Nature, Origins and Development* (Cambridge: Cambridge University Press, 1990).

Blair, T., 'The Key to GM is its potential, both for harm and good', *Independent on Sunday*, 27 February 2000.

Bloor, D., *Knowledge and Social Imagery* (London: Routledge and Kegan Paul, 1976).

Bonhoeffer, Dietrich, *Christology* (London: Collins, 1978).

Bonhoeffer, Dietrich, *Letters and Papers from Prison* (London: SCM Press, 1971).

Borgmann, Albert, 'The Moral Significance of the Material Culture', in Feenberg and Hannay, *Technology and the Politics of Knowledge*, 85–93.

Borgmann, Albert, 'Prospects for a Theology of Technology', in Carl Mitcham and Jim Grote (eds), *Theology and Technology: Essays in Christian Analysis and Exegesis* (Lanham and London: University Press of America, 1984), 305–25.

Borgmann, Albert, *Technology and the Character of Contemporary Life: A Philosophical Inquiry* (Chicago: University of Chicago Press, 1984).

Bowler, P., *The Invention of Progress: The Victorians and the Past* (Oxford: Blackwell, 1989).

Boyd Group Draft Discussion Paper, *Genetic Engineering: Animal Welfare and Ethics*.

Brock, W., *The Fontana History of Chemistry* (London: Fontana, 1992).

Brooke, J., *Science and Religion: Some Historical Perspectives* (Cambridge: Cambridge University Press, 1991).

Brooke, J., '"A Sower Went Forth": Joseph Priestley and the Ministry of Reform', in Truman Schwartz and McEvoy, *Motion toward Perfection*, 21–56.

Brooke, J., '"Wise Men Nowadays Think Otherwise": John Ray, Natural Theology and the Meanings of Anthropocentrism', *Notes and Records R. Soc. London*, 54, 2000, 199–213.

Brooke, J. and G. Cantor, *Reconstructing Nature: The Engagement of Science and Religion* (Edinburgh: T&T Clark, 1998).

Bruce, D. M. 'Ethics Keeping Pace with Technology', in R. Cole-Turner (ed.), *Beyond Cloning : Religion and the Remaking of Humanity* (Harrisburg, USA: Trinity Press International, 2001), 34–49.

Bruce, D. M., and J. T. Eldridge, 'The Role of Values in Risk Perception in the GM Debate', in M. P. Cottam, D. W. Harvey, R. P. Pape and J. E. Tait (eds), *Foresight and Precaution* (Rotterdam: Balkema, 2000).

Bruce, Donald M. and Anne Bruce (eds), *Engineering Genesis:*

The Ethics of the Genetic Modification of Non-Human Species (London: Earthscan, 1998).

Bruegemann, Walter, *The Land: Place as Gift, Promise and Challenge in Biblical Faith* (Philadelphia: Fortress Press, 1977).

Buber, M., *Good and Evil: Two Interpretations* (New York: Scribner's, 1953).

Bud, R., *The Uses of Life: A History of Biotechnology* (Cambridge: Cambridge University Press, 1993).

Burke, E., *A Philosophical Enquiry into the Origin of our Ideas of the Sublime and Beautiful* (Oxford: Blackwell, 1987).

Carlile, R., *Lion*, 2, 1828, 488–9.

CEC, *White Paper on Growth, Competitiveness and Employment* (Brussels: Commission of the European Communities, 1993).

Cerezuelle, D., 'La critique de la modernité chez Charbonneau', in P. Troude-Chastenet (ed.), *Sur Jacques Ellul* (Bordeaux: L'esprit du Temps, 1994), 61–74.

Chadwick, E. C. R., M. Levitt, M. Whitelegg, H. Häyry, M. Häyry and J. Lunshof, *Cultural and Social Attitudes to Biotechnology: Analysis of the Arguments, with Special Reference to the Views of Young People* (European Commission: Directorate-General Science, Research and Development, EUR 18491 EN, 1998).

Challis, P., *Genetic Engineering and Its Applications: Some Theological and Ethical Reflections* (Cambridge: Wesley House, 1992).

Chossudovsky, Michel, *The Globalisation of Poverty: Impacts of IMF and World Bank Reforms* (Penang: Third World Network, 1997).

Christian Aid, *Selling Suicide* (London: Christian Aid, 1999).

Church of Scotland, 'The Society, Religion and Technology Project Report on Genetically Modified Food', *Reports to the General Assembly and Deliverances of the General Assembly 1999*, 20/93–20/103, and Board of National Mission Deliverances 42–5, 20/4 (Edinburgh: Church of Scotland, 1999).

Churchland, P. and T. J. Sejnowski, 'Perspectives on Cognitive Neuroscience', *Science*, 242, 1988), 741–5.

Clark, J., 'Eleanor Ormerod (1828–1901) as an Economic Entomologist: "Pioneer of Purity even more than of Paris

Green"', *British Journal for the History of Science*, 25, 1992, 431–52.

Clark, John, 'The Dialectical Social Geography of Elisée Reclus', *Philosophy and Geography*, 1, 1997, 117–42.

Clark, Stephen, *The Political Animal: Biology, Ethics and Politics* (London: Routledge, 1999).

Clarke, A., 'Is Non-Directive Genetic Counselling Possible?', *Lancet*, 338, 1991, 998–1001.

Cole-Turner, Ronald, *The New Genesis: Theology and Genetic Revolution* (Louisville, KY: Westminster/John Knox Press, 1993).

Coleman, W., 'Providence, Capitalism and Environmental Degradation: English Apologetics in an Era of Economic Revolution', *Journal of the History of Ideas*, 37, 1, 1976, 27–44.

Commission of the European Communities, *Science and Governance* (Brussels: 2001).

Cooper, D., 'Intervention, Humility and Animal Integrity', in Holland and Johnson, *Animal Biotechnology*, 145–55.

Cooper, D. E., 'Intervention, Humility and Animal Integrity', in Holland and Johnson, *Animal Biotechnology*, 145–55.

Crick, F. H. C., *Of Molecules and Man* (Seattle: University of Washington Press, 1966).

Crisp, R. and M. Slote, *Virtue Ethics* (Oxford: Oxford University Press, 1998).

Crouch, M., 'Lessons from the Field', *Science and Public Affairs*, October 1999, 19–21.

Darbyshire, Stuart, 'In Defence of Animal Experimentation', originally published in *Living Marxism*, 115, November 1998.

Dawkins, R., *The Extended Phenotype: The Gene as the Unit of Selection* (Oxford: Oxford University Press, 1982).

Dawkins, R., *The Selfish Gene* (Oxford: Oxford University Press, 1976).

Dawkins, R., *The Selfish Gene*, 2nd edn (Oxford: Oxford University Press, 1989).

Dawn, Marva, 'Chronicles of the Problems of Civilization', *Sources and Trajectories*.

Deane-Drummond, C., *Biology and Theology Today: Exploring the Boundaries* (London: SCM Press, 2001).

Deane-Drummond, C., 'Come to the Banquet: Seeking Wisdom in a Genetically Engineered Earth', *Ecotheology*, 9, 2000, 27–37.

Deane-Drummond, C., *Creation through Wisdom* (Edinburgh: T&T Clark, 2000).

Deane-Drummond, C., *Genetic Engineering for a New Earth* (Cambridge: Grove Books, 1999).

Deane-Drummond, C., 'Reshaping Our Environment: Implications of the New Biotechnology', *Theology in Green*, 5, 1995, 19–33.

Deane-Drummond, C., *Theology and Biotechnology: Implications for a New Science* (London: Geoffrey Chapman, 1997).

Devlin, P., *The Enforcement of Morals* (Oxford: Oxford University Press, 1965).

Dobbs, B. J., *The Janus Faces of Genius* (Cambridge: Cambridge University Press, 1991).

Dodd, C. H., *The Parables of the Kingdom* (Welwyn, Hertfordshire: Nisbet, 1961).

Donaldson, L. (Chair), *Stem Cell Research: Medical Progress with Responsibility: A Report from the Chief Medical Officer's Expert Group Reviewing the Potential of Developments in Stem Cell Research and Cell Nuclear Replacement to Benefit Human Health* (London: Department of Health, 2000).

Dormann, C., 'BES Lecture at Leeds: An Open Letter to Professor Beringar', *British Ecological Society Bulletin*, 31, 2, 2000), 17–18.

Douglas, Mary, *Purity and Danger* (Harmondsworth: Penguin, 1966/1970).

Dreyfus, H. L. and S. E. Dreyfus, 'What Is Morality? A Phenomenological Account of the Development of Ethical Expertise', in D. M. Rasmussen (ed.), *Universalism vs. Communitarianism: Contemporary Debates in Ethics* (Cambridge, MA: MIT Press, 1990), 237–64.

Dreze, Jean and Amartya Sen, *Hunger and Public Action* (Oxford: Clarendon Press, 1989).

Dryzek, J., *Discursive Democracy: Politics, Policy, and Political Science* (Cambridge: Cambridge University Press, 1990).

D'Silva, J., 'Campaigning against Transgenic Technology', in Holland and Johnson, *Animal Biotechnology*, 92–102.

Dulap, Willis, 'Two Fragments: Theological Transformations of Law, Technological Transformations of Nature', in Carl Mitcham and Jim Grote (eds), *Theology and Technology* (Lanham, MD: University Press of America, 1984), 231–3.

Dupré, L., 'Spiritual Life in a Secular Age', in M. Douglas and S. Tipton (eds), *Religion and America: Spiritual Life in a Secular Age* (Boston: Beacon Press, 1983), 3–13.

Dworkin, R., *Life's Dominion: An Argument about Abortion and Euthanasia* (London: HarperCollins, 1993).

Dyson, A., 'Genetic Engineering in Theology and Theological Ethics', in A. Dyson and J. Harris (eds), *Ethics and Biotechnology* (London: Routledge, 1994), 259–71.

Elder, G., *Chronic Vigour: Darwin, Anglicans, Catholics, and the Development of a Doctrine of Providential Evolution* (Lanham: University Press of America, 1996).

Ellul, J., 'Chronicle of the Problems of Civilization', in M. Dawn (ed.), *Sources and Trajectories* (Grand Rapids: Eerdmans, 1997), 13–22. (This is a translation of an early article, 'Chronique des problèmes de civilisation', *Foi et Vie*, 44, 6, 1946, 678–87.)

Ellul, J., 'Political Realism (Problems of Civilization III)', in Dawn, *Sources and Trajectories*, 51–84 ('Problème de civilisation III: Le realisme politique', *Foi et Vie*, 45, 7, 1947, 698–734).

Ellul, J., *Présence au monde modern: Problèmes de la civilisation post-chrétienne* (Geneva: Roulet, 1948).

Ellul, J., *The Presence of the Kingdom* (London: SCM Press, 1951; Colorado Springs: Helmers & Howard, 1989).

Ellul, J., *The Technological Bluff* (Grand Rapids: Eerdmans, 1990).

Ellul, J., *The Technological Society* (New York: Alfred A. Knopf and Random House, 1964).

Ernst & Young, *Biotechnology's Economic Impact in Europe: A Survey of Its Future Role in Competitiveness* (London: Ernst & Young, 1994).

Environmental Data Services (ENDS), 'Applying a Biodiversity

Brake to Genetically Modified Crops', *ENDS Report*, 289, February 1999, 21–7.

Environmental Data Services (ENDS), 'Government Still Struggling to Master the Biotechnology Agenda', *ENDS Report*, 292, May 1999, 28–32

Environmental Data Services (ENDS), 'The Spiralling Agenda of Agricultural Biotechnology', *ENDS Report*, 283, August 1998, 18–30.

EPCAG (European Biotechnology and the Public Concerted Action Group: J. Durant, coordinator), 'Europe Ambivalent on Biotechnology', *Nature*, 387, 26 June 1997, 845–7.

ESRC Global Environmental Change Programme, *The Politics of GM Food: Risk, Science and Public Trust*, Special Briefing No. 5 (Brighton: University of Sussex, 1999).

Eurobarometer, 'The Europeans and Biotechnology', report by INRA(Europe)-ECOSA, for EU, DG Research, Brussels, 15 March 2000.

European Federation of Biotechnology, *Ethical Aspects of Agricultural Biotechnology*, report to Task Group on Public Perceptions (The Hague: EFB, 1999).

European Province of the Society of Saint Francis, *Celebrating Common Prayer: A Version of the Daily Office* (London: Mowbray, 1992).

Excellence and Opportunity: A Science and Innovation Policy for the 21st Century, Cm 4814 (London: HMSO, 2000).

Fackenheim, E., *God's Presence in History* (New York: New York University Press, 1970).

Feenberg, Andrew, *Critical Theory of Technology* (New York and Oxford: Oxford University Press, 1991).

Feenberg, Andrew, *Questioning Technology* (New York and London: Routledge, 1999).

Feenberg, Andrew, 'Subversive Rationalization: Technology, Power and Democracy', in Feenberg and Hannay, *Technology and the Politics of Knowledge*, 3–22.

Feenberg, Andrew and Alistair Hannay (eds), *Technology and the Politics of Knowledge* (Bloomington and Indianapolis: Indiana University Press, 1995).

Fenn, R. K., *Liturgies and Trials* (Oxford: Blackwell, 1982).

Flanagan, K., *Sociology and Liturgy: Re-Presentations of the Holy* (Houndmills, Basingstoke: Macmillan, 1991).

Fergusson, D. and M. Sarot (eds), *The Future as God's Gift: Explorations in Christian Eschatology* (Edinburgh: T&T Clark, 2000).

Frey, R., 'Organs for Transplant: Animals, Moral Standing, and One View of the Ethics of Xenotransplantation', in Holland and Johnson, *Animal Biotechnology*, 190–208.

Frye, N., *The Great Code: The Bible and Literature* (London: Ark, 1983).

Fullick, P. and M. Ratcliffe (eds), *Teaching Ethical Aspects of Science* (Southampton: Bassett Press, 1996).

Gaskell, G. and N. Allum, 'Sound Science; Problematic Publics? Contrasting Representations of Risk and Uncertainty', *Politeia*, 17, 63, 2001, 13–25.

Genetic Intervention on Human Subjects (London: The Catholic Bishops' Joint Committee on Bioethical Issues, 1996).

Gibbons, Mike, 'Science's New Social Contract with Society', *Nature*, 402, 6761 (Suppl), 1999, C81–C84.

Goddard, Andrew, 'Obituary: Jacques Ellul 1912–1994', *Studies in Christian Ethics*, 9, 1996, 140–53.

Golinski, J., *Science as Public Culture: Chemistry and Enlightenment in Britain, 1760–1820* (Cambridge: Cambridge University Press, 1992).

Golinski, J., 'The Secret Life of an Alchemist', in J. Fauvel, R. Flood, M. Shortland and R. Wilson (eds), *Let Newton Be!* (Oxford: Oxford University Press, 1988), 147–67.

Graham-Rowe, D., 'Possums on the Pill: Contraceptive Carrots Will Stop the Spread of Marauding Marsupials', *New Scientist*, 4 March 2000, 18.

'The Green Man', editorial, *New Scientist*, 2240, 27 May 2000, 3.

Grove-White, R., 'New Wine, Old Bottles? Personal Reflections on the New Biotechnology Commissions', *Political Quarterly*, 72, 4, 2001, 466–72.

Grove-White, R., P. Macnaghten, S. Mayer and B. Wynne, *Uncertain World: Genetically Modified Organisms, Food and Public Attitudes in Britain* (Lancaster: Centre for the Study of Environmental Change (CSEC), Lancaster University, 1997).

Grove-White, R., P. Macnaghten and B. Wynne, *Wising Up: The Public and New Technologies* (Lancaster: Centre for the Study of Environmental Change, Lancaster University, 2000).

Grove-White, R. and B. Szerszynski, 'Getting Behind Environmental Ethics', *Environmental Values*, 1, 4, 1992, 285–96.

Grove-White, R. and B. Wynne, *Science, Culture and the Environment* (Lancaster: Lancaster University, CSEC, 1998).

Gumperz, J. J. and D. Hymes (eds), *Directions in Sociolinguistics: The Ethnography of Communication* (New York: Holt, Rinehart and Winston, 1972).

Gunton, Colin, 'Dogmatic Theses on Eschatology', in Fergusson and Sarot, *Future as God's Gift*, 139–43.

Gunton, Colin E., *The Triune Creator: Historical and Systematic Considerations* (Edinburgh: Edinburgh University Press, 1998).

Habermas, J., *Moralbewusstsein und Kommunikatives Handeln* (Frankfurt am Main: Suhrkamp Verlag, 1983).

Habermas, J., *The Theory of Communicative Action*, Vol. 1, *Reason and the Rationalization of Society*, tr Thomas McCarthy (London: Heinemann, 1984).

Hall, D. J., *Imaging God: Dominion as Stewardship* (Grand Rapids: W. B. Eerdmans, 1986).

Hall, P. M., *Narrative and the Natural Law: An Interpretation of Thomistic Ethics* (Notre Dame and London: University of Notre Dame Press, 1994).

Hammnon, Ross and Lisa McGowan, 'Ghana: The World Bank's Sham Showcase', in Kevin Danaher (ed.), *Fifty Years Is Enough: The Case against the World Bank and the International Monetary Fund* (Boston, MA: South End Press), 78–84.

Hannaway, O., *The Chemists and the Word* (Baltimore: Johns Hopkins University Press, 1975).

Hanson, M., 'The Depths of Reason: Biotechnology's Challenge to Public Policy', *Science and Spirit*, 10, 5, 2000, 22–3.

Haraway, Donna, *Simians, Cyborgs and Women: The Reinvention of Nature* (London: Free Association Books, 1991).

Hardy, D., 'The God Who is with the World', in F. Watts (ed.), *Science Meets Faith* (London: SPCK 1998), 136–53.

Hardy, Daniel W., 'Eschatology as a Challenge for Theology', in Fergusson and Sarot, *Future as God's Gift*, 151–8.

Harris, M., *Cows, Pigs, Wars & Witches: The Riddles of Culture* (Glasgow: Fontana/Collins, 1974/1977).

Harrison, P., *The Bible, Protestantism and the Rise of Natural Science* (Cambridge: Cambridge University Press, 1998).

Harrison, P., 'Subduing the Earth: Genesis 1, Early Modern Science, and the Exploitation of Nature', *Journal of Religion*, 79, 1999, 86–109.

Harvey, Graham, *The Killing of the Countryside* (London: Random House, 1998).

Hauerwas, S., 'Happiness, the Life of Virtue and Friendship: Theological Reflections on Aristotelian Themes', *Asbury Theological Journal*, 45, 1, 1990, 5–48.

Hay, H. A., *Essentials of Behaviour Genetics* (Oxford: Blackwells, 1985).

Heaton, E. W., *Solomon's New Man* (London: Thames and Hudson, 1974).

Hefner, Philip J., *The Human Factor: Evolution, Culture, and Religion* (Minneapolis: Fortress Press, 1993).

Heidegger, M., *The Question concerning Technology and Other Essays. Translated and with an Introduction by William Lovitt* (New York: Harper Colophon, 1997).

Hemmming, L. P., 'Quod Impossible Est! Aquinas and Radical Orthodoxy', in L. P. Hemming (ed.), *Radical Orthodoxy: A Catholic Enquiry* (Aldershot: Ashgate, 2000), 76–93.

Hinshelwood, R. D., *A Dictionary of Kleinian Thought*, 2nd edn (London: Free Association Books, 1991).

Holland, A. and A. Johnson (eds), *Animal Biotechnology and Ethics* (London: Chapman & Hall, 1998).

Hornig Priest, S., 'Popular Beliefs, Media and Biotechnology', in S. Freidmann, S. Dunwoody and C. Rogers (eds), *Communicating Uncertainty: Media Coverage of New and Controversial Science* (Mahwah, NJ, and London: Lawrence Erlbaum, 1999), 95–112.

House of Lords Science and Technology Committee, *Science and Society*, HL 38 (London: HMSO, 2000).

House of Lords, Select Committee on Science and Technology, *Science and Society* (London: HMSO, March 2000).

Hunter, M. (ed.), *Robert Boyle Reconsidered* (Cambridge: Cambridge University Press, 1994).

Hursthouse, R., *On Virtue Ethics* (Oxford: Oxford University Press, 1999).

Imutran, Novartis, *Animal Welfare: Xenotransplantation – Helping to Solve the Global Organ Shortage* (Cambridge: Imutran Ltd, 1999).

Irwin, A. and B. Wynne (eds), *Misunderstanding Science* (Cambridge and New York: Cambridge University Press, 1996).

Jacobs, M., 'Environmental Valuation, Deliberative Democracy and Public Decision-Making Institutions', in J. Foster (ed.), *Valuing Nature? Economics, Ethics and Environment* (London: Routledge, 1997), 211–31.

Jardine, N., *The Birth of History and Philosophy of Science: Kepler's A Defence of Tycho against Ursus, with Essays on Its Provenance and Significance* (Cambridge: Cambridge University Press, 1984).

John Paul II, 'The Ethics of Genetic Manipulation', speech to World Medical Association, *Origins*, 13, 23, 17 November 1983, 339.

Johnson, A., 'Needs, Fears and Fantasies', in Holland and Johnson, *Animal Biotechnology*, 133–42.

Junker-Kenny, M. and L. S. Cahill (eds), *The Ethics of Genetic Engineering* (London: Concilium/SCM Press, 1998).

Kaul, D., 'Eco-News from across the World: Eco-Feminism in the Nordic Countries', *Ecotheology*, 2, 1997, 100–8.

Keil, F. C., *Semantic and Conceptual Development: An Ontological Perspective* (London: Harvard University Press, 1979).

Keller, Catherine, *Apocalypse Now and Then* (Boston: Beacon Press, 1996).

Kendon, A., R. M. Harris and M. R. Key (eds), *Organization of Behavior in Face-to-face Interaction* (The Hague: Mouton, 1975).

Kerr, A., S. Cunningham-Burley and A. Amos, 'Drawing the Line: An Analysis of Lay People's Discussions about the New Genetics', *Public Understanding of Science*, 7, 1998, 113–33.

Kerr, A., S. Cunningham-Burley and A. Amos, 'The New Genetics: Professionals' Boundaries', *Sociological Review*, 45, 1997, 279–303.

Knight, D., *The Transcendental Part of Chemistry* (Folkestone: Dawson, 1978).

Kramnick, I., 'Eighteenth-Century Science and Radical Social Theory: The Case of Joseph Priestley's Scientific Liberalism', in Truman Schwartz and McEvoy, *Motion toward Perfection*, 57–92.

Krimsky, S., S. Golding and D. Golding (eds), *Social Theories of Risk* (New York: Praeger, 1992).

Ladd, G. E., *Jesus and the Kingdom: The Eschatology of Biblical Realism* (London: SPCK, 1966).

LaFollette, Hugh and Niall Shanks, *Brute Science: Dilemmas of Animal Experimentation* (London: Routledge,1996).

Lash, S., 'Risk Culture', in B. Adam, U. Beck and J. van Loon (eds), *The Risk Society and Beyond: Critical Issues for Social Theory* (London: Sage, 2000), 47–62.

Lash, S., B. Szerszynski and B. Wynne (eds), *Risk, Environment and Modernity: Towards a New Ecology* (London: Sage, 1996).

Layton, D., E. Jenkins, S. Macgill and A. Davey, *Inarticulate Science? Perspectives on the Public Understanding of Science and Some Implications for Science Education* (East Yorkshire: Studies in Education Ltd, 1993).

Leach, J., J. Lewis, R. Driver and C. Wood-Robinson, *Opinions on and Attitudes towards Genetic Screening: A, Pre-Natal Screening (Cystic Fibrosis)*, Working Paper 5 (Leeds: CSSME, University of Leeds, 1996).

Lee, Martha F., *Earth First! Environmental Apocalypse* (Syracuse, NY: Syracuse University Press, 1995).

Lee, Martha F., 'Environmental Apocalypse: The Millenial Ideology of "Earth First!"', in Thomas Robbins and Susan J. Palmer (eds), *Millenium, Messiahs and Mayhem: Contemporary Apocalyptic Movements* (New York and London: Routledge, 1997), 119–37.

Leopold, Aldo, *A Sand County Almanac and Sketches Here and There*, first published 1949 (paperback edition New York: Oxford University Press, 1968).

Levidow, L. and S. Carr, 'How Biotechnology Regulation Sets a Risk/Ethics Boundary', *Agriculture and Human Values*, 14, 1997, 29–43.

Levitt, M., 'Drawing Limits: Contemporary Views on Biotechnology', *Journal of Beliefs and Values*, 20, 1, 1999, 41–50.

Levitt, M., 'Natural Ways Are Better: Adolescents and the "Anti-Obesity" Gene', *Science and Engineering Ethics*, 3, 3, 1997, 305–15.

Lewis, J., R. Driver, J. Leach and C. Wood-Robinson, *Understanding of Basic Genetics and DNA Technology*, Working Paper 2 (Leeds: CSSME, University of Leeds, 1997).

Lindberg, D., 'On the Application of Mathematics to Nature: Roger Bacon and His Predecessors', *British Journal for the History of Science*, 15, 1982, 3–25.

Linzey, A., *Animal Theology* (London: SCM Press, 1994).

Linzey, A., 'Human and Animal Slavery: A Theological Critique of Genetic Engineering', in P. Wheale and R. McNally (eds), *The Bio-Revolution: Cornucopia or Pandora's Box* (London: Pluto Press, 1990), 175–88.

Lisska, A. J., *Aquinas's Theory of Natural Law: An Analytic Reconstruction* (Oxford: Clarendon Press, 1997).

Lloyd, I., 'The Tyranny of the L-shaped curve', *Science and Public Affairs*, February 2000, 14–15.

Lock, R., C. Miles and S. Hughes, 'The Influence of Teaching on Knowledge and Attitudes in Biotechnology and Genetic Engineering Contexts', *School Science Review*, 76, 276, 1995, 47–59.

Lowe, Walter, 'Prospects for a Postmodern Christian Theology: Apocalyptic without Reserve', *Modern Theology*, 15, 1, 1999, 17–24.

Macer, D., *Shaping Genes* (New Zealand: Eubios Institute, 1990).

MacIntyre, A., *After Virtue: A Study in Moral Theory* (London: Duckworth, 1985).

MacIntyre, A., *After Virtue: A Study in Moral Theory*, 2nd edn (London: Duckworth, 1985).

MacKinnon, Donald, 'Objective and Subjective Conceptions of

Atonement', in F. G. Healey (ed.), *Prospect for Theology* (Welwyn: James Nisbet, 1966), 167–82.

Making Our Genes Fit: Christian Perspectives on the New Genetics (London: Methodist Church, 1999).

Martin, J., *Francis Bacon, the State, and the Reform of Natural Philosophy* (Cambridge: Cambridge University Press, 1992).

Martin, S. and J. Tait, *Public Perceptions of Genetically Modified Organisms* (London: Department of Trade and Industry, 1992).

May, R., 'Science and Public Policy', lecture to EXPO, Hanover, Germany, July 2000.

May, R., *Scientific Advice to Government* (London: Department of Trade and Industry, 2000).

Merton, R., 'Science, Technology and Society in Seventeenth-Century England', *Osiris*, 4, part 2, 1938, 360–632; republished New York: Harper, 1970.

M'Gonigle, M., 'A New Naturalism: Is There a (Radical) "Truth" Beyond the (Postmodern) Abyss?', *Ecotheology*, 8, 2000, 8–39.

Milbank, J., '"Postmodern Critical Augustinianism": A Short *Summa* in Forty-Two Responses to Unasked Questions', *Modern Theology*, 7, 3, 1991, 225–37.

Milbank, J., 'Sublimity: The Modern Transcendent', in Paul Heelas (ed.), *Religion, Modernity and Postmodernity* (Oxford: Blackwell, 1998), 258–84.

Miller, H., *The Testimony of the Rocks* (Edinburgh: Nimmo, 1869).

Ministry of Agriculture, Fisheries and Food, *The Ethics of Genetic Modification and Food Use*, chairman John Polkinghorne (London: HMSO, 1984).

Ministry of Agriculture, Fisheries and Food, *Report of the Committee on the Ethics of Genetic Modification and Food Use* (London: HMSO, 1993).

Ministry of Agriculture, Fisheries and Food, *Report of the Committee to Consider the Ethical Implications of Emerging Technologies in the Breeding of Farm Animals* (London: HMSO, 1995).

Moltmann, Jürgen, *The Coming of God: Christian Eschatology* (London: SCM Press, 1996).

Moltmann, Jürgen, *God in Creation: An Ecological Doctrine of Creation* (London: SCM Press, 1985).

Moody, C. J. E., 'Drawing Near', *Theology*, 103, 2000, 243–50.

Morea, Peter, *Personality: An Introduction to the Theories of Psychology* (London: Penguin Books, 1990).

Moreno, J. D., *Deciding Together: Bioethics and Moral Consensus* (Oxford: Oxford University Press, 1995).

Morris, B., *Anthropological Studies of Religion: An Introductory Text* (Cambridge: Cambridge University Press, 1987).

Murdoch, I., *The Sovereignty of Good* (London: Routledge and Kegan Paul, 1970).

Murphy, N., B. J. Kellenberg and M. T. Nation, *Virtues and Practices in the Christian Tradition: Christian Ethics after MacIntyre* (Harrisburg: Trinity Press International, 1977).

Nash, James, *Loving Nature: Ecological Integrity and Christian Responsibility* (Nashville, TN: Abingdon, 1992).

Nature: Editorial, 'GM Foods Debate Needs a Recipe for Restoring Trust', *Nature*, 398, 6729, 1999, 639.

Nelson, D. M., *The Priority of Prudence: Virtue and Natural Law in Thomas Aquinas and the Implications for Modern Ethics* (University Park: Pennsylvania State University Press, 1992).

Nelson, D. M. and J. Finnis, *Natural Law and Natural Rights* (Oxford: Clarendon Press, 1980).

Nelson, J. R., *On the New Frontiers of Genetics and Religion* (Grand Rapids, Michigan: William B. Eerdmans Publishing Company, 1994).

Newton, I., Portsmouth Collection MS Add. 4003, Cambridge University Library.

Northcott, Michael S., *The Environment and Christian Ethics* (Cambridge: Cambridge University Press, 1996).

Northcott, Michael S., *Life after Debt: Christianity and Global Justice* (London: SPCK, 1999).

Nowotny, H., P. Scott and M. Gibbons, *Re-Thinking Science: Knowledge and the Public in an Age of Uncertainty* (Cambridge: Polity, 2001).

Nuffield Council on Bioethics, *Genetically Modified Crops: The Ethical and Social Issues* (London: The Nuffield Foundation, 1999): website http://www.nuffield.org.

Nuttall, N., 'China sows the seeds of GM crop expansion', *The Times*, 29 February 2000.

Oakeshott, M., *Rationalism in Politics and Other Essays* (London: Methuen, 1962).

O'Connor, James, 'The Second Contradiction of Capital', *Natural Causes: Essays in Ecological Marxism* (New York: Guilford Press, 1998), 160–1.

Olofson, A., 'Public Attitudes and Biotechnology', paper to European Sociological Association, workshop on Social Theory, Risk and Environment: Istanbul, Turkey, September 2000.

O'Neill, O., 'Kant after Virtue', *Inquiry*, 26, 1984, 387–405.

O'Neill, O., *Towards Justice and Virtue: A Constructive Account of Practical Reasoning* (Cambridge: Cambridge University Press, 1996).

Oster, M., 'The "Beame of Divinity": Animal Suffering in the Early Thought of Robert Boyle', *British Journal for the History of Science*, 22, 1989, 151–79.

PABE, *Public Attitudes towards Agricultural Biotechnologies in Europe*, final report of project with five partner country teams (Spain, Italy, Germany, France, UK), funded by EU, DG Research, Brussels, December 2000, coordinated by B. Wynne and P. Simmons, Lancaster University – also in *Politeia*, 16, 60, 3–29; also on www.pabe.com .

Pacey, A., *The Maze of Ingenuity: Ideas and Idealism in the Development of Technology* (Cambridge, MA: MIT Press, 1976).

Page, R., *God and the Web of Creation* (London: SCM Press, 1996).

Peacocke, Arthur, *Theology for a Scientific Age: Being and Becoming – Natural, Divine and Human*, 2nd enlarged edn (London: SCM Press; and Minneapolis: Fortress Press, 1993).

Pearce, F., 'Opinion Interview: Feeding Africa', *New Scientist*, 2240, 27 May 2000, 40–3.

Personal Origins (London: Church of England Board for Social Responsibility, 1985).

Peters, T., *Playing God? Genetic Determinism and Human Freedom* (London and New York: Routledge, 1997).

Pickstock, C., *After Writing: On the Liturgical Consummation of Philosophy* (Oxford: Blackwell, 1998).

Pinckaers, S., *The Sources of Christian Ethics*, tr Sr Mary Thomas Noble, 3rd edn (Edinburgh: T&T Clark, 1995).

Porter, J., *Moral Action and Christian Ethics* (Cambridge: Cambridge University Press, 1995).

Porter, J., *The Recovery of Virtue* (London: SPCK, 1994).

Porter, J., 'What the Wise Person Knows: Natural Law and Virtue in Aquinas's *Summa Theologiae*', *Studies in Christian Ethics*, 12, 1, 1999, 57–69.

Porter, R., *Doctor of Society: Thomas Beddoes and the Sick Trade in Late-Enlightenment England* (London: Routledge, 1992).

Priestley, J., *A Free Discussion of the Doctrines of Materialism and Philosophical Necessity in a Correspondence between Dr. Price and Dr. Priestley* (London: Johnson and Cadell, 1778).

Principe, L., *The Aspiring Adept: Robert Boyle and His Alchemical Quest* (Princeton: Princeton University Press, 1998).

Raine, Kathleen, *William Blake* (London: Thames and Hudson, 1970).

Rappaport, R. A., 'Veracity, Verity and *Verum* in Liturgy', *Studia Liturgica*, 23, 1, 1993, 35–50.

Ratcliffe, M., 'Teaching Ethical Aspects of Science: Evaluation of Case Studies' (unpublished paper).

Rayner, E., *Human Development: An Introduction to the Psychodynamics of Growth, Maturity and Ageing*, 3rd edn (London: Unwin Hyman, 1986).

Reiss, M. J., 'The Ethics of Xenotransplantation', *Journal of Applied Philosophy* (in press).

Reiss, M. J., 'Human Sociobiology', *Zygon*, 19, 1984, 117–40.

Reiss, M. J., 'On Suffering and Meaning: An Evolutionary Perspective', *Modern Believing*, 41, 2, 2000, 39–46.

Reiss, M. J., 'What Sort of People Do We Want? The Ethics of Changing People through Genetic Engineering', *Notre Dame Journal of Law, Ethics & Public Policy*, 13, 1999, 63–92.

Reiss, M. J. and R. Straughan, *Improving Nature? The Science and Ethics of Genetic Engineering* (Cambridge: Cambridge University Press, 1996).

Reiss, M. J. and S. D. Tunnicliffe, 'Conceptual Development', *Journal of Biological Education*, 34, 1999, 13–16.

Report on the Implications of Cloning for the Welfare of Farmed Livestock (FAWC: December 1998).

Rinsland, H. D., *A Basic Vocabulary of Elementary School Children* (New York: Macmillan, 1946).

Roberts, J. M. and M. J. Forman, 'Riddles: Expressive Models of Interrogation', in J. J. Gumperz and D. Hymes (eds), *Directions in Sociolinguistics: The Ethnography of Communication* (New York: Holt, Rinehart and Winston, 1972), 180–209.

Rogers Brambell, F. W., *Report of the Technical Committee to Enquire into the Welfare of Animals Kept under Intensive Livestock Husbandry Systems* (London: HMSO, 1965).

Rollin, B. E., *The Frankenstein Syndrome: Ethical and Social Issues in the Genetic Engineering of Animals* (Cambridge: Cambridge University Press, 1995), 172.

Rollin, Bernard, *Animal Rights and Human Morality* (Buffalo, NY: Prometheus Books, 1981).

Rosch, E. and C. B. Mervis, 'Family Resemblances: Studies in the Internal Structures of Categories', *Cognitive Psychology*, 7, 1975, 573–605.

Rossi, P., *Francis Bacon: From Magic to Science* (London: Routledge, 1968).

Royal Commission on Environmental Pollution, *Response to the Review of the Framework for Overseeing Developments in Biotechnology* (London: RCEP, 1999).

Royal Commission on Environmental Pollution, *Setting Environmental Standards*, Cm 4053 (London: HMSO, 1998).

Rubenstein, R., *After Auschwitz: Radical Theology and Contemporary Judaism* (New York: Bobbs-Merrill, 1966).

Russell, W. M. S. and R. L. Burch, *The Principles of Humane Experimental Technique* (London: Methuen, 1951).

Safeway, *A Guide to Safeway Double Concentrated Tomato Purée Produced from Genetically Modified Tomatoes* (London: Safeway, undated, c. 1997).

Santmire, H. Paul, *The Travail of Nature* (Philadelphia: Fortress Press, 1985).

Schnädelbach, H., *Philosophy in Germany 1831–1933* (Cambridge: Cambridge University Press, 1984).

Schofield, R., 'The Professional Work of an Amateur Chemist: Joseph Priestley', in Truman Schwartz and McEvoy, *Motion Toward Perfection*, 1–19.

Schumacher, E. F., *Small is Beautiful: Economics as if People Mattered* (London: Abacus, 1974).

Scott, Peter, 'Beyond Stewardship? Dietrich Bonhoeffer on Nature', *Journal of Beliefs and Values*, 18, 2, 1997, 193–202.

Scott, Peter, 'The Future of Creation: Ecology and Eschatology', in Fergusson and Sarot, *Future as God's Gift*, 89–114.

Scott, Peter, 'Imaging God: Creatureliness and Technology', *New Blackfriars*, 79, 928, 1998, 260–74.

Scott, Peter, *A Political Theology of Nature* (Cambridge: Cambridge University Press, 2002).

Scott, Peter, 'The Technological Factor: Nature, Redemption and the Image of God', *Zygon: Journal of Religion and Science*, 35, 2, 2000, 371–84.

Scott, Peter, *Theology, Ideology and Liberation: Towards a Liberative Theology* (Cambridge: Cambridge University Press, 1994).

Searle, J. R., *Speech Acts: An Essay in the Philosophy of Language* (Cambridge: Cambridge University Press, 1969).

Shannon, C. E. and W. Weaver, *The Mathematical Theory of Communication*, 2nd edn (Urbana: University of Illinois Press, 1962).

Shapin, S., *A Social History of Truth: Civility and Science in Seventeenth-Century England* (Chicago: University of Chicago Press, 1994).

Shapin, S. and S. Schaffer, *Leviathan and the Air Pump: Hobbes, Boyle and the Experimental Life* (Princeton: Princeton University Press, 1985).

Shiva, Vandana, *Monocultures of the Mind: Biodiversity, Biotechnology and the Third World* (Penang: Third World Network, 1993).

Shortland, M. (ed.), *Hugh Miller and the Controversies of Victorian Science* (Oxford: Oxford University Press, 1996).

Sigmund, P. E., 'Thomistic Law and Social Theory', in P. E. Sigmund (ed.), *St Thomas Aquinas on Politics and Ethics* (London and New York: W. W. Norton, 1988), 180–8.

Singer, P., *How Are We to Live?* (Oxford: Oxford University Press, 1997).

Sloan, Philip R. (ed.), *Controlling Our Destinies: Historical, Philosophical, Ethical and Theological Perspectives on the Human Genome Project* (Notre Dame: University of Notre Dame Press, 2000).

Slote, Michael A. and Roger Crisp (eds), *Virtue Ethics* (Oxford: Clarendon Press, 1997).

Slovic, P., *The Perception of Risk* (London: Earthscan, 2000).

Slovic, P., 'Reflections on the Psychometric Paradigm', in S. Krimsky and D. Golding (eds), *Social Theories of Risk* (New York: Praeger, 1992), 78–92.

Smith, J. A., 'Beyond the Divide between Cognition and Discourse: Using Interpretative Phenomenological Analysis in Health Psychology', *Psychology and Health*, 11, 1996, 261–71.

Smith, P. K., H. Cowie and M. Blades, *Understanding Children's Development*, 3rd edn (Oxford: Blackwell, 1998).

Smithson, M., *Ignorance and Uncertainty: Emerging Paradigms* (Berlin: Springer Verlag, 1989).

Sober, E. and D. S. Wilson, *Unto Others: The Evolution and Psychology of Unselfish Behavior* (Cambridge: Harvard University Press, 1998).

Soil Association, *Contrasting the Use of Genetic Engineering in Medicine and Agriculture*, Soil Association Briefing Paper (Bristol: Soil Association, 1999).

Sonntag, O., 'Religion and Science in the Thought of Liebig', *Ambix*, 24, 1977, 159–69.

Sperry, R. W., 'Psychology's Mentalist Paradigm and the Religion/Science Tension', *American Psychologist*, 43, 1988, 607–13.

Sperry, R. W., *Science and Moral Priority* (Oxford: Blackwell, 1983).

Stansfield, D., *Thomas Beddoes M.D. 1760–1808* (Dordrecht: Reidel, 1984).

Statman, D., *Virtue Ethics: A Critical Reader* (Edinburgh: Edinburgh University Press, 1997).

Stevenson, P., 'Animal Patenting: European Law and Ethical Implications', in Holland and Johnson, *Animal Biotechnology*, 288–302.

Straughan, R. and M. Reiss, *Ethics, Morality and Crop Biotechnology* (London: Biotechnology and Biosciences Research Council (BBSRC), Department of Trade and Industry, 1996).

Sykes, Stephen, 'Ethical Reference Points for Scientific Developments', *Crucible*, 39, 2000, 1–8.

Szerszynski, B., 'On Knowing What to Do: Environmentalism and the Modern Problematic', in S. Lash, B. Szerszynski and B. Wynne (eds), *Risk, Environment and Modernity: Towards a New Ecology* (London: Sage, 1996), 104–37.

Szerszynski, B., 'Risk and Trust – the Performative Dimension', *Environmental Values*, 8, 2, 1999, 239–52.

Szerszynski, B., J. Urry and G. Myers, 'Mediating Global Citizenship', in J. Smith (ed.), *The Daily Globe: Environmental Change, the Public and the Media* (London: Earthscan, 2000), 97–114.

Tait, J., *More Faust than Frankenstein: The European Debate about Risk Regulation for Genetically Modified Crops*, SUPRA Paper no. 6 (Edinburgh: University of Edinburgh, 1999).

Tangwa, G. B., 'Globalisation or Westernisation? Ethical Concerns in the Whole Bio-Business', *Bioethics*, 13, 1999, 218–26.

Tannen, D., *Talking Voices: Repetition, Dialogue, and Imagery in Conversational Discourse* (Cambridge: Cambridge University Press, 1989).

Teilhard de Chardin, P., *Le Milieu Divin* (London: Collins, 1957).

Theisen, W., 'John Dastin: The Alchemist as Co-Creator', *Ambix*, 38, 1991, 73–8.

Thomas, K., *Man and the Natural World* (Harmondsworth: Penguin, 1984).

Thomas, S., 'The Global Resurgence of Religion and the Role of the Church of England in World Politics', *Crucible*, July–September 2000, 149–69.

Thomas Aquinas, *see* Aquinas.

Thompson, Paul, *The Spirit of the Soil: Agriculture and Environmental Ethics* (London: Routledge, 1995).

Thomson, R., 'Diversity, Values and Social Change: Renegotiating a Consensus on Sex Education', *Journal of Moral Education*, 26, 1997, 257–71.

Tiles, M. and H. Oberdiek, *Living in a Technological Culture* (London: Routledge, 1995).

Topham, J., 'Science and Popular Education in the 1830s: The Role of the *Bridgewater Treatises*', *British Journal for the History of Science*, 25, 1992, 397–430.

Trinkhaus, C. E., *In Our Image and Likeness: Humanity and Divinity in Italian Humanist Thought* (London: Constable, 1970).

Truman Schwartz, A. and J. McEvoy (eds), *Motion toward Perfection: The Achievement of Joseph Priestley* (Boston: Skinner House, 1990).

Tucker, G. A., 'Improvement of Tomato Fruit Quality and Processing Characteristics by Genetic Engineering', *Food Science and Technology Today*, 7, 2, 1993, 103–8.

UK Office of Science and Technology, *Guidelines for the Procurement of Scientific Advice for Policy*, update (London: Department of Trade and Industry, 2000).

Van den Bossche, M., 'Technique, esthétique et métaphysique', in Troude-Chastenet, *Sur Jacques Ellul*, 251–70.

Wainwright, G., *Doxology: The Praise of God in Worship, Doctrine and Life – a Systematic Theology* (London: Epworth Press, 1980).

Wainwright, G., 'The Language of Worship', in C. Jones, G. Wainwright, E. Yarnold and P. Bradshaw (eds), *The Study of Liturgy* (London: SPCK, 1992), 521–2.

Wall, Derek, *Earth First and the Anti-Roads Movement* (London and New York: Routledge, 1999).

Walton, D., 'Genetically Modified Futures', *British Ecological Society Bulletin*, 31, 2, 2000, 14–16.

Webster, C., *The Great Instauration: Science, Medicine and Reform 1626–1660* (London: Duckworth, 1975).

Weil, S., *Gravity and Grace* (London: Routledge, 1952).

The Wellcome Trust Medicine in Society Programme, *Public*

Perspectives on Human Cloning (London: The Wellcome Trust, 1998).

Wenham, G., *Word Biblical Commentary*, Vol. 1 (Milton Keynes: Word (UK), 1991).

Wertz, D. and J. C. Fletcher, 'Attitudes of Genetic Counsellors: A Multinational Survey', *American Journal of Human Genetics*, 45, 1988, 592–600.

Weyembergh, M., 'J. Ellul et M. Heidegger le prophète et le penseur', in Troude-Chastenet, *Sur Jacques Ellul*, 75–100.

Wiggins, D., 'Nature, Respect for Nature, and the Human Scale of Values', *Proceedings of the Aristotelian Society*, 100, 1, 2000, 1–32.

Williams, B., 'Must a Concern for the Environment be Centred on Human Beings?', in *Making Sense of Humanity and Other Philosophical Papers 1982–1993* (Cambridge: Cambridge University Press, 1995), 233–40.

Williams, J. R., *Christian Perspectives on Bioethics: Religious Values and Public Policy in a Pluralistic Society* (Ottawa: Novalis, 1997).

Williams, R., 'God and Risk', in R. Holloway (ed.), *The Divine Risk* (London: DLT, 1990), 11–23.

Wilson, E. O., *Sociobiology – the New Synthesis* (Cambridge, MA: Belknap Press/Harvard University Press, 1975).

Wimsatt, W. C., 'Robustness, Reliability and Multiple-Determination in Science', in *Knowing and Validating in the Social Sciences: A Tribute to Donald Campbell* (San Francisco: Jossey-Bass, 1981), 124–63.

Wynne, B., 'Expert Discourses of Risk and Ethics on Genetically Manipulated Organisms: The Weaving of Public Alienation', *Politeia*, 17, 62, 2001, 51–76.

Wynne, B., 'Frameworks of Rationality in Risk Management: Towards the Testing of Naïve Sociology', in J.Brown (ed.), *Environmental Threats* (London: Frances Pinter, 1989), 93–110.

Wynne, B., 'Knowledge in Context', *Science Technology and Human Values*, 16, 1, 1–21.

Wynne, B., 'May the Sheep Safely Graze? A Reflexive View of the Expert–Lay Knowledge Divide', in S. Lash, B. Szerszynski and B. Wynne (eds), *Risk, Environment and Modernity: Towards a New Ecology* (London: Sage, 1996), 44–83.

Wynne, B., *Risk Management and Hazardous Wastes: Implementation and the Dialectics of Credibility* (London and Berlin: Springer, 1987).

Wynne, B., 'Risk, Technology and Trust: On the Social Treatment of Uncertainty', in J. Conrad (ed.), *Society, Technology and Risk* (London, Arnold, 1980), 83–117.

Wynne, B., 'Uncertainty and Environmental Learning: Reconceiving Science and Policy in the Preventive Paradigm', *Global Environmental Change*, 2, 1, 1992, 1–22.

Žižek, S., *The Fragile Absolute* (London: Verso, 2000).

Subject Index

Name Index

Scripture References Index

367